# The Rochdale Thunderbolt
## A story of Triumph and Tragedy

Jack Doughty has had a varied and interesting career. He played professional Rugby League with Oldham, but following a serious injury he moved into amateur acting before graduating to television and a number of appearances at Oldham Repertory Theatre. From this he went on to performing song and dance routines in Music Hall. This was followed by a dramatic change in direction when he became involved in professional boxing, opening a gym at Bacup, Lancashire in the mid-eighties. In 1988, Jack opened a new gym at Rochdale, before leaving there in 1993 to open a boxing gym at Shaw, Oldham.

For the past eighteen years Jack has managed and trained fighters, producing several champions. Though he also stages regular small hall shows in order to develop young boxers, he has always been far more interested in training techniques and spends much of his time in the gym.

Apart from the theatre and sport Jack was always interested in reading and studying crime and his first venture into print reflected this with *Come at once – Annie is dying* (1987). This was followed by the hard-back version of *The Rochdale Thunderbolt* (1991), a biography of the boxer Jock McAvoy. He had a marked success with another biography *The Rochdale Hangman and his victims* (1998). In 2002, he published *The Manchester Outrage – A Fenian Tragedy,* a well researched and graphic account of the murder, in 1867, of Sergeant Brett near Belle Vue, Manchester and the capture, trial and execution of those responsible. Jack has also written a radio play for the BBC, *The Shadow of Slim*, and a stage play, *The Cato Street Conspiracy*, which was performed at The Little Theatre, London. He is now working on his autobiography.

# The Rochdale Thunderbolt

## A story of Triumph and Tragedy

Jack Doughty

**Jade Publishing Limited,**
5, Leefields Close, Uppermill, Oldham, Lancashire, OL3 6LA.

This revised impression published in paperback by Jade Publishing Limited 2004.



ISBN 1 900734 31 1 The Rochdale Thunderbolt.
– A Story of Triumph and Tragedy (Pbk).

Printed in Great Britain
Typeset by
Jade Publishing Limited, Oldham, Lancashire.

British Library Cataloguing in Publication Data
Doughty, J.,
The Rochdale Thunderbolt
– A Story of Triumph and Tragedy – Rev. ed.
Includes bibliography and index.
1. McAvoy, Jock 2. Boxers – England – Rochdale – Biography
I. Title
796.8'3'092

ISBN 1–900734–31–1

Dedicated
to the memory of
my father
JAMES DOUGHTY

# Contents

# Acknowledgements

When I first embarked on the research for this book I soon discovered that though most of the people I approached were delighted to tell me what they knew about Jock McAvoy, alias Joe Bamford, there were some who were more than a little reticent when it came to being interviewed and others who seemed downright obstructive, even hostile. When pressed, these people simply refused to talk, one man bluntly informing me that he had no intention of helping me "dig up dirt".

As a great McAvoy admirer, that was the last thing I intended to do, but I also realised that I could not tell half a tale, and that if the McAvoy story were to be told at all, then it had to be told in full. A whitewash job would be totally unacceptable, and in any case would never ring true. Nor would the complex character behind the controversial figure who was known to the public as 'The Rochdale Thunderbolt' ever fully emerge if the more unpalatable side of his nature and somewhat turbulent private life were swept under the carpet.

Quite apart from the writing itself, my research occupied over two years of ploughing through old newspaper files going as far back as the early twenties, days spent at St. Catherine's House, London, in the Births, Deaths and Marriages section, plus scores of interviews, not all of which proved fruitful, though I very much appreciate the fact that all of these people found the time to talk to me.

I'm especially grateful to the late Harry Mullan, former editor of *Boxing News*, who gave me access to the files, with permission to use anything I needed, and also to the *Boxing News* staff, who were so helpful and friendly during my two visits to Langham Street.

I was in contact with ace record compiler, the late Vic Hardwicke from an early stage in my research, and in constant touch while combing through the files of various libraries up and down the country as I attempted to track down every single contest McAvoy ever engaged in. This at times required painstaking detective work and comparing notes with Vic certainly helped clear up many problem areas. In the end we were able to agree on all points.

As neither of us could manage to trace contests which purportedly took place against Tommy Welsh or Walsh and Teddy Hey, these could not, of course, be included. The former, in fact, is something of a phantom, for no other contests have come to light involving a boxer of that name from Royton, and it is certainly not the Tommy Walsh who fought out of Liverpool during the twenties, who was only around bantam or featherweight. The case of Teddy Hey may well be similar to those of Freddie Heighton of Delph and Hal O'Neill of Pendleton, each of whom was billed to meet McAvoy in contests which never took place.

Apart from Vic's renowned record-keeping expertise and vast knowledge of boxing, I was very much impressed by his bubbling enthusiasm and obvious love of the game. I'm very grateful for all his help and advice, which proved invaluable.

I would also like to thank the following people, who helped in varying degrees with information or photographs:

Albert Tolley, who started off being interviewed and became part of the story, Joe Rostron, a real gentleman of the ring, Mrs Nellie Dodman, Ron Dodman, Don Waters, Jack and Vera Pilkington, Joe Horridge, Jack Petersen, Frankie 'Boy' Holt, Arthur 'Ginger' Sadd, Raymond Cole, Jack and Margaret Ryan, Arthur Henson, Harold Henthorn, Joe Myers, Jack Travis, Paddy Lyons, Nat Basso, Jack Trickett, Johnny Sullivan, John Fleming, Tony Reddy, Harold Brown, Mervyn Mason, Mrs Nellie Ratchford, Beryl Cook, Margaret Danson, Florence Danson, James Briggs, Frank Turner, Arthur Ashworth, Eddie Jones, Bert Hollows, Jack Kershaw, Charlie Henderson, Vera Ellison, Bernard Fahy, John Cole, Albert Crabtree, Thomas Terry, James Coney, Mary Hurst, Mr B. J. Redmond, Mrs N. Jackson, Clifford Astin, Doris Cookson, Bob Hartley, Ernie Whittaker, Joe Riley, Billy Tansey junior, Joan Hunt, Audrey Smethurst, Brenda Dyson, Phyllis Wolnica, Hilary Taylor, Willie Loveridge and Len Collinge.

I am also very much indebted to my faithful secretary, Sheila Whitworth, who is without doubt the most conscientious, serene and even tempered person I've ever known, attributes which are very necessary when working with an impatient, temperamental and at times even irritable author.

Jack Doughty,
January, 2004

# Illustrations

There are 45 pictures between pages 60 and 61, 35 pictures between pages 160 and 161 and 37 pictures between 266 and 267.

All copyrights are acknowledged and permission was sought, and granted, to reproduce the pictures shown in this work.

Cover design by Danny Doughty.

# Preface

As a young lad I was very much influenced by my dad, who was keen on most sports, especially boxing. Through him I was brought up on the exploits of great fighters like Jimmy Wilde, Ted 'Kid' Lewis and Jim Driscoll, outstanding ringmen who had been prominent many years before. In the days before television we would spend many an evening discussing these legendary exponents of the Noble Art and comparing them with current champions such as Joe Louis, Rocky Marciano and Ray Robinson. We had no radio, but fortunately for us the lady next door, a widow by the name of Mrs McCormick, was a keen fight fan. As she was very deaf her wireless was always turned up to full volume, which was just as well, as my father was also somewhat hard of hearing. The result was that the two of us were able to listen to the commentary of Raymond Glendenning with inter-round summaries by W. Barrington-Dalby with our ears pressed against the wall without missing a word.

From my father I also learned all about the famous Royton Stadium, where Jock McAvoy began his career. Along with other members of our family my Dad had followed the Royton boxing during the twenties and early thirties, and in particular the fortunes of the two Ovey (Overton) brothers, Walter and Charlie, the latter being related to us by marriage. When I knew him, much later, Uncle Charlie, as we all called him, was a stocky, benign sort of character whose battered features always seemed to be wreathed in a pleasant bemused smile. Uncle Charlie had been one of the Royton heroes, who, like most of the other local lads of his day, had fought for a few bob because it was so badly needed. Yet, he also loved the game for itself, for he enjoyed a good scrap and is remembered by old timers as one of the hardest, most fearless battlers ever to step into the Royton ring.

While this book is essentially an exploration of the life and character of Jock McAvoy, a truly great fighter, it would be fair to say that it is also, in a way, a tribute to the army of unsung heroes of the ring, men like 'Cyclone' Charlie Ovey, who fought their hearts out week in and week out for a few paltry shillings. They were the backbone of the game; the men for whom I and many others have the greatest admiration and respect. They, almost as much as the famous Jock McAvoy himself, were the inspiration behind the writing of *The Rochdale Thunderbolt*.

# Chapter 1

## The Mystery surrounding McAvoy's birth

Jock McAvoy always claimed to have been born Joseph Bamford in Burnley on November 20th 1907, though numerous writers over the years have given the year as 1908.

Embarking upon the research for this book I immediately set out to clear up this apparently simple, yet very important point, and ran into a brick wall. No birth is recorded of a Joseph Bamford anywhere in the country on either of the above dates, nor in any month or year around this period.

The obvious answer seemed to be that the parents had simply not bothered to register the birth. Realising that I would be forced to dig deeper, just in case, I nevertheless decided to press on rather than hold up the work, and solve the mystery later – if indeed there was a mystery to be solved.

Every other birth or death certificate I searched for I eventually found, but Joe Bamford's was to prove so hard to trace that the entire book was almost completed before the truth about his birth finally came to light.

Joe's mother was born at Pendleton, Salford, in 1872. The daughter of Robert and Ellen Ginty, she was christened Mary Ellen, but was known throughout her life as Nellie. She was exceptionally good looking as a young woman, with jet black hair and strong Irish features, her Irish ancestry, in fact, being something of which she was always extremely proud.

Times were very hard and those out of work had to be prepared either to travel to wherever labour was required or risk finishing up in the Workhouse, which is most probably why Nellie Ginty arrived in Burnley, where she found a job as a weaver. In February 1893, when she was twenty, Nellie gave birth to a daughter. The father was George Hardacre, a local man who also worked in the mill. The child was christened Rose Ellen and the address given on the birth certificate is number 20 Lisbon Street, Habergem Eaves, Burnley. But though the couple were living together there is no record of any marriage having taken place. Both parents loved the child dearly, but their own relationship was already deteriorating rapidly, and it appears more than likely that Nellie was the main cause of this, for we do know that while George was a steady, quiet sort of man, Nellie tended to be somewhat promiscuous. She had never been short of male admirers, and did little to discourage their attentions, despite the fact that she was now a mother, with the inevitable result that the couple soon broke up and went their separate ways, although George remained very close to his daughter and never lost contact.

While Nellie, in all probability, continued to have her share of men friends, she in no way neglected the child, and as far as is known did not become involved in another permanent relationship until some years later when she met Joe Bamford and set up home with him at No. 30 Luther Street, in Burnley. Bamford, a powerfully built man of middle height, was a labourer who worked at any job he could get, usually in the building trade, but quite frequently as a carter.

In 1907 Joe junior was born. He was an exceptionally large baby, well over ten pounds, and although the birth occurred on the 20th of November it was not registered until December 30th, some six weeks later, which is not particularly unusual, although in this case it's probable that Nellie was undecided as to just what name should go on the birth certificate. In those days Nellie's conduct would have been looked on as quite scandalous, so the couple no doubt considered the situation very carefully before committing themselves.

Registrars are totally dependant upon the information given to them by the parent or parents, and Register offices have always displayed signs pointing out that any person giving false information to the Registrar 'will be liable to prosecution'.

As Nellie's daughter had, quite correctly, always been known as Rose Hardacre, it's more than likely that Nellie had also continued to use the same surname. The parents then, were in something of a quandary when it came to filling in the birth certificate. In the end it was decided to leave out the name of the father altogether, so that particular column is crossed through. The child's christian name is entered as Joseph, after his true father, while the mother gave her name as Mary Ellen Hardacre, formerly Ginty, the result being that the infant was officially registered as Joseph Hardacre, though Bamford was without doubt the natural father.

At last the mystery was solved. The date of birth was November 20th 1907, and though the infant, who would later become famous as Jock McAvoy, most certainly began life as Joseph Bamford, his birth was never registered in that name. This fact has remained unknown ever since, even to members of the family, for though many people in Rochdale later came to know his step-sister, Rose, and were aware that her maiden name was Hardacre, it was never realised that Joe had once shared the same name, officially at least. It's more than probable that Joe himself never knew the truth about his birth, for in those days people went to great lengths to keep such things hidden.

One sad and pathetic figure to emerge from all this is George Hardacre, by all accounts a thoroughly nice, gentle sort of man, who, after losing his family, appears to have led a most unhappy existence. George not only retained the greatest love for his daughter Rose, but also became very much attached to her children later on, and even to Joe Bamford Junior, the son of the man who ultimately replaced him.

The break-up of George Hardacre's relationship with Nellie also led to the loss of his home, and for the rest of his life he lived in lodging houses and Salvation Army hostels, constantly moving around, but always keeping in touch with the family he had lost. In later years, when Rose had children of her own, Joe Bamford senior was known to them as Grandad Bamford, while George Hardacre was always referred to as Grandad George. Joe Bamford senior, a kindly man himself, never seemed to resent George turning up unexpectedly to visit, and always made him welcome.

When Joe junior was born his parents were by no means young, the father, in fact, at forty-one, was approaching middle-age, and there can be no doubting the fact that from the beginning he was thoroughly spoiled, particularly by the mother, in whose eyes he could do no wrong.

The results of this over-indulgence by the two loving parents were soon to become apparent. If Joe didn't want to go to school he just didn't go, and nothing short of being dragged there would make him. In everything, he had to have his own way, and if he didn't get it he could make life hell for those around him. Not that the father was a weak man, far from it, but when problems arose he was often out at work, and after getting his own way with Nellie, Joe could be pretty certain that she would be unlikely to mention anything to her husband.

It seems very clear that these mistakes, made by the parents when the boy was at such a tender age, most certainly had a lasting effect on his personality, and go a long way towards explaining the reasons for his behaviour in later life. The chronic impatience, at times arrogant, belligerent attitude and explosive temper, which were to manifest themselves as Joe grew up, can be traced directly back to his formative years.

While Joe was still quite young the family moved to the nearby town of Barnoldswick, just over the Yorkshire border, where Joe senior found employment with a local builder. Nellie also went out to work, as a weaver, leaving Joe to be 'minded' by a kindly neighbour, Mrs Alice Entwistle. Rose, who by this time was in her teens, was also working in the cotton mill.

The family lived in Collin Street, known locally as 'Chinatown', because of the steam laundry which operated there, and when he was old enough Joe was sent to Gisburn Road Junior School, close by, later moving on to the newly built St. Joseph's Catholic School. Quite a big lad for his age, he tended to be rough and boisterous and was keen on most sports, especially football. Though not particularly skilful, he was always wholehearted and hated to lose.

As young Joe grew up he became very close to his father, whom he admired very much, in particular for his exceptional strength and powerful physique. Joe Bamford senior was also a man with a great love and understanding of animals, especially horses and dogs, which he undoubtedly passed on to his son, for in later life Joe would exhibit infinitely more patience with animals than he ever did with people.

Though the elder Bamford was a hard and conscientious worker, the years immediately following the first World War were lean indeed, and steady employment was very hard to come by, especially in a town the size of Barnoldswick. Feeling that the prospects were likely to be better in a large city, the Bamfords packed their meagre belongings and travelled south to Manchester, where Nellie had some relatives, the Ryans, a large family of youngsters who had been left orphaned. Rose, who remained in Barnoldswick, was by this time well into her twenties and already a widow. She had married a man named Alf Trayford, who died during the time of the Great War, leaving her with two young children, Rose and Leonora.

The Bamfords, unable to get work or suitable accommodation in Manchester, were soon on the move again, this time to Rochdale, where they managed to find lodgings with an old lady who lived in a back alley known as Turner's Yard, eventually taking over the tenancy when the old lady either died or moved out. Young Joe, then around twelve years old, was sent to St. Patrick's School, just a few streets away. The Bamfords arrived in Rochdale at a time when the mills there were booming and trade generally was enjoying an upsurge.

It's not known precisely what sort of work Joe senior found, but it's fairly certain that Nellie got herself fixed up in one of the local mills nearby. The family now settled down at last and less than two years after this were reunited with Rose, who by this time had remarried. Her new husband was Jim Pilkington, a weaver, who, though a very hardworking man, just could not find regular employment in Barnoldswick. The birth of another child, a boy named Jack, did not help the financial situation, and Jim Pilkington, like many others at that time, was forced to tramp to nearby towns in a desperate attempt to find work.

One day, finding himself in Nelson, he decided to set off for Rochdale, having heard, possibly from the Bamfords, that hands were wanted in the mills there. The fact that Rochdale was approximately 18 miles away does not appear to have deterred him in the slightest.

In any event, Jim Pilkington soon forgot about his sore feet when he was taken on at the Dunlop cotton mill. It's more than likely that the Bamfords put their son-in-law up for the first few weeks following his arrival, perhaps longer. In 1921, however, when his son Jack was one year old, Jim Pilkington managed to rent a house at No. 3 Ogden Street nearby, and was then able to send for his family. Later on, in the mid-twenties, the Pilkingtons were lucky enough to get one of the first corporation houses built in the Queensway district, and on their moving out, the Bamfords took over the house in Ogden Street. The two families kept in close touch, Rose's children continuing to see a lot of their grandparents and also Joe Bamford junior, who was, of course, their uncle.

Next door in Ogden Street lived Mrs Annie Dodman, a widow, and her son and daughter-in-law with their young family. The daughter- in-law, Mrs Nellie Dodman, who was ninety years of age when interviewed by the author, but still extremely sharp mentally, remembered the Bamfords very well. According to her, Joe senior was a nice, quiet man, 'a real gentleman', though she was none too keen on his wife, whom she found rather pushy and a tough character, with whom few of the neighbours were inclined to argue, especially over the children, for no matter what mischief young Joe might get up to she always sided with her son. As far as the mother was concerned he was never in the wrong, and anyone who suggested otherwise risked incurring Nellie Bamford's wrath.

Ogden Street was on the fringe of a district known as The Mount. It was the Irish section of the town, populated by large, mainly poor, families, living in rather squalid housing conditions. Most of the kids from The Mount and the surrounding areas were Catholic and went to St. Pat's, where the parish priest was Father Murphy, a firm but kindly man who was well liked and who took a great interest in the boys and their sporting activities. Young Joe soon made friends with the other lads in the district and knocked about a lot of the time with two sets of brothers, the Collinge's and the Davies's, with Len Collinge his closest mate.

On leaving school at fourteen Joe went to work at the Townhead Mill, which was no more than a few yards from his home, but does not appear to have settled very well, for after no more than a few weeks he left, and over the next three or four years drifted from one job to another, working as a labourer for the local Corporation Transport Department, in an artificial silk mill and at various other occupations, without ever finding anything that really suited him.

He does not appear to have relished the tedium of steady employment, in addition to which his temper was already beginning to get him into all kinds of bother, for if local folklore is to be believed he lost at least two jobs after arguments with foremen, during which he is alleged to have used his fists.

Joe's own version of at least one of these incidents, related some twenty-odd years after the event, reads very much like a John Wayne movie script, with the teenage Bamford slugging it out with a mature man who outweighed him by several stones, and ending with the two of them on their knees, collapsing in a heap from sheer exhaustion, before slowly dragging themselves upright again and grinning at each other in mutual respect and admiration.

While the above scene was almost certainly inspired by Joe's regular visits to the local picture palace, there is no doubt that he did get himself into trouble even in those early days, on one occasion striking his foreman, a man named Wolfenden, and getting himself fired on the spot.

Joe was a tough lad alright, and an ambitious one. He realised soon after starting work that a regular job was not for him, though he had very little idea about alternative ways of making a living. He had always had a great admiration for top sportsmen, especially speedway riders and boxers. Jack Dempsey, then Heavyweight Champion of the World, was the one he admired most of all, and whose exploits he never tired of reading about. Joe longed to emulate his idol, but had no idea if he had the necessary ability to succeed. Still, there was plenty of opportunity to find out, for Rochdale, like most working class towns in the country in those days, had its fair share of boxing clubs, and though facilities were poor and equipment sparse, there was plenty of enthusiasm amongst the local lads and every possibility of getting bouts if one showed any sort of promise, though the competition was fierce.

It's at this point that a great old-timer enters the story in the shape of John Willie Ryan, or 'One-round' Ryan, as he was often called. Ryan was an old fairground fighter whose lethal right hand was no doubt responsible for the 'One-round' tag.

It seems very surprising that John Willie Ryan was never even mentioned in Jock McAvoy's own account of his early years, for Ryan most certainly had at least something to do with his introduction to the rudiments of boxing. Born at Bradford, Yorkshire, in 1886, of Irish parents, John Willie started to box on the fairgrounds when quite young and soon became known throughout the county for his skill and hitting power.

He had been married only a short time when tragedy struck, his young wife being burnt to death in a fire. Many years later, when living in Rochdale, Ryan was again involved in a fire, when he rescued two children from a blazing house at great personal risk, and finished up in the Infirmary with burns to his face and hands.

Some years prior to this latter incident he had remarried, settling down in Rochdale with his new wife, Margaret O'Connor, a local girl, and raising a family in Middle Lane, which was quite close to Ogden Street.

John Willie, a big, broad shouldered man with hands like shovels, worked in the building trade, but despite family commitments and a full time job, he still managed to devote a great deal of his time to boxing. It was in his blood and whenever a fair came to town he was always there, standing outside the boxing booth, ready to challenge the biggest man on the platform. As he was well known to the booth proprietors he was usually either avoided or invited to join them for the week.

On one occasion, while standing on the platform himself, Ryan was challenged by one of the locals, who, though well aware of his reputation, nonetheless still fancied his chances, misguidedly believing that John Willie, by this time in his fifties, was very much a spent force who would present very few problems to a bold young scrapper like himself.

As Ryan was much the heavier man he was instructed to go easy on the challenger and carry him for a couple of rounds, but as often happens in such situations, the novice, after having things all his own way in the early exchanges, began to grow in confidence.

When John Willie retreated into a corner, covering up, his opponent, believing that he was now in total command and that the grey-haired veteran had had enough, began to take liberties. Egged on by his noisy friends, he began to sneer at Ryan, calling him a coward and daring him to stand and fight.

There was only one way out and John Willie took it. Peering from behind his gloves, he noted that his tormentor, between quick bursts of eye-catching if ineffectual flurries of punching, would glance into the crowd in the direction of his wildly cheering supporters. He was basking in his new found glory and thoroughly enjoying himself. But while his eyes were averted John Willie carefully measured his man, and as the local hero turned to resume hostilities, a solid right hander, delivered with pin-point accuracy, exploded on his exposed chin. Down went the bantam cock – spark out.

John Willie insisted afterwards that he had not put his full weight behind the blow, but the knockout nevertheless resulted in some anxious moments for the booth proprietor, for it was some time before the unfortunate challenger was able to leave the ring, after which he had to be walked up and down by his mates for another ten minutes or so before he had fully regained his senses.

But John Willie Ryan was by no means a violent man. He was in fact a gentle giant, very quiet, courteous and well liked. He was a man who loved the sport of boxing and would spend hours teaching the young lads all he knew about the game. Over the years he coached at make-shift gymnasiums all over the town; at South Lane, Buckley Lane, in an upper room at the Derby Hotel and in a cellar in Holland Street in the town centre. All these gyms were within a stone's throw of Ogden Street, where Joe Bamford lived, and we know for a fact that Joe went along with the other lads, including Eddie Strawer, later to become a great McAvoy rival, to the Holland Street cellar.

With the help of a friend, Johnny Scully, who handled what little correspondence was involved, Ryan arranged contests for some of the lads at small halls in the area. Scully, who could do a bit himself when the occasion arose, was the brother-in-law of Joe Walsh, another well-known local fighter, who later tried his hand at promoting.

Though Joe Bamford's first recorded contest was on November 6th 1927, when he was not far short of his twentieth birthday, it's quite possible that he took part in the odd bout prior to this. For one thing, nineteen was rather an advanced age for a beginner in those days, when most of the lads took up the game professionally at fifteen or sixteen and could have as many as fifty to a hundred fights behind them before they reached twenty. On the other hand, boxing was just one of several sports in which Joe was interested as a teenager. He was very keen on soccer and also played amateur Rugby League, so it could well have been the case that he did not in fact take part in any serious scrapping before reaching his late teens.

McAvoy's own account states that he first became interested through two brothers, Charlie and Stan Hall, who had rigged up a gymnasium in the cellar of their home in Holland Street. He also mentions that the Halls occasionally fought at the Royton Stadium in Oldham. Here again there is a probable connection with John Willie Ryan, for Ryan regularly took boys along to fight at the Stadium, and seconded them. The purses involved were very meagre and Ryan never took a cut. He was just interested in the sport for its own sake. To pass on his vast knowledge and watch the lads in action was reward enough for him.

Holland Street, close to the town centre, where most of the lads lived, was at the heart of an area which abounded with rough pubs, pawn shops and cheap lodging houses, one of which was kept by the parents of Johnny King, later to become British and Empire

Bantamweight Champion. Though born in Manchester, Johnny was brought up in Rochdale and learned his boxing at Royton.

To say that young Joe Bamford put his heart and soul into those early sessions in the Holland Street cellar would be putting it mildly. From the very beginning he gave it everything, tearing like a mad bull into any lad who was willing to spar with him, and not always getting the better of things, for some of the regulars were older and more experienced than he was and quite capable of handling him. But Joe was hard and not easily put off. Very often sheer determination would keep him going, until, with his opponent all but exhausted, he would begin to get the upper hand and really punish the other lad, when he would have to be restrained and reminded that it was just a sparring session and not total war.

Joe knew that his mother was none too keen on him boxing, yet he soon began to wonder just what his chances might be if he were to take up the game seriously. For a long time he hesitated, while toying with the idea of going along to the Royton Stadium in nearby Oldham, where J. B. Tolley, the well-known local promoter, staged boxing every Sunday. To pull on the gloves and experience the thrill of fighting in front of a big crowd really excited him. It took some months, however, for him to pluck up enough courage to take the plunge.

# Chapter 2

## Royton

The suburb of Royton lies on the main route from Oldham to Rochdale. Like Shaw, which is only a mile or so away, Royton played a very prominent part in the great cotton boom, when huge fortunes were made by a few while the vast majority lived just above starvation level, toiling away uncomplainingly in the mills, working long hours and being thankful that they had a job, as thousands were on the dole.

In the early twenties Royton was little more than a village, with no particular claim to fame. Yet long before the decade was out it was to become known, not only throughout the North, but all over the country, and this surprisingly enough, in the tough cynical world of professional boxing. During that period Royton was without doubt one of the most famous and certainly the most unique fight centre in Britain.

One man was responsible for this. One man, who started it all, built it up and nursed it through good times and bad, and saw it reach a euphoric peak before the bubble finally burst and the inevitable downward spiral began.

His name was Joe Tolley. Joe Tolley – Promoter, Manager, Referee, Matchmaker, Master of Ceremonies, Boxing Correspondent, Entrepreneur and Showman – and what a showman!

Ask any local boxing fan of the older generation about Royton in the twenties and early thirties and he'll tell you he remembers it well. He'll tell you that the great Jock McAvoy, Johnny King and 'Cast Iron' Casey fought there, plus a host of others, including a whole string of local scrappers who never reached the top, but who were every bit as tough and talented as many who did. He'll tell you how exciting and how popular those Sunday afternoon shows were, with people from every walk of life attending, and charabancs (coaches) from all over the North rolling up.

If you then ask him just where the boxing was held he'll more than likely tell you that it was at the old Royton Stadium, 'At the bottom of Dogford Road there.' This is where the confusion begins.

If you should make further inquiries you'll find that the more knowledgeable, or those with clearer recollections, will recall that there was also a boxing arena in another part of Royton, 'Down Middleton Road somewhere.' Most seem very vague though, regarding exact locations, and after following up numerous leads I began to realise that there had certainly been at least two Royton Stadiums, and possibly three arenas where boxing shows were held. In the end I found there had actually been four.

However, I might never have discovered this had I not had the good fortune to find Albert Tolley, son of Joe.

Albert himself was quite a remarkable man. Aged seventy-eight, at that time, he was still slim, fit, clear thinking and very articulate. A lifelong sportsman, he managed fighters, boxed a bit himself, played table tennis for many years and later became a keen ballroom dancer. From him I not only learned quite a lot about McAvoy's early career, but also a large and very important part of the fascinating story of the rise and fall of boxing in Royton.

The Royton story is, of course, the Joe Tolley story, for Tolley was at the root of it all and built up an immense following, though later, others, who knew nowhere near as much about the game as he did, would come along to cash in on its popularity and eventually succeed in putting him out of business and into bankruptcy.

Joe Tolley was born in 1883 at Winsford in Cheshire, and was illegitimate. His mother, Hannah, only sixteen or so at the time, got herself into trouble through a young man of some means named Bamford*, whose family promptly sent him off to America for a spell, to get him out of the way. He apparently liked the life there and decided to stay.

All this was related to young Albert many years later by Joe Tolley, who told his son that Bamford had never returned to England, having been shot dead in a New York saloon around the turn of the century. When Albert asked the reason for the slaying Joe simply told him, 'For speaking out of turn'.

The infant was christened Joseph and given his mother's name of Tolley, with the father's surname as his middle name. Joe's mother was illiterate, and he himself could barely read or write when he left school, round the age of nine. Amazing then, that he was able, in later years, to earn a part of his living by writing for newspapers, both in this country and abroad, having taught himself as best he could.

* No connection with the Bamfords of Burnley.

Joe and his mother later moved to Warrington, where Hannah met and married John Maloney, a labourer and former prizefighter, who undoubtedly kindled in Joe an early interest in boxing.

For some reason the family moved to Oldham, possibly in search of work, settling in the village of Royton. They were very poor, even for those times, a situation not helped by the fact that Maloney was a Catholic and believed in large broods, eventually producing eight children of his own, two of whom became professional fighters. He himself had fought with bare knuckles and looked scornfully on what he called 'these 'ere cream puffs' who boxed with 'pillows' on their fists.

In 1900, while the Boer war was on, Joe Tolley joined up as a militiaman in the Royal Lancasters. He was not sent abroad, but served ten years as a part time soldier, being discharged in 1910 'on completion of engagement'.

Having already done some professional boxing and also qualified as a referee, he was keen to make a career in the sport, and whenever the opportunity arose he would involve himself with local promotions, helping out in any way he could, just to learn the ropes and gain as much experience as possible.

Joe never had a steady job, although he was employed off and on in the local cotton mills as a cop picker. By this time he was married to Ellen Floyd, a girl he had known in Warrington. They lived in Spencer Street at the rough end of the village, in a one-up-one-down cottage, and over a period of thirteen years or so Ellen gave birth to four children, Albert, born in 1912, being the youngest.

Ellen was never happy in Royton. She saw very little of her husband, for Joe was seldom at home. When he wasn't at work he would either be out on boxing business or just enjoying himself. Though not a heavy drinker, he had a keen eye for the ladies, and the fact that he was now a married man with a family does not appear to have inhibited him in the slightest. Joe's philandering and uncaring attitude eventually wrecked the marriage, for when Albert was only three months old the couple separated, Ellen returning to her relatives in Warrington with the two eldest children, while Albert and his four year old sister, Josephine, were left behind in Royton with their father. Joe solved the problem by moving what was left of his family in with the Maloneys, who occupied a cottage in Union Street, just off the Middleton Road.

Some time after this Joe managed to rent a large end terraced, also in Union Street, with four spacious upper rooms. Known as Meanock House, it was a property previously occupied by the Meanocks, a theatrical family, the departing thespians having left behind a pile of old costumes and stage props, which proved ideal playthings for the army of kids who made up the Maloney-Tolley clan.

The break-up of the family must have been a terrible wrench for Ellen and her children, but it was no doubt necessary on economic grounds alone. As for Joe Tolley, it's doubtful if the parting weighed too heavily on him, for he was always busy, and Albert claims that his father could never settle down to a quiet evening at home throughout his entire life. From being a young man, almost until the time of his death, he would be either out on business or with a woman.

Albert did not see his mother again for seventeen years. Even then it was only a chance meeting, for he and his father had stopped off at Warrington to visit one of his sisters while on their way to Liverpool Stadium. Finding Ellen in attendance, Joe simply turned to Albert and said, 'This is your mother'.

But for Albert it was not an emotional meeting. The woman standing before him was a stranger.

By the time the Great War broke out Joe Tolley was doing a bit of part time journalism, as one of the Lancashire contributors of the trade paper '*Boxing*', though this amounted to little more than sending in the results and details of shows in his area. The war had been going on for about two years before he got back into uniform, though he rose quickly to the rank of Corporal. There was not much time for sport during that bloody conflict, but Joe somehow managed to fit in some boxing and became a P.T. instructor, finishing the war as a Sergeant-Major, being demobbed in February 1919, after serving in France.

Back home there was little work to be had for a man without a proper trade in his hands, but Joe was a very resourceful fellow. Apart from his work as a boxing correspondent, which actually brought in very little, he was by this time a leading referee and was also involved in the organisation of local shows then being held at the old Olympic Skating Rink and the Oldham Drill Hall.

In addition, he was attempting to establish boxing in the village of Royton, where any number of eager young lads were keen to put the gloves on. Whenever he could get hold of a room of any kind; a hut, or an old barn, Tolley would instruct the locals and arrange bouts between them.

This was really the beginning and there is no doubt that, despite his impoverished state, Joe had promotional ambitions of his own even then. In the early twenties he saw the chance to make a start, albeit a very modest one.

On the opposite side of the street from Meanock House, which the Maloneys and the Tolleys still occupied, stood a small factory which repaired packing cases for the cotton mills. Joe arranged to rent the upper floor, where he started a boxing school. This tiny arena was to become the first Royton Stadium.

Conditions were spartan and the equipment very basic indeed. Strips of wood were nailed to the rough walls to serve as bars, there were a couple of heavy bags, home made, hanging from the exposed beams, and apart from a few battered medicine balls and skipping ropes, the only other piece of equipment was an inflatable dummy with a heavy rounded hollow base, which rolled over then bounced back again when punched. An assortment of worn out old boxing gloves completed the inventory. There was no toilet or shower, just a tap on the wall and one tiny dressing room containing a massage bench.

The gym soon attracted quite a number of local lads as well as some from outlying districts, but as there were already a number of clubs in the area, including the Oldham Boxing Club and the Broadway Boxing Club, in nearby Chadderton, Tolley felt that it would take a while to develop. In a surprisingly short space of time, however, the lads were flocking in and clamouring for Joe to stage his first show.

According to Albert, the makeshift ring which Joe erected was so small that the boxers had no alternative but to stand and fight. As many as 200 people could be packed into the 'Stadium', but because of poor ventilation and the fact that almost everyone smoked in those days, the back windows had to be removed or people could quite easily have suffocated. The only way into this loft was via a flight of rickety wooden steps running up the outside of the building.

Shows were held each Sunday morning and a silver collection taken, though usually the hat was returned to Tolley full of the old silver threepenny bits, so there was very little chance of the new promoter becoming a tycoon overnight.

Tolley's first venture was named The Royton Boxing Club and over the next couple of years or so it became well known throughout the area, with a growing band of supporters keen to watch the local scrappers slug it out, the boys themselves being eager to show what they could do and earn a few shillings into the bargain.

The club was, in fact, such a success that Tolley was soon looking for bigger premises. He found them no more than fifty yards away, in the shape of a long room above Ben Barns' skip and case making works higher up Union Street. This building, which still stands today, later became a sawmill and is now unoccupied, was infinitely better than the old club and could hold three or four times the number of people. Again the entrance was by way of a flight of wooden steps leading up to the one small door. In the yard at the back Tolley erected a primitive urinal out of old sheets of corrugated iron, but did not bother about drainage.

The New Royton Boxing Club opened its doors in 1925 and was an even bigger success than the first one. In this period many promising fighters were developed. They came from as far away as Ashton-under-Lyne, Rochdale, Middleton, Shaw and Lees, and usually walked there and back, for very few could afford the tram fare. Some had jobs in the cotton mills, but many more were out of work.

Those lads who were good enough to fight on the bills were allowed to use the training facilities free of charge, while others were expected to contribute towards the club's upkeep by paying a subscription of a few pence per week. There was so little money about in those days, however, that Tolley considered himself very lucky when someone paid up.

The club was open most days and every night in the week except Saturday and Sunday, with a show each Sunday afternoon.

Before very long great local rivalry had been built up and many 'money matches' were made for as much as ten and twenty pounds aside, the boxers having to rely on someone to back them, which was not usually a problem, so keen was the local interest.

Among the more prominent scrappers developed at Royton during the twenties to early thirties were Joe Myers, 'Kid' Lees, Harry Riley, Jimmy Travis, Johnny Nolan, Johnny Melia, Billy Mounders, 'Cyclone' Charlie Ovey and Walter Ovey (Overton), 'Stoker' Lawrie Sharples, Joe Sharples, Billy 'Cast Iron' Hague, Tommy Woods*, Billy Cook, Louis and Jock Callan, Willy Walsh, Tommy Maloney and Phil Milligan, all from Oldham, and Billy Cakewell (Capewell), Matty Cox, Jack 'Tod' Sloane, Young Tierney, Roy Hilton and Sam Pearson from Hollinwood.

* Not to be confused with the Oldham heavyweight of the 1960s.

From the Shaw-Royton area came Harold Ratchford, Mick Ester, Syd and Billy Longworth, Walter and Mickey Maloney (Young Mickey), Bert, Dick and Asa Hilditch, Teddy Bodell, Billy and Roland Bowcock, Jean Locatelli (Jimmy Haigh), 'Battling' Bennett, Jim Costello, Tom Durnford, Freddie Hilton, Fred and Jack Northfield and Stan 'Spud' Murray.

Nearby Middleton provided Jim Dagnall, 'Seaman' Harry Wolfe, Jim Byron, Bob Braid, Sam Fidler, and Billy and Tommy Tansey, while from Rochdale came Joe Walsh, Eddie Strawer, Martin Gallagher, Joe Fleming, Johnny Eccles, Joe Crompton, Mickey Clarke, Joe Horridge, George 'K.O.' Turner and Johnny King, plus Joe Rostron from Heywood.

From the Ashton-under-Lyne area came Harold Smithson, Jack Davies, Billy Raybould, 'Cush' Davies, Billy Griffin and Billy Pritchard, 'The Fighting Postman' from Stalybridge.

Of the above mentioned, 'Cast Iron' Hague and Jimmy Travis fought with some success in America. In 1927, Hague, only twenty-five, was described as a veteran, and no wonder. Over the previous five years or so he had been fighting week in and week out, and usually engaged in what could only be described as blood baths, slogging away until either he or the other man dropped.

Phil Milligan was a great little flyweight who later fought in the highest class, taking on Peter Kane, Jackie Paterson, Benny Lynch and Terry Allen, all World Champions.

Several of the Middleton lads lived in the same street, a situation which led to fierce local rivalry.

Two of the most enthusiastic Royton fighters were Joe Tolley's stepbrothers, Walter and Mickey Maloney*, both of whom fought in good class. In 1920 Walter lost on points over ten rounds to the great Len Johnson, the coloured Manchester fighter, and in 1925 met Len Harvey at the world famous National Sporting Club in London. Walter was K.O.'d in one round, though this was no disgrace, as the clever Cornishman would go on to become one of Britain's greatest ever champions.

Walter's brother, known as Young Mickey, was a flyweight, skinny as a beanpole, but with a punch like a sledgehammer. He was also as hard as nails, and though a fast mover, usually preferred to stand and slug it out. This did not serve him well in the long run. He was just too tough for his own good and took so many hard blows that his

* Sometimes billed as Malone.

career, which began at the age of fourteen, was virtually over by the time he was twenty.

Mickey was fighting long before Joe Tolley opened his first boxing club and on one occasion was engaged to box an exhibition with Jimmy Wilde, who was World Champion at the time and without doubt the greatest flyweight ever. Mickey saw the exhibition as a chance to make a name for himself and went all out to flatten his famous opponent. Wilde, however, was far too clever to be caught napping. He was easily able to avoid Young Mickey's haymakers and could have disposed of the local fighter in short order had he so wished.

Having experienced the Welsh Wizard's genius at first hand, Mickey came out of that fight a much wiser man and with the greatest respect for Wilde, later describing to Albert Tolley the way in which the champion had drawn him onto his punches 'like a magnet', then picked him off as easily as if he'd been a novice.

This was also one of the secrets of Wilde's awesome punching power, for apart from leverage, his timing was immaculate, an opponent often being caught flush on the chin just as he moved in to take advantage of an apparent opening left by the crafty little Welshman.

Johnny King first took up the game when he was fourteen and lived in Rochdale. He was taught and trained at Royton, and apart from the odd defeat was successful from the start. He did not remain long with Joe Tolley, however, before moving on to Harry Fleming's gym at Collyhurst, Manchester. Brought along gradually by Fleming, he eventually succeeded in winning the British and Empire Bantamweight titles, and came very close to taking the World crown from 'Panama' Al Brown.

Albert Tolley had no intention of making a career out of fighting himself, though he had won a local schoolboy title and later engaged in a number of professional contests. But from the age of fourteen he was involved in the day to day running of the club, for on leaving school he went to work for his father full time, doing the office work, helping to organise the shows and later driving Joe and his fighters to out of town venues.

Joe Tolley could never be bothered to learn how to drive. He was just too busy and too impatient. So he gave Albert the money and told him to get a license.

'There was no test then,' Albert told me, 'you just sent a five bob postal order off to Preston and back came this parchment. It was as simple as that.'

Each Monday morning, while Albert and his Dad set about preparing the bill for the following Sunday, Young Mickey, who never had a regular job, would sweep up and carry out all the other menial tasks around the club.

Albert had also learned to type, and early in the week would have to get his copy ready for the printers. As soon as the posters and hand bills were delivered later in the week he would distribute them to the various pubs, clubs and shops in the area. Then, assisted by Young Mickey and sometimes Billy Mounders, another of the boxers, he would go around the town fly-posting those which were left over.

But all the hard work and planning was certainly paying off, the new club going from strength to strength, with the Sunday afternoon shows now beginning to attract a more varied clientele, including theatrical people, businessmen, doctors and professional footballers.

Even the toilet situation had improved, separate ladies and gents conveniences having been installed, which was very necessary, for among the regular customers were a growing number of female fans.

As well as promoting, managing most of the fighters and refereeing, Joe Tolley also acted as matchmaker and MC., and was adept at getting the crowd all fired up and buzzing with anticipation. A born showman, he was quick-witted, entertaining and never at a loss for words.

He was also an extremely busy man, and as well as running his own operation was in increasing demand all over the country, away two or three times a week, travelling by train while Albert looked after things at Royton.

Medical supervision in boxing was almost non-existent in those days, and Albert recalls an incident involving the Rochdale flyweight, Johnny Eccles, who was knocked out in a bout at Uppermill, just over the border in Yorkshire. Afterwards, he was in such bad shape that he had to be carried out of the stadium and transported to Joe Tolley's house in Royton. Still in a semi-conscious state, he was laid out on a couch to 'sleep it off'. There is no doubt that he should have been taken to the hospital, or at the very least a doctor called. Instead, he was made as comfortable as possible before Joe and the family went off to bed. Next morning, Albert, then just a lad, came downstairs to find the boxer still asleep. Fortunately, little Johnny eventually came round and was apparently none the worse for his frightening experience. This incident, and the way it was handled, could quite easily have had serious consequences for all concerned, and in 1925 a terrible tragedy did, in fact, occur, which shocked and saddened, not only local boxing fans, but the whole of Royton and the surrounding area.

Matthew Ratchford was seventeen, and like his brother Harold had been boxing for a number of years, going back to the time when they, along with several other local kids, had been hoisted up into the ring at professional shows and encouraged to 'get stuck in' while the crowd roared them on. These miniature battlers became known as the Royton Midgets, and from their ranks emerged some pretty formidable fighters, the most talented of whom was without doubt Harold Ratchford. Two years older than his brother Matt, Harold, known as Royton's 'Wonder Boy', was a highly skilled performer, even as a teenager. A superb boxer, he was so quick and clever that opponents found it almost impossible to lay a glove on him, let alone nail him with a solid punch. Matt, on the other hand, though a more than useful boxer, was not nearly so dedicated. A bobbin carrier at the King Mill, Royton, he fought only spasmodically, and after a lay-off of several weeks, sometimes months, he would be back in the gym, his interest having returned, and would then have a few contests before dropping off again.

In the autumn of 1925, Matt, who had done very little boxing over the previous eighteen months, resumed training and took part in three contests in the space of three weeks or so, one at nearby Shaw and two at Royton.

On Sunday afternoon October 25th he was matched with John Green, another Royton lad of similar experience and class, in the semi-final of a 7-stone competition arranged by Joe Tolley, the winner to receive a 400-day clock and the runner-up a cup. The referee was Captain J. S. Codlin, an experienced official who handled the contest in his usual competent fashion. The fight, though hard, was not particularly brutal, the only sign of damage being that both boys bled slightly from the nose. By the third round, however, Ratchford was beginning to take a beating, and at this juncture the referee decided to call a halt and award the decision to Green.

The loser left the ring unassisted, remarking to one of the officials, Jack Crossan, that he was quite all right. On reaching the dressing room he lay on a trestle table while Tommy Corrigan, the club masseur, sponged him, then gave him a rub down, there being no baths or showers on the premises. While this was going on Ratchford complained of pains in his head. Soon after this, while getting dressed, he suddenly collapsed in an unconscious state. The boy's father, who was in the hall, working as a second in one of the corners, was immediately sent for, while efforts were made to revive him. Joe Tolley was soon on the scene but could do little to help. The stricken fighter did come round for a few seconds, before sinking away again.

Young Albert, only thirteen years old at the time, was playing outside in the street while all the drama was taking place, but remembered the incident and seemed to recall that an ambulance arrived to take Matt Ratchford to the hospital. The newspaper records of the time, however, tell a slightly different story. After lying in the dressing room for roughly three-quarters of an hour, the boxer was removed to his home, which was quite close by, and a local medical man, Dr Holden, sent for. After examining the patient the doctor told his mother that he would be all right after a good night's sleep. During Sunday evening he was conscious some of the time, but spoke only a few words. As he was no better the following morning the doctor was again summoned. By now it was clear that the patient's condition was quite serious and an ambulance was soon on the scene.

Matt Ratchford was admitted to the Oldham Royal Infirmary at 4.15pm that day, unconscious and obviously in a very bad way. Shortly before six o'clock on the following evening the young boxer died.

At the inquest it was stated that death was due to cerebral haemorrhage. The bout had been governed by National Sporting Club rules and 8oz. gloves used. Captain Codlin stated that although the contest had been quite a rugged affair, there were no knockdowns and neither boy had taken excessive punishment. He had only stopped the fight because Ratchford was so far behind on points that he had no chance of winning.

John Green, who lived in nearby Spencer Street and worked as a piecer at the Fir Mill, Royton, had been a close friend of his deceased opponent, the two of them having been out together on the evening before the contest. The dead boy's father, Robert Ratchford, a barber, said that the bout had been properly conducted. The contestants had been around the same weight and the fight was fair in every way. A verdict of "death by misadventure" was returned.

Ratchford's family were naturally distraught, and Harold's mother pleaded with him to seriously consider giving up the game. Severely shocked by what had occurred, he was certainly in no fit state mentally to make a positive decision on his future as a boxer. I was told by a member of the family that Harold gave up for well over a year following the tragedy, but in fact the records show that he was back in the ring exactly six weeks later, outpointing Ernie Barker at Royton over fifteen rounds. Still, six weeks was a long time to be out of the ring in those days, and no doubt it was also a question of economic necessity. We do know that Harold Ratchford was a very popular fighter and that Joe Tolley was constantly receiving requests for his services. So, upsetting as this horrifying episode had undoubtedly been, both boxer and manager very soon put that tragic Sunday behind them and carried on as before.

# Chapter 3

## Alias Joe Bamford

No one, of course, realised it at the time, but Sunday, November 6th 1927, was to prove a momentous day indeed for the Royton Boxing Club. For on that day nineteen-year-old Joe Bamford from Rochdale walked through the door for the first time.

It was a Sunday morning, and he had come over from Rochdale with a mate. Bamford's pal, who claimed to have some experience, spoke to Joe Tolley, who told him that the pair of them would have to have a trial before being considered for a contest.

Bamford was told to strip off and found himself facing the promoter's step-brother, Young Mickey Maloney. Though much the lighter man, Mickey was a seasoned scrapper and tore into the attack from the first bell, peppering the newcomer with stinging left jabs and darting around him at such speed that Joe hardly managed to lay a glove on him.

At the end of four hectic but very frustrating rounds he was somewhat surprised to be offered a fight on that afternoon's bill, his friend being told to come back another time.

Before going on that day Bamford was asked his name, and, fearing that his mother might find out and not wanting to upset her, he decided to borrow the name of another great idol of his, Kid McCoy, or at least part of it, for he asked Tolley to announce him as Jack McCoy.

Tolley didn't mind at all, but got things a bit mixed up when making his ring announcement and introduced the new lad as 'Jock McAvoy from Rochdale'.

The name, of course, stuck. Though to close friends and relatives he always remained Joe Bamford.

From this point on, however, it will be simpler and less confusing to the reader if we refer to him as McAvoy, or Mac, as he was known in the fight game and to the general public.

That afternoon McAvoy was matched with Billy Longworth of Royton and came out throwing punches non-stop from the first bell.

Returning breathless to his corner, he was dumped on his stool by a second, who then showered him with water, wiped his face with a towel and told him to slow down and pick his punches.

The advice went unheeded, for when the bell rang for round two McAvoy bounded from his corner like a tornado, and though most of his haymakers missed by a mile, one at last somehow connected, stretching Longworth out on the canvas for the full count.

The debutant was very pleased with himself and asked Tolley how he had done.

'You were too big for him,' snapped the promoter, handing him his purse. 'You can come back next week if you like.'

That McAvoy was too big for his opponent there can be no doubt, for at that time he was at least ten and a half stone, while Billy Longworth weighed nine stone odd and was a novice himself, though by no means as green as Mac.

As for the purse, as near as can be ascertained it would be around seven shillings and sixpence*.

Thus began a long and fruitful relationship between two men who had much in common, although neither of them realised it at the time.

McAvoy went home to Rochdale elated with his win and raring to go again, putting in some hard, enthusiastic training and hoping to get another fight the following Sunday.

It was, however, three weeks before he got his next chance, this time against Bert Hilditch, a lad from nearby Shaw, and one of three brothers, all of whom boxed at Royton. While McAvoy had just turned twenty, his opponent was a mere youngster of seventeen, though already an experienced pro with a string of wins to his credit, and was the only man to have beaten 'Stoker' Sharples (of whom more will be heard later) up to that time.

When he met McAvoy though, Hilditch was not much more than a lightweight, and soon found that he'd picked a tartar in the new lad from Rochdale, who was very tough indeed and started where he'd left off in his previous contest, throwing caution to the wind and just wading in.

Hilditch's experience saw him through the first few rounds all right, and also enabled him to land some well-placed shots of his own. Bert soon found, however, that he was up against a lad who seemed to possess tremendous strength, and as he himself began to slow down he had little option but to stand there and trade punches.

* 37½p in today's money.

It had now developed into a gruelling contest, and though the Rochdale boy could not manage to put his opponent away, he did, in the end, outlast him, Hilditch eventually running out of steam and being put down several times in round six, prompting the referee to call a halt.

Weary, but flushed with success, McAvoy could hardly wait to be given his next assignment.

In those early days at Royton McAvoy would turn up at the gym in the hope of finding some good sparring, but this did not work out. In the first place the best and most experienced boxers at the club did not go in for much sparring, they didn't need to. Under Tolley's management they were constantly in demand, some fighting as often as two and three times a week. That left only the other novices and the second-raters, and once McAvoy became known around the club there were very few among them who were willing to get into the ring with him. For one thing he was too big for most of the locals, Tolley's boys being mostly on the small side*; flyweights, bantams, feathers and lightweights, with very few heavier men around. McAvoy, on the other hand was a big welterweight and still growing.

The other reason was that with Mac there was no such thing as a sparring session. He always went at it as though the world title was at stake, going all out to hammer any man they put in front of him, whether he was a big fellow or the smallest boxer in the gym.

In these circumstances it is not difficult to understand why there was so little sparring available for him. The truth is, that although there were any number of tough lads around the gym, they were all well aware that sparring partners taking the sort of punishment that Mac was dishing out usually got paid for it. Consequently Mac soon dropped off going to Royton between fights, but continued to train in Rochdale.

By contrast little Phil Milligan was never away. Phil lived in the West Street area of Oldham. It was a tough neighbourhood which the police always patrolled in twos. There were some rough families living in and around West Street and the Milligans were among the roughest. Like the Lynches up in Glasgow they were fighters and drinkers, though in his early days Phil never touched a drop himself.

He was dead keen on boxing, and after finishing work at the Sun Mill, Chadderton, where he was employed as a little piecer, he would

* This was hardly surprising, for then the average Lancashire man stood about five foot five or six and weighed around nine stone.

dash home, have a quick bite and a 'swill' at the slopstone, before grabbing his kit and rushing off to Royton.

When Albert arrived to open up for the evening's training Phil would usually be standing on the doorstep, a paper parcel under his arm containing shorts, pumps and a dirty towel.

After skipping, shadow boxing and bag punching he could hardly wait to get into the ring, and like McAvoy, he always gave it everything. After going three blistering rounds with one sparring partner, Phil would lean back on the ropes and wait for the next man to climb in. He was never satisfied until he'd taken on every fighter in the gym.

'In fact,' Albert told me, 'some of the other lads were inclined to make themselves scarce when Phil was in the gym, even the bigger ones.'

Though he weighed not much over seven stone at that time, little Phil had the heart of a lion, and there is no doubt that he would not have thought twice had he been called upon to fight it out with McAvoy. But of course, even Joe Tolley would never have allowed that. Somebody might easily have been killed.

'Phil would never leave the place until we were ready to close up around ten o'clock,' recalls Albert. 'Night after night he'd be at it. He used to knock hell out of 'em. And of course he was taking plenty himself, but that never bothered him. He loved it.'

Though McAvoy may have been short of sparring he was by no means neglecting his training. In his own way he was very keen and had managed to rig up a makeshift gym in a derelict house close to his home, which he rented for a few coppers per week. There he fashioned a punchbag out of an old sack stuffed with rags and other bits of rubbish. As well as pounding this for round after round he also put in many hours of skipping and shadow boxing.

Having invested in a manual on boxing by Jack Dempsey, the fighter he admired above all others, Mac devoured every word in it. Words were not the only thing he devoured, for as well as practicing interminably every move and punch illustrated in the book, he also ate huge quantities of the oatmeal bread which Dempsey advocated. Many years later he told a reporter, 'After a fortnight the stuff was coming out of my ears and I started to develop boils.'

Meanwhile, Mac was keen to fight as often as possible, but here we run into something of a mystery regarding his record, for though his next recorded contest was against Billy Chew of Darwen, on January 27th 1928, McAvoy himself claimed to have taken part in a number of other contests between beating Bert Hilditch on November 27th 1927 and the Billy Chew fight.

There are several versions of McAvoy's record knocking about, every one incorrect in some respect or other*. Almost all of them begin in 1928, which throws the whole thing out from the start, for there is absolutely no questioning the fact that McAvoy's career commenced at Royton in 1927.

The only record which comes close to anything like authenticity is one which does actually start on the correct date of November 6th 1927. After the Hilditch contest, however, that too goes astray, listing two other contests, both in December 1927. These were purportedly against Tommy Welsh (Shaw) and Bill Lee (Wrexham), at Royton and Rhyl respectively.

Careful checking, however, reveals that the Lee fight took place on February 28th 1930, ending in a win for McAvoy on a three round knockout, while no record of a fighter by the name of Tommy Welsh from Shaw appears to exist. There was a Joe Walsh of Rochdale, who was very well known, and also a Billy or Willie Walsh of Oldham, who was only a flyweight, so it's hardly likely to have been either of these. If such a contest did take place, then Tommy Welsh or Walsh was probably a local novice, who, like many others, had just a handful of fights before realising that he had little chance of making the grade and quickly vanished from the scene.

So far as can be ascertained McAvoy did not fight again following the Hilditch contest until he met Billy Chew two months later.

Joe Tolley at that time had his hands full looking after the Royton club's better known fighters, who were now in wide demand, as well as his numerous other activities. Of course, Joe certainly knew a prospect when he saw one, and obviously decided that McAvoy was already capable of going ten rounds in better class. Matching him with Chew, however, turned out to be a bad mistake.

Mac trained hard for the contest, perhaps too hard, for he seemed slow and listless on the night and took quite a pasting from the very capable Chew, a tough Lancashire miner with plenty of experience behind him.

As usual McAvoy tore into the attack from the opening bell, only to be met by a long left jab that was as solid and jarring as it was

* See note regarding the late Vic Hardwicke in acknowledgements.

accurate. No matter how hard he tried in the opening rounds Mac could not seem to get going, and though he refused to be disheartened, battling away for three minutes of every round, he was making no impression at all on the crafty Chew, who was letting him tire himself out.

By round six Mac had begun to slow down, while Chew, now in full control, was handing out a systematic beating. In round seven Billy stepped up the pace, a lightning right hand putting Mac on the canvas for the first time. But though tired out and bleeding badly from the nose he refused to take a count and was up immediately and ready to carry on, though by now he had barely enough strength left to raise his arms to defend himself. At the round's end he was just about all in, and after the minute's rest, during which he was hurriedly cleaned up by his second, it was all he could do to get up off his stool. On being pushed out by his corner when the bell rang for round eight, he was so dead beat that he was forced to hold up his hand in surrender.

Mac later claimed that he had tired himself out that afternoon by playing football in the snow, in the mistaken belief that it would enhance his stamina for the fight, but there seems little doubt that he had been well and truly beaten. Clearly the result of overmatching.

Billy Chew was no mug. Though there was very little difference in their ages he knew far too much for Mac at that time and handled the Rochdale man with ease. Chew didn't look much like a fighter, but once inside the ropes he was an accomplished craftsman. He came from a very poor background indeed and gave the impression that with someone behind him he might well have gone a long way in the game.

The defeat was without doubt a serious setback for McAvoy, who took it very much to heart. Later he was to state that his mother got to know of his boxing activities and was so upset that he gave it up for the next eighteen months.

This is not quite correct. When he returned home after fighting Billy Chew there is very little doubt that Nellie would have been upset when she saw the state of her only son's features, for Chew had really worked him over. She probably pleaded with him to pack it in, and after such an emphatic defeat he must have had more than a few misgivings himself. However, there was one more contest to come before he left the game for a spell, for within a couple of months he had regained his confidence enough to go in with Teddy Cox of

Todmorden, knocking him out in seven rounds at Todmorden Drill Hall, on March 19th 1928.

Around this time McAvoy was being pursued by a rugged local fighter named Freddie Heighton, who was also something of a character. Heighton came from the village of Delph, near Oldham, and was prepared to take on just about anything on two legs. He was very fond of issuing challenges, and though quite a tough customer and a very hard hitter, he had come to grief himself a few times, usually through stepping out of his class; like the night he was hammered by Jock McFarlane of Bolton and knocked down a dozen times in all before the fight ended.

Freddie, who had a full time job as a navvy, was a very busy fighter who always seemed to be surrounded by controversy. Once, at Royton, he was involved in a double knockout when fighting Mick Ester of Shaw, both fighters collapsing to the canvas after an horrific clash of heads, and neither being in a fit state to continue.

Heighton had heard all about the new sensation from Rochdale and couldn't wait to get a crack at him, telling all and sundry just what he intended to do to Mac and offering to back himself for £25 aside. McAvoy indicated that he was willing and the match was duly arranged, though according to the posters the side bet was for £10. Unfortunately, it was a fight which never came off, though the reason why is not clear.

According to Freddie he encountered McAvoy outside the stadium on the day of the fight and was astonished to be told that although Mac was quite fit there would be no contest between them that afternoon, as Joe Tolley had refused to let it go on. Heighton then went on to state that he was very angry and told McAvoy to take off his jacket and he'd fight him on the spot.

It would seem extremely unlikely that Tolley would call off such a money spinning contest between two big punching rivals. More likely it was Mac himself who pulled out for some reason or other, and didn't like to admit it.

In any event, further efforts were made to get the fight on over the following weeks, but nothing concrete materialised. In the end it was stated in a local paper that the proposed clash had been called off altogether, McAvoy having failed to cover Heighton's money for the third time.

After disposing of Teddy Cox in March 1928, therefore, McAvoy disappeared from the fight scene and was not heard of again until the summer of 1929.

# Chapter 4

## A Unique Arena

McAvoy was not the only one under pressure at this time. For over a year Joe Tolley had been fighting a running battle with the Lord's Day Observance Society, whose members, outraged at the very idea of people actually enjoying themselves on the Sabbath, especially through such a barbarous pastime as prizefighting, were dedicated to closing Tolley down, he and his cohorts being referred to in a letter to the local newspaper as 'the dregs of humanity'.

Boxing, of course, could be termed a brutal sport, and the Royton fans certainly loved hard slugging matches with plenty of blood and guts. In those days a boxer had to be in a very bad way indeed before a referee would even consider stopping a contest, and Albert could clearly recall many fights which he described as 'absolute slaughter', with one or other of the combatants refusing to go down or 'give in', despite being covered in blood and practically out on his feet. To the Lord's Day Observance people the roar of the crowd must have sounded like the whoops of the bloodthirsty as the Roman gladiators clashed in a fight to the death.

Most of the time Joe Tolley just ignored his critics, but when they failed to make an impression by drawing the public's attention to the scandalous and disgraceful performances being staged at Royton on a Sunday afternoon, Tolley's enemies decided to try other tactics, attempting to get their own way by informing the authorities that the club was a fire trap.

Unfortunately they were quite right, it was. With only a small door at the far end of a loft over a hundred feet in length, it would have been quite impossible to evacuate several hundred people quickly in the event of a fire, and the truth was that Tolley, giving little or no thought to even basic fire and safety precautions, was packing them in like sardines. But Joe could see the writing on the wall and set about looking for other premises while stalling for time. In any case it was clear that he would soon be hard pressed to accommodate all who wanted to see the fights, so popular had the new venue now become.

Not far away in Middleton Road, standing well back from the main carriageway and directly opposite the Church Inn, was an old weaving shed, backing onto the Grape and Vine cotton mills. Many years before it had closed down and become derelict, but during the First World War had been taken over and renovated by Brookes' Bakery of Manchester. As it was now again unoccupied, Tolley approached the bakery company and managed to fix up a deal, leasing the property and adjoining yard at a very nominal rent indeed.

The place was vast; capable, in fact, of holding well over 2,000 people comfortably. There was a huge yard at the rear, surrounded by a high wall, which Tolley estimated would take at least 5,000 in the event of outdoor boxing being staged.

As Joe strutted proudly around his new empire, Albert at his side, his fertile brain was working overtime. The possibilities were endless. Already a master plan was forming in his mind. Without pausing to reflect on the sad fact that he lacked the wherewithal to make the dream a reality, Joe lost no time in outlining the details of his scheme to the newspapers.

Accordingly it was announced in the press that the new stadium, scheduled to open its doors in the early part of 1928, would be fitted with all the latest gymnasium equipment, also baths, open air running track, tennis courts and motor park.

In the meantime Albert and the lads set about clearing out the old weaving shed, which had a number of gaping holes in its glass roof and was overgrown with weeds inside, although the stone floor was basically sound. Once the place was tidied up and the roof repaired they were ready to move in and Joe was already planning the first show.

The new arena was named Royton Stadium and opened in the spring of 1928. It was to be Tolley's final move, and proved to be an inspired one, with boxing in the area reaching an all-time peak over the next four years.

Soon they were ready to open, by which time one local newspaper, after interviewing Joe Tolley, claimed that the new Royton Stadium was the third largest boxing hall in the North and Midlands, with its '2,000 elevated seats'.

This seating claim was something of an exaggeration, the layout being as follows: several rows of bentwood chairs were arranged around the ringside, the price of those closest to the ring being three shillings, with the two shilling seats a little farther back. Beyond this the one shilling customers were accommodated on slightly elevated plank seating. These were on three sides of the arena, leaving one end free for standing room at sixpence. In wintertime the place was very cold and several large braziers were used to heat it up before the fans arrived.

Joe Tolley's career in boxing had now really taken off. With the new stadium open and doing well he was able to leave more to Albert and spread his wings. He was by far the busiest boxing referee in the country, and a regular at Liverpool Stadium, Morecambe Winter Gardens and many other venues, including the Gaiety Theatre in Douglas on the Isle of Man, where, in 1928, a Manx Boxing Syndicate, which had big plans to put Douglas on the map as a major fight centre, also appointed him matchmaker. In addition, he had begun accepting engagements in Ireland, and travelled to Dublin and Cork on a number of occasions.

Most of the matches he made in Douglas involved his own fighters, and over the next few years Royton boxers made the trip as a team, often accompanied by Albert. As well as work it was also a holiday for the lads, who might not otherwise have had the opportunity to travel so far. They really enjoyed those trips and made good money.

A typical Douglas bill in 1928 read as follows:

| | | |
|---|---|---|
| **Joe Walsh (Rochdale)** | **V** | **Ted Thomas (Newcastle)** |
| **Roland Bowcock (Shaw)** | **V** | **Billy Mounders (Oldham)** |
| **Johnny King (Rochdale)** | **V** | **Tich Cain (Douglas)** |
| **Syd Longworth (Royton)** | **V** | **Harry Killner (Douglas)** |

Several of Joe Tolley's fighters were now in big demand. Harold Ratchford, probably the most talented man in the stable, was beating many top men and pressing for a title fight. The trouble was that there were so many outstanding fighters in the country at every weight in those days that the odds against reaching the top were very great indeed.

Harold started at thirteen in 1920 and worked his way through the weights from fly to lightweight, building up a tremendous record. He was at his best around the age of eighteen, when he was said to be absolutely superb and highly accomplished in every facet of the game. Like most of his contemporaries he often fought much bigger men and never worried about giving weight away.

Though his record shows a total of nearly 300 traceable contests there were probably a good many more which went unrecorded. Harold himself claimed 532, but this total no doubt included booth bouts, which don't count on a boxer's record. However, the correct figure would appear to be somewhere between three and four hundred, a staggering total, though by no means unique in that era.

Harold retired in 1934, having enjoyed a fine career, the high points of which were undoubtedly his two wins over Aldo Spoldi, one of Italy's all-time greats. That Ratchford never got the chance to fight for a major title was a gross injustice.

The fact that he finished up with a flat nose and a couple of cauliflower ears was by no means a true reflection of his ability, for these were sustained when he was close to the end of his career. Training had become a chore, he was nowhere near as fit as he had been in his younger days and found himself getting caught with punches which he would previously have evaded with ease. He knew then it was time to get out.

Harold kept himself in excellent shape for the remainder of his life, and when turned sixty underwent a three-day examination at the Manchester Royal Infirmary as part of an investigation into the lasting effects of ring combat. He came out of it with flying colours, being pronounced a hundred per cent fit both physically and mentally.

Some people claimed that Joe Tolley was a bad manager. That he overmatched his fighters and put them into the ring too often and for too little money. Looked at in greater depth this does not appear to have been the case at all. Joe controlled as many as fifty fighters at any one time, at least thirty of whom would be boxing during any given week. At the foot of his letterhead was the slogan:

*"Never be stuck for a substitute, any weight, any class, write, 'phone or wire.., any time, any day".*

Not that he needed to rely on substitute jobs for his fighters, for he had so many contacts all over the country that he could guarantee the majority of his boys at least a fight a week. They wanted the work and it was normal in those days for a pro to fight often. If a boxer was forced by injury to lay off for a few weeks he was considered to be making a comeback on his return to the ring.

The purses may appear small by today's standards, until looked at more closely, for a boxer in Ratchford's class could earn as much as a pound a round.

By the late twenties Harold was making a good living travelling all over the country, often fighting twice, sometimes even three times a week and having to turn down many lucrative engagements, being booked up months ahead. Fighting ten and fifteen rounders, often at the top of the bill, he was earning well over twenty pounds a week during the season, an enormous amount of money in the twenties and thirties, especially when compared to a working man's wage in the cotton mill say, which could be anywhere from twenty-two shillings (£1-10) to two pounds ten a week (£2-50).

Of course the fighters certainly earned their money, and quite a number finished up punchdrunk, but whether Tolley exploited them or not, he certainly gave them the opportunity to earn excellent wages, provided they possessed a talent for boxing and were dedicated enough.

One thing is certain; there was more to it than just the money, for almost every one of these lads was dead keen and loved to fight. During the summer, many, including Ratchford, would travel the country with the fairground boxing booths.

On fight days at Royton the regular timekeeper was Jim Hall, father of Terry Hall, the ventriloquist, who, along with his dummy, Lennie the Lion, became famous many years later on stage and television.

Tommy Corrigan, a stocky, powerful individual, acted as trainer and rub-down man. Corrigan, a local cotton mill worker, had boxed himself and had a sound knowledge of the game. Full of enthusiasm, he would spend hour after hour putting the raw novices through their paces. He also worked as a second on the Royton shows, a duty for which he usually received sixpence per boxer.

When Royton fighters were booked to appear out of town they were often driven to the venue by Albert Tolley, especially if a number of them were on the same bill. At other times they were told to make their own way and would then go by train. If a boxer had no money for the fare, which was often the case, Joe Tolley would let him have a 'sub'. This would later be repaid out of his purse, which the fighter or his trainer would collect, giving Tolley his commission on returning home. The manager's cut was two and sixpence in the pound (12½p), but Joe only charged this when he placed a boxer on another promoter's bill, never when his boys fought at the Royton Stadium.

Recalling the times when a group of Royton fighters would travel away together, Albert said that following the weigh-in, usually around mid-day, they would all go for lunch, preferably to a Lyon's cafe, if there was one in the town, and Joe Tolley would let them order any meal they wished.

'He believed in letting them have just what they fancied. He always said it was good for their morale, especially if they'd had to take weight off. They might drink half a bottle of milk, then soup, then have a fry-up if they felt like it.

'After that we'd take them for a drive and they would also take a nice leisurely stroll during the afternoon. At teatime they'd have a light meal, perhaps egg on toast say, then just take things easy before going to the stadium.

'Of all the lads, McAvoy had the biggest appetite. How he could eat! I remember us going into a cafe in… Rhyl, I think it was, and Mac ordered this mixed grill. Well, the waitress brought the meals over to us, and almost before the rest of us had got started, his had gone. Aye, just wolfed it down he did, then said he was still hungry. I had to order him another. He was just greedy.

'Mind you, he always gave the impression that if there was owt' goin' he'd make sure he got his share – especially if somebody else was paying.'

One of the lads whom Albert regularly took to the old Liverpool Stadium was 'Cyclone' Charlie Ovey, of Oldham. Though he seldom trained, Charlie, a cotton mill worker, could be relied on to turn out at a minute's notice. According to Albert he was never any trouble. Never argued about money, giving weight away or who he was fighting, and always gave a good account of himself.

If the car was broken down they would travel by train and when the programme finished late it was a rush to get to the station before the last train for Manchester pulled out at around eleven o'clock. If they missed it there was no alternative but to settle down in the waiting room and attempt to get an hour or two's sleep while waiting for the milk train, which did not leave until several hours later. During the night the police would drop in from time to time and clear out anyone sleeping rough who did not possess a rail ticket.

Albert recalls how miserable those long nights were, shivering in that cold, shabby and thoroughly depressing waiting room at Lime Street station. Yet Charlie never complained, he just took it all in his stride.

Once, in the middle of the night, Albert was suddenly aware that Charlie was shaking him gently and woke up to find his companion lolling back contentedly and smiling to himself. Irritably, Albert asked, 'What is it?' Charlie just nodded his head, and Albert, following his gaze, was horrified to see a couple of large rats not more than a few feet away.

'That was Charlie, nothing ever worried him. While I slept he'd been watching these rats as they made a meal of some scraps that were lying about on the floor.'

As far as the Liverpool Stadium fans were concerned Charlie Ovey was tops. Though they really knew their boxing and liked to see a class performer in action, they also admired guts, a quality Charlie possessed in abundance. Stocky and strong, he was certainly lacking in finesse, but though often out-boxed he was never beaten until the final bell. He could be miles behind on points and taking a real hiding, but he would never give up. Quite often, after his opponent had all but punched himself out while trying in vain to put Charlie away, the rugged Oldhamer would begin to come into his own and severely punish his man.

Shorter than the majority of his opponents, Ovey usually had trouble getting to close quarters, especially against a good boxer, though he never minded taking a dozen punches if it meant getting near enough to land one of his own, for Charlie, a powerful hitter, only needed to connect with one clean shot to turn the tide his way.

On one occasion he was taken over to Liverpool by Albert as a trial horse for a local fighter named Charlie Smith, a young and highly promising featherweight from Birkenhead, who was carrying all before him and dispatching his opponents in quick time.

For nine rounds things went according to the script, with Smith boxing brilliantly and jabbing the head off the stocky hard man from Oldham. Then out of the blue Ovey landed one of his 'specials' and the young hopeful went out like a light.

Convinced that their man had been caught with a lucky punch, the Liverpool camp immediately arranged a return for the following week. Unfortunately for Smith, Ovey again found his chin with that sleep-producing right hand, effectively putting an end to the Merseysider's title aspirations.

Soon after this Charlie spoiled another outstanding record, a local newspaper reporting that: 'It took 'Cyclone' Ovey less than three rounds to ruin the Championship ambitions of Young Lundy of Haslingden.'

Following this and other K.O. wins, Ovey was being described in the press as 'One of the most dangerous punchers in the country today.'

But despite his phenomenal hitting power, which resulted in a remarkable run of knockout wins in the late twenties, Charlie was not destined to reach the top. The closest he ever came to competing in higher class was in gaining a win and a draw against Bill Beynon, a former British Champion, who was by then well past his best.

Charlie took far more punishment than was good for him and showed the effects of it in later years. He was so tough that he could proudly lay claim to never having been knocked off his feet in a long and gruelling career.

On the Sunday afternoon shows at Royton there were always far more boxers eager to fight than there were places on the bill, and many of those not booked would still turn up with their gear just in case someone dropped out at the last minute. If there happened to be a few quick knockouts a couple of extra contests could be arranged without any trouble.

One well known scrapper who never failed to put in an appearance was Billy Mounders*, who had no regular employment and lived in a local lodging house. Billy was another who didn't bother to train, yet would take a fight at a minute's notice and could always be relied upon to give value for money. Possessing a rather prominent nose, which must have presented quite a target to his opponents, Mounders was also something of a comedian and a great favourite with the fans.

On one of his shows Joe Tolley billed Mounders as 'The Old Warhorse', matching him with Sam Aarons 'The Smiling Hebrew' from Manchester's Cheetham Hill, for what he termed 'The Comic Championship'.

The antics of these two, who were no mean scrappers when they chose to get down to serious business, had the crowd rolling about with laughter and afforded a nice touch of comic relief from some of the hard slogging contests taking place that afternoon.

With a bigger, better stadium Tolley now saw the opportunity to put into operation many of the grandiose plans and novel ideas which he had been turning over in his mind for a long time.

In March 1928 he announced to the press that he was putting up a belt for 7-stone men, open to all in Great Britain. There were quite a large number of entries, the eventual winner of the competition being Harold Henthorn of Oldham, who beat Jack Wint in eight rounds in the final.

* Pronounced Maunders.

This fight was so keenly contested that a return was arranged over fifteen rounds for £20 aside. Tolley again staged the match and announced that the referee would be Owen Moran, whose presence alone was responsible for ensuring a packed house. An all-time great, the little man from Birmingham was given a rousing reception by the enthusiastic Royton crowd.

Again Henthorn won, and followed this up by sensationally knocking out Johnny King in 30 seconds, including the count, at Oswaldtwistle, later that year, this being the outcome of King's challenge to any fighter in England at his weight.

Henthorn, an outstanding prospect, was badly handicapped by his lack of size, for he was no more than what was then termed a 'paper-weight'. It was a weight class that existed, as there were many small men around in those days, though it was never really recognised. Henthorn was a full stone short of the flyweight limit, and, unlike Johnny King, never grew, being therefore unable to progress as a fighter.

At a time when coloured people were a rare sight on the streets of this country Tolley engaged the services of popular 'Darkie' St. Clair and Alf Langford, known as 'The Black Demon'. He also brought in Constant Le Favourt, a charismatic Frenchman, who caused a major upset on his debut by knocking out local favourite Jim Byron* of Middleton, and became a big hit at Royton.

Other popular visitors were Danny Finn 'The Fighting Harp', a tattooed Irishman who had campaigned successfully in America, Dom Volante, the Liverpool Italian, Jack 'Cast Iron' Casey, the 'Sunderland Assassin', Paddy Slattery, Middleweight Champion of Ireland and Deno Guselli, another Anglo-Italian, based at Barrow-in-Furness.

In March 1928 Tolley staged an Irish/Jewish bill, which read as follows:

| | | |
|---|---|---|
| **Danny Finn (Dublin)** | **V** | **Curly Cliffe** |
| **Martin Gallagher (Rochdale)** | **V** | **Major Nadler** |
| **Jim Costello (Royton)** | **V** | **Joseph Rosenberg** |
| **Harry McLaughlin (Oldham)** | **V** | **Eli Rappstein** |
| **Phil Milligan (Oldham)** | **V** | **Nipper Caplan** |

* In the return fight, in Durham, Byron got his revenge, winning in four rounds.

Recalling that two one-legged men had fought on a bill at Warrington some twenty years before, Tolley decided that such a contest might prove to be something of a draw at Royton. Using the local rivalry angle he put on a much publicised clash between World War One veterans Reggie Humphreys of Middleton and Alf Flanagan of Oldham, who, despite his handicap, acted as trainer to the Higher Moor Rugby League Club. Tolley's publicity mentioned that 'both were handy scrappers before the war'.

This was not the only degrading display that Tolley put on, for he would always be willing to stage challenge matches between men who wished to settle an argument, knowing full well that they would be sure to attract additional custom from the local pubs. He even went so far, on one occasion, as to allow a contest between two women, and another time two men fought over a woman, who was present at the ringside and finished up going off with the loser.

Such unsavoury goings-on did the promoter very little credit by today's standards, but Tolley, an out and out showman, was always looking for something different, anything with either curiosity value or a touch of comedy to add an extra dimension to his shows.

Each summer he would take a team of boxers to Delamere Forest in Cheshire for the annual carnival, where, as well as staging contests, he would don the gloves himself and treat the crowds to a very skilful exhibition of the noble art. As he was now in his late forties and a heavy smoker the bout would be mercifully brief and Tolley would finish puffing and panting but quite pleased with himself. He liked to keep his hand in and was always willing to visit police stations and army barracks to give instruction on unarmed combat.

By the spring of 1929 the Royton Stadium was a huge success, and though the latest gymnasium equipment, baths and tennis courts etc., had failed to materialise, a running track had, in fact, been added, at practically no expense at all, for the crafty Tolley had been up to his usual wheeling and dealing.

Noting that it was the regular practice of the cotton mills to have load after load of ashes removed from their premises to the local tip, the Royton promoter lost no time in visiting the mill offices and informing them that he would be quite willing to take a few tons off their hands free of charge.

Within a matter of days the whole of one side of his yard had been banked up in such a way as to not only make an ideal running track, but also to afford a clearer view of the ring for standing spectators when the outdoor shows were put on.

Next, Tolley approached the Belle Vue management in Manchester and persuaded them to let him have an old ring at a knockdown price. This ring, which was elevated, had previously graced Belle Vue's King's Hall, and many great fighters had ducked under its ropes, including Phil Scott, Ted 'Kid' Lewis, Len Johnson, 'Boy 'McCormick and Johnny Curley.

Tolley was now taking bookings from fans from as far away as Yorkshire, Staffordshire and North Wales. They came in ever increasing numbers and by every mode of transport. Often it was a case of how many bodies could be crammed in before the doors were closed.

Albert Tolley, who collected the money and tickets at the door, was quite often unable to get a clear view of the ring himself once his duties were finished. On one occasion he was very disappointed at finding it impossible to gain a good vantage point for a contest which he and hundreds of others had been looking forward to, an epic battle between local rivals Harold Ratchford and 'Cast Iron' Hague. In desperation Albert went outside and climbed a drainpipe, then making his way to a spot directly above the ring, he was able to settle down and watch the fight through the old weaving shed's glass roof.

The commencement of the outdoor shows in 1929 enabled Tolley to pack in even more people during the summer months. The big problem, of course, was the uncertainty of the weather. If the day was fine and warm a portable ring would be erected in the mill yard. By mid-day a decision would have to be taken as to whether or not it was likely to remain dry. If rain threatened and looked like setting in for the afternoon the show would, of course, be held indoors. But if the weather appeared favourable it would be a case of all hands on deck, for the seats would then have to be carried outside and arranged around the ring before the crowd began to arrive.

The Royton Stadium was now indeed unique. For what other arena in the country could switch the show either indoors or outdoors at half-an-hour's notice?

# Chapter 5

## Eliza

With the bitter memory of that first defeat beginning to fade, McAvoy's thoughts began to turn again to boxing. He still found the idea of a regular job rather irksome and began to wonder if he had in fact been somewhat hasty in his decision to stay away from Royton.

Apart from boxing though, he was keenly interested in motor bikes and had his first one around the age of sixteen, a patched-up affair which he and his friend Len Collinge had spent many a long hour repairing and fiddling about with, while dreaming of becoming famous dirt-track riders like those who hurtled around the track at Rochdale's Athletic Grounds on a Saturday evening in front of crowds of ten and twelve thousand. Men like 'Skid' Skinner, 'Riskit' Riley* and Oldham's daredevil, Clem Beckett.

If Mac had possessed enough money to purchase a decent motor bike he might never have bothered about returning to boxing at all. As it was he still did a bit of sparring now and again with the local lads, but his presence did not arouse much enthusiasm, for he was too strong and too rough for most of them and could never hold back, getting himself all fired up and grunting and snorting like a wild bull as he tore in.

Quite apart from sport, McAvoy was always keen on girls, his impressive physique and dark good looks making him very popular at the local picture houses and dance halls.

It was during this period that he began to see quite a lot of Eliza Jarman. Eliza, small, dark and attractive, was the daughter of Billy Jarman, a bookie's runner, who lived in Rosemary Place, near the town centre. There is no doubting the fact that the two were very much attracted to each other, but it's by no means certain that McAvoy would have agreed to get married had they not discovered that Eliza was pregnant.

The ceremony took place in November 1928, at St. Patrick's Church. The witnesses were Tommy Jarman, Eliza's brother, and

* Riley was also a professional boxer, while Beckett, reckless and game for anything, went off to the Spanish Civil War and lost his life.

McAvoy's step-sister, Rose Ellen Pilkington. Mac was four days past his 21st birthday, while Eliza, who worked in the cotton mill, was 18.

For a time they lived in Ogden Street with McAvoy's parents, as most young couples were forced to do in those days, while trying to get a rented house of their own. Next door lived old Mrs Dodman. Her daughter-in-law Nellie and family had by this time found a place in nearby South Lane, but still spent a lot of time at the old lady's house, especially Ronnie, Nellie's son, who called at his grandmother's every night after school.

The Dodmans took to Eliza from the start. She was a pleasant, friendly sort of girl, who seemed happy enough living with her in-laws. But those who knew McAvoy, including the Dodmans, were well aware that it did not take much to trigger off a temper which could be almost uncontrollable at times, and when friction began to occur between the newly-weds Nellie Bamford would always take her son's side, which did not help matters.

Eliza got along particularly well with her father-in-law, though Joe Bamford senior, now in his sixties, was a quiet man who preferred to stay out of things rather than get involved in family arguments. For many years he had made a living selling firewood from a pony and cart, but later, while working as a navvy, had sustained an injury to his lower leg which resulted in permanent damage, for the wound never healed and was a terrible sight in later years, when he would sit in his chair day in and day out, a virtual cripple.

As for McAvoy, the one thing about Eliza that really irritated him was the fact that she had taken up smoking. Though very popular among men at that time it was still frowned upon where women were concerned. Their arguments over it became so bad that Eliza was at times forced to retreat to the privacy of the outside toilet to indulge her habit. Even then it had to be done surreptitiously, for if her husband found out there was sure to be a blazing row, and Mac would not think twice about giving her a hard slap, which would effectively end the argument and result in tears. This sort of behaviour by his son did not please Joe senior at all, but there was very little he could do about it, and he was no doubt relieved when the young couple found a house of their own in Rosemary Place.

Both Joe and Nellie Bamford were much loved by their own families, especially Jim and Rose Pilkington and their children, whom they saw often. Jack Pilkington, who was, in fact, McAvoy's nephew and called him Uncle Joe, was very close to his Grandad and Grandma Bamford, and spent a lot of time in their company. It did not take Jack long to realise, even as a young lad, that apart from over-indulging her son, his Grandma had one other great weakness – Guinness.

Being an outgoing type of woman, it's quite probable that she enjoyed the company as much as she did the drink, but she certainly loved to sit in pubs and would have been there every day in the week had she possessed the necessary funds.

On arriving home she could become very argumentative indeed, and would quickly turn on any member of the family who dared contradict or disagree with her.

Old Joe was very tolerant at these times and would sit reading in his chair, waiting for her to come home. He would never scold or criticise her in any way, but would help her off with her coat, then listen patiently to her inebriated chatter while he made her a drink of tea.

Early in 1929 Eliza gave birth to a son. They called him Joe, after his father and his grandfather. Perhaps it was the need to earn a few extra shillings, or the realisation that at twenty-one, and with increasing family responsibilities, time was running out on him if he ever intended to make his mark as a sportsman. Whatever the precise reason, McAvoy decided that boxing was more of a possibility than dirt track racing and made up his mind to go along and talk to Joe Tolley again.

Tolley, though busy as ever, seemed pleased to see him. He told Mac that he could get fights for him and that if he was really serious about making something of himself he might even be prepared to sign him to a contract and manage him.

Mac was soon booked to box again and trained like a demon for his first comeback fight. His opponent was Frank Ormerod of Nelson, the contest taking place at the New Market Stadium, Burnley, where regular Thursday night shows were held.

McAvoy made the trip over the moors from Rochdale on the pillion of Len Collinge's motor bike. It was a long bumpy ride over narrow winding roads, but that didn't bother Mac one bit. He was all keyed up and eager to get there.

The fight didn't last long, for at the bell McAvoy flew at Ormerod like a tiger and punished him severely before dispatching him to the canvas with a tremendous right. The luckless local lad hardly moved a muscle as the referee – none other than Joe Tolley – counted him out.

Mac's next outing was against Jack Ogden of Chadderton, who possessed plenty of know-how and boxed well in the opening round. Round two, however, saw McAvoy connect with a perfectly timed right hand to the chin which shook Ogden and prompted him to back-pedal. Mac soon caught up with him and had him down several times before finishing him off in round three.

McAvoy's victory must have been particularly pleasing to Tolley, for Ogden was a protégé of Tom Chapman's Broadway Boxing Club at Chadderton, a rival outfit which staged Saturday night shows. Though the Broadway Club presented no real threat to him at that time, Tolley knew that the Chapman family were ambitious, and had detected more than a hint of jealousy in their attitude towards him and the success his promotions were now enjoying after many years of hard, slogging work as he laid the foundations.

Following the Ogden bout Tolley gave McAvoy the opportunity to avenge his only defeat, putting him in with Billy Chew again, at Burnley, over ten rounds. This time Mac was much fitter and better prepared. He was also learning fast and it was noticeable in the early rounds that the extra experience gained since their last contest eighteen months previously had made all the difference.

Chew, supremely confident after beating McAvoy so decisively in their first bout, made no attempt to box his man, but went all out to impose his authority from the opening bell. This suited Mac perfectly, and for the first six rounds the spectators were treated to an all-out war, with both men soaking up plenty of punishment and neither prepared to give an inch.

In round seven a burst glove halted the proceedings for several minutes, and on the resumption, McAvoy, who appeared to have benefited most from the rest, began to get on top, eventually gaining a clear points victory.

A week later Tolley got his man booked at the Winter Gardens, Morecambe, where the well known Harry 'Kid' Furness was match-maker. Mac was very excited at the prospect of fighting at a bigger, out of town venue and was determined to make a big impression. The fight was to be over ten two-minute rounds against a character known as 'Basher' Bargh. Mac and a couple of other boxers on the same bill met in the centre of Manchester and were picked up by Furness in a taxi. Various other fighters were collected along the way and packed in like sardines. Operating in this way Furness made sure that everyone would turn up, for he had most of his programme crammed into the one vehicle by the time it arrived in Morecambe. It also kept the expenses down.

Harry Furness, a small man of boundless energy and confidence, was known throughout the game as the most tight-fisted paymaster of them all. Yet he was so well connected and influential that few fighters or managers turned down his offers of work, even though the purses involved were invariably on the small side.

When Mac's turn came to go on that night he found himself facing a very confident and formidable looking opponent. Bargh was a local with a big following and a string of knockout victories to his credit. He appeared in no doubt that McAvoy would be added to the list, nor were his supporters, who cheered loudly when the Basher was introduced by the M.C.

Bargh started tossing his big bombs from the opening bell, but soon found that he was forced to take a few as well, the first three rounds being fairly even. In the fourth McAvoy connected with a jarring uppercut. It was beautifully executed and shook the Basher down to his bootlaces. That punch proved to be the turning point, and as Bargh's supporters grew quieter the local favourite was subjected to a thorough beating.

The Basher, however, could take it as well as dish it out and simply refused to go down. Eventually he was forced to take a short count, but was quickly on his feet again and ready to carry on. At that point the referee wisely stepped between them.

Harry Furness was so impressed by McAvoy's performance that he was invited back two weeks later and set off for Rochdale that night feeling very pleased with himself. On being dropped off in Piccadilly, Manchester, it was back to earth with a bump, for at that time in a morning there was little or no public transport on the roads and Rochdale was twelve miles distant. Unless he was lucky enough to get a lift in one of the newspaper vans there was nothing for it but to walk the whole way.

As Mac set off on the first stage of his long tramp he could think of nothing else but the fight, re-living each round and savouring again every moment of the contest. He could hardly wait to get back to Morecambe two weeks later. He did not know it then, but a mishap during his next assignment would have a profound effect upon the rest of his career.

Jack Jukes came from Tyldesley, near Leigh, in Lancashire, and had a somewhat patchy record, which, as is very often the case, did not tell the whole story. He was one of the fighters who travelled in the taxi from Manchester, so he and Mac found themselves sitting next to each other on the two hour journey to Morecambe.

All friendliness was, of course, forgotten when they faced each other in the ring that night, and Mac soon discovered that Jukes was no pushover. A tough, experienced scrapper, he seemed impervious to punishment as he bored in bobbing and weaving, American-style. Eventually, however, McAvoy began to wear him down and at last managed to drop his man for a short count. On rising Jukes ducked and dived in an effort to evade Mac's lethal punches. One big right, aimed at his jaw, caught him on the top of the head. Jukes was a hard man and the blow proved more damaging to Mac than it did to the recipient. A pain such as the Rochdale man had never experienced before seemed to shoot straight up his arm. He knew immediately that some sort of damage had been done and was unable to use the right hand again for the remainder of the fight. Yet he still won with plenty to spare, having Jukes down twice more from left hooks before the referee finally stopped it in the sixth.

The hand was badly swollen and so painful that Mac got very little sleep that night. Later he was to claim that his hands were never bandaged in his early fights and blamed this for the damage that was done to them, which was to give him serious problems throughout the rest of his career. McAvoy also claimed that he wore neither gum shield nor protective cup in those days.

Though a boxer is responsible for providing his own gear it seems inconceivable that a man of Joe Tolley's experience would have allowed him to enter the ring without having his hands taped and bandaged. The answer may well lie in the fighter's own foolishness, for Mac never liked being told what to do, even when it was clearly in his own best interests, and was always a very difficult man to handle. He was well aware that his manager was one of the wisest and most knowledgeable men in the business, but this did not stop him from arguing with Tolley.

When booked to fight away from home on one occasion, for example, he was told to report to Royton Stadium, from where he would be taken to the venue by car, along with several others. When Mac arrived he was accompanied by a friend, probably Len Collinge.

Joe Tolley was none too pleased and pointed out that there was no room for an extra body, as he did not want his boxers to be cramped up and uncomfortable during the journey. McAvoy simply refused to see the sense in this and delivered an ultimatum, 'If he can't go, then I don't go.'

After much arguing, Tolley, realising that Mac was not going to budge and that time was fast running out, finally gave way and the friend was grudgingly accommodated*.

This incident clearly illustrates just how awkward and stubborn McAvoy could be. Tolley was not always present when his boxers fought away from home, but there was always a trainer or second there to tape and bandage the boxers. So if McAvoy's hands were left unbandaged as he claimed he would have no one but himself to blame.

Even if Tolley had not had his finger in several pies he could not possibly have accompanied his fighters on every occasion, as so many were appearing in various parts of the country each week, but there is no possibility that he would have failed to impress on both seconds and fighters the importance of correct taping and bandaging.

However, whether Joe Tolley made sure that McAvoy's right hand was fully healed or not before putting him on again is another matter. As the manager he was certainly responsible for that. In fact, Mac was back in the ring some three weeks later, knocking out Bob 'Tiger' Ennis of Halifax, a tough looking customer who outweighed McAvoy by a stone at least, in one round. How well the hand had healed we don't know, but as it was no longer painful Mac pronounced himself fit to fight. A week later he was in action again, beating 'Seaman' Douglas of Warrington. The ex-sailor put up a game display but was eventually ground down by the purposeful McAvoy and forced to retire after six rounds.

Joe Tolley now staged a rubber match between his rising star and Billy Chew at Royton, in a top-of-the-bill contest over fifteen rounds. The distance did not bother Mac. He was by now a more experienced, better conditioned fighter, and looked forward eagerly to confirming his superiority over the Darwen 'Iron Man'. The fight created a lot of interest and a packed house greeted the contestants as they made their way to the ring.

Chew was as surprised as the fans to find that McAvoy, instead of tearing forward in his usual slam-bang style, was boxing behind a

* The inclusion of Mac's friend proved fortuitous, as the car broke down on the way home and he was able to fix it. This makes it more likely that the friend was Len Collinge, who was very adept with anything mechanical.

straight left. This tactic could well have been prompted by caution, with Mac somewhat dubious about letting his right hand go in view of the problems he'd been experiencing with it.

Whatever the reason, McAvoy's new style proved very effective, and though forced to travel the full distance he ran out a comfortable winner, with Chew having to take a fair amount of punishment in the later rounds. It was an exceptionally good performance, particularly in view of the fact that Chew had grown some and now weighed close to twelve stone.

McAvoy stated later that although his hands were well bandaged on this occasion, the right was so badly swollen after the fight that the glove had to be cut off in the dressing room, and that Joe Tolley told him to take a long rest until the hand was properly mended.

Again there is a lapse of memory here, for the newspaper records show that McAvoy travelled to Fleetwood the following day to take on Jack Ogden a second time. There is no doubt that he packed far too much power for the Chadderton man, so the fact that the best he could manage was a points victory over ten rounds clearly indicates that the right hand was still very sore. It's more than likely, therefore, that the removal of the glove with scissors followed the Ogden, rather than the Chew fight, otherwise, if the hand had been so badly swollen the day before, there would have been no question whatsoever of Mac fighting at Fleetwood so soon afterwards.

It must have been after the second Jack Ogden fight then, that Tolley ordered a long rest to enable the hand to heal. This amounted to just over two months, during which time, McAvoy, with the encouragement of a string of excellent wins behind him, now concentrated on building up his stamina through exercise and road-work while he waited for the hand to improve.

Eventually the swelling reduced and the hand appeared to return to normal. The unfortunate truth was, however, that it would never be normal again. Mac would have trouble with both hands throughout his career, particularly the right.

It has been claimed by several people who knew him that Mac did not have particularly strong hands to begin with. They have even been described as being smallish and delicate. If that was the case then another factor must be taken into account – his tremendous punching power. He would not have been the first fighter to suffer with his hands for this reason.

McAvoy himself said that his thumbs were so short that he could never find a glove that fitted him comfortably, and that this was the reason he developed the habit of repeatedly tugging at the thumbs of his gloves with his teeth during a contest. If this was in fact so, then those who insist that his hands were on the small side might just be right.

Whatever the reason behind the hand problems though, one thing is crystal clear. While bearing in mind the fact that a fighter in those days would be loath to give up a good pay day, it was surely pushing it a bit to have boxed a total of twenty five rounds in two days so soon after sustaining such a painful and troublesome injury, and Mac would live to regret it.

In 1929 big changes were taking place in British boxing. In May of 1928 Joe Tolley had been among those invited to London by the Earl of Lonsdale when the council of the Board of Control met to form a new body for Britain and the British Empire, to be constituted and run along the lines of the Jockey Club. The Prince of Wales and Lord Lonsdale were to become stewards and one of the main objectives was to ensure that all boxers and bone fide officials became licensed. It took until the following year, 1929, before the Board was finally reconstituted. Joe Tolley had, in fact, been a founder member of the original Control Board and as one of the best known, most respected men in boxing was very much involved in its reconstitution.

Ironically, however, during the course of generally tidying things up and resolving various anomalies in the game the question of Joe Tolley holding so many licenses was called into question, the most glaring conflict of interests being the fact that Tolley was refereeing contests involving boys under his own management. After much discussion it was decided that this state of affairs could not be allowed to continue, but Joe himself soon figured out a way to get around the problem. He simply gave up the manager's license, at the same time instructing Albert to apply for one.

As Albert was only eighteen, Tolley was taking a real chance, for in those days anyone under twenty-one was considered immature and not even allowed to vote, so the Board could quite easily have turned down the application. That they did not was no doubt due to the influence of Joe Tolley. Albert thus became probably the youngest person ever to hold a manager's license.

Upon the license being granted the released boxers were then instructed by Tolley to sign up under Albert's management, though they knew full well of course that nothing had really changed. All went smoothly until it came to getting McAvoy's signature, then the problems started. Although never actually refusing to sign his name to the new contract, Mac somehow contrived to keep on putting it off, causing Joe Tolley to become very nervous, for he was well aware that although McAvoy was still in the novice class his promise was such that certain other people would have been only too pleased to get their hands on him. Tolley knew that something would have to be done quickly, and, having got Mac's verbal agreement, he sent Albert over to Rochdale with the contract. Arriving at the tiny cottage in Rosemary Place, Albert found the house locked up, and after getting directions from a neighbour made his way to the home of McAvoy's parents. Nellie, who was nursing her grandson, young Joe, then only a few months old, told Albert that her son and his wife had had a bust-up and that Eliza had walked out. Mac had promptly left the baby in his mother's charge and gone out himself. She had no idea when either of them would be back. Albert realised that even if he found McAvoy the possibility of getting the contract signed while the boxer was up to his neck in domestic problems was fairly remote. There was nothing for it but to return to Royton with the document unsigned. Joe Tolley was very angry and a few days later Albert was back in Rochdale with orders not to return without McAvoy's signature.

This time McAvoy was at home and apparently reconciled with his wife. Albert did not, however, get the impression that Mac was particularly pleased to see him. While the fighter looked over the contract, frowning as he did so, Albert sat there uncomfortably. Glancing around the room, he noted that it was rather sparsely furnished, much as one would have expected, bearing in mind that they were a young married couple just getting a home together. At length McAvoy somewhat dubiously signed the contract, and Albert, breathing a sigh of relief, was glad to take his leave and hurry back to Royton with the good news.

# Chapter 6

## More Tolley Magic

Though by now acknowledged as an outstanding prospect, McAvoy was by no means the only exciting fighter in the Royton camp, and while he was laid off and waiting for his hand to mend some of Tolley's other stars were causing quite a stir in fistic circles.

Lightweight Tommy Maloney for example, who came from the village of Lees, had beaten the best that the booming fight centres of Manchester and Salford could offer, including such formidable fighters as Billy Marchant, Ike Bradley, Al Kenny, Mick Keogh, Johnny Roach, Dan Kelly and Terry Donlan. By the summer of 1929, Maloney, tagged 'Oldham's Wonder Boy', had accounted for no less than seventy opponents and was barely eighteen years of age.

'Stoker' Sharples, a welterweight, was another local fighter with a big reputation and a long string of wins on his record. In May 1929 Sharples won four contests in four days, beating Jim Lee (Gorton) over fifteen rounds, Jim Dagnall (Middleton), one round, Jack Ogden (Chadderton), three rounds, and Terry Donlan (Manchester), ten rounds, to break the record of Young Mickey, who had won four scheduled fifteen rounders some years before in five days.

Mickey's record was, however, superior, in that each of his opponents had been knocked out inside four rounds. They were Billy Hindley, Jimmy Buck, Young Lundy and Johnny Witts.

Two other Rochdale lads, George 'K.O.' Turner and Eddie Strawer (pronounced Stroyer), were also beginning to make their mark. Turner, who had flattened nine of eleven opponents, was being compared to McAvoy, one newspaper stating that 'Rochdale now has two knockout merchants, who are sure to meet in the near future'.

Eddie Strawer, however, a promising middleweight, saved Mac the trouble, beating Turner twice in quick succession, once on a two round knock-out, to put himself firmly in the picture, at the same time lining up a lucrative match with McAvoy at a later date.

Both Strawer-Turner contests were staged at Royton, Tolley's astute matchmaking having a lot to do with the tremendous interest being shown by the public in these intense local derbies which he had so cleverly built up.

At the same time a growing number of his fighters were gaining reputations further afield, and there is no doubt whatsoever that had Tolley concentrated on promoting and managing he would have achieved far more than was ultimately the case. But he seemed unable to resist being involved in every facet of the game, and though his refereeing and matchmaking activities brought in regular money, it was his flair as a showman that really stood out.

Tolley was never at a loss for ideas and 1929 was a wonderfully exciting year at Royton, with numerous thrilling contests and novelty spots which drew the crowds in their thousands.

In February Tolley announced that he would present the 'Jem Mace Cup' to the winner of a competition to be staged at the Stadium later that month. This cup, according to Joe, was presented to Jem Mace 'when he beat Tom King for the Championship of England* over sixty years ago', and was now in his possession.

How Tolley came by such a rare item was never explained, nor is there any record of its authenticity being questioned, but when the competition reached its climax and was won by Wilf Duckworth of Hollinwood, the said trophy was duly presented, and is now quite probably gathering dust in someone's attic.

After engineering an eagerly-awaited money match between Bert Hilditch and Mick Ester, both from Shaw, Tolley decided to give it an extra touch by engaging the services of Johnny Basham, a former British Champion and outright winner of a Lonsdale belt, as referee.

The Royton fans, always thrilled to have a renowned fighter in their midst, gave Johnny a great reception when Joe Tolley introduced him as 'the finest welterweight this country has ever produced'.

Unfortunately the old champion was much less popular when the fight was over, having incurred the displeasure of Ester's supporters by giving the decision against him in a very even contest. Of course, Basham knew his stuff, and explained afterwards that he would never give a decision in favour of any boxer who repeatedly landed with the open glove.

In June, 1929, Tolley was very pleased at being appointed referee for the first boxing show ever held at Winsford, Cheshire, his birthplace. Soon after this he was engaged by a leading American publication to rate all British boxers for them, and not long afterwards accepted the

* This contest took place on the 28th January 1862, King failing to come to the scratch after 43 rounds.

job of British correspondent for two other publications, one Belgian, the other, *The Boxing Blade*, being based in Canada.

Yet despite all this extra work he still could not bring himself to turn down engagements of any kind. He had maintained strong connections with the army, and for many years had gone to camp for fourteen days each year with the Welsh division of the Local Defence Volunteers to act as 'P.T. Instructor, Boxing Specialist and Sports Promoter'.

In the summer of 1929, when he was up to his neck in work, the last thing he needed was to have to drop everything and go off to camp. Yet giving it up went very much against the grain. So instead of tendering his resignation, he accepted, then informed the army that he was 'rather busy at the moment', and sent Bert Hilditch to Cardigan Bay in his place. It was his way of hanging onto the job and making surc that nobody else stepped in.

After what was considered a lengthy lay-off of two months McAvoy returned to the ring on December 2nd 1929 to take on Jack Harrison*, brother of Tommy, a former British Bantamweight Champion of the early twenties. The fight took place at Hanley and Mac forced his man to retire in four rounds, the hand giving him no problems at all.

During that same month he took part in a further five contests, beating 'Soldier' Jones in two rounds at Rhyl, Ted Abbott in six at Blackburn, Lud Gresvig, a Norwegian import, also in two, at Royton, all three on retirements, and five days later was slugging it out with tough Billy Horner at Preston.

Horner, a very determined fighter, put up much sterner resistance, standing toe to toe with McAvoy for the first three rounds and giving him all the trouble he could handle. In the fourth, however, Mac's speed, strength and greater variety of punches began to take effect on the rugged Leeds man, who went back to his stool in such a sorry state that his corner refused to allow him to come out for the fifth round.

McAvoy's fifth and final bout of the year, against Griff Williams of Denbigh, proved to be one of the toughest. Both men boxed well in the early rounds, which were fairly even. Mac's hands were feeling a bit sore, prompting him to rely a lot more on skill rather than his more familiar slam-bang tactics. By the seventh, however, he appeared to be very much on top and was beginning to get through

* Not to be confused with Jack Harrison of Rushden, British Middle weight Champion 1912-13.

with some telling shots, but in the following round Williams showed his resilience by coming back strongly and nailing McAvoy with a heavy right to the jaw which visibly shook him. The Welshman, however, failed to follow up his advantage and by the ninth Mac was again in charge, severely punishing the local man to head and body. The last round was fought at a blistering pace, with Williams at first giving as good as he got and catching Mac with a couple of hard left hooks for which he paid dearly as McAvoy again hammered him about the body. The decision, a draw, appeared somewhat unfair as far as Mac was concerned, for though Williams had put up a game show, the visitor had clearly proved himself the better man.

Tolley opened the year 1930 by matching his man with 'Marine' Davies of Portsmouth, in what was described as McAvoy's biggest test so far. Davies was reported to be as quick as a bantamweight and to carry a heavy punch. He had beaten such capable performers as George Stevens, Jack Pettifer and Ted Williams, who held a decision over Phil Scott, the reigning Heavyweight Champion. On the debit side Davies had been outclassed by Billy Chew on his only other visit to the North.

The contest took place at Royton on January 12th, and it quickly became apparent that the Rochdale K.O. king carried the heavier artillery, for Davies was soon under fire and took a real battering before being dispatched in the sixth. It was the unfortunate Marine's introduction to the 'dream punch', for he had never previously been knocked out.

Next came Sid Aldridge of Bath, who had little to offer and was counted out in four rounds at Preston after taking a heavy shot to the body.

In early February, at Haslingden, McAvoy again met Jack Ogden, confident that he would not have to travel the distance this time. Though just a little sore after each contest, his hands were holding out well and he had every intention of putting Ogden away in short order.

Mac was in for a shock, however, for Ogden, a hard and accurate puncher himself, waited for McAvoy to come rushing in with all guns blazing, which he did. When the big right came over Ogden blocked it neatly and countered with a perfectly timed delivery of his own which landed flush on the chin and sat Mac down on the seat of his pants. Finding himself on the canvas was a new experience and one which he did not enjoy at all. More shocked than hurt, he was back on his feet almost instantly and chasing after the clever Chadderton man, who kept his cool, boxing behind a ramrod left jab and keeping Mac at bay for the remainder of the round.

In the second McAvoy at last managed to find an opening, a fast combination setting Ogden up for the finisher, a tremendous left hook to the body which ended the contest.

Mac was next booked to meet Deno Guselli, at Royton, but when the popular Italian from Barrow-in-Furness was forced to pull out due to injury his place was taken by Andy Ross, also from Barrow, who must have regretted making the trip. Ross was subjected to a thorough trouncing before being knocked out in round five. Later that week, at Preston, Mac, though well on top, was forced to go twelve rounds against Fred Oldfield of Doncaster, winning comfortably on points. Two weeks later, at Rhyl, he destroyed Bill Lee of Wrexham in three rounds, Lee being stopped for the first time in his career.

Early in March 1930 Joe Tolley received a telephone call asking if McAvoy would step in at short notice at Penrith. After accepting the match Tolley dispatched young Albert to Rochdale to find Mac and inform him of the trip. It was an assignment Albert did not relish at all, for he always found McAvoy very awkward to deal with.

Mac was not always an easy man to contact. He spent most of his time on the dole and might be just about anywhere during the day-time, but on this occasion, on arriving at his house, Albert was told that Mac had found a job, and after a bit of sleuthing tracked him down to Queensway, Rochdale, where he was working as a navvy on a major road building scheme.

When told that Joe Tolley wanted him to travel to Cumberland the following evening Mac asked how much he was getting, and when Albert informed him that he would be receiving something in the region of £8, including travelling expenses, he scowled and said, 'I'll bet the fellow I'm replacing was on more than that.'

According to Albert, 'That was just like Mac. Always grumbling and never satisfied. He just didn't seem to understand why a small hall in a place like Penrith, no more than a village really, couldn't pay as much as Royton Stadium say. Or why Royton couldn't afford as much as Morecambe Winter Gardens. He didn't want to understand, that was the top and bottom of it.

'He was always very cynical, as if he thought you were trying to fiddle him all the time. And don't forget, he was going up there on his own and drawing the money himself. It wasn't as if me or my Dad were getting the purse, then giving him his cut.'

McAvoy did, however, make the trip, travelling by train to Penrith, where boxing was held at the Market Hall, in a ring pitched at floor level. There was no canvas covering over the boards, which were very rough and uneven. Looking across to the opposite corner Mac found himself facing Bill 'Shocker' Bowman, a man of around thirteen stone.

Evading Bowman's bull-like rushes and wild swings for the first two rounds, Mac, having sized his man up, caught him with a powerful right cross as he tore in at the start of the third, knocking him out and breaking the tough Cumbrian's nose in the process.

Three days after the Cumberland trip Mac was booked to take on Jack Haynes of Birmingham at Wolverhampton, but when this contest fell through he travelled instead to Stourbridge, where he met Fred Blything of Wolverhampton, outpointing him over fifteen rounds.

Next it was Jack Wilkinson of Warrington, flattened in two rounds at Royton, then Fred Oldfield again, the Yorkshireman being forced to retire after eight rounds, suffering from what turned out to be a broken rib, which says much for the power of Mac's body punching.

McAvoy was still growing and by now weighed close to eleven stone, but had no trouble giving weight away and regularly took on much bigger men.

Fighting out of a crouch, chin tucked well down, Mac always came forward throwing plenty of leather and had developed a good variety of punches. He was also fast, and, unlike many big hitters, possessed a sturdy chin himself. As well as having great natural stamina he was always superbly conditioned for his fights and usually managed to wear down any opponent he failed to knock out in the early rounds. He had discovered that body punching could be very effective in slowing a man down, and also that it was a lot easier on his vulnerable hands.

McAvoy's fame was beginning to spread, although it's not quite clear at what point the newspapers began to refer to him as the 'Rochdale Thunderbolt'. Still, it was an apt description and no exaggeration, for only four of his victims up to that point had managed to last the distance. As one local newspaper put it, 'Not since the days of Young Mickey has this district turned out a fighter with a punch like McAvoy's.'

This was certainly true, but despite his very impressive record, Mac was, in a sense, still in the novice class. In those days the competition was so fierce that no fighter ever reached the top without having got there the hard way. By that time he would probably have engaged in perhaps a hundred contests or more, and would be a skilled and experienced craftsman.

McAvoy though, was something of an exception. Having started late, he was in a hurry. He had worked hard, learned quickly and was fast developing into a top class fighter. Most important of all though, was the fact that he possessed the answer to all arguments – explosive punching power.

Joe Tolley in fighting pose, aged about twenty, soon after the end of the 19th century.

An outdoor sparring session at the Royton quarry. Joe Tolley, left, with Young Mickey. Old John Mahoney, Joe's stepfather, is second right.

A Royton group in the early twenties, with a very young Harold Ratchford sitting next to Kid Lees. Joe Tolley is on the front row, third from the right.

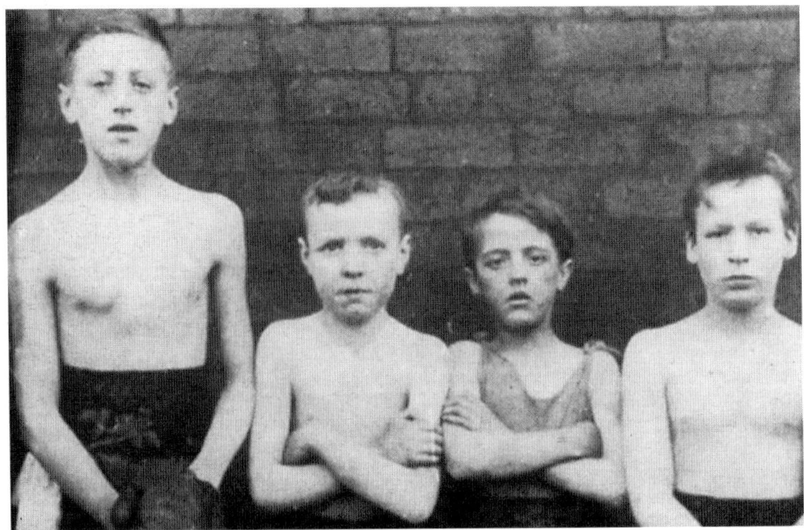

Albert Tolley, extreme left, as a successful schoolboy boxer.

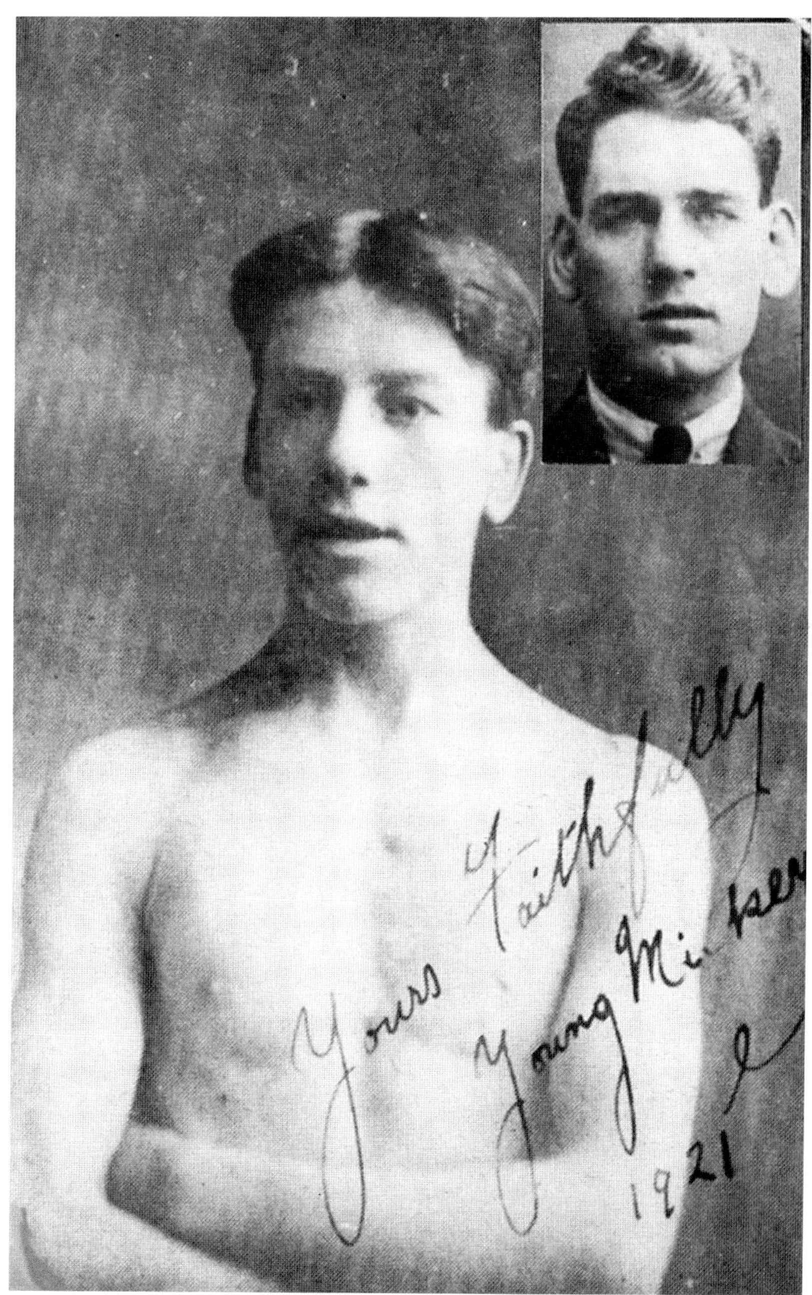


Joe Tolley's stepbrothers; *Above:* Young Mickey, who was burned out by the time he was twenty. *Inset:* Walter Maloney, who fought Len Harvey.

Phil Milligan with 'Wigan' Jud, a local character better known for training greyhounds than fighters.

The author outside the old skip and case-making works in Union Street, Royton, the upper floor of which became Joe Tolley's second 'stadium'.

The Ovey brothers, Walter *left,* and 'Cyclone Charlie.

1.5

Inside the old weaving shed at Middleton Road, Royton. Harold Ratchford *right*, with 'Spud' Murphy.

The mill yard – Joe Tolley's open air stadium in the late twenties.

Joe Horridge

The legendary John Willie Ryan, who taught and trained many local fighters in the twenties and thirties.

Young Joe Chapman

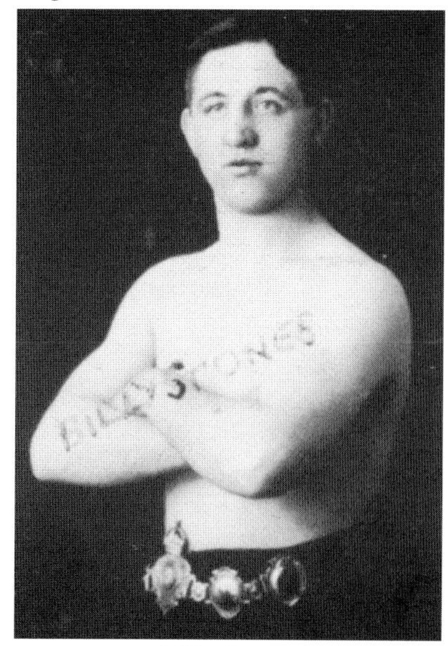

Billy Stones

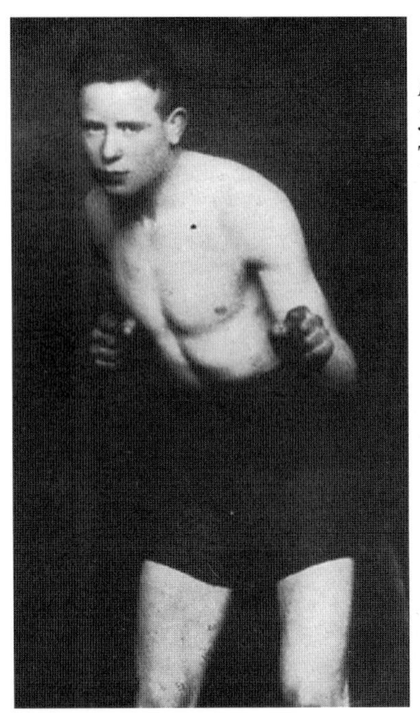

*Left:* Jimmy Travis

*Right:* Billy Tansey

Joe Crompton

Jim Byron

'Seaman' Harry Wolfe

Deno Guselli

Lawrie 'Stoker' Sharples

Harry Riley wearing his Lancashire Flyweight Championship belt.

*Left:* Local tough guy, Freddie Heighton, who tried unsuccessfully to get McAvoy into the ring on a number of occasions.

*Right:* 'Rugged' Roy Hilton

1.10

1.11

*Left:* Harold Henthorn, conqueror of the great Johnny King. *Above centre:* A young Johnny King in his Royton days. *Below centre:* Bert Hilditch, an early McAvoy victim at Royton. *Right:* Billy Bowcock, a Royton favourite.

Some Royton scrappers from the 1920s.

Tommy Allen

Billy Beaver

Joe Walsh

Wilf Duckworth

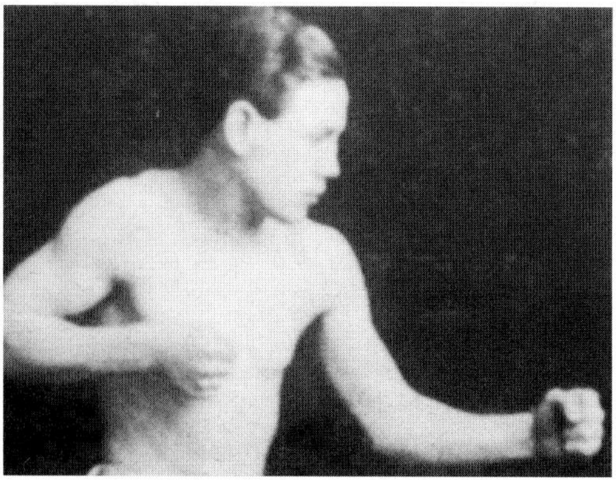

George Houghton

Some Royton scrappers from the 1920s.

Mick Ester

Teddy Bodell

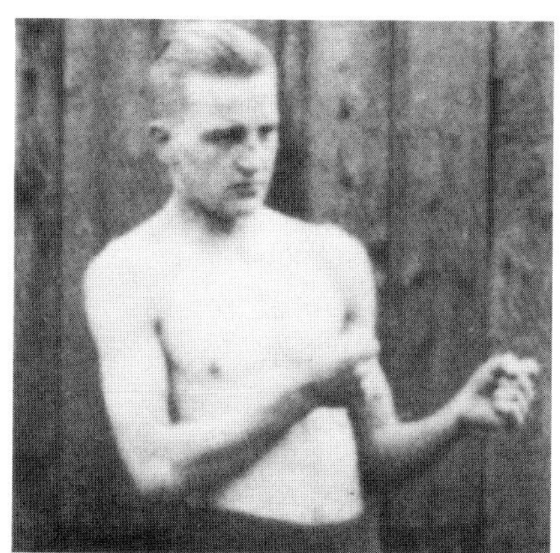

Jean Locatelli

Billy Mounders, Royton's Comic Champion.

Albert Tolley as a young man.

Joe Tolley, left, with popular Kid Lees.

Jim Eastham

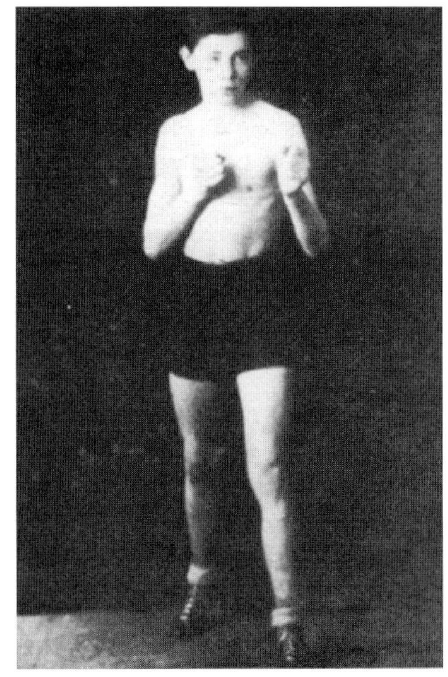

Joe Myers

Joe Walsh on the canvas against Eddie Strawer at Royton.

Eddie Strawer is counted out as McAvoy leans back on the ropes..

Johnny Nolan

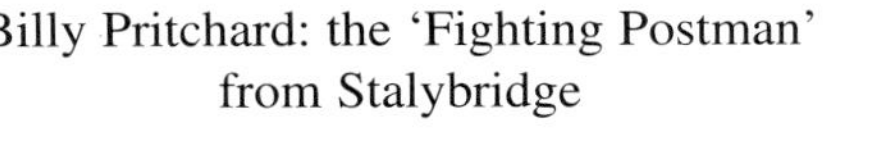

Billy Pritchard: the 'Fighting Postman' from Stalybridge

Billy Griffin

# Chapter 7

## Storm Clouds

There can be no doubting the fact that any success Tolley had achieved up to this point had been very hard earned. In a long and difficult struggle to establish himself, over a period of nearly thirty years, he had not made a great deal of money, but no one could argue with the fact that in his numerous careers and enterprises, all involving the fight game, Joe Tolley was unrivalled. An outstanding referee and M.C., and acknowledged as one of the foremost authorities on boxing in the country, he had now emerged as a great entrepreneur and showman. But at a time when the jewel in his crown, Royton Stadium, was reaching its peak of success and popularity, storm clouds were beginning to appear on the horizon, the source of Tolley's impending troubles being the Chapman family of Chadderton.

Up to this point Tom Chapman had been no more than a minor local rival, and by no stretch of the imagination could he be considered serious opposition when it came to staging shows. The Broadway Club, with its Friday evening promotions, was quite successful in its own small way, but no more competition to Tolley than any of the other local fight clubs in the district. Joe Tolley was top man, there was no question about that, with the Royton Stadium in a class of its own, renowned throughout the country. The size of the gates at Royton and the quality of the bills were on a different plane altogether than anything else in the area.

But the Chapmans were casting envious eyes in the direction of Royton, and, unknown to Tolley, were already making plans to move in on his territory.

Tom Chapman had two sons, Tom junior and Joe, an outstanding flyweight who had boxed several times at London's world famous National Sporting Club, where only the best Northern fighters were invited to appear. Known as 'Young' Joe Chapman, he was an extremely tough little battler, but another who took far too much punishment for his own good.

Joe's brother Tom was a completely different proposition. A successful builder, he possessed a keen business brain and was determined to succeed as a big time promoter, though getting the better of Joe Tolley appears to have been his main objective in life.

From what later transpired it would seem that Chapman's strategy was well planned, and though his knowledge of the game was negligible compared to Tolley's, he certainly thought big. More important still, perhaps, was the fact that the Chapman finances were on a much sounder footing than were those of his rival, and this in the end was to prove a decisive factor in the power struggle which was to develop over the next couple of years.

In the latter part of 1929, Chapman, who had been involved with boxing promotions at the Middleton Drill Hall, announced that he would be staging shows at the Castle Rink, Bloom Street, Oldham, a hall which would later become well known as the Majestic Ballroom, or the 'Ticker'.

Chapman had made up his mind to feature big name fighters on his bills once the new venture was firmly established. In the meantime he would take a leaf out of Tolley's book and attempt to capture the interest of the fans by pitting local scrappers from various districts in the area against each other.

At the same time he realised that Tolley had something he did not possess – a McAvoy. There may have been an abundance of talent on the Royton shows each Sunday afternoon, but it was becoming increasingly obvious that the biggest drawing card of the lot and by far the most exciting performer, was the Rochdale Thunderbolt. With his fierce all-action style and lethal fists, McAvoy was now just about the hottest property on the local fight scene and one of the finest prospects in the country.

In Chapman's opinion though, indeed in the opinion of many good judges, there was one local fighter who possessed an even greater all-round talent than McAvoy, a man who was surely bound for the very top.

That man was Joe Rostron of Heywood, a fighter with forty-odd contests behind him, of which he had won all but three.

Rostron was first introduced to the game at Jack Lord's Boxing Academy behind the Friendship pub in Heywood, Lancashire. He had always been keen on boxing, having been encouraged by his father, and soon became one of the Academy's outstanding pupils. A stroke of good fortune for Rostron was the fact that Billy Hunter, an up and coming young fighter from Salford, regularly used the Heywood gym, as well as boxing on the small local shows promoted by Jack Lord, for Billy was the son of Sam Hunter, an outstanding trainer, and Sam, along with Joe Goodwin, another gifted boxing tutor, would often hold coaching sessions at the Heywood club. Rostron's father, Harold, a former sprinter, wrestler and champion weight-lifter, also took Joe along to work out under the supervision of Teddy McGuiness, at the Jewish Boys' Club in Cheetham Hill, Manchester.

It was from these venerable veterans of the ring, for whom he had the greatest admiration and respect, that Joe learned the skills that would make him one of the best fighters at his weight in the country.

One night at Heywood, not long after he had passed out of the novice stage, Rostron entered a competition in which he emerged the winner of a silver cup, beating three opponents in one night in the same ring.

Joe gradually developed into a fine all-rounder fighter. He had everything, toughness, speed, a fair punch, great skill and the right temperament. Though only nineteen, he was in great demand and had already received a number of offers to fight on the Continent and in America.

Even more important, he was now operating under the banner of the Broadway Club and Tom Chapman junior was determined that no effort or expense would be spared in building Rostron up into the Castle Rink's biggest attraction and a challenger for Jack Hood's British Welterweight title.

The irony, as far as Joe Tolley was concerned, was that he himself had been instrumental in launching the Heywood lad's career in 1925, when Rostron had made his debut at the original Royton Stadium against Billy Mounders, whom he defeated on points over six rounds.

Chapman's opening show at the Castle Rink took place in January 1930, with Rostron topping the bill against Doncaster's Mike Maloney, whom he polished off without too much trouble, confirming a previous victory over the Yorkshireman at Haslingden, two months before. Maloney, a tough all-action scrapper, never had a chance and took a count in every round before being halted in the fourth. Chapman was elated. His new star had certainly captured the interest of the local fans, for the new venue was packed to the doors, with many having to be turned away.

Against Maloney, Rostron showed that he was in a different class and well worthy of a shot at Hood's title. Chapman announced that he would open negotiations immediately on Rostron's behalf, but as it turned out Hood's people were more interested in meeting American Jackie Fields for the World title, a contest which was expected to take place that summer.

Chapman nevertheless did manage to pull off a nice stroke of business by featuring Jack Hood on his next show, paying the British Champion a fee of £25 to box an exhibition with young Rostron, who acquitted himself exceptionally well. Hood himself was so impressed that he offered to engage Joe as his sparring partner in the lead-up to his anticipated World title shot.

In the meantime Rostron was booked to meet Jim Pearson of Bamber Bridge, one of the most feared middleweights in the country, at Manchester's Free Trade Hall. Though considered superior in speed and skill, there was some doubt as to whether Rostron could give weight away to such a tough, experienced opponent. He would be conceding almost a stone to a man whom few middleweights could stand up to, let alone a welter.

The cool, determined Rostron, however, performed brilliantly on the night, his neat boxing and lightning hand speed drawing appreciative applause from the knowledgeable Manchester crowd. Nevertheless he did not have things all his own way by any means, and was forced to take a few solid shots as they went the full distance of fifteen rounds. The decision, a draw, was considered an excellent result against a fighter of Pearson's standing and Rostron followed it up a month later by stopping Joe Lynch, the rugged Glaswegian, in eight rounds at Hanley.

Lynch had just returned from America, where he had been an outstanding success, beating, among others, Tully Moore, in a never to be forgotten contest in Boston.

Lynch fought in true American two-fisted style, but was made to order for the clever Rostron, who boxed him to a standstill.

Tom Chapman was naturally delighted with these results, and quite confident in his belief that he now controlled, not only the area's hottest fistic property, but a future British Champion.

Yet despite this success and that of his new venture at the Castle Rink, Chapman was far from satisfied. He was still determined to depose his arch rival, Joe Tolley, and only a matter of weeks after his first Oldham promotion he announced that he had taken over the old Tram Shed at Dogford Road, Royton, only a stone's throw from

Tolley's now famous Royton Stadium. Not content with this, Chapman had also made up his mind to stage his shows on a Sunday afternoon, traditionally the Stadium's fight day.

This was a senseless and totally unnecessary move and must have come as a body blow to the Tolleys, who had always operated on a shoestring, for they were well aware that money was the least of Chapman's worries. They realised only too clearly that they were now up against it, for it was obvious that Chapman would use his financial muscle to squeeze them out by offering bigger purses than they could afford. He would be in a position to stage more attractive bills and would therefore be quite likely to win over many of Tolley's regulars.

Joe Tolley, however, remained defiant, and determined that he would very quickly see off the young upstart from Chadderton. He still controlled some of the district's best fighters, and had given the public excellent value for money over the years. Based on this knowledge he was confident that the majority of his patrons would stand by him.

When McAvoy's next opponent, Hal O'Neill of Pendleton, was unable to appear, Tolley somewhat reluctantly accepted Jim Pearson as substitute, and Mac travelled to Preston determined to go one better than Joe Rostron by decisively beating Pearson. Unfortunately things did not quite work out.

Despite the fact that he had only managed a draw against Rostron, the ringwise Pearson was by far the most formidable opponent McAvoy had yet faced. As well as being taller than Mac he was much heavier, and had the reputation of being one of the hardest hitting middleweights in the North.

One man who could certainly attest to this was Royton favourite 'Darkie' St. Clair, whose jaw had been broken by Pearson the previous year.

But McAvoy was afraid of nobody and started confidently, even having Pearson on the canvas as early as the first round, though he was up without a count and soon fighting back strongly. A good straight puncher, Pearson constantly drove his jarring left jab into McAvoy's face, following up with solid right crosses which visibly shook Mac but failed to discourage him.

After three rounds the Bamber Bridge man began to get well on top, and though McAvoy rallied in the eighth he was unable to penetrate Pearson's tight defence and finished the contest bleeding heavily from the nose, a clear points loser.

It was a result over which the Chapman camp shed few tears. They had not only moved onto Tolley's own doorstep, but had now had the satisfaction of seeing his star attraction humbled by a fighter who had only been able to manage a draw against their own top boy not many weeks before.

Everything was going according to plan, with Chapman's new stadium almost ready for its grand opening, scheduled for March 30th 1930. According to the advance publicity it would be capable of accommodating several thousand fans and boasted garage space for over fifty cars and charabancs.

Chapman announced that as well as featuring prominent local fighters he would bring big names to the town and also run talent-finding competitions, informing the local press that 'any boy showing promise will be tutored and coached with a view to fighting for higher honours'.

Of course, he was merely copying Joe Tolley's methods. Tolley had started these competitions many years before, prior to opening his first stadium in fact, discovering such outstanding local talent as 'Kid' Lees, Vivian Bethel, 'Young' Mickey, Harry Riley, Johnny King, 'Cyclone' Ovey, Harold Ratchford, Joe Myers and Tommy Maloney among others.

If Chapman made one mistake it was in naming his new stadium the National Sporting Club, or N.S.C. A sharp letter from London soon caused him to think again, the Royton club being hurriedly re-named the Northern Sports and Boxing Club, or N.S.B., as it would henceforth be known.

Before the opening date luck deserted Joe Rostron when the opportunity to fight Jack Hood suddenly appeared out of the blue. When Londoner Alf Mancini pulled out of his contest with the Welterweight Champion the fight was offered to Rostron, who was reluctantly forced to decline, having suffered a badly damaged ear in a previous engagement.

Former champion Harry Mason then stepped in and surprised everyone by beating Hood on points. In a scrappy, untidy affair the crafty Leeds man employed his usual spoiling tactics to out-manoeuvre Hood, who appeared sluggish and fought well below his best. Fortunately for the champion his title was not at stake, but the result obviously hurt his World title aspirations, for the Fields fight never did materialise.

Nor was Rostron fit to appear on Chapman's opening show at the new Royton venue, though he was introduced from the ring and received a big reception. Top of the bill saw Irishman Barney Tooley beat Accrington's Jack Marshall on points.

On the same afternoon, only a few hundred yards away at Joe Tolley's Royton Stadium, Eddie Strawer was living up to his billing as one of the North's most promising middleweights by knocking out Fred Williams of Manchester in two rounds.

# Chapter 8

## The Clash with Rostron

McAvoy's defeat by Pearson, though disappointing, was regarded by Tolley as nothing more than a temporary set-back, which would probably do McAvoy no harm at all. A good learning fight in fact. At any rate he was soon back in action, knocking out Ted Lewis, a Wiganer, taught and trained at Royton, in six rounds at the Stadium, and tough Welshman Dai Beynon in five at Blackburn. Tolley's star attraction was back on the winning trail again.

Despite the opposition close by, the Royton Stadium shows were still very well attended, which was hardly surprising, for a typical Stadium bill would feature as many as nine bouts. Over seventy rounds of top class boxing. That was going to take some beating, but Tolley knew he would have to pull out all the stops to prevent his arch rival from taking the bulk of his trade.

Joe was in no rush to match his man with Joe Rostron, not for the moment at least, though it was one fight the fans were clamouring to see. In any case it would have been a very difficult one to put together, for Tolley had no intention of doing business with the Chapmans at any price. He was well aware of McAvoy's vast potential, but felt that it would perhaps be as well not to put him in with a man of Rostron's class too soon. The problem was that Mac had a mind of his own.

On April 25th, 1930, McAvoy travelled alone to Preston to fight a return with Jim Pearson, determined to set the record straight. On reporting for the weigh-in he was told that the doctor had refused to pass Pearson fit and that they were searching for a substitute.

At six-thirty that evening Joe Rostron received a telegram from the Majestic Theatre, Preston, asking if he would be prepared to fight McAvoy that night. Rostron, always ready and willing, immediately hired a taxi and arrived in Preston at 8.45.

If Joe Tolley had known what was going on, the fight would, in all probability, never have taken place, but Mac did not feel inclined to back out, despite being well aware of Rostron's reputation. The Heywood man was a few pounds lighter, but very experienced and a superb boxer. McAvoy, on the other hand, could at least be confident that he carried the heavier punch, and had every intention of making it count. He was sick to death of hearing about Joe Rostron and couldn't wait to get in there and have a crack at him.

From the opening bell McAvoy attacked his man ferociously, going all out to land the big one early on. But Rostron was by far the cleverest fighter he had come up against and was easily able to cope with Mac's rushes, always remaining cool under pressure and evading the punches by the merest movement of the head, so that they either fell short or just whistled past his ear.

Every time Mac missed he was made to pay, and Rostron, a speedy and deadly accurate counter puncher, hurt him with jolting body shots when in close. At other times Rostron's left hand was never out of his face. It seemed that the harder Mac tried the more frustrated he became. At the end of twelve rounds he had been well beaten and knew it, admitting later that the only thing more depressing than the disappointment of defeat was the thought of what Joe Tolley would have to say when he discovered that Mac had taken the fight.

Tolley of course, was very angry, particularly with the Preston promoters, whom he felt had pulled a fast one. He warned Mac that he must never again accept a change of opponent without first getting his manager's consent.

For once McAvoy didn't argue. He knew he'd been taken for a ride and was anxious to get back into the ring and start winning again. Tolley told him to take it easy for a couple of weeks and that his next pay day was likely to be the biggest he'd ever seen. From the look in Joe's eye Mac knew that he was working on some crowd-pulling scheme, which was intended, not only to draw a big gate, but also to give him the edge over Chapman. For though he always insisted that competition was healthy for the game, Tolley was clearly unhappy about the way the opposition was gaining ground in Royton. He knew that, generally speaking, they were paying the fighters better money than he was. Joe Rostron's purses, for example, at the N.S.B. were averaging twenty to twenty-five pounds, which was substantially more than McAvoy was getting at the Stadium, Mac's pay at that time usually being a pound a round. Tolley also knew that Chapman was no philanthropist, and that he was paying over the odds just to beat Joe Tolley.

So far Joe had held his own, but it was getting harder, and he was well aware that he was under pressure to keep on coming up with the goods, otherwise he might be in danger of losing, not only his customers, but perhaps some of his fighters as well, when their contracts came up for renewal.

In fact, there was a possible threat to both camps looming, for those solid citizens entrusted with the saving of souls in Royton were again on the warpath, a situation that might never have arisen had Chapman not appeared on the scene to aggravate the problem. To make things even worse the outraged cries of the holy ones had been heard in the council chamber, with the result that at Chapman's opening show a group of Royton councillors were seen to gather at the bottom of Dogford Road, not far from the N.S.B. entrance, to observe for themselves the arrival of the fans and take note of their behaviour.

It did not help matters when two youths roared up on a noisy motorbike belching black smoke, and asked one of the councillors where the boxing was being held.

When the show ended that day Tom Chapman appealed to his patrons to disperse in a quiet and orderly manner in view of the controversy raging around the question of Sunday boxing in the district.

Not long after this the Vicar of Royton, Mr W. Rowe, spoke out against boxing in one of his sermons. Apparently he took great exception to the fact that Oldham had laid on special trams to carry the fight fans to Royton on Sundays for the shows.

'The day of rest,' he said, 'is rapidly becoming a day of disturbance. It will be a sad day indeed for the people of this country if the old idea of the sabbath is swept away.'

Tom Chapman was cock-a-hoop over McAvoy's defeat at the hands of his top boy and immediately advised Joe Rostron to postpone his proposed American tour and stay at home in the hope of getting a title shot. As far as he was concerned his fighter was not only a leading contender, but also the district's top drawing card. Tolley did not go along with this at all. Though he fully appreciated the fact that Rostron was an outstanding all-round performer, who might well become a champion, he was also aware that in the moody, difficult to handle McAvoy, he had something special – a man with dynamite in his fists. It was a quality the fans found irresistible, and one they would travel miles to see.

At the same time Tolley accepted the fact that after the two recent defeats McAvoy's stock had slumped very low indeed, and decided that something spectacular had to be done to put the 'Rochdale

Thunderbolt' back in the spotlight, otherwise there was no telling how many of the fans might now decide to drift off in the direction of Dogford Road on a Sunday afternoon instead of patronising the Stadium.

Joe was certainly planning something big, but in the meantime he could still manage to concoct the usual novelty attractions, which seemed to come to him so effortlessly.

One week it would be Morris Dancers in the ring, then a top boxing personality to referee a major bout, such as Len Johnson, who was very talented and extremely popular. On another occasion he put on a Black v White bill, a very unusual spectacle in those days. Then on a sunny afternoon in May 1930, Dom Volante of Liverpool and Italy appeared in the Stadium ring to a rapturous reception. Volante was then in preparation for his British featherweight title fight against Johnny Cuthbert*. Just back from a highly successful American tour, the versatile Italian, a talented musician, stepped into the ring at the interval and treated the delighted fans to selections from opera on his mouth organ. It was another example of the Joe Tolley genius and the fans loved it.

In the spring of 1930 Tolley made the match that local fans had been waiting for. The two Rochdale men, McAvoy and Strawer, would fight it out in the open air in a contest that Joe knew would outsell anything Chapman was likely to come up with.

Strawer, a regular at the Stadium, had put together an impressive record. As well as disposing of George 'K.O.' Turner in quick time he had also knocked out or stopped a whole string of good men, including Jack Ogden, Jack Jukes, 'Seaman' Higham, 'Shocker' Bowman and the Dutchman, Con Van Leowen. Eddie had also drawn with Billy Chew and outpointed Deno Guselli and 'Stoker' Sharples, prompting one newspaper to describe him as the greatest middleweight prospect unearthed in the district for many years.

In arriving at this conclusion, the writer did not, perhaps, take McAvoy into account, as he was well short of 11st. 6lbs at that time, and hovering somewhere between Welter and Middleweight.

There was tremendous local support for both boys, with McAvoy sure that he could knock his rival out, and Strawers backers equally confident that their man would emerge the winner.

With both McAvoy and Strawer going well, Tolley had been in no hurry to match them. He had simply bided his time, while allowing interest in the contest to build up. Now, because of the urgent need to combat the Chapman menace, he decided that the time had come.

* Volante lost on points over 15 rounds.

In the meantime, Joe Rostron fought a return with Jim Pearson at the N.S.B. and raised his stock still higher by beating him comfortably on points. That day the Stadium staged a very ordinary bill, which, naturally enough, in view of the big fight just down the road, failed to excite public interest. The N.S.B., on the other hand, was forced to close its doors at 2.30, with many being turned away. It was clear that Tolley now needed the Strawer-McAvoy set-to very badly indeed.

May 25th, 1930, turned out to be the perfect day for the big fight. It was warm and sunny with not a cloud in the sky, so the likelihood of rain forcing the show indoors was very remote indeed, which was just as well, for there would have been no hope of accommodating the expected crowd in the old weaving shed.

By mid-day, with cars and charabancs beginning to arrive in great numbers and droves of people pouring into Royton by public transport and on foot, it was clear that Joe Tolley was all set to draw his biggest gate ever. This, in fact, turned out to be the case.

As far as the purse money received by the principals is concerned, this is very difficult to determine. McAvoy claimed that he and Strawer received only £6 each, while a newspaper at the time, in reporting that contracts were to be signed at the Swan With Two Necks public house in Rochdale, mentioned that they would be fighting for a 'record purse', with the winner getting 60% and the loser 40%. But in a newspaper interview in 1971 Albert Tolley was quite positive that McAvoy had received £30, his biggest purse up to that time, and that the Stadium had grossed £129, by far the highest figure ever taken there in gate receipts, which normally averaged sixty to seventy pounds.

Jack Dare of Liverpool, a class 'A' referee, and one of the most experienced officials in the country, was chosen to handle the eagerly awaited battle. There was no doubt as to where the majority of the fans were headed that afternoon. It was Chapman's turn to play to a sparsely filled hall, while at the Stadium's open air arena the fans stood shoulder to shoulder like a football crowd, in their shirt sleeves, enjoying the sunshine as they watched the preliminary contests and waited in eager anticipation for the big fight. Naturally enough the noisiest fans in the Stadium were the two Rochdale factions, and Strawer's father, a big red-faced man who tended to be rather loud and aggressive, was the noisiest of the lot. It was always 'our Eddie this and our Eddie that'. Now here he was close to the ringside, telling all and sundry that he was Eddie Strawer's dad and bragging about what Eddie was going to do to McAvoy, whom he clearly considered had been receiving more than his fair share of attention from the press and public.

There was a minor drama just before the contestants appeared for the main event. On the other side of the wall at the top end of the old mill yard was a building in which the horses used to remove ashes from the mills were stabled. In charge there that day was a cocky young fellow named Finnerty, who sported tattoos on his arms and wore a thick belt with a huge buckle, which he often used on any animal that disobeyed him. Though not a big man, Finnerty fancied himself as a tough guy and had irritated Joe Tolley on a number of occasions.

When Joe spotted him perched on the wall, waiting for the big fight to begin, he immediately left the Stadium and went around to the stables to confront the gatecrasher, informing him that he must either pay or get down from the wall. Finnerty had no hesitation in telling Tolley just what he could do with his ultimatum, and harsh words were exchanged. By this time, young Albert, feeling very apprehensive, had arrived on the scene to find Finnerty squaring up to his father. Joe Tolley, well schooled in all forms of unarmed combat, and not too particular about his methods, quickly put an end to the brief scuffle by head-butting the intruder, before calmly returning to the Stadium and climbing into the ring to introduce the main eventers. Albert was appalled at what he considered to be unnecessary violence, but had to admit later that it had the desired effect, for young Finnerty was never a problem after that.

On another occasion, while announcing an unpopular verdict, Joe was attacked from behind by an irate second, who caught him in a cross-buttock throw and slammed him to the canvas. Almost before he had regained his feet most of the Tolley/Maloney clan, females included, were in the ring and laying into the bewildered cornerman for all they were worth. Joe soon restored order and the afternoon's boxing continued without any further problems.

Strawer appeared very nervous as he waited in his corner for the contest to begin, while McAvoy, always edgy himself until the bell rang, danced around, shadow-boxed and tugged at the thumbs of his gloves with his teeth.

Mac attacked his man from the start, but failed to land any really telling punches early on. Strawer certainly knew how to handle himself.

He was a clever boxer with a pretty fair dig, and his use of the ropes, now almost a lost art, was an outstanding feature of his work.

After three or four rounds Eddie settled down and began to gain in confidence to such an extent that he even began to trade punches with Mac. This proved quite successful until he ran into a right cross in round eight which shook him badly. Strawer now started to box on the retreat with McAvoy stalking him, ready to move in for the kill the moment an opening appeared. In round ten, after taking several full-blooded hooks to the body, Eddie was caught with another right, flush on the chin. From the moment it landed everyone in the arena knew that the fight was over. There was now absolutely no doubt about who was Rochdale's top fighting man.

Outside the ring, old man Strawer, who could be something of an embarrassment to his son at times, was kicking up quite a fuss, for some reason taking exception to McAvoy's tactics and issuing the direst threats at the top of his voice. As soon as he heard what was going on Mac attempted to get at Strawer senior, and would certainly have punched him had he not been restrained by his handlers and hustled off to the dressing room.

Eventually, the elder Strawer was calmed down, but as he was obviously not satisfied with the result, Joe Tolley agreed to match the two boys again at a later date.

Violence outside the ring was nothing new to Joe Tolley. At the time of the incident with the Stadium gate-crasher, who must have been twenty-odd years his junior, Joe was forty-seven and had seen more than his fair share of trouble over the years. Not that he ever went looking for it. He just seemed to run into it from time to time. When that happened he never backed off, no matter how big or menacing the opposition, with the result that he sometimes took a beating himself. More than once he was forced to defend himself against an irate husband, though this did little to cool his ardour, for he could never resist bringing his not inconsiderable charm into play when a good looking woman, whether married or single, crossed his path.

Always a snappy, if somewhat conservative dresser, he could often be seen around Royton wearing a bowler and smartly cut dark suit. Joe's stylish attire, coupled with his straight-backed military bearing, tended to give him a rather dandified appearance, which had the effect of raising the hackles of the rougher element among the young men who lived down Sandy Lane, then very much the poorer end of the village, where even a collar and tie was considered posh.

One Saturday night he was accosted by four or five youths as he made his way home, and in the scuffle that followed Tolley finished up getting the worst of it. Knowing where each one of his assailants lived, Joe went down Sandy Lane the following day and knocked on a door. When a woman answered it he asked to see her son, who came out to be met by a swift punch on the nose. This performance was repeated at several other houses, until honour had been satisfied, after which no further late night accosting took place as far as Joe Tolley was concerned.

A month after the Strawer fight McAvoy beat Billy Green of Pontypridd at Morecambe, the fight being stopped in round fourteen with Green in no shape to defend himself.

Afterwards Mac's right hand felt very sore and he was forced to withdraw from a proposed bout with 'Seaman' Jim Cox of Wigan. Tolley, confident that a short rest would put things right, then booked a return contest with Jim Pearson. However, a month later, in July 1930, Eddie Strawer got his re-match rather unexpectedly when Pearson was forced to withdraw from his scheduled fight with Mac at the Stadium.

This time it turned out to be very one-sided, with Eddie on the deck in the opening round. After taking a count of nine he recovered well and gave a very good account of himself until the fifth, when Mac put him down again with a terrific body punch. It was clear that Eddie would not last much longer, and in round six the fight ended when a vicious left hook put him clean out of the ring, with no hope of beating the count.

Eddie Strawer, a more than useful middleweight, fought on and compiled an excellent record, though never reaching the top. Several veteran fight fans have claimed that Strawer was every bit as talented as McAvoy, but believe that Eddie had an inferiority complex where Mac was concerned. This could well be so, but Albert Tolley probably put his finger on the truth when he told me that the real difference between them was not only McAvoy's punching power, but his killer instinct.

Albert, who did not get on very well with Mac, stated: 'Although we were connected for a long time, he never liked me and I didn't like him. I disliked his arrogant attitude, his morals and his massive ego; but as a fighter – superb. His punching was lethal, and though he could take a punch himself, he didn't like being hit, especially in the face. When he was hurt, that was when he was at his most dangerous. If an opponent caught Mac and shook him you could see it in his face – sheer hatred. I'd say to myself, this is it. This fellow's had it now, and I was usually right. He'd bite at his gloves, snarl, then tear in like a wild animal and just batter 'em into submission.'

At the end of July 1930 McAvoy ran up against a tough one in Nottingham's George Porter, a hard puncher who could also box a bit. Porter forced Mac to travel the full distance of fifteen rounds, and though the Rochdale man got the verdict and had the satisfaction of putting his opponent down twice in the later rounds, he knew he'd been in a fight.

Tolley had no complaints. He was slowly moving his fighter up in class and realised that they could not expect a knockout every time. Seaman Jim Cox was present and stepped into the ring to challenge the winner. Tolley was pleased to accept, and Harry 'Kid' Furness announced that the contest would take place at the same venue, Morecambe Winter Gardens, the following month.

Prior to this, however, McAvoy had a date with Doncaster's 'Farmer' Jackson, at Royton. Jackson claimed to have fought over 200 contests, out of which he had lost only a handful, never having been stopped. Sure enough he proved to be as hard as nails. Mac hit him with just about every punch in his repertoire and had him on the canvas a number of times but was unable to keep him there, the rugged 'Farmer' managing to last out the full twelve rounds, though he was in a sorry state at the finish.

For the Cox fight, billed as a final eliminator for Joe Lowther's Northern Middleweight title, McAvoy had a weight advantage of 5lbs over his opponent, who came in at a pound over eleven stone. For Cox, normally a welterweight, this was on the heavy side, while McAvoy, still filling out, was now very comfortable at 11st. 6lbs.

Joe Tolley advised Mac not to be in too much of a rush, as the experienced Cox was a skilled campaigner who knew every trick in the book. As Tolley expected, the veteran bided his time, allowing McAvoy to come to him, covering up cleverly as Mac opened up with the heavy artillery, then suddenly stepping in with rapid combinations of his own, which, though not damaging, certainly took Mac out of his stride.

Having failed to find the Wiganer's well-guarded chin, Mac concentrated more and more on the body as the fight wore on, and eventually this tactic began to pay dividends, Cox wincing as those murderous hooks thudded into his ribs. At the end of twelve absorbing rounds McAvoy was declared the winner and official challenger for Joe Lowther's crown. First though, he was given the opportunity to reverse the decision Jim Pearson had gained against him, Joe Tolley arranging the contest for September 14th at Royton. Tolley then dashed off on another refereeing tour, creating something of a record by handling six principal contests in six days, all in different towns.

The Royton promoter certainly had a busy schedule, and as he had just been appointed examining officer of the British Referees' Association, it was clear that he was about to become even busier. In addition to his promoting, M.C.'ing, matchmaking, refereeing and unofficial managing, he was also on the councils of the Referees' Association and the British Boxing Board of Control. The last thing he needed was yet another appointment. But as Tolley considered this latest one a great honour, he didn't even consider turning it down. As always, he was delighted to accept.

There was much excitement at Royton on September 14th 1930, as the fans poured into the Stadium in great numbers. They were expecting to see a real battle, and when McAvoy was involved they were seldom disappointed. But the question was, could the local favourite now accomplish what he had failed to do six months previously at Preston – get the better of the tough, ringwise Jim Pearson?

McAvoy's plan was simple. He would go tearing in from the start, making sure that Pearson did not get the chance to settle. As it turned out these tactics worked perfectly, though Mac was forced to take a few in order to get in close. As usual he made the body his main target, hammering away with both hands until Pearson began to weaken.

In the seventh a tremendous right under the heart stopped the Bamber Bridge man dead in his tracks, and Mac was able to put over the finisher, Pearson falling forward on his face, out to the world. He was so stunned that it was some time before he could be removed from the ring.

The referee, Mr Jack Smith of Manchester, who also acted as matchmaker at the Free Trade Hall, was very impressed, and immediately offered to book Mac for a series of fights at the Manchester venue. Smith predicted that the 'Rochdale Thunderbolt' would become a champion for sure.

McAvoy's first contest at the Free Trade Hall was against Billy Delahaye of Pontypridd, who lasted less than two rounds in the face of Mac's thunderous punching. Three days later, after polishing off Patsy Flynn in the third at Preston, he was informed that he would be appearing on the next Free Trade Hall bill, and was delighted to learn that his opponent would be none other than Joe Rostron.

As Rostron's natural weight was well under 11st., McAvoy would be required to get down to 11st. 2lbs, but this did not worry him. He knew he could easily take off four or five pounds and remain strong. He had gained considerably in experience since the Rostron defeat and was confident that he could turn the tables. Joe himself had run up a string of nine wins since beating McAvoy, his victims being Jim Pearson (twice), Albert Johnson, brother of Len (twice), Dick Burt, Jim Cox, Bonny Evans, Fred Oldfield and Jack Haynes. He had, however, suffered a set-back only a month before in one of the biggest money matches ever staged in the North of England, being outpointed over fifteen rounds by Ben Marshall of Newport at the Royton N.S.B.

Marshall, a Welsh Champion of gypsy blood, was a seasoned scrapper who craftily allowed Rostron do all the work in the opening rounds. From the halfway stage he started to fire back, and Rostron, who had knocked up his right hand early in the contest, began to get the worst of it, Marshall outlasting him to take a clear points decision.

The loss to the highly-regarded Welshman was not considered too serious, but with the McAvoy fight just over three weeks away Joe's damaged hand was the cause of much concern in the Rostron camp. However, after resting it for a week or so Joe was able to resume training in the knowledge that the injury appeared to be healing and would probably give no further trouble.

Rostron's father, normally a very sensible sort of man, who took a great interest in his son's career, was guilty of grossly under-estimating the opposition here, for he confidently told Joe, 'Don't worry lad, if necessary you can lick this fellow with one hand.'

Though the injury had responded to treatment and the hand felt sound enough by the time he climbed into the Free Trade Hall ring, Rostron knew that it was not quite back to normal, and had made up his mind to use it sparingly, firmly believing that he could outpoint McAvoy with his educated left. But going in against a man as dangerous as McAvoy with only one good hand proved to be a grave mistake. The Heywood 'Hurricane' had a very poor night, boxing well below his best, while McAvoy, a much improved fighter, constantly found the target with both hands, forcing Rostron to give ground as he attempted to hold off his eager tormentor. Joe came under such pressure that there were times when he had no option but to bring his right hand into play, and quickly discovered that it was of little use to him. By some miracle, and certainly a great deal of cleverness, Rostron managed to keep out of serious trouble until late in the fourteenth round, when, backed up against the ropes and covering up, with his right hand held high and left arm protecting his body as McAvoy came at him, he suddenly felt Mac lift his left elbow. The next moment Joe thought his ribs had caved in as McAvoy banged a piledriver of a right hand into his body. Rostron had never been hit as hard in his life and was sure that his ribs must be broken. At that moment he was badly winded and in agony, but before Mac could follow up, the bell rang. Rostron, in great pain, could hardly summon up enough breath to get back to his corner, and would certainly have been stopped had that punch come a little earlier in the round.

Joe must have been very apprehensive as he left his stool for the fifteenth and final session. Sure enough, Mac came after him like a tiger, throwing punches from every angle as Rostron back-pedalled, desperately trying to keep out of the way of Mac's ferocious fists as the final three minutes slowly ticked away. He had still not recovered his breath when the fight ended, and considered himself very fortunate indeed to have lasted the distance.

That night Rostron discovered just how formidable McAvoy really was. Summing up many years later, Joe described Mac as a great natural fighter, who seldom threw wild punches, but always worked for his openings, picked his shots and hit correctly with the knuckle part of the glove, getting his full weight behind almost every blow. He did not consider McAvoy to be a rough or dirty fighter, explaining that when Mac lifted his arm to create the opening for that pulverising body punch he had simply brushed it out of the way and banged in the right to the short ribs. There was no holding involved. It was just a well executed move.

To his credit Rostron never attempted to use the hand injury as an excuse for his defeat. On the contrary, he had nothing but praise for McAvoy, admitting that he had been well beaten and expressing the opinion that no man of Mac's weight ever punched as hard.

'It was like being hit with a sledgehammer,' said Joe. 'When that punch landed all the breath went out of my body. It was just like a football being punctured. I'll tell you straight, I couldn't bend down to tie my own shoelaces for a week. What power that man had. Strong as a bullock and almost unstoppable.'

Of course, Joe Rostron, a very modest man, was so good himself that he would undoubtedly have given McAvoy a much harder time with two good hands, and it says much for his skill and courage that he was able to go fifteen rounds with such a dangerous puncher in the circumstances. Mac, however, was rapidly reaching true championship class, and would soon leave his rival far behind.

The 'Rochdale Thunderbolt' was now ready for Joe Lowther, the fight being booked for the Morecambe Winter Gardens in October, 1930. Unfortunately, Lowther's title would not be at stake, although there was no reason why it should not have been, but that was the way they did things in those days. Very often a challenger was expected, not only to fight his way through all the other contenders, but to prove himself against the champion as well before he was allowed a shot at the title.

McAvoy later confessed to getting a bad attack of nerves before the fight, far worse than he had ever experienced previously, with the result that he contributed very little to the opening rounds. By the third he was beginning to loosen up and punished Lowther severely, opening an ugly looking cut over the Yorkshireman's eye.

Badly handicapped, Lowther was forced to box on the retreat, using his superior skill to keep the fight at long range. With McAvoy doing the chasing and picking up most of the points, he eventually ran out a comfortable winner, the champion being credited with no more than three of the fifteen rounds.

Lowther was not satisfied, insisting that the cut, which had troubled him for most of the contest, had ruined his chances. Joe Tolley was quite happy to offer him a re-match, providing the title was at stake next time, and there the matter rested.

A proposed match with Harry Mason, recent conqueror of Jack Hood, failed to materialise, which was a great pity, for it would have been an intriguing contest. Mason, a former British Champion at Light and Welterweight, was one of the craftiest fighters ever to lace on a glove, and would certainly have brought the best out of the up and coming McAvoy.

Before the year 1930 was out Mac had added three more wins to his record, outpointing 'Seaman' Jim Cox again, this time over fifteen rounds at the Stadium, stopping Tate Evans of Maesteg in the fifteenth in Manchester, and knocking out Newcastle's Jim Johnson in two rounds, again at Royton.

At the beginning of January, 1931, Tolley brought 'Shocker' Bowman down from Penrith to take on McAvoy for a second time.

Having disposed of the big Cumbrian so decisively on the first occasion, Mac was obviously fancied to do even better this time, especially as Eddie Strawer had also beaten Bowman in the interim. But as often happens in boxing, things did not work out as anticipated. From the confident way he started you would never have believed that Bowman was facing a man who had flattened him in three rounds only a few months before. The 'Shocker' had come to fight and stood toe to toe slogging it out with Mac for most of the contest. Despite going down for a nine count in round seven and coming under heavy fire thereafter he was still upright at the finish, McAvoy being awarded a clear points verdict.

Next came the opportunity to box at the famous Liverpool Stadium, this being the original arena in Pudsey Street, against Charlie McDonald, a coloured fighter from Sunderland. McAvoy was keen to do well in front of the very knowledgeable local fans, and won on points over fifteen rounds. But as it turned out the contest was a dull, boring affair, with neither man impressive, a bout of influenza being blamed by the Royton camp for their man's lack-lustre showing.

Mac was disappointed. He was anxious to get more fights at the larger halls, where the money was better and the possibility of being thrust into the national spotlight much more likely. The break came quicker than expected, however, when Tolley arranged a contest at the King's Hall, Belle Vue, Manchester, against Dick Burt of Plymouth, billed as Middleweight Champion of the West of England.

Mac was back to his best that night. He was out to redeem himself and poor Burt was made to pay for the below par performance against McDonald, coming under pressure from the start and seldom managing to trouble McAvoy, who was in devastating form and on top in every round. Burt was tough and took his punishment without showing any signs of wilting until the eighth round, when the constant bombardment finally began to take its toll, the plucky West Countryman being hammered to the canvas several times before the referee accepted his retirement.

Mac's demolition job on Burt did not go unnoticed by the Belle Vue promoters, who had big plans, and were very keen, not only to use the best talent available, but to get their hands on it if possible. For the moment though, they were quite happy just to sign up the Rochdale wonderboy for a further contest, to take place at the end of the following month.

In the meantime it was back to the bread and butter fights at Royton, with Mac facing Charlie Keeling of Nottingham. After a promising start, during which he gave as good as he got, Keeling ran into one of Mac's specials, a right flush on the chin that put him down for an eight count. Rising on shaky legs, he was met by another crunching right, this time to the body, and sagged to the canvas to be counted out in round three.

In later years Charlie ruefully recalled his trip to Royton, saying he was not at all sure that he had received a square deal, in view of the fact that Joe Tolley, as well as being the promoter, matchmaker, M.C. and McAvoy's unofficial manager, was also the referee, and allowed his fighter plenty of leeway when it came to rough tactics, including some very dubious body punching which tended at times to stray dangerously close to the kidney region.

McAvoy's next outing at Belle Vue was against Paul McGuire from Sunderland. This time things went rather badly. Having developed into a devastating body puncher, he now invariably made this area his main target, and after being well in command of the early action Mac was unfortunate enough to get himself disqualified for hitting low in round four. Only four days after this he outpointed Jim Cox for the third time, over twelve rounds in Bolton, and a fortnight later was back in Morecambe to face Sonny Doke, a tough southpaw from Battersea whom Mac found very difficult to fathom. Nevertheless he still got the better of things in a hard contest over fifteen rounds.

Around this time it was announced in a local newspaper that McAvoy had opened his own School of Boxing in Baron Street, Rochdale. Just what sort of 'school' it was is not clear, but Mac was doing his own training there, helped by, among others, Benny Sutcliffe, a Rochdale Hornets Rugby League player, who fancied his chances with the gloves and was brave enough to get into the ring with McAvoy for sparring sessions.

Training not more than a few hundred yards away, in an upper room of the Derby Hotel, under the keen eye of a Mr Todd, described as his backer, was Eddie Strawer, eager to re-establish himself as the district's number one middleweight. Apart from his two losses to McAvoy, Strawer was doing well, and had seen off a number of worthy opponents over the previous months in various parts of the country.

McAvoy was now boxing at least once, sometimes twice, a month. Having advanced to the status of leading contender, engagements were less frequent but better paid. Not that he was earning anything like big money, but at least he could feel that at last he was getting somewhere.

The fact that he was a married man with a young family did not, however, keep him home in the evenings. He had always liked nice clothes whenever he could afford them, and now that he was earning a few bob he tended rather to indulge himself. He and Len Collinge, sporting all the latest American-influenced styles, could be seen regularly on a Friday or Saturday night strolling through the town centre, dressed to kill. Len, like McAvoy, was big and good looking and the two of them were naturally very popular with the girls, especially Mac, who was now becoming something of a local celebrity. He liked to be seen out and about and enjoyed the music and the atmosphere of the dance halls – as well as the girls of course, but he would never drink or smoke. To Mac, getting to the top was the most important thing in his life, and though he would never be the type to sit at home by the fireside, he certainly did not overdo the late nights, but looked after his body and was always in superb physical condition.

Charlie Henderson, several years younger than McAvoy, and a former pupil of St. Patrick's school, recalls that Mac, although on his way up in the world, still identified very strongly with his roots. Charlie remembers how, as a teenager, he played football with the other local lads on a piece of ground known as Cronkyshaw Common, using any sort of patched-up ball they could lay their hands on. One day they were standing on a street corner when McAvoy came by and stopped for a chat, asking why they weren't playing on 'Cronky'. On learning that they had no ball, he asked how much one would cost, then gave Charlie eleven shillings to go and buy it.

Charlie returned with a magnificent leather football, purchased for ten and sixpence. Mac told him to keep the sixpence change, at which Charlie was both astonished and delighted. 'Well,' he says, 'a tanner was a lot of money to me in them days.'

McAvoy then joined in the game, getting stuck in for all he was worth. He was a hero to the lads, who, as well as thoroughly enjoying his company, finished up the proud owners of a real leather caseball.

# Chapter 9

## Bankruptcy

With Joe Tolley all was far from well. Over the past few months he had been steadily losing money. At first, the fact that a rival promoter had come onto the scene appeared to make very little difference. But it was inevitable that in the end something would have to give. With the advent of the N.S.B. he had naturally lost a few customers, for it was obvious that the fans would be curious enough to want to go along and take a look at the new set-up. Having seen it they would be back at the old Stadium the following week, unless there was a particularly attractive bill on at Chapman's place, although usually, whatever Chapman had to offer, Tolley could top it. He was the master showman. The man who could get up there in the ring, address the audience, laugh and joke with them, engage in entertaining repartee with ringside patrons, outwit and silence the hecklers and give his customers a wonderful sporting afternoon out. But perhaps most important of all was the fact that Tolley controlled the majority of the district's top fighting men. This, more than anything else, is what gave him the edge.

Tolley must have been livid when Chapman had the audacity to move into Royton and run shows on the same afternoon. He must also have cursed the man for a fool. Either the customers would split and both promoters would struggle along on half empty houses, or one of them would fall by the wayside. After a few weeks though, it certainly appeared that Tolley was in very little danger. The reason for this was that Chapman, who had nothing like the flair of a Joe Tolley, made the mistake of attempting to copy his rival. Belt competitions, personalities invited along to the shows, novelty acts – once he even had his brother Joe perform an Indian club-swinging act in the ring while shadow boxing – and various other gimmicks, which all added up to nothing more than second rate Joe Tolley. On top of this, while attempting to develop local rivalry among the fighters, he found himself, in the main, with the lesser lights of the district.

If this state of affairs had continued, Chapman would, in all probability, have closed down within a few months, but he was well fixed financially and could afford to dig in and wait to see who cracked first. It was this financial stability that Joe Tolley lacked. In other words he was very vulnerable and any serious drop in revenue would be likely to find him struggling.

Chapman must have realised that now he had established himself the time was right to take the next step. Starting with Ben Marshall he began to book more 'name' fighters from out of town, while still using the local rivalry angle for his supporting contests. It was an excellent formula, made possible by Chapman's ability to finance the operation, for he could afford to gamble where Tolley couldn't. From the moment he embarked on this policy Joe Tolley's gates began to nosedive and he was on the slippery slope.

Even before this though, Tolley was feeling the pinch. In April 1931 the Sessions Court of the Salford Hundred decided that defendants J. B. Tolley and T. A. Chapman were guilty of conducting illegal boxing shows, binding them over to be of good behaviour for twelve months.

The same day both promoters announced that the boxing programmes would continue. Chapman then withdrew from management of the N.S.B. and Tolley made a statement to the effect that he no longer had any part in the running of the Royton Stadium, but would be present on fight days as M.C.

On the following Sunday, April 26th, certain ingenious measures were taken, which, it was hoped, would keep them within the law. No admission charges were made, but people could come in and then pay for a seat, so long as it was reserved.

In the midst of this odd state of affairs boxing continued at both arenas, while Chapman made bigger plans and Tolley continued as before, featuring the best fighters in the district, with McAvoy his biggest drawing card, and leaving Albert to do the donkey work while he chased around all over the country on M.C.'ing and refereeing trips, and fulfilling his role of boxing correspondent in between times.

Though Albert was unaware of it at the time his father was experiencing acute financial difficulties. His earnings were quite substantial, if not high, but there were two major problems, the first of course being that the Stadium was now losing money. The second was the fact that Tolley was rather a big spender. He was well known in towns all over the country and had become friendly with many show business people who attended the fights. He had always been a great womaniser and Albert later admitted that his father had had a female friend in just about every town he visited on a regular basis. That added up to quite a few women, for he was on the road practically every week, and when at home he often spent his evenings in Manchester, where he was more than friendly with a certain well known radio and big band singer.

None of this was conducive to thrift, so it was hardly surprising that Joe had begun to experience money worries. While all was going well at the Stadium there was no problem, but once the crunch came and Chapman started to turn the screw Tolley began to find himself in real trouble. He told no one, but made the fatal mistake of approaching a money lender in the forlorn hope that he could hold out until things took a turn for the better. In fact he was merely postponing the inevitable, for things were about to get worse – much worse.

In the early part of 1931 Tom Chapman began to experiment with All-in-Wrestling, putting it on as a sort of second feature to the boxing. This was in fact a sound idea, for at that time this form of wrestling was becoming all the rage. It was a sport which had caught on in a big way in Europe and America. It incorporated very few of the old wrestling rules and was certainly nothing like the sort of contrived stuff we see today, the object then being to wear your opponent down, kicking and punching being allowed.

A large and curious crowd turned up on the first occasion to witness a titanic struggle between Johann Fessan and 'Tiger' Billy Snowball. Their reactions seemed to indicate that they had enjoyed it and wanted to see more.

Though boxing was Joe Tolley's passion as well as his business, he was always a firm believer in giving the public what they wanted. In any case All-in-Wrestling was becoming so popular that he did not feel that its inclusion in his programmes would be too much of a gamble and might well go a long way towards bolstering the attendances. If he was going to do it though, he had to go one better than Chapman. So with this in mind Joe got in touch with Billy Riley, landlord of the Crispin Inn in Wigan and a man who claimed to be the first All-in-Wrestling Champion of the World, a title won in America.

Riley made his first appearance at Royton Stadium on April 5th 1931, against 'Strangler' Harris of Tyneside.

A local newspaper, in announcing the contest, claimed that 'many local wrestlers are turning to the All-in style, and some good ones should be turned out, as Oldham and Wigan are traditionally the homes of the grappling game'.

This tit-bit of information no doubt originated from Joe Tolley, who also let it be known that he himself was not unfamiliar with the sport, having acted as boxing and wrestling coach to the British Army while on wartime service in France. When the two maulers climbed into the Stadium ring to do battle they were given their final instructions by the versatile Tolley, who acted as referee.

On a number of occasions after this, Riley, who ran a School of Wrestling in Wigan, brought over a team of grapplers to make up bills of half wrestling, half boxing, which for a time went down very well with the fans. Though it helped Tolley's desperate situation somewhat, the crowds were still steadily dwindling. The truth was that despite the great popularity of boxing at that time Tolley was suffering because he was being forced to share his customers with Chapman. With both promoters running on the same day and in the same district, there just weren't enough fans to make it a paying proposition. It was obvious that in the end one promoter would be forced to close down.

In mid-April McAvoy was back at Royton Stadium, where he made short work of Bedford's Johnny Seamarks, knocking him out in three rounds. At Belle Vue the following month he was matched with Fred Shaw of Shipley, Yorkshire, an outstanding middleweight and one of the few men to have beaten the formidable Frenchman, Marcel Thil. Shaw, a very experienced performer, had never been put down, let alone stopped, and took McAvoy's best punches without flinching, then banged back with some jolting ones of his own. But though Shaw's toughness and know-how kept him in the fight, it was Mac's tremendous workrate that tipped the scales in the end, giving him a well merited points victory.

Next came a return with Sonny Doke, this time at Royton over twelve rounds. In the previous ten days Doke had defeated Frank Ogden (Salford) and Joe Woodruff of Accrington, one of the hardest middleweights around.

Nevertheless Mac was determined to put Doke away this time and trained hard at the Baron Street gym, doing his roadwork at Hollingworth Lake, a local beauty spot which would later become the setting for his training camp.

From the opening bell Doke commenced to frustrate the eager McAvoy, much as he had done in their first meeting. As well as fighting southpaw he also had an awkward style and a very strong chin. Try as he might McAvoy could do little with the tough Southerner, who defied all Mac's efforts to put him on the canvas and received a great ovation from the crowd for his courage, though Mac got the verdict after twelve very hard rounds.

McAvoy's hands were still troubling him and moving up in class had not helped at all, for whenever he was forced to go through ten or fifteen rounds of hammer and tongs slogging he found that the hands were usually very sore for some days afterwards.

Next on the list was Dutchman Con Van Leowen, who claimed to be cruiserweight and ex-middleweight champion of his country. On arriving in Britain, Van Leowen had knocked out heavyweight Tom Stribling in four rounds and followed this by beating Welshman Jack Thomas, another heavyweight. Only a few weeks before the meeting with McAvoy he had defeated the promising Manchester fighter, Ian Ritchings, who was also a well known speedway rider. A measure of the Dutchman's ability can be gleaned from the fact that Ritchings had managed to stop Sonny Doke in eight rounds.

None of these statistics were of much interest to McAvoy, who set about the much bigger Van Leowen with great relish. For the first four rounds he met with stern resistance, but in round five Mac's pulverising body punches had his opponent hanging on desperately and taking so much punishment that he did well to get through the round, at the end of which his corner called the referee over and pulled their man out.

That day the police visited both the Royton Stadium and the N.S.B. while boxing was in progress, taking down the names, addresses and occupations of everyone concerned in running the shows, from referees to seconds and even doormen. The police presence, which the promoters considered to be further harassment, was naturally causing some concern, especially to Tolley, for attendances that day at both arenas could only be described as moderate.

Mac, of course, was concentrating on his own career and had thrown out a challenge to any middleweight in the country. Welterweight Champion Jack Hood, meanwhile, made a bid for Len Harvey's Middleweight crown, taking him the full distance of fifteen rounds at the Albert Hall before losing on points. Though Hood showed tremendous gameness he was soundly beaten and did well to last the course.

Harvey, rather than Hood, was now Mac's target, for he had grown into a solid middleweight and felt confident that he was ready. The problem was that Harvey was more interested in chasing the World title, especially since Mickey Walker had relinquished it owing to weight-making problems.

McAvoy now prepared to leave for Ireland to take on Jack O'Brien of Belfast, but first made a brief visit to the Rochdale Hornets' Rugby ground, where he K.O.'d Yorkshireman Jack Bottomley in 55 seconds in an open-air charity show. It was one of the few times that his father saw him in action, for Joe senior now seldom left the house, though he was very interested in his son's career and followed it closely in the newspapers.

The O'Brien contest took place at Tolka Park, Dublin, bad weather keeping the attendance down to around five thousand. But sparse as it seemed in such a large stadium, the noisy Irish spectators roared their man on from the start, O'Brien being so fired up that he was able to drive McAvoy back during the first two rounds.

But Mac was confident enough. He knew that once he landed solidly the Irishman would know all about it. His chance came sooner than expected, for in round three O'Brien swung over a big right hand and missed, losing his footing on the wet slippery canvas. Mac was in like a flash, catching O'Brien with a vicious right to the jaw which put him down so heavily that his head struck the boards with a sickening thud. Amazingly the game Irishman managed to stagger to his feet, but before McAvoy could do any further damage the towel came fluttering into the ring.

On returning from Ireland Mac learned that he was to meet Joe Lowther again. This time Lowther's Northern Area Title would be at stake and the fight would take place at Belle Vue. It was not the big one, but at least if he could beat Lowther again he could call himself a champion.

Determined to stop Lowther this time and also to impress the big Manchester crowd, McAvoy rushed in at the opening bell, catching the champion cold with a stinging right to the jaw. Lowther, backing off, was forced on to the ropes, where Mac, instead of steadying himself and picking his shots, flailed away wildly, missing with many more punches than he landed. The bell sounded with Lowther half out of the ring and in serious trouble.

A smart boxer, the experienced Leeds man now attempted to keep the fight at long range, but whenever McAvoy could trap him against the ropes Lowther came in for some heavy punishment about the body. By the eighth this had begun to have its effect, and seeing his opponent fading, Mac increased the pressure, bombarding Lowther from all angles. Finally, a superbly timed right hand to the body finished the job, the champion slumping to the canvas just as his seconds threw in the towel.

Just one week after the Lowther fight excerpts from this and the Johnny King versus Pat Gorman fight, also on the Belle Vue bill, were shown at the Colosseum Cinema, Rochdale, and it was announced that McAvoy would make a personal appearance at the Friday evening performance.

Mac obviously relished the publicity and all the adulation. He was now a well known local figure and just loved to be seen and recognised.

In the summer of 1931 Joe Tolley's financial problems finally caught up with him. He had been having a very bad time of it, and though never the type of man to let people know he was worried, he must have been feeling the strain nevertheless. He had now tried just about everything he could think of to save his beloved Royton Stadium, even turning it into a keep-fit club during the week in a desperate last ditch effort to produce some much needed revenue. Here again he was very far ahead of his time. Fifty years or so later health clubs would become big business, but in the poverty stricken thirties the idea was doomed to failure. In the end Tolley realised that he was working hard all week at his other activities just to keep the Stadium going, and slipping deeper and deeper into debt. He knew he was fighting a losing battle and that the end was in sight.

After taking legal advice, Joe decided to file a voluntary bankruptcy petition, but first, certain arrangements had to be made. The house in Union Street was not owned by him, it was rented, and it would have been very difficult to prove that anything in it belonged to Tolley, the Maloney family still being in residence.

At the Stadium there was an old Royal portable typewriter in the office. This he gave to Albert, telling him to remove it from the premises without delay. Everything else of value he quietly disposed of himself, leaving only one item to be considered – the car. A Morris saloon, it was at that moment standing in Mills' garage in Royton, where Albert had taken it for an engine overhaul.

Tolley thought things over very carefully, then told Albert to get the car back as quickly as possible. On going round to the garage, however, Albert found that it could not be removed as the engine was stripped down, and it was several days later, after repeated visits to the garage, that he was able to drive the vehicle away.

Joe Tolley then instructed his son to go out and sell it for the best price he could get, his parting words being, 'Whatever you do don't bring it back here.'

Albert called at several garages before he was able to dispose of it to one Ralph Renton, of Hollinwood. Renton, a tough businessman, soon sensed that young Albert was desperate, and after a trial run offered to 'take it off his hands' for a very modest sum. Albert had no option but to accept.

At a meeting of creditors, held at the Official Receiver's Office in Manchester soon afterwards, Joe Tolley was described as a forty-eight year old former boxing promoter, now out of work, which was, of course, far from the truth. It was stated that he had net liabilities of £222.1s.10d and assets of £28.10s.10d, leaving a deficit of £193.11s.0d. The debtor attributed his failure to local trade depression and also the decline in business following his summons under the Sunday Observance Act, which had had a further damaging effect on attendances at the Stadium.

Of the unsecured debts, over £91 was owed to money lenders, while a sum of £51.13s.7d was shown as being owed to J. B. Mills of Royton, for repairs to the car, a debt that was never paid.

The Stadium was closed down for good and after a few years returned to its former derelict state, a sad and forlorn reminder of those great days and the many talented and colourful fighters who had performed there.

Though it was a bitter blow as far as the Tolleys were concerned, Joe was never one to be on his knees for very long. He soon put his troubles behind him and carried on. He was, as always, in great demand as a referee, matchmaker and M.C. and had no intention of allowing the stigma of bankruptcy to cramp his style. Throughout his entire working life a large part of his earnings went undisclosed as far as the tax people were concerned, though they were on his trail at various times. But although he hardly ever paid any tax, they never succeeded in catching up with him.

'The amazing thing,' Albert told me, 'was that no matter what financial straits or what trouble he was in, he never appeared to be worried, and always seemed to have plenty of money in his pocket.

'He didn't use banks very much, and whenever he was paying for anything he'd pull a roll of notes out of his back pocket as thick as your fist. In fact, I never felt that there was really any need for him to have gone bankrupt at all.'

This is no doubt true, for although the deficiency stated was quite a substantial amount for those days, it was by no means a frightening sum to a man of Joe Tolley's ingenuity. The fact was though, that he had already borrowed from money lenders earlier in 1931 in an effort to keep the Stadium afloat. When he realised that he was failing in his efforts to stem the tide he obviously realised that there was very little point in sinking funds into an enterprise which was losing money every week. He therefore decided to cut his losses, cease trading and concentrate on other, more profitable areas of the boxing business.

One thing is quite certain. If Tom Chapman had not come on the scene it's extremely unlikely that Joe Tolley would ever have found it necessary to shut up shop and declare himself bankrupt. What must have been particularly galling to Tolley was the thought that he was now leaving his arch rival with a clear field to cash in on what he himself had built up over the years.

Several weeks later Joe surprised his son by announcing that he had decided to pay a visit to the N.S.B. to see for himself just how things were going. Albert knew they would not be welcome, but Joe insisted that he go along. Of a much more reserved disposition than his father, Albert was somewhat apprehensive as they approached the officials' entrance that afternoon, accompanied by one of Joe's lady friends.

If they had gone in at the public entrance there would have been no problem, but being in the business Joe had no intention of paying. He had probably never paid to get into a boxing show in his life, and had no intention of doing so now.

At the door Albert's worst fears were confirmed when they found their way barred by a huge man whom Chapman employed as a bouncer. The big man recognised Joe Tolley immediately and told him that they couldn't pass without tickets. But Joe was not one to be put off that easily and an argument ensued, much to Albert's embarrassment. Eventually the bouncer went away to consult his boss. Chapman was not too keen to have Joe Tolley around the place. On the other hand he was anxious to avoid any unpleasantness which might result in adverse publicity, and Joe was by this time quite steamed up. So reluctantly Chapman gave the order to let Tolley and his party through.

Joe just grunted contemptuously as he strode past the bouncer and into the hall. He had been in boxing for thirty-odd years and if he wished to see a show he'd see it, and no doorman or anyone else was going to stop him.

At a later date Tolley was actually called upon to referee at the N.S.B., though not at the request of Tom Chapman. When asked to officiate there, Joe did not refuse and was quite happy to go along, though he was probably just about the last man Chapman wanted to see up there in the ring taking a prominent part in his shows.

Tolley, meanwhile, remained on the old merry-go-round. He wouldn't have been happy doing anything else, for boxing was his life. He was steeped in the game and loved it, despite the ups and downs. And though he took plenty out of the game he certainly put a lot more back into it.

After the Stadium closed, for example, although still exceptionally busy, he was always ready to give any keen young lad a lesson or two in self-defence, and started quite a number of local men, including one or two ex-boxers, on the road to becoming licensed referees, coaching them in his own time.

It is also a remarkable fact that of the five Northern Championship belts fought for between the Great War and 1931, when the Stadium closed its doors, four were won by fighters who started their careers at Royton under Joe Tolley. They were 'Kid' Lees (Oldham), Billy Pritchard (Stalybridge), Johnny King and Jock McAvoy, both from Rochdale, while the only other official belt winner, Jim Learoyd of Leeds, was twice defeated by Royton favourite Harold Ratchford, who was half a stone lighter.

Amazingly, even the fifth belt finished up, in a way, in Royton hands, when the formidable Jack Davies, of Ashton-under-Lyne, defeated Learoyd at Morecambe in the summer of 1932, to win the Northern Junior-Lightweight title. Davies, who twice beat Ratchford, was another who began his career at Royton under Joe Tolley.

Premises or no premises, Albert Tolley had a stable of fighters to run, though they were still unofficially controlled by his father. Without training facilities it now became necessary for them to work out wherever they could, quite a few going to Willie Walsh's gym near Mumps Bridge, Oldham. Walsh, still an active fighter, and an old Royton product himself, was only too pleased to be in a position to help.

There was no vehicle, of course, to transport them to out-of-town shows and all business had to be conducted from the house at No. 16 Union Street, Royton.

They were still sending fighters all over the country, to places such as Newcastle, Morecambe, Blackpool, Rhyl, Barrow and even the

National Sporting Club on occasion. Sometimes a complete team of boxers would be sent out, as was the case in August 1931, only a month after the bankruptcy hearing, when Albert booked a group of his boxers to appear on a Wigan bill, plus another party to open a new stadium in Leeds only a few days later. All this, of course, was done through Joe Tolley's network of contacts and organised by the supposedly out-of-work promoter.

# Chapter 10

## The Contract

It was in 1931, soon after McAvoy had won the Northern Area title, that Joe Tolley and his ace drawing card finally reached the parting of the ways. There is, in fact, an intriguing and highly controversial story surrounding the way in which the contract changed hands, and indeed in whose hands it actually finished up.

The story concerns a secret meeting which took place at Belle Vue in 1931, at which the contract was sold for cash. Albert Tolley kept the details of this meeting to himself for the best part of sixty years. Even after such a passage of time he was very reluctant to speak out, and did so only after much deliberation.

Those concerned were obliged to keep the meeting quiet because McAvoy's managers, both the official and the unofficial, were required to be present, as well as the most important member of the Belle Vue Syndicate, who was at pains to conceal his involvement.

According to the rules of the British Boxing Board of Control, a contract is not transferable. Should a manager agree to let his fighter sign up with another manager, providing all three parties, that is, both managers and the boxer, are in agreement, then the existing contract is terminated by the manager who holds it, simply writing a letter to that effect to the Board of Control. The remaining period of the contract being thereby cancelled, the boxer is then free to sign a new contract with the second manager. It is important to note here that a boxer is not permitted to sign for any sort of group or syndicate, but may only enter into an agreement with a manager licensed by the British Boxing Board of Control.

According to McAvoy, in an article written nearly twenty years after the event, it was 'put to him' that he could take a short cut to the top by more closely associating himself with the Belle Vue people. Apparently, the Manchester manager, Harry Fleming, who was known to have very close ties with the Belle Vue set-up, approached him, offering to take over his affairs, provided Mac could come to an amicable agreement with Joe Tolley.

McAvoy stated that he then talked it over with his manager, who readily agreed that he would do a lot better by moving into more influential circles, that he had no wish to stand in his way and was prepared to relinquish his claims. He then went on to say, 'It was a very sporting gesture on Joe Tolley's part, and one I shall never forget. I was now in a position to come to financial terms with him over the transaction and we parted the best of friends.'

This, of course, gives the impression that Tolley was quite happy to stand aside, and that McAvoy was therefore able to buy back his contract and sign up with Harry Fleming.

Such an over-simplification of what actually transpired over McAvoy's change of management cannot be allowed to go unchallenged, as it amounts to nothing less than a gross distortion of the facts, which is why Albert Tolley eventually agreed to reveal the true story behind McAvoy's change of management.

Considering Mac's vast potential, that contract was a very valuable document indeed, for it was quite obvious to everyone in the fight game that he was headed for a British title at least. Joe Tolley was no mug. Even if he had felt that without the co-operation of the big promoters it was going to be a long hard slog, he would never have been so 'sporting' as to surrender the contract that easily. After all, he had discovered McAvoy and brought him from obscurity to championship class, and if Tolley had not been Mac's promoter as well as his manager this might not have been possible.

True enough, Tolley had been forced to shut up shop and needed money, but even if he saw the writing on the wall and realised that sooner or later he would have to let Mac go, he was not the sort of man to give up the contract simply because he felt it would be in the fighter's best interests. He was not that noble, nor could he afford to be.

The contract was drawn up sometime after the reconstitution of the British Boxing Board of Control in 1929, and though Albert admitted that, over sixty years on, he was unable to recall just how long a period it covered, he was certain that at the time of the meeting at Belle Vue there were still at least a couple of years left to run. Joe Tolley was entitled to a percentage of McAvoy's earnings, and as McAvoy was now Northern Area Champion and fighting at least a couple of times a month, this represented quite a sum as far as Joe Tolley was concerned. So, if he was prepared to sell his interest, it would certainly have had to be well worth his while, and neither Harry Fleming nor McAvoy was in a position to come up with the kind of money that would be required to clinch the deal. So who would? Quite obviously the people who wanted McAvoy most – the Belle Vue Syndicate. Of course, they could have waited until the contract ran out, but they were very anxious that no one else should beat them to it.

This so-called syndicate was apparently made up of Henry Illes, the licensed promoter, Jack Madden, matchmaker, Harry Fleming, official manager of, among others, Jackie Brown and Johnny King, and Norman Hurst, one of the country's leading sports journalists.

It would appear, however, that Illes had very little to do with it. His position was that of manager of the Belle Vue complex, and as such he held the license to promote at the King's Hall. Madden, a former fighter himself, was the one who dealt with all the boxing business and put on the shows, while Fleming, assisted by another former fighter, Jack Bates, looked after the boxers and trained them at his own gymnasium in Collyhurst. Later, a well-equipped gym within the Belle Vue complex was set up and placed at his disposal.

The real power behind the organisation, however, was Norman Hurst, a man whose involvement in boxing went back a good many years. Hurst wrote for the *Daily Dispatch* and the *Empire News*, whose sports coverage was excellent. He was also believed to be the ghost writer for certain other papers which carried articles by well known sporting figures.

Though Hurst could obviously not afford to have his connection with the syndicate made public, it was well known in boxing circles that he was not only involved, but was in fact the main man, who provided the financial backing and made all the major decisions. In other words, a shadowy figure who remained discreetly in the background pulling the strings.

One thing is quite clear. If Harry Fleming had not thrown in his lot with the Syndicate he would have been in exactly the same position as Joe Tolley. For though quite successful as a manager-trainer, even before Norman Hurst came on the scene, he needed a powerful organisation behind him to have any chance at all of breaking into the big time.

Originally just a trainer, Fleming had simply moved into management as his Collyhurst stable grew and became more successful. He still spent a considerable amount of time in the gym, where he excelled as a sort of trainer-coach. With the addition of Jack Bates, who developed into a fine trainer himself, Harry was able to devote more time to the business side. But though more than capable of handling the day to day running of the stable, it was always apparent to those who had dealings with him that if a major decision had to be made Harry could never commit himself on the spot. He would always have to 'get back to you', it then being assumed that he would be making a telephone call.

Norman Hurst could usually be reached either in Manchester or London, where he spent a good deal of his time. All week he would pound out his articles for the sports pages, and who could blame him if the names of the Belle Vue boxers, notably King, Brown and later McAvoy, were constantly in the news. The thousands of words churned out on these three fighters, built up their images, helped sell them to the public and must have been worth a fortune in terms of free publicity.

Once Joe Tolley decided to let his fighter move on, a meeting was arranged at Belle Vue, and Tolley travelled down there accompanied by Albert, and Harold Ratchford, who was there as a witness. On arrival, they were taken upstairs to a private room in the Belle Vue Hotel. Albert recalls that Harry Fleming was present, also McAvoy.

Not until all were assembled did Norman Hurst make his entrance, and after some polite conversation the meeting got down to business, Albert gaining the distinct impression that his father and Hurst had previously spoken together, as everything appeared to be cut and dried.

Hurst, who did all the talking, began by briefly summarising the achievements of the Belle Vue set-up and outlining some of the exciting plans they had for the future. Then, after acknowledging the very important part played by Joe Tolley in McAvoy's career up to that point, he went on to say that in his opinion Mac had all the makings of a world class fighter. With an influential organisation behind him, which would ensure that he was properly handled and the right opportunities put his way, there was virtually no limit to the heights he might reach.

The eloquent Mr Hurst then assured McAvoy that, provided he was prepared to work hard under the guidance of Harry Fleming, they would guarantee that he would be a British Champion within two years, and earn a great deal of money into the bargain. McAvoy at once indicated that he was keen to sign up. A document was then produced and laid down before him on the table. McAvoy glanced over it rather vaguely, nodding, while Hurst carried on talking, outlining the contents.

The new agreement was based on an American idea. It was known as a fifty-fifty contract, which meant that a fighter's earnings were split down the middle between boxer and management. On hearing this Mac's face clouded, but after being told that the management would assume responsibility for all outgoings, including managers', trainers' and seconds' wages, plus expenses connected with training, travelling, accommodation, meals, sparring partners etc, he seemed happier, and nodded his acceptance. McAvoy's hesitance was hardly surprising, for Joe Tolley had never taken more than 12½%, or half-a-crown (12½p) in the pound, as his commission, a very modest percentage indeed.

It has been claimed that McAvoy never worked under a fifty-fifty contract until he went to America in 1935, but according to Albert Tolley this is incorrect. Albert could clearly recall Norman Hurst explaining this form of agreement to McAvoy that day in the Belle Vue Hotel, and was present when McAvoy signed the contract.

Harry Fleming then added his name, the signatures being witnessed by Albert and Harold Ratchford. With the transaction completed, Norman Hurst handed over to Joe Tolley a roll of banknotes. He also peeled off a tenner and gave it to McAvoy, 'to be going on with'. Albert and Harold were each presented with a five pound note. After that it was handshakes all round followed by a celebratory drink.

Albert left the meeting feeling very pleased. As he pointed out, 'Five quid was a lot of money in those days. Especially to a lad of nineteen.'

He knew better than to ask how much his father had received for the contract, and Joe never volunteered that information, though he appeared well satisfied.

Getting himself into what McAvoy considered to be the big league was a great boost for him. He was eager to please and Harry Fleming was greatly impressed with the way he set about his gym work. Harry had no idea then, but once Mac settled in and became familiar with the set-up he would prove just as awkward and difficult to handle as he had always been.

Harry Fleming, like his brother John and his father before him, had begun his working life as a cooper, developing an interest in boxing as he grew up and later running his own gym in Collyhurst. His working partnership with Jack Bates, whom he had formerly managed, was to prove highly successful, and though the opportunities were provided for them by Norman Hurst and the Belle Vue Syndicate, there is no doubt that they were more than equal to the job of managing and training the outstanding talent in their stable.

By the early thirties the Fleming camp had the use of a spacious, well-equipped gymnasium within the Belle Vue complex and plans were in the pipeline to set up a training camp at Hollingworth Lake, Rochdale, in the run-up to important fights.

Now training full time under the experienced eye of Fleming, McAvoy must have benefited greatly from working so closely with a man like Jack Bates, who had been a more than useful fighter himself and could teach Mac all the tricks of the trade. With good quality sparring he was soon coming on by leaps and bounds and looking forward eagerly to his next contest.

At the end of August, 1931, McAvoy was matched with the clever Hebrew from Stepney, Jack Hyams. A crafty, experienced campaigner, formerly known as 'Kid Froggy', Hyams was not much more than a welterweight and had no intention of slugging it out with the powerful McAvoy. He knew all there was to know about in-fighting and had no trouble tying Mac up in the clinches. Whenever he was tagged Hyams would immediately 'claim' his man, who found it very difficult to produce his best against a fighter who refused to stand and trade punches. Even when attacking, Hyams tended to hit and grab, making it a very frustrating evening for the eager McAvoy. By the middle rounds, however, Mac was beginning to find the target, causing the Stepney man to hang on desperately. In the end referee Ben Green had had enough and disqualified the Londoner for persistent holding.

A week later Mac was back at Belle Vue to face Welsh Middleweight Champion, Jerry Daley, who had been knocked out by Len Harvey less than two months before in three rounds. Daley, a stocky, willing scrapper, knew only one way to fight and met McAvoy head-on in the centre of the ring, where they punched it out toe to toe.

Playing McAvoy's game, however, was the worst mistake he could have made, for though the Welshman was very tough it was soon evident that he could not compete with Mac when it came to firepower and before the session ended he was backed up in a corner taking a fearful pounding and looking in some distress. Within seconds of the commencement of round two Daley was flat on his back from a devastating right to the jaw, with no chance whatsoever of beating the count.

A month after this McAvoy was matched with Alfred Pegazzano, a French-Italian, who held the French Middleweight title, and a man described as 'the toughest McAvoy has yet faced'.

After an uncharacteristically quiet opening round Mac suddenly cut loose in the second, raining punches on the surprised Continental from all angles and having him down a number of times before the round ended. Pegazzano came out somewhat apprehensively for round three to be battered around the ring unmercifully. He was on the canvas in a helpless state when the referee stepped in and stopped the contest.

McAvoy was next given the chance to reverse another decision when he was re-matched with Paul McGuire at the Tower Circus, Blackpool. Mac never liked the idea of having a blot on his record and was keen to get McGuire back in the ring. Things looked very ominous for the Sunderland man from the moment he left his corner. Without wasting any time on sizing up his opponent Mac tore straight in and subjected McGuire to a tremendous two-handed battering, finally putting him down with a bump just before the round ended. Round two had barely begun when McGuire, after taking a couple more heavy right handers, held up his hand in surrender.

Less than two weeks after this McAvoy was scheduled to meet ex-Seaman Albert Harvey at Belle Vue. When Harvey pulled out his place was taken by Billy Adair, a tough blond whom Mac did not need to go looking for. Billy was only too willing to make a fight of it, but found that these tactics did not pay against a man with McAvoy's punching power and lasted less than two rounds, taking some heavy punishment about the body before being put down for keeps.

Mac's next three fights were all at Royton, but this time, of course, at the N.S..B., where he would be appearing for the first time. Now Chapman had it all, even Joe Tolley's top drawing card on his show, and he was determined to make the most of it, bringing in an army of joiners to re-fit the whole place, with seating all round. He could now claim that the N.S.B. was one of the largest, most up-to-date arenas in the country, with a seating capacity of 3,000. One thing was certain. With McAvoy on the bill there would be very little danger of those seats being unoccupied.

Mac's sparring partners were nineteen-year-old Tommy Woods, described as Oldham's 'Young Carnera', Alf Robinson, the Smithfield Market heavyweight, Jack Davies of Bolton, 'Tod' Sloane (Hollinwood), Pat Murray, (Stockport) and Tommy Burgon of Todmorden. Burgon, a butcher, was a big burly fellow, who, though not a boxer, was a close friend of Mac's and liked to spar with him occasionally.

They certainly earned their money, McAvoy was almost as ferocious in the gym as he was in a real contest. Throughout his career, finding sparring partners would always prove a problem, for very few men were prepared to be subjected to the sort of treatment Mac handed out.

The first of these three contests should have been against Alf Noble, a cruiserweight from Bermondsey, but when Noble withdrew due to injury Mac found himself facing old foe Sonny Doke, the man who had twice taken him the distance and made him look bad into the bargain. This time Mac, determined to put the Londoner in his place once and for all, had no intention of being kidded by Doke and his awkward southpaw style.

At the opening bell Mac left his corner like a rocket and immediately put Doke under heavy pressure, finding him with fast punches from both hands to head and body, and having him in some trouble early on.

In the opening rounds the Battersea man visited the canvas several times before the end came early in the fifth, Doke's seconds throwing in the towel as he was again floored. There would have been no need for the referee to count in any case, as it was quite some time before Doke came to.

The following month, at the same venue, McAvoy was matched with Welshman Glen Moody, but was again obliged to accept a substitute when Moody went down with the 'flu, his place being taken by Ernie 'Red' Pullen of Cardiff. Mac received something of a shock when Pullen flew across the ring at the opening bell and belted him with a left hook that put him on the ropes in his own corner. It was one of those moments when, with anger blazing in his eyes, he waited for his opponent to follow up his advantage, then nailed him with a left hook to the ribs followed instantly by a crippling right under the heart. They were tremendous sledgehammer blows which had Pullen gasping and grimacing with pain. As his hands came down a right to the jaw floored him for nine, and on rising the bewildered

Welshman was immediately dropped again. He was out cold even before he hit the canvas.

It was another stunning victory for the 'Rochdale Thunderbolt', who was more than living up to his nickname. The big problem now was finding a middleweight, or even a light-heavyweight, capable of extending him. 'Cast Iron' Casey was offered a purse of £250 to take Mac on at Belle Vue, but declined, holding out instead for a title fight with Len Harvey.

The previous month Casey had clashed with Marcel Thil, the tough Frenchman, at the Royal Albert Hall, on a bill topped by Nel Tarleton. In that fight the Sunderland man took punches on the chin that would have felled an ox, but kept on coming back into the fight and threatening to belt out Thil with his powerful right hand, which he threw frequently, if somewhat crudely. Thil, a competent boxer and a very hard man, won on points in the end, and both fighters must have impressed Len Harvey, who was sitting at the ringside.

At this particular point in his career, Harvey was not at his most popular. Earlier that year, 1931, he had visited America, where he had taken part in three contests, losing them all, Vince Dundee (twice) and Ben Jeby, having beaten him on points. Though it was alleged by the Harvey camp that a couple of the decisions were of a rather dubious nature, the truth appears to have been that Len's upright British style and cautious approach to the job were not to the liking of the Americans at all, the sheer aggression of his opponents counting very much in their favour.

Since then Harvey had managed to redeem himself to some extent by outpointing Jack Hood and scoring knockout wins over Rene Devos and Jerry Daley.

It was clear that fighting his way back into the World title picture would not be easy, though efforts were being made to persuade Vince Dundee, a leading contender, to come to London so that Len might have the opportunity of gaining revenge with an English referee in charge. At the same time he was being pressed to defend his British title against either Casey or McAvoy, his only credible domestic challengers, and very formidable ones at that.

Meanwhile, the world title situation was changing rapidly. Jeff Dickson, the Paris-based American promoter, had brought Vince Dundee to Europe to fight Marcel Thil. When Thil licked the American, Harvey realised that if he could also beat Dundee the way would be clear for him to take on Thil for the vacant title.

All these plans were shattered, however, when Len was struck down by a serious kidney infection while in training. Jack Hood was brought in and held Dundee to a draw.

It was several weeks before Harvey recovered and was able to take to the ring again, K.O.'ing Fred Shaw in November, 1931. He was now in a position where he could no longer turn a blind eye to his domestic obligations and signed to meet Jack Casey, the contest to take place at Newcastle in February 1932.

# Chapter 11

## A Shot at the Title

McAvoy's first fight of 1932 was against Jack Marshall of Accrington, a very tough customer and hard puncher. Marshall was quite a bit bigger than Mac, standing six feet and weighing nearly 12 stone, but this made little difference. Mac set about him the moment the bell rang and blasted Marshall out in two rounds, in a contest refereed by Gus Platts of Sheffield, himself a former British and European Champion.

Two weeks later McAvoy got to fight the other Harvey, ex-Seaman Albert, at Belle Vue, in what promised to be a much sterner test. Harvey, a former Navy champion, who had beaten men of the calibre of Jack Bloomfield and 'Cast Iron' Casey, certainly knew how to look after himself. Though some of Harvey's own work tended to be rather negative, he was a very difficult man to catch cleanly, and Mac spent fifteen frustrating rounds trying to pin him down and nail him with a solid shot. In the end he had to be content with a points victory.

Jack Etienne, of Belgium, was McAvoy's next opponent. A hard, durable battler, who had given Len Harvey plenty of problems before being forced to retire in the thirteenth, Etienne was obviously unimpressed by Mac's reputation and made it plain from the start that he was quite prepared to walk in and have a go.

For the first couple of rounds, the Belgian, who seemed to dwarf McAvoy, more than held his own and was looking very confident until Mac caught him bang on the chin late in the third. Though Etienne took it well, it was obvious that the punch had shaken him and he was very glad to hear the bell. The minute's rest seemed to make all the difference, however, for he recovered well, Mac being forced to take some heavy right handers himself as Etienne fought back strongly. He was still there at the finish, with McAvoy being adjudged the winner after fifteen hard rounds.

Despite the fact that Mac had been obliged to go the distance it was still a good performance, considering that he had given away over half a stone to a man who had not only extended Len Harvey, but had also beaten Jack Hyams and Len Johnson.

The previous month Harvey had outpointed Jack Casey over fifteen rounds in a non-title fight, the Board of Control having refused to sanction the match as a British title contest. But if they were doubtful of Casey's worthiness as a contender, those doubts were quickly dispelled by the tremendous show the Sunderland man produced in making Harvey fight every inch of the way.

Now it was McAvoy's turn, Belle Vue clinching the deal by offering the champion a four figure purse, and though this meant that Mac's earnings from the fight would be on the small side, it was felt that the opportunity to lay hands on the title was not to be missed. If he won, Mac would be able to cash in at a later date, so he was quite happy to sign on the dotted line.

During the special preparations for what would be his greatest test so far McAvoy stayed at Harry Fleming's home, while training at the Belle Vue gym. A good deal of time was also spent at Hollingworth Lake, a local beauty spot, where the air was bracing and the terrain ideal for road work. At Walsden, not far away, Mac engaged in wood chopping sessions, his rippling back and shoulder muscles drawing admiring comments from the locals. Mac had always possessed a good physique, but now, as he reached the absolute peak of fitness, his body could only be described as magnificent. Around five foot ten, he was powerful, yet beautifully proportioned in the upper body, with slim, muscular legs.

As training progressed Mac was becoming increasingly difficult to handle, grumbling and complaining all the time, and with the day of the big fight drawing closer he grew even more edgy and irritable. This is quite normal during the final days of a fighter's preparation, but with McAvoy it went far beyond the norm, everyone around him having to be very careful as to how they behaved and what they said to him, for he was liable to explode at the slightest thing.

On the Wednesday afternoon prior to Monday, March 21st, the date of the big fight, a special workout took place at Belle Vue for the benefit of the press.

In contrast to Len Harvey, who always treated his sparring partners with the utmost consideration and respect, and would never take liberties, Mac was, as usual, in a very mean mood and ready to punish severely any man who dared get into the ring with him, sparring session or not.

After going two rounds with Fred Shaw*, to whom he administered a real hammering, Mac sparred a round each with Tim Ryan of Manchester, Bud Larney of Salford and P. C. Henderson, a Manchester City Police amateur, who quickly retired with blood streaming from his nose.

He also did some shadow boxing, skipping and floor exercises, greatly impressing everyone with his wonderful condition. Shrewd judges among the newsmen gathered expressed the opinion that Harvey would certainly have to perform a great deal better than he had against Casey if he expected to retain his title.

Len Harvey was a world class fighter, and without any question one of the finest ever produced in this country. Though brought up in Devonport, near Plymouth, and billed at various times as coming from Plymouth or London, Len was, in fact, a Cornishman, born at Stoke Climsland, near Golberdon, in July, 1907, making him roughly four months older than McAvoy. Unlike Mac, however, he had commenced his ring career early, at the tender age of twelve in fact, making his debut at the old Cosmopolitan gym in Plymouth.

Over the next nine years he engaged in more than eighty recorded contests as he grew into a tall, strong, muscular middleweight, winning the British title in 1929 with a seventh round knockout of Scotland's Alex Ireland. Since then he had defended it against Jack Hood no less than three times, winning twice on points and being held to a draw on the third occasion, and also against another Scot, Steve McCall, who had been forced to retire after nine rounds.

Harvey was a master boxer with a defence that was said to be almost impregnable, and though it cut no ice with the Americans, Len's style was extremely effective. Len usually preferred to bide his time, and would never let the punches go until he saw a clear opening. Then he could be devastating, and though Casey, driven on by the fanatical Geordie supporters, had given him a very hard fight, it is interesting to note that one of Len's perfectly timed and executed right handers to the chin had put the 'Iron Man' on the canvas for the first time in his career.

There was no question about it, McAvoy was about to face a man who was clearly in a different class than any he had previously come up against, and only by producing an outstanding performance would he stand any chance at all of toppling the champion.

*While helping with McAvoy's preparation, Shaw was training for his forthcoming contest with Joe Rostron, the two having previously fought a draw. Rostron won the return on points.

One thing the challenger was assured of was tremendous support, not only from Rochdale, where excitement was at fever pitch, but the whole of Lancashire, and in particular, Manchester, which had developed into one of the country's leading fight centres, due largely to the success of Harry Fleming and the Belle Vue Syndicate. Up to this point the Fleming stable could boast a British and European champion in flyweight Jackie Brown, while Johnny King* was considered a good bet for the British bantamweight crown. So Fleming's ambition to manage three champions would indeed become a distinct possibility if McAvoy could manage to dethrone the great Len Harvey.

On the day of the fight a telegram was received at Belle Vue, which read:

> IT WOULD BE VERY NICE IF YOU COULD WIN AND BRING FAME TO MY NATIVE TOWN. GOOD LUCK LAD – GRACIE.

When McAvoy arrived for the weigh-in he was in tip-top condition, but complained that his left hand felt a bit sore. It was nothing serious though, and didn't appear to bother him at all during the fight.

It was now that he met Len Harvey for the first time, Mac's impression being that he looked very young, pale and dignified. He must also have taken note of Harvey's impressive physique, and in particular his powerful shoulders, as the champion stepped onto the scales.

Harvey was just on the weight, while McAvoy was comfortably inside it at 11st. 3¼lbs. Len was a big middleweight and it was whispered in fistic circles that he was finding it very hard to get down to eleven-stone six. This was quite true, for he would be fighting for the light-heavyweight title the following year. On this occasion though, he had managed the weight without too much trouble, even stepping onto the scales in a pair of slippers.The contest was an extremely important one as far as Harvey was concerned. That same evening at the Palais des Sports in Paris, Marcel Thil was fighting Jack Hood in what was considered to be an eliminator for the World title. As Harvey had beaten both men he was obviously very much in the running himself, despite the ill-fated American trip, and the last thing he could afford was to slip up against McAvoy. Most critics agreed, however, that unless Len was prepared to show more aggression than he had in recent fights, he would not only find himself out of the

* King beat Dick Corbett to gain the British and Empire Bantamweight titles later the same year, while Brown went on to win a World title.

World title picture, but could, in fact, be in danger of losing his British crown. It would not be easy, for as well as being extremely tough and a heavy puncher, like Casey, McAvoy was a far better boxer than the Sunderland man, which all added up to a very hard night's work as far as Harvey was concerned.

Belle Vue was packed to the doors, with hundreds having come by special train from Rochdale to cheer their hero on to what they firmly believed would be a great victory. Eliza was there, looking very nervous as she waited for her husband to come into the ring.

When Mac finally appeared he was met by a roar that threatened to lift the roof off. The champion also received a warm reception from the sporting Manchester crowd as he climbed through the ropes. It was a wonderful occasion, and the atmosphere in the packed hall was electric as the crowd waited, tense with anticipation, for the contest to begin.

Harvey stood quietly in his corner, looking cool and composed, while McAvoy limbered up and went through his usual glove-biting ritual. When the champion was introduced by the M.C. he merely bowed to the crowd. Mac, nervous and a little agitated, trotted to the centre of the ring, looking awkward and embarrassed, nodded jerkily, then jogged back to his corner. He was wound up like a coiled spring and seemed greatly relieved when the preliminaries were over and the bell rang to send them on their way.

As the combatants met in the centre of the ring the stark contrast in styles was instantly apparent, the champion, tall and erect in the classical fighting pose, while McAvoy crouched low, head down, bobbing and weaving his way in, ready to strike the moment he came within range. Harvey waited calmly as Mac pressed forward, winging in hooks with both hands in an effort to find his opponent's ribs. Harvey backed off, then tied McAvoy up as they came together, the challenger wrestling fiercely to disentangle himself and batter away to the body at the same time.

Mac was rather surprised to discover that most of his best work was being done at long range, for the moment the two became involved in close quarter exchanges it was evident that Harvey was vastly superior. His short, sharp body shots made Mac gasp, and he was very adept at holding with one hand while punching with the other, at the same time making sure that the referee was unsighted.

In addition to his great skill, Harvey was a very strong man indeed, having at one time won a contest involving the World's Grip Record. Mac now felt that vice-like grip on his arm – on the referee's blind side of course*. Then Harvey, after getting him off balance, would give a sharp tug and McAvoy would stumble forward, straight into a jarring right cross. Though Mac and his corner knew exactly what was going on, it was obviously not so apparent to the referee, Jim Kendrick of London, who did not issue any warnings.

Once McAvoy realised that he was being made to look like a novice at close quarters he was only too eager to break away in order to give himself punching room. Then, as he weaved his way in again, he would be met by solid left jabs which jerked his head back. Still he pressed forward, forcing Harvey to give ground, his raw aggression and fierce determination showing up well against the apparent cautiousness of the champion.

During the first round Mac went down on one knee from a slip caused by his eagerness to go in and trade punches, but as he steadied himself he gradually began to get the range, finding the target with short sharp combinations as he bustled in, keeping Harvey under constant pressure.

This pattern continued for the first four rounds, then in round five came a sensational incident which almost ended the fight. As McAvoy tore in Harvey suddenly fired back, catching Mac with a superb left hook and forcing him back against the ropes. A following hook just failed to connect, and as the two fighters became entangled Harvey somehow contrived to bundle McAvoy through the ropes and out of the ring.

To Mac it must have seemed like a nightmare. One moment he was swapping punches, the next he was outside the ropes and almost standing on his head. Turning a complete somersault, he landed half on his feet and half among the spectators, before finishing up on the floor. Quickly realising what was happening, he then attempted to climb back into the ring, assisted by one of his seconds, who was immediately warned by the referee to stand clear. Scrambling desperately onto the ring apron, Mac somehow managed to get back through the ropes just in time to beat the count.

There was no question of Harvey following up his advantage, for Mac at once went looking for *him*, charging after the champion with all guns blazing, pushing him back and landing some telling blows.

* In those days the thumb was not attached to the main part of the glove as it is today, making it possible for a fighter to get a good grip on his opponent's arm.

Whenever he was in danger, however, Harvey was always able to tie Mac up and employ his dubious tactics, causing Harry Fleming to complain loudly to the referee as the session ended.

For the next five rounds McAvoy continued to attack, driving the champion before him and scoring with crisp punches to head and body. All the best work was coming from the challenger, while Harvey, though often forced to clinch, never became ruffled, but kept his head as McAvoy flailed away, waiting patiently for the storm to blow itself out. But this did not happen, for Mac's strength and stamina were truly phenomenal, and by waiting for his opponent to tire Harvey merely succeeded in falling further behind on points. McAvoy was beginning to get the upper hand and knew that if he could keep it up he would leave Belle Vue that night with the Lonsdale belt. At the end of every round Mac returned to his corner to the accompaniment of deafening applause from the partisan crowd, who were delighted with his efforts and willing him to win.

After ten rounds had been completed McAvoy was not only in front, but very much in command, and Harvey's corner pleaded with their man to step up his workrate and take the play away from the challenger. Over the next couple of rounds Len's boxing was much sharper, though McAvoy continued to be the aggressor. At this stage there was very little in it, but round thirteen was to prove the turning point.

McAvoy was still attacking strongly, switching from head to body and had Harvey backed up against the ropes, when the champion, apparently weary, suddenly dropped his arms to his sides. Mac, though obviously surprised, saw it as his big chance and moved in for the kill. Then bang! A tremendous right from Harvey caught him flush on the chin, stopping him dead in his tracks and causing him to stagger back. He was badly hurt but refused to go down, though his legs were like jelly.

Amazingly, the champion failed to follow up his advantage. He had knocked out many men during his career and knew that the punch he had just delivered was one of the hardest he had ever connected with. He was so sure that McAvoy would go down and stay there that for a second or two he just stood and watched as Mac lolled back against the ropes, struggling to keep his feet. After what seemed an eternity Harvey at last moved in to apply the finisher as the stunned challenger covered up, ducking and diving to avoid the blows raining in on him. At the first opportunity he grabbed Harvey and held on to him until his head had cleared. Before the round was over McAvoy appeared to have recovered and was fighting back gamely at the bell.

That one punch, however, had turned the fight around completely, and from then until the final bell the champion took complete charge, boxing superbly and scoring repeatedly with rapier-like lefts interspersed with stinging hooks and right crosses. In those last two rounds McAvoy had to summon up all his considerable courage. He just gritted his teeth and hit back with everything he had, but the fight was clearly slipping away from him. Harvey was now in full control and cruising to victory. When the referee, without hesitation, went over to the champion and raised his arm at the finish, there were many dissenting voices among the crowd, and some booing. The scoring was very close, but Jim Kendrick had obviously decided that Harvey's work in the last five rounds had wiped out the substantial lead McAvoy must have established in the earlier part of the fight. Not too many of the 7,000 crowd were in agreement with him, but one man who did feel Harvey just about deserved the verdict was Mac himself. Though naturally disappointed, he lost no time in crossing the ring, throwing his arms around the champion and warmly congratulating him.

Mac now found himself the hero of the hour, despite the fact that he had been returned the loser. Back in the dressing room he was hugged by his wife, who told him that he had put up a wonderful performance, which had made her feel very proud. Excited people pushed their way in, slapping him on the back and congratulating him. It was more like the winner's dressing room than the loser's.

Harvey had been disappointing, fighting only in spasms and doing just enough, but no more, while Mac, going all out to make a real fight of it, had forced the pace from the start, never letting up, even after being out on his feet in the thirteenth. If the contest had been held in America there is absolutely no doubt that he would have got the verdict.

According to the following day's newspapers, Harvey had been too obsessed with defence, and had very little chance of winning a World title on the form shown against McAvoy.

In Paris Marcel Thil had avenged a previous loss to Jack Hood by stopping him in the seventh round on a cut eye, it then being announced that Thil would meet 'Gorilla' Jones for the World Middleweight title on June 11th. So for the time being Harvey would have to take a back seat in any case.

As for McAvoy, he knew that as far as effort was concerned he had given everything, but felt that he might have clinched it had he managed to keep a firmer grip on himself and attempted to land cleaner, more decisive punches instead of just tearing in and banging away.

The truth was that he had performed magnificently, and there is no doubt that until he stopped that thunderous Harvey right in the thirteenth he was well on his way to a decisive victory. Harvey's experience had been the deciding factor, Mac having fallen for one of the oldest tricks in the game. Yet the fact remained that he had taken that punch flush on the chin, delivered with all the strength of Harvey's powerful shoulders behind it, and had not only remained upright, but had actually come fighting back. In doing so he had shown that as well as being exceptionally tough and durable, he also possessed the sort of courage necessary to become a great champion.

After the fight, Dan Sullivan, Harvey's manager, took Mac on one side and told him that he would be the next middleweight champion.

The following morning he was the toast of Rochdale. Apart from slight facial bruising he looked none the worse for having travelled fifteen torrid rounds the night before. As usual though, one of his hands was badly swollen and would have to be rested. As Mac relaxed at the local baths, he told reporters that he would now take a short break, but was anxious to secure a return with Harvey in the near future, as he felt that he would have the beating of him next time.

# Chapter 12

## 'Cast Iron' Casey

In the weeks following the Harvey fight Mac was able to spend more time with his family. He was also kept busy with public appearances locally and always received a tremendous reception when introduced from the ring at various Northern boxing venues.

After a month or so the hand was feeling a lot better and he was able to do some light training. His next assignment was again at Belle Vue; a top of the bill contest against Edwin John of Chelsea, son of the famous painter, Augustus John, in May 1932, nearly two months after his epic battle for the title.

Edwin John, an artist himself, appeared very much out of place in a boxing ring, being tall and scholarly looking, with a long pale face. But with his very upright stance and lengthy reach he turned out to be extremely awkward to pin down. Whenever McAvoy got close John showed remarkable agility in skipping rapidly away from the danger zone.

Mac was far below his best in this contest or he would surely have put his opponent away within a couple of rounds at the most. He had been suffering from boils and looked very listless. Also, after what was for him an unusually long spell of inactivity, his timing was way off, many of his big punches either missing the target completely or landing just as John pulled away.

John himself, however, failed to land a worthwhile punch and would have been quite content to last the distance. After a couple of rounds Mac began to warm up, and though his work was still ragged he managed to put the artist down for eight in the third. From then on McAvoy stalked his man, looking for the opportunity to bang over that big punch.

John, a clever boxer with a decent record, was finding Mac far too strong for him, but in round six he suddenly decided to stop running and stand his ground, catching McAvoy with a sharp left hook to the jaw. That was enough! With a snarl, Mac unleashed a tremendous right, which, though aimed at the chin, was slightly mistimed and struck John on the mouth, causing blood to gush out and the referee to call an immediate halt. After a doctor had inspected the damage the stoppage was confirmed, and though John indicated his willingness to continue it would have been quite out of the question, for the lower lip was very badly split and later required several stitches.

Next on the menu came Bill Hood, known as 'The Plymouth Rock', not only because of his rugged countenance and rock hard body, but also because of the fact that he had proved himself extremely durable in the course of a very busy career which had started in the famous West Country booth of Sam McKeown.

Though the possessor of a somewhat patchy record, he had been in with some pretty tough customers and was never an easy man to get the better of. 'The Rock' had contested almost a hundred battles against the likes of George Rose, Trevor Burt, 'Seaman' Tommy Long, 'Kid' Kelly and Archie Sexton, all highly-rated scrappers, and had just returned from America, where he had engaged in some really hard fights and acquitted himself well. Unfortunately he had come home with very little to show for his efforts and was anxious to start earning. Taking on a man of McAvoy's calibre would be no easy pay day, but after the experience gained in the States Hood considered himself capable of standing up to any middleweight in the country, even the noted puncher from Rochdale.

Jack Casey was at Royton that afternoon and was introduced from the N.S.B. ring as the next challenger for McAvoy's Northern Area title.

Hood began cautiously, but soon discovered that he could reach McAvoy with his accurate left jab. Had he persisted with this tactic the fight might well have gone a few rounds, but the West Countryman was no 'Fancy Dan' and was quite prepared to swap punches with Mac. However, after taking a couple of hefty digs to the body which made him gasp, he was forced to back off. After him came Mac, warming to his task. Bang... a ramrod left stopped him short, but only momentarily. In he drove again, hammering away to the mid-section. Hood, scorning defence now, met him head on, slamming in a left and right to the body. Though the blows appeared to have little effect, Hood was encouraged enough to stand there and trade, giving as good as he got as both men scored with ferocious body punches. But the Plymouth man's bravado was to prove his undoing, a sizzling right to the jaw dropping him for an eight count just before the round ended.

It was clear that the fight was as good as over, and though Hood now attempted to return to his long range boxing he had little chance of keeping Mac at bay and was soon in desperate trouble. After a series of strength-sapping body blows had brought his hands down, a right to the jaw, which landed with a sickening thud, put him away for keeps. 'The Rock' was spark out and it was some time before they could bring him round. At last, after a worrying few minutes, he had recovered enough to be assisted from the ring, though still very unsteady on his feet.

One of the first to congratulate the winner was Jack Casey, but though he must have been impressed with Mac's showing he was certainly not worried. Casey was a real tough guy. Though not much above eleven stone, he had no qualms about going in with far bigger men than himself, even heavyweights, and would have taken on a gorilla. A great favourite in the North-East, Casey fought just like one of the old bare-knuckle breed. He was so tough that he seldom bothered to evade punches, and many a hardened scrapper finished up with sore hands after a few rounds of pounding away at Casey's iron jaw and rock-like cranium. It was just like punching a brick wall. Jack never wasted his time learning the finer points of the Noble Art. His sole aim was to get close enough to land one of his pile-drivers, for he carried dynamite in either hand, and when he managed to connect cleanly it was usually curtains for the recipient. Fighting Casey could be a very unnerving experience, for he had plenty of patience as well as apparently limitless stamina, and would stalk an opponent for round after round, taking punches flush on the chin without even blinking, while waiting for the one opening that would bring the fight to an abrupt conclusion.

But despite these amazing attributes Casey had been beaten on quite a number of occasions by faster, cleverer men who were smart enough to keep things at long range while piling up the points. Starting in the late twenties he had barred no one and had licked some of the best men around, including such notables as Joe Woodruff, Joe Lowther, Fred Shaw, Jack Haynes, 'Seaman' Harvey, Jack Marshall, Sandy McKenzie, 'Red' Pullen, Glen Moody, Del Fontaine and Archie Sexton. Not one of them had managed even to shake Casey, let alone put him down, and some of the above named could really hit. Later he would go on to beat Jack London, Reggie Meen and Tommy Farr, each one of whom succeeded in winning the British Heavyweight title.

Both Casey and McAvoy were on the next Royton show, the country's leading middleweight contenders sharing joint top billing, with Casey taking on Billy Thomas, a Welshman who had just returned home after winning the New Zealand Middleweight title, and McAvoy tackling Sandy McKenzie of Glasgow.

It was the most expensive bill ever staged in the area and drew a record crowd. With no Joe Tolley promotion to worry about Chapman was now able to spread his wings, and his enterprise certainly paid off, as bookings poured in from all over the North of England. Chapman's prices that day were 2/-, 3/-, 5/-, and 7/6d.

As fight time approached all the surrounding streets were jammed with cars and charabancs, and great excitement built up as the fans filed in through the gates of the N.S.B.

There was plenty to shout about once the fighting got under way. Of the principals, McAvoy appeared first. His opponent, McKenzie, was considered a real hard man, who claimed to have taken part in over 200 fights, but against McAvoy he failed to last one round.

The Scot, however, still managed to accomplish something that very few men had. For when McAvoy, opening with his familiar body attack, forced him into the ropes, McKenzie amazed the crowd by fighting back like a tiger and in turn driving McAvoy to the other side of the ring until his back was up against the ropes. The locals could hardly believe it, for they had seldom seen Mac take a backward step. But before McKenzie could press home his advantage McAvoy set himself solidly and banged in hard punches with both hands. There then followed a brief burst of toe to toe slogging, before the courageous Scot was sent reeling into the ropes. As he straightened up Mac stepped in and finished him off with a right to the chin.

Casey would do well to top that performance, especially as Thomas's pre-fight publicity claimed an impressive record, stating that whatever happened he would be there at the finish.

As it turned out though, the 'Sunderland Assassin' proved just as devastating as McAvoy in his own unique way. His opponent flattered to deceive in the opening round, spearing Casey with a long raking left, and when danger threatened, Thomas, quick and elusive, was able to glide out of harm's way. Casey, calm and composed, plodded after him as the Welshman darted in and out. Then, as he bounced off the ropes, one of the ring stabilizers gave way and the proceedings were halted while it was repaired. Meanwhile, Casey, quite unconcerned, waited patiently in the centre of the ring.

When hostilities were resumed Thomas got on his bike again, while Casey, in curiously unhurried fashion, walked after him, taking punch after punch, some bang on the chin, without batting an eyelid, and just waiting for the chance to get in one of his own. When it came it travelled less than a foot, but Thomas went down as if he'd been shot. Rising shakily at nine he was dropped again, this time by a short, sharp left hook, at which point he was saved by the bell.

At the start of round two Thomas was immediately put down again and on regaining his feet decided to fight back, but was soon on the canvas once more when he failed to connect with a haymaker of a right and lost his footing. Casey then moved in, completely ignoring Thomas's punches, and dropped him with such force that the referee didn't even bother to count.

The results of these two exciting contests naturally evoked much speculation around the hall, with Chapman expressing the hope that his bid to stage the clash between McAvoy and the Sunderland hard man would be successful, but as it turned out the N.S.B.'s purse offer was topped by Belle Vue. Nevertheless, Chapman was enjoying the spotlight and had several other big shows lined up.

Joe Tolley, meanwhile, no doubt still hoping to get back into the promoting business, had accepted an invitation to organise a charity show at the Oldham Athletic football ground. Most of the boxers were locals, with Harold Ratchford topping the bill against Sam McVey, a West Indian. Tolley used his influence to bring in Jimmy Wilde as referee and an added attraction.

The show was held in the summer of 1932 and Tolley was counting on a fine, sunny day to ensure a big crowd. What he got was exactly the opposite – thunderstorms and heavy rain, which came at just the wrong time and kept the crowd down to a few hundred, a rather pathetic sight in a stadium then capable of holding forty-odd thousand.

The ring, pitched in front of the main stand, was soon awash, and by the time the principals came on it was so saturated that Ratchford and McVey had great difficulty keeping their feet, slipping and sliding all over the place as they threw punches or attempted to evade them.

Jimmy Wilde refereed the contest wearing an overcoat, and looked every bit as miserable and bedraggled as the boxers long before the finish, when he raised Ratchford's hand at the end of twelve rounds of sheer purgatory.

The show had been an absolute disaster, but Tolley, though naturally disappointed, still made sure of some favourable publicity by pointing out to the press that he had been the first man to bring Jimmy Wilde to Lancashire. He had boxed Jack Birch of Oldham at the old Olympic Skating Rink, Union Street, before the First World War. On a later trip Wilde had boxed exhibitions with Royton's Young Mickey and Joe Walsh of Rochdale, at the Oldham Drill Hall. The former World Flyweight Champion, then a popular, highly-paid referee, said he enjoyed visiting Oldham as he had many friends and also relatives in the district, and was always sure of a warm welcome.

Only a few days after the Royton show, erstwhile Casey victim, Billy Thomas, again tempted fate by climbing into the ring with McAvoy at Blackpool. The fight lasted into round three before the referee mercifully called a halt to the slaughter after Thomas had been put down a number of times.

Early in June 1932, Marcel Thil won a version of the World Middleweight title, beating American negro, 'Gorilla' Jones, in Paris. He was immediately challenged by Len Harvey, who was at the ringside.

Jeff Dickson, the flamboyant Paris-based American promoter, made plans to stage the contest at London's White City Stadium, dealing directly with Harvey, as Len's contract with Dan Sullivan had come to an end and had not been renewed.

On the same bill Dickson matched McAvoy with Carmello Candel, a leading French middleweight. Mac was delighted. He had never been to the big city and looked forward very much to the experience and also the chance to prove that he merited another crack at Harvey. If Len managed to beat Thil, Mac could well find himself fighting for the World title.

As Harvey was now unattached, Jeff Dickson suggested that he take over the handling of his affairs, but getting involved with a fast talking, slick operator like the American was not Harvey's style at all, and he graciously declined, later signing up with the well-known manager, Charlie Rose.

The clever Cornishman had previously beaten Thil and was confident that he could again prove his superiority over the tough Frenchman. But in the intervening four and a half years Thil had improved immeasurably.

After being outboxed for the first three rounds, and having his right eye closed as early as the first, Thil, strong and rugged, marched forward relentlessly, constantly hammering Harvey about the body.

The British Champion claimed later that the Swiss referee had allowed Thil to get away with murder in the close quarter exchanges, while he himself had been warned a number of times. The truth was, that if anything, the referee had been lenient towards Harvey, who again employed his old trick of holding and hitting. In other words it was the McAvoy fight all over again, the only difference being that this time Harvey did not get the verdict. By boxing on the retreat he had allowed the Frenchman to take the initiative, Thil forcing Len back against the ropes time after time and subjecting him to more punishment than he had taken in any previous fight.

McAvoy found Candel a tough customer and failed to put him away, but won by a wide margin over ten rounds. He was now after Len Harvey again, though disappointed that Harvey had lost to Thil, but first was committed to defending his Northern Area title at Belle Vue against Jack Casey.

The fight naturally created tremendous interest, McAvoy, with home advantage, being considered a slight favourite. Like Casey, Mac was tough as teak, but more mobile, and though he could never be described as scientific, was undoubtedly the more skilful of the two. Neither had ever been put down for the full count, McAvoy probably having come nearest to it in that fateful thirteenth round. But now, as he faced Casey across the ring, Mac must have been wondering if he could become the first man to K.O. the 'Iron Man from Sunderland. At the weigh-in McAvoy scaled 11st. 4½lbs to Casey's 11st. 2¾lbs, both men being in perfect physical shape.

From the start Casey was clearly outboxed, but still walked forward in his usual indomitable style, taking everything that came his way in an attempt to get in close. When he did it was only to be stopped by a blockbuster of a right to the jaw that would have flattened most heavyweights. For a split second Casey appeared to stagger, but quickly pulled himself together and marched forward again.

The contest now developed into the punishing battle it had always promised to be, with the contestants pounding away at each other in the centre of the ring. Casey was a hard man alright, but he was taking far too many heavy blows, and as round followed round, McAvoy, whose work was generally sharper and more varied, was forging further and further ahead.

Then came the sensational fourteenth. Suddenly switching his attack from head to body, McAvoy doubled Casey up with a battery of fierce punches, the Sunderland man slipping to the canvas as his seconds yelled out loudly that the blows had been low, a claim disregarded by the referee, Mr Tom Gamble, who ordered the fighters to box on. As Casey slowly regained his feet, McAvoy, confident that he had at last found his opponent's weak spot, rushed in and banged in several more vicious shots to the body. As Casey again went down the referee spun round on McAvoy and indicated that he was disqualified.

The decision, which appeared to come as a great shock to McAvoy, who naturally pleaded his innocence, was certainly a severe set-back, making 1932 a year to forget. He had scored some devastating knockouts, but had lost the two fights that really mattered, as well as his Northern Area title. In view of the fact that Mac had been well ahead on points it was all the more disappointing, and the disqualification could perhaps be considered somewhat dubious in view of the fact that the referee had not even warned McAvoy after Casey had gone down the first time. It appeared very much as if he had been influenced by the cries of foul from Casey's corner.

The 'Sunderland Assassin' was now favourite to get a second shot at Harvey's title, with McAvoy, at least for the time being, out of the picture. Local rival Eddie Strawer was also pushing his claims for national recognition. Though he had lost to Joe Rostron and also dropped a disputed decision to Jack Casey, whom he was keen to meet again, Eddie had accounted for some formidable opposition, including former McAvoy victim Jack Marshall, 'Bombardier' McDonald, Jack London, Horace Woolmer, Sonny Doke and Scottish Champion George Gordon, whom he beat in nine rounds in Glasgow.

Strawer was said to have lost all his old cautiousness, a factor which had certainly told against him in the McAvoy fights. Against Casey, Eddie had fought with plenty of fire and felt that he had every right to be in the title picture. This view though, loudly expressed to all who would listen by Eddie's father, was not quite realistic, for Strawer would have had to get past McAvoy to be taken seriously as a contender, and as one old Rochdale fight fan put it, 'Eddie couldn't have licked McAvoy if Mac had had one hand tied behind his back.'

As things turned out neither Rochdale man was given a look-in when the Board met to name two contenders for Harvey's title, Jack Casey being nominated to fight Archie Sexton, of Bethnal Green, in a final eliminator.

Albert Tolley was still striving gamely to keep together a dwindling stable of fighters which included Harold Ratchford, Deno Guselli,

Jean Locatelli, Billy Cook, Billy and Syd Longworth, Jack Lister, Tommy Woods, 'Battling' Bennett, Jim Shaw, Teddy Bodell, Fred Dyer and the old warhorse, Billy Mounders.

Albert himself donned the gloves again to help out as a sparring partner as Ratchford prepared for his contest with the talented Jack Davies of Ashton-under-Lyne, and was in such good form that he decided to enter a nine-stone belt competition at Heywood. Billed as Bert Tolley, he surprised a lot of people by knocking out Jim Astley of Middleton in one round. In the semi-final, however, Albert was himself stopped by Heywood's 'Gunner' Riley, a mature fighter, who proved far too strong for him.

After that Albert concentrated once more on running the stable, but with the halcyon days of the Stadium now very much in the past, a lot of the interest had gone out of it for him. However, with no trade, and little prospect of something else coming along, he had no choice but to carry on, encouraged by his father, who was quite determined not to let the stable, which he had worked so hard to put together, break up. He was still dashing up and down the country, covering hundreds of miles almost every week, for in those desperate days of depression boxing was really booming, with dozens of fight clubs in most areas and scores of young men ready and eager to don the gloves and earn a few shillings.

By this time Albert was courting. His fiancée, Ada Merry, was, however, very unhappy with the situation, and gave him an ultimatum. Either he go out and find a proper job or there would be no wedding. As he had had his fill of boxing in any case, it would not have been too difficult a decision to make, had it not been for his father. He was the fly in the ointment. For not only did he expect Albert to remain single for as long as it suited Joe himself, but he had every intention of carrying on with the stable come what may, and with his own considerable commitments he needed Albert very badly, especially as Albert held the manager's license.

In the end Ada won, and Albert, much against his father's wishes, got himself a job at Ben Barns' Skip and Case Making works in Union Street, the same building which had housed the second Royton Boxing Club. He had always been handy at joinery, and starting work as a packing case maker, Albert soon settled in and was glad he had made the break. Though turned twenty, it was the first real job he had ever had.

Albert had never really had a proper home. With no mother, living with grandparents, uncles, and sisters, his father always away, he now looked forward to having a house of his own. In the thirties though, this was much easier said than done, and it would be another three years before he could afford to go ahead and get married.

The few remaining fighters on the books were informed that Albert was finishing and told to make other arrangements for themselves. For a while the stable remained more or less intact, with Tommy Corrigan continuing as trainer in any old cellar or loft where they could hang a punchbag. Eventually though, the Royton boys broke up, going their own separate ways.

It was the end of Joe Tolley's dream, but not quite the end of an era as far as Royton was concerned, for the N.S.B. still flourished, and would carry on for another couple of years before it too had run its course and would finally close its doors.

# Chapter 13

## A Second Chance

Despite his bitter disappointment at the disqualification against Casey, closely followed by the announcement that the Sunderland man would be in line for a return with Harvey if he could manage to win his eliminator against Sexton, Mac was soon back in the ring.

Two weeks after the Casey fight he beat Welshman Tom Benjamin on an August Bank Holiday show at Blackpool Football ground, Benjamin's corner throwing in the towel in round five after their man had taken a terrific pounding and been on the deck several times. Harry Fleming's other stars, King and Brown, also recorded wins on the same programme.

At the end of that month ex-policeman George Brown of Stepney took McAvoy the distance, withstanding a heavy bombardment along the way. Mac found the Londoner very cagey and surprisingly resilient. Though under heavy fire for most of the contest he simply refused to go down, surviving a torrid last three rounds to finish well beaten but still on his feet. Brown was warmly applauded for his gameness by the enthusiastic Morecambe crowd.

There were two fights the following month, September, against Billy Roberts of Bishop Auckland and Phil Green of Bath. Roberts turned out to be another game 'un and attacked McAvoy from the start, but soon ran into the heavy artillery and was put down for an eight count. He visited the canvas twice more in the opening round and several times in rounds two and three, before signalling to the referee that he had had enough.

On Harry Barlow's promotion at the Palace Theatre, Rawtenstall, Phil Green was dropped twice in the first round by devastating body punches, but managed to survive to the bell. In round two the slaughter continued, the referee stopping the contest with Green on the canvas and in some distress.

In those days a crowd did not readily accept an early stoppage and pandemonium broke out in the hall. This went on for some time, until eventually Green himself managed to quieten things down. Coming to the centre of the ring after he had recovered somewhat, he made a short speech, assuring the crowd that he would have been unable to continue even if the referee had not called a halt, as he was badly hurt, and adding that he had never been hit so hard in his career. At this the spectators seemed satisfied and the booing turned to applause.

McAvoy's next opponent, Tommy Moore, was also put away inside three rounds, and was in such a bad way that he had to be taken from the Morecambe Winter Gardens to the local hospital. Again it was body punching that did the damage, but Moore soon recovered and was allowed home.

Jack Casey, meanwhile, had disposed of Archie Sexton in seven rounds at Newcastle and was lined up for a second crack at Harvey's title. McAvoy knew he would have to wait until the two had settled their differences, but felt confident of getting a shot at the winner. In the meantime he was keeping busy.

There were three more wins in 1932. Against Ted Coveney, K.O. 'd in four rounds at Blackburn, Mihail Fubea, a Rumanian, stopped in four at Belle Vue, the referee calling a halt after Fubea had slumped to the canvas following a heavy blow under the heart, and German middleweight Hans Siefried, who gave McAvoy a hard time before losing on points at the Albert Hall.

In December, Harvey again met Casey at Newcastle, with local promoter John Paget packing the New St. James' Hall and the fight-mad Geordies all set to roar 'Cast Iron' Jack on to victory.

Since losing to Marcel Thil, Harvey had comfortably disposed of Belgian light-heavyweight, Theo Sass, 'Seaman' Harvey and Glen Moody, and looked in great shape. The determined Casey, however, marched forward in his usual fearless style, completely ignoring the champion's ramrod left as it thudded into his rugged visage. Occasionally he would get in a telling punch of his own, but in most of the early rounds was completely outboxed by the immaculate Harvey.

As the contest wore on, however, it was becoming clear that Casey's tremendous workrate and all-out aggression had begun to close the gap. As the twelfth round opened Jack marched forward yet again to the accompaniment of the Geordie roar and managed to tag Harvey with one of those lethal right-handers smack on the jaw. The champion sagged at the knees and staggered back against the ropes as the crowd went wild.

Yet despite the deafening yells, imploring him to go in and finish it, Casey unaccountably hesitated, possibly recalling a similar situation at Belle Vue, when the crafty Cornishman had lured McAvoy onto that sucker punch. But Len was genuinely hurt, and that moment of hesitation probably cost Casey the title, for by the time he decided to move in Harvey had begun to gather his wits and was able to use his vast experience and cunning to fiddle his way out of trouble. Casey tried desperately to land another big punch, but the speedy Harvey kept on the move and for the remainder of the contest had only to stay out of the way of Casey's haymakers while picking up the points with his educated left hand, to run out a clear winner.

There was some concern in the Harvey camp after the fight at the state of the champion's right hand, which had been damaged as early as the sixth round, when Casey had stopped three successive piledrivers, all bang on target, which had merely bounced off the cast iron jaw as Jack plodded nonchalantly forward. Within a couple of weeks, however, the swelling and bruising had almost disappeared, and Harvey was ready to resume training.

McAvoy, having fought fourteen times since his losing title bid, and winning all but the controversial contest against Casey, now felt that he was entitled to a return with the champion, and was therefore very disappointed to learn that Harvey had been matched with Eddie Phillips of Bow in an eliminator for the Light-heavyweight title, left vacant due to Jack Petersen having decided to move up a weight, after beating Reggie Meen to become British Heavyweight Champion. The winner of the Harvey/Phillips contest would then meet Harry Crossley of Mexborough, a former champion, for the Light-heavyweight crown.

Harvey was, of course, perfectly entitled to take this step, as he would not be obliged to defend his middleweight title again for six months, but not content with this, Charlie Rose, Harvey's new manager, also issued a challenge to Jack Petersen, obviously confident that the brilliant Cornishman was capable of winning titles at three different weights.

While he waited for another chance, Mac knew he would have to keep fighting and winning, and began 1933 by stopping Glen Moody*, brother of Frank, a former British Middle and Light-heavyweight Champion, at Belle Vue in the sixth round.

A fortnight later Les Ward of Woking was flattened in six rounds at Royton, and the following week Cardiff's Ernie 'Red' Pullen again

* Harvey had previously achieved an identical result against the Moody brothers, stopping both in six rounds.

took his life in his hands, this time lasting three rounds before being K.O.'d at Blackburn. Mac finished the month of February with an eight round knockout victory over Leonard Steyaert of Belgium, at Belle Vue, after which he was given some very good news. Len Harvey had agreed to waive his six months grace and would give McAvoy another shot at the middleweight title on March 27th, only a fortnight after his meeting with Eddie Phillips.

It's quite probable that Harvey, contemplating a permanent move up to the heavier division, felt that this would be his last opportunity to cash in on the middleweight title, and after getting the McAvoy return out of the way he could then forget about making weight and concentrate on bulking up to contest the two heavier titles.

By contrast the McAvoy camp had only one goal in mind; to win that Middleweight title and Lonsdale belt. One of the first things that Harry Fleming did was to engage an additional coach. Rene Devos was a Belgian with a wealth of experience, who had earned some big purses in America in the twenties. Being a shrewd man, Devos had invested most of it, only to suffer badly from the effects of the Wall Street crash.

Rene was something of a scholar, having a great thirst for knowledge and a passion for languages. He always said that he hated fighting in a country where he couldn't understand what the spectators were shouting about. Starting his ring career at fourteen he had made sure that his education was not neglected, and claimed to be proficient in Flemish, English, Dutch, French and German. He had also passed an elementary examination in Spanish.

Rene had been in the ring for sixteen years, continuing his education in between engagements, but on reaching the age of thirty and finding that there was less and less money in the game, he was at that time considering retirement and had begun to take an interest in training fighters, having worked very closely with Marcel Thil, who had benefited greatly from his coaching.

On arriving in Manchester Devos was provided with lodgings in Whitley Road, Collyhurst, where he immediately set about writing an article for a French newspaper about his visit. Amazingly, he had never heard of Blackpool, and was promised a visit there by Harry Fleming. Regarding his work with McAvoy, Devos said that his philosophy was that every fighter had his own individual style, so each one should be trained differently.

He could also claim to be something of an expert on Len Harvey, or at least on Harvey's punching power, as the British champion had knocked the Belgian out in one round in June 1931 at the Albert Hall. In addition to Devos, Harry Smith, a coloured fighter from New York, was brought in as an extra sparring partner.

McAvoy now settled down to a month of rigorous training leading up to the title fight, his usual mean and awkward attitude soon very much in evidence. As always, he showed his sparring partners no mercy, and was very dubious when constantly told how good Devos was supposed to be and what a difference his coaching would make. After several sessions in the ring with the experienced Belgian though, Mac began to understand what Harry Fleming had been getting at, for Devos turned out to be an excellent tutor and was able to impart to Mac many tricks of the trade picked up in American rings. After several sessions McAvoy's in-fighting was showing distinct signs of improvement, and when Devos demonstrated how to throw an opponent off balance with a slight pull or push when coming out of clinch, Mac's thoughts must have gone back to his first meeting with Harvey. The new coach also worked on blocking and evading punches, and it soon became obvious that when added to Mac's aggression, speed and punching power, the extra polish would make him a very formidable fighter indeed.

With the talented Belgian in the camp the training was much more interesting, and as he began to reach peak fitness Devos confidently predicted that Mac would not only take the title, but would go on to even greater things. At this point, however, with everything going so well, Len Harvey requested a postponement.

Things had not quite gone according to plan in the eliminator against Eddie Phillips. Though a clear favourite at the outset, Harvey had found Eddie a difficult proposition. After falling behind early on Phillips had fought back strongly to earn a draw. To complete his misery Harvey had knocked up his right hand again and knew that to face an opponent as ferocious as McAvoy when less than a hundred per cent fit would be asking for trouble. The Board of Control accordingly put back the date to April 10th, giving the champion only two extra weeks' grace.

Harvey was none too happy, but then neither was Mac. Having to slow down his training schedule just when he was reaching peak fitness was a big blow, especially to a man of McAvoy's temperament.

It made him even more edgy and difficult to handle than usual, which was saying something. To make matters worse, a week or so later, Harvey asked for a further postponement, saying he was not at all happy about the hand, but after an examination by the Board doctor he was informed that the contest must take place on the newly agreed date.

The presence of Rene Devos in the camp now assumed a new importance, for the Belgian turned out to be quite a character, with a keen sense of fun, and his American style humour and witticisms certainly helped lift Mac's spirits and keep him on the rails.

As usual Jack Bates put in a great deal of hard work as he concentrated on Mac's conditioning in the weeks leading up to the fight, and must have had mixed feelings as the big night drew closer, for he knew that he would not be at Belle Vue, owing to the fact that Johnny King was fighting at Newcastle on the same date and Bates would be required in his corner. This unfortunate state of affairs had been brought about by Harvey's request for a postponement.

Although in strict training and working harder than ever before, McAvoy still found time for the odd diversion, particularly if there was a touch of glamour involved. So when a group of enterprising ladies hit upon the novel idea of inviting the handsome young fighter to MC. a dance they had organised in aid of the Mayoress of Rochdale's appeal for clothing for the families of the unemployed, he was only too pleased to oblige, and cut quite a dash as he moved gracefully around the dance floor of the Provident Hall before the admiring gaze of the many females present.

On the evening of April 10th, 1933, Belle Vue's King's Hall was one seething mass of humanity, with every seat sold and hundreds standing around the back and in the aisles. Quite apart from the main contest, an excellent bill had been put together, the chief support being a return between Jack Casey and Archie Sexton. In the dressing room McAvoy was naturally very edgy as he endured the long wait, while Harvey, who was again favoured to retain his title, appeared, as always, calm, confident and unruffled.

In the hall the atmosphere was tense. It was a warm, clammy evening, and the thick pall of cigarette smoke which hung heavily in the air simply refused to be moved by the battery of electric fans dotted around the arena.

At just turned 9.15 a great burst of cheering rang out as the challenger appeared and made his way to the ring, resplendent in an orange and gold dressing gown. Harvey soon followed, wearing a much more subdued gown of black and purple. Then, while the champion cast a nonchalant eye over the crowd and Mac shuffled about nervously in his corner, the M.C. called Rene Devos and Harry Smith into the ring and introduced them.

There had been some wrangling over the choice of referee, Charlie Rose having immediately put in a protest on learning that the contest would be handled by a local man, Arthur Myers of Manchester. But Harvey, slightly irritated at Rose for making a fuss over what he himself considered a minor matter, persuaded his manager to withdraw his objection.

As he waited to be introduced McAvoy was probably more keyed up than he had ever been in his life. He was determined to leave the Belle Vue ring with the Lonsdale belt around his waist and nothing short of a major disaster was going to stop him. In the opposite corner the apparently unconcerned Harvey quietly limbered up. Though the champion must have been nervous himself, he showed no sign of it, but was just as determined as Mac. That belt meant everything to him. He had already won one outright and had two notches on a second, so victory over the 'Rochdale Thunderbolt' would make this also his own property.

From the start Harvey seemed again set on fighting a defensive battle. Still, he held the title. It was up to the challenger to try and take it away from him. To everyone's surprise, however, McAvoy showed little inclination to take the initiative. For five rounds the contest followed the same pattern, with Harvey feinting, moving away, clinching and apparently reluctant to get involved, while Mac, though constantly pressing forward, was throwing very little in the way of worthwhile punches. About the only thing of any consequence that happened during the early rounds was that Harvey connected with a low blow, for which he was warned by Mr Myers. But the fact that Harvey threw so few punches meant that Mac had very little opportunity to try out his new defensive skills.

Harvey, no doubt worried about his right hand, had obviously made up his mind to take as few chances as possible. If McAvoy came to him he was confident that his clever defensive work would see him through, while he picked up points with that brilliant left hand.

But Mac had no way of knowing just how fragile Len's right hand was, and with painful memories of the trap he had been drawn into in their previous encounter, he had no intention of being 'old-headed' a second time. The result was that the first third of the fight turned out to be unbelievably dull, and by round six, the referee, who must have become as bored as the crowd, stopped the contest and called for more action from both men.

Harvey nodded, but carried on in the same negative fashion, while McAvoy decided from that moment on to forget his caution and go all out to make a fight of it. At least there was one aggressor now, though sure enough, Mac ran into a steady stream of stiff left jabs as he tore in. But it was noticeable that he was beginning to push Harvey back, and was certainly having more success in breaking through the champion's superb defence than he had had in their first contest. Several times Harvey found himself driven back against the ropes, where Mac pounded away to the body.

In the seventh McAvoy created a sensation by almost bundling Harvey over the top rope. Had he not stepped back at this point the champion could well have finished up among the ringside spectators.

Mac was now fighting with something like his old style, throwing caution to the wind and just pressing forward, battering away with both hands. Harvey's defensive class was now very apparent, but it was the challenger who was catching the eye and slowly but surely getting on top. Though Harvey threw very few right hand punches the forceful McAvoy was continually picked off by that ramrod left and the occasional jarring left hook to the head and body.

Round nine, and Mac threatened to end the fight there and then when he caught Harvey with a tremendous right to the chin. Again Harvey staggered back against the ropes as the crowd roared for Mac to go in and finish it. But though he threw everything he had at the retreating champion he was unable to nail him with a really decisive punch, and despite being under constant pressure, Harvey was at no time badly hurt. In the last two rounds, knowing that he was behind on points, Harvey fought hard in an effort to turn the tide, but made little impression on the determined McAvoy, whose telling body punches were again very much in evidence.

At the final bell, while the referee carefully totted up his scorecard, the fighters waited anxiously in their corners for the verdict. After what seemed an eternity Mac could see Arthur Myers walking towards him. At the same moment he was aware of the rising swell of emotion within himself and then the sudden roar of the crowd, coming first in one tremendous blast, then mounting to a crescendo which seemed to go on and on, until it could only be described as sheer pandemonium. Mac's head was in a whirl as his overjoyed seconds yelled in his ear, 'You've won, you've won!'

Len Harvey came across immediately to congratulate him, while the cheering and clapping continued unabated as people climbed into the ring and surrounded his corner. Then Mac found himself lifted shoulder high and carried around the ring in triumph.

It was quite some time before order was restored and Mac could be officially declared the winner and new champion. He was brought to the centre of the ring, then, amidst scenes of great emotion, the magnificent gold Lonsdale belt was placed around his waist and he proudly posed for the photographers. After that an attempt was made to get him out of the ring and down the steps. Then, surrounded by his seconds and a battery of policemen, he was hustled up the aisle with great difficulty as people pushed and shoved, trying desperately to get close enough to touch the newly-crowned champion.

The dressing room was so crowded with friends and well-wishers that Mac was barely able to get in himself, and it took quite a while before they could be persuaded to leave. Later, Len Harvey called in, shook Mac's hand warmly, wishing him luck and telling him with a smile, 'You're the champion now. Your troubles are just beginning.'

Len then showed McAvoy his right hand, which was badly swollen, although he had hardly used it all night.

Harvey had held the title for just under over four years. He had been a fine champion and was destined to achieve even greater honours. In an interview with reporters Harvey said that in his opinion it had been a very close contest and that he considered McAvoy fortunate to have got the verdict. Mac, however believed that he had clearly had the better of it, and had won convincingly. He added that he was very pleased to have brought the title to Rochdale.

Rene Devos told the newsmen that Mac had been a marvellous pupil and had fought like a true champion, his body attack having worn Harvey down.

'I hope he won't be content,' said Devos, 'with winning just the British title.'

The fight itself might not have been a thriller, but this had been more than off-set by the euphoric scenes following the announcement that McAvoy was the winner and new champion. All in all it had been a wonderful night, never to be forgotten by the legion of Manchester fight fanatics who witnessed it, and would speak of it with great pride for the rest of their lives.

There were three other contests on the bill that night, each one a cracker. Ted McGuire (Manchester) knocked out Tommy Ireland (London), Joe Rostron was retired by his corner with a cut eye against Ronnie Headley, the Canadian Welterweight Champion, and Archie Sexton outpointed 'Cast Iron' Casey, then promptly issued a challenge to McAvoy.

# Chapter 14

## Champion

McAvoy was at last Champion, and determined to be an active one. He meant to go on training hard and keeping busy, but he also intended to enjoy the feeling of being a champion and the fame and recognition it brought. Wherever he went in the North of England he was immediately spotted and surrounded by admirers. Constantly being asked for his autograph, posing for photographers, presenting prizes at various functions, going up on stage at some local theatre or kicking off a football match, all made it a marvellously exciting time.

Did all this success and adulation go to his head? The answer is that it undoubtedly did. To go from being a poor boy, battling his way up through the small halls, compiling an amazing record of knockouts along the way, then finally defeating a great champion like Len Harvey, was perhaps just too big a transition for a lad of his temperament to cope with. It was bound to have an effect on his personality.

Mac had always been cocky and something of an egotist, but now, as he went on to even greater success through the thirties, his behaviour in public could at times be arrogant, offensive and often violent.

There was also a cynical side to him, and he was not slow to notice that many who had looked down their noses at him in earlier days were now falling over themselves to get close to him and bask in the reflected glory. He just about tolerated such people, but had little time for them, and very often it showed. Throughout his life he would never be altogether comfortable with people other than those of his own kind – working class. With them he could laugh and joke, and swear a bit if he had a mind to, which he often did.

Mac enjoyed a good night out, and was always very keen on cars, having had a series of bangers of various types since the battered motor bike he'd started out with in the early Royton days. Now he got rid of his old box-type Singer and bought a big flashy American job, in which he proudly roared around the cobbled streets and local country roads. Cars, in fact, along with horses, were to become a lifelong passion and would also be at the root of quite a number of scrapes he was to find himself in over the years.

As far as can be ascertained, Mac was never in any kind of trouble as a youth, nor in his early days as a fighter, but after winning the title in 1933, his name was never out of the newspapers for long, very often for the wrong reasons. There were times when even the most trifling incident would be blown up out of all proportion, both by the newspapers and by word of mouth, simply because he was a public figure. Mac considered this a great injustice, but apparently failed to realise that as a well-known sportsman he had a duty to make sure that his behaviour in public was always exemplary and above reproach. But he was no Len Harvey by any stretch of the imagination and never learned to master his explosive temper.

One thing Mac never did was neglect his training, being in superb condition for practically all his fights. He might have grumbled a lot in the gym and been a difficult man to control, but he certainly got stuck into his work, giving a hundred per cent at all times and never wishing to lay off for very long between contests, for he just loved to fight.

A couple of weeks after beating Harvey he was raring to go again. Of course, Mac was naturally keen to cash in on the title, but quite apart from that, once all the cheering and the back-slapping had died down he could hardly wait to get back into training to prepare for his next outing, a fifteen rounder against Jack Hyams at The Ring, Blackfriars.

From the start Hyams adopted his customary spoiling tactics. The Stepney man, an extremely skilful boxer, was well aware of McAvoy's power and had no intention of getting in the way of one of those big bombs. Hyams was doing plenty of holding and McAvoy had a very hard time trying to prise himself loose. The result was a rather untidy affair which did not please the spectators.

In round six Mac managed to find an opening, nailing Hyams with a sizzling hook to the body. Down went the East Ender, grimacing with pain and claiming that he had been hit low. The referee disagreed and began to count, whereupon Hyams made a miraculous recovery, regaining his feet at eight and back-pedalling rapidly. And though Mac chased him for the rest of the fight, occasionally shaking his man with solid body shots, Hyams managed to steer clear of further trouble, McAvoy getting the decision at the end of fifteen unmemorable rounds.

For his next contest Mac was booked by the National Sporting Club to face Oddone Piazza, Middleweight Champion of Italy, at London's Olympia, on a bill packed with champions and topped by stablemate Jackie Brown, who had won the World Flyweight title the previous year and would be defending it against Valentin Angelmann of France. British Bantamweight Champion, Johnny King, was down to meet Bobby Leitham of Canada for the vacant Empire title, and 'Panama' Al Brown, World Bantamweight Champion, was matched with Dave Crowley in a non-title clash. Last, but by no means least, was a return between Len Harvey and Eddie Phillips, this time for the British Light-heavyweight title, the Board having unaccountably overlooked the unfortunate Harry Crossley, who was left waiting in the wings.

Brown, King and McAvoy all won on points, but with each contest going the distance it was after midnight before Harvey and Phillips entered the ring, Harvey outpointing his old rival to gain a second British title. Though Phillips fought with great spirit and had the satisfaction of putting Harvey down for a short count, the Cornishman's class told in the end and he finished well on top.

As for McAvoy, he was not only forced to go the full ten rounds, but suffered the indignity of a knockdown from a sharp right to the chin early in the fight. None the worse for this unexpected reverse, Mac, as usual, tore straight into the attack, belting Piazza about the body, but was given a difficult time by the taller Italian, who boxed behind a neat left hand, occasionally banging over a dangerous looking right cross which caused McAvoy plenty of problems. Though not one of his better performances, it was still a creditable, if hard won, victory.

Before his next contest McAvoy found himself in court, being sued for £70 damages by one Frank Schofield, for personal injuries sustained in a road accident. Schofield, described as a spinner, had been struck by McAvoy's car in Rochdale Road, Royton, and thrown into the air. After finishing up in the hospital he had been off work for fourteen weeks.

On leaving a public house the plaintiff had apparently attempted to cross the road, and on reaching the tram lines had stopped to allow a car travelling from the direction of Rochdale to pass by. The driver of this vehicle had sounded his horn, causing Schofield to panic and step back into the path of McAvoy's car, which was going in the opposite direction.

Schofield's case was considerably weakened when it was revealed that on being carried into a nearby house he had said, 'It's my own fault. I didn't look where I was going.'

So, in spite of the fact that the plaintiff was able to produce two witnesses to testify that the new Middleweight Champion was travelling at an excessive speed, the court found in favour of the defendant, awarding costs against Schofield. Though not a particularly serious case, it was the beginning of a lengthy series of court appearances, and one of the rare occasions McAvoy was to come out on the right side.

When Oddone Piazza lost his Italian Middleweight title to Clemente Meroni, the new champion was matched with McAvoy at Belle Vue. A couple of days before the contest was due to take place, however, it was announced that Mac had been forced to withdraw due to an attack of boils. His place was taken by the very busy Archie Sexton, who was on a winning streak, having accounted for such good quality fighters as Johnny Summers, Joe Lowther, and of course, 'Cast Iron' Casey. Sexton easily beat Meroni, who turned out to be a very moderate performer.

Topping the Belle Vue bill that night was Johnny King, challenging for 'Panama' Al Brown's World Bantamweight title in the open air in front of twenty thousand people.

Brown was something of a freak. Though weighing only 8st. 6lbs he stood six feet and possessed arms of an incredible length, making him an extremely difficult man to get near. In attempting to work his way in close right from the start, King ran into a tremendous uppercut which seemed to come from the champion's bootlaces. Down went the Manchester favourite as if he'd been shot, managing to struggle to his feet as the count reached eight. From this point on King fought like a terrier, but found the champion almost impossible to pin down.

Brown was a real box of tricks and gave a marvellous exhibition to completely outbox the gallant local man, pouring in a constant stream of left leads and sizzling hooks which came from the most unlikely angles. Amazingly, on the few occasions that King managed to get in close, he discovered that the versatile Panamanian was equally adept at infighting, and always came out of it second best. Johnny was dropped several times more, but refused to stay down. Then, after looking just about exhausted by the eighth round he began to come more into the fight, as Brown, having failed to put his man away, began to slow down himself. Roared on by the excited Manchester crowd, King took on a new lease of life. The lanky Negro was tiring rapidly as the contest drew to a close, but was still far too elusive to be nailed by a solid shot and finished a deserved points winner.

Though the following day's sports pages naturally concentrated on Johnny King's courageous title challenge, it was also reported that McAvoy had not been the victim of an attack of boils after all, but had pulled out of his contest with Meroni because he was not satisfied with the money he was getting.

On the day before the Belle Vue show he had contacted Harry Fleming by telephone and told him that he was unhappy with the size of his purse. According to McAvoy, Fleming had told him that if he didn't wish to fight they could always get Archie Sexton. McAvoy then angrily told him, 'All right then, you'd better get Sexton.'

When interviewed by reporters Fleming told them, 'I'm very surprised at McAvoy's attitude. This is a terribly unjust thing he's done. I'll tell you straight. If I were to publish the figures involved you'd be astounded. The purse was a big one. His money was there. I'm waiting for McAvoy to give me an explanation. I'm not going to see him.'

There is no record of whether McAvoy did contact his manager or *vice versa*. Most probably Norman Hurst stepped in to have a quiet word in the wayward boxer's ear, for the dispute was soon settled, with Mac back in the ring a month later to confirm a previous win over ex-P.C. George Brown, the durable East Ender again managing to stay the distance.

Since Archie Sexton's decisive victory over Casey, the Londoner's livewire manager, Johnny Sharp, had been pushing hard to get his fighter a crack at the title, but the Belle Vue camp made sure that McAvoy received his full six months grace before agreeing to a defence, the date then being set for October 9th 1933.

It was an extremely important contest as far as Mac was concerned, and he was determined to be in the best possible condition for it. With several weeks in which to prepare, he set up his training quarters at Hollingworth Lake. Around this time he acquired an Alsatian named Peggy, which he found to be a great source of pleasure. Mac had far more patience with animals than he had with people and spent hours playing with his new friend. Peggy accompanied him on his road-work, then would sit in the gym while he trained, an apparently interested spectator and certainly his most adoring fan.

Mac loved Hollingworth Lake. It was a place he had known as a youngster and he was always happy there. It was well away from the smoke of the cotton mills and the air was crisp and clear.

The party was accommodated at the Lake Hotel, and Mac's daily routine began at eight a.m. with coffee and toast. Within half an hour or so he would be walking on the lake shore, doing deep breathing exercises, then would set off to run right round the lake, a distance of over two miles. After finishing with a fast sprint he would have a further session of breathing exercises, then proceed around the lake again, walking and running, as much as three or four times as his training reached its peak.

After completing his roadwork Mac would have a bath and a rub down, then eat breakfast and rest until noon, when he would have a light lunch, usually fish. By early afternoon he would be in the gym, a large wooden building which normally served as the hotel cafe. Once the bag work, skipping and shadow boxing were out of the way he would set about his sparring partners with great relish. On this occasion he had plenty of variety, with Paul Schauffer, a tough slugger from Winnipeg, providing the heavier opposition and Jack Lord and Alban Mulrooney to speed him up. Chief sparring partner was Glen Moody, selected because his style was very similar to that of Archie Sexton. As usual they earned their money, with each succeeding session more gruelling than the last, as fight day drew closer and Mac became meaner and more savage.

Lightweight Harold Ratchford was also in attendance to help with training generally. Ratchford, whose career was more or less over, sparred with McAvoy on occasion and amazed the champion with his speed and cleverness.

Mac would finish each day's training with a hard, grinding session of floor exercises and would have dinner, his last meal of the day, around five-thirty. He later stated that after completing his training for the day he would often swim all the way across the lake, but this was not mentioned in any reports on his training at the time, and would appear to be something of an exaggeration to say the least. For one thing that lake is icy cold in the middle of the summer. At the end of September to early October it would feel like the Arctic Ocean. Still, Mac was a pretty hard fellow – perhaps he did occasionally take a quick dip.

After dinner McAvoy and his party would either play cards, listen to the radio or visit a local cinema. Most nights though, Mac would play his records on a gramophone he had brought along. He was very keen on music and built up quite a collection over the years, mostly crooners and dance bands.

As the day of the fight drew closer, Mac, as always, became edgy and irritable. One day after training was over he walked into the dining room and asked if his dinner was ready. On being told that he would have to wait a few minutes he flew into a rage and finished up banging his fist down on the table before striding off angrily and leaping into his car. Setting off with a roar, the big American job screeched down the narrow winding lane which encircles the lake at a tremendous speed. Harry Fleming's heart must have been in his mouth as he watched his fighter endanger his own life and possibly other peoples' as he worked off his temper. After a while the wayward walloper returned, and strolling into the dining room, sat down and ate his meal as if nothing had happened.

Archie Sexton, meanwhile, was being hailed in the newspapers as a hero, after diving into the sea at Shoeburyness, in Essex, where he was in training, and saving the lives of two children.

On the Wednesday, five days before the fight, Mac was again impressive in his workout, at which a number of sportswriters were present, lining up his three main sparring partners, Moody, Schauffer and Lord and taking them on one after the other.

Compared to when he had first arrived at the lake a couple of weeks before he appeared considerably faster in his movements and generally sharper in all his work. There was no doubt that the invigorating air of Hollingworth Lake had acted as a tonic in itself, and helped to get Mac in just about the finest condition of his life. Archie Sexton would have to be at his very best to have any chance at all of taking the title.

When McAvoy arrived for the weigh-in at 2 o'clock on Monday October 9th, 1933, he was tense as usual, but raring to go. He was very keen to get another notch on that magnificent Lonsdale belt, and both fighters also had the added incentive of knowing that promoter Jeff Dickson had made an offer to match the winner against Marcel Thil, for Thil's International Boxing Union World Middleweight title.

Archie Sexton was certainly a worthy challenger for McAvoy's crown. The son of Jimmy Sexton, a bare-knuckle scrapper who fought many times in the North of England, and the father of Dave Sexton, later to become famous as a football manager, Archie had begun his career at the Columbia Boxing Club in Hoxton and turned professional in 1926 after winning an open competition. Apart from boxing, Sexton was a fine swimmer who had represented London at the age of thirteen.

Going into the McAvoy fight Sexton had taken part in 174 contests and been beaten only 12 times, scoring 84 knockouts.

A buzz of expectant excitement ran through the crowd of over six thousand which packed the King's Hall as the fighters entered the ring, and though McAvoy was clearly the fans' favourite, the sporting Belle Vue patrons gave the visitor a warm reception. They were looking forward to what they had every reason to believe would be a superb contest, but were in for a disappointment, for it became obvious almost from the start that both fighters had decided to play a waiting game.

McAvoy was clearly hoping that Sexton would come to him, and was lying in wait to catch the challenger with the heavy artillery as he came in. Sexton, however, had no intention of playing McAvoy's game, and stood off, waiting for Mac to make the first move, with the result that round one turned out to be something of a non-event.

Realising that he was going to have to make all the running, McAvoy took the offensive at the start of round two and was stopped short by a hard left to the face. Still Archie held back. It was obvious that he intended to let Mac do all the forcing while he conserved his energy and picked up points along the way. The problem was that Sexton was not prepared to do anything at all. The East Ender was very clever with his defensive work, but apart from the odd counter he could not have thrown more than half a dozen decent punches in the first five rounds.

After the wonderful display he had put on in the same ring against Casey only a few months before, Sexton was a big disappointment. Slow moving, ever ready to seek safety by going into a clinch at every opportunity, the Bethnal Green man was cautious to the point of appearing apprehensive, which was perhaps not so surprising, considering McAvoy's fearsome reputation as a puncher. The spectators however, were becoming restless, and by round seven some scathing remarks were heard from a section of the crowd, with a derisive cheer going up whenever Sexton showed even the slightest inclination to get involved, which was not very often. Even the sight of a cut over McAvoy's left eye failed to spur him into action and the round ended as tamely as the previous ones.

Mac himself was trying hard to inject some life into the proceedings but was not looking impressive and realised that if the fight went the distance it would do his reputation no good at all, overwhelming though the points margin in his favour would undoubtedly have been. During the middle rounds, as Mac stepped up the pace, he would occasionally run into a stiff left jab followed by a stinging right cross and found these punches so powerful that he must have wondered why Sexton never followed them up.

For nine rounds the fight followed the same pattern, with McAvoy attacking and banging away to the body whenever he could prise open Sexton's airtight defence, and Archie concentrating on defence and doing as little as possible, in the hope, no doubt, that Mac would eventually tire.

But Mac was now so intent on making a show that he was quite prepared to take chances as he stormed in. In the tenth, as McAvoy set up another big attack, Archie loaded up and belted the champion flush on the chin with every ounce of power he could muster. The crowd gasped as Mac staggered, momentarily stunned, but again Sexton made no effort to follow up.

It took McAvoy only seconds to recover from that tremendous punch, then in he went, battering away furiously at his surprised opponent. Backing away rapidly Sexton soon felt the ropes at his back and tried to clinch, but there was no escape. Mac was fired up now and poured in the leather, smashing his way through Sexton's defences with both hands. Many of the punches struck the Londoner's arms and gloves, but a fair number found the target, thudding into his body and causing him to double up as he tried desperately to hold off the rampaging McAvoy, who now proceeded to set Sexton up for the finisher, rapidly switching his attack to catch his man with a flurry of heavy blows to the head, putting him halfway through the ropes. As Archie straightened up and attempted to clinch Mac connected with a murderous right uppercut to the jaw that seemed to come up almost from the floor. Sexton dropped to his knees, then pitched forward on his face. He never moved, the count over the prostrate challenger being a mere formality. After that his seconds rushed across the ring and carried their man to his corner, where it took several minutes before he was restored to consciousness.

Later, Sexton, who had failed completely to rise to the occasion, expressed his own disappointment at his performance, telling reporters, 'I don't know what was the matter with me tonight. I just couldn't do a thing right.'

As for McAvoy, he had managed to save the day by producing a thrilling finish to what had been a very disappointing contest right up until the final round, dispatching his opponent in such devastating fashion that the excited crowd appeared to forget all about the tedium of the earlier rounds and cheered him to the echo. It was notch number two on that prized Lonsdale belt.

Since losing to McAvoy, the talented Joe Rostron, though very much in the shadow of his dynamic local rival, had continued to campaign very successfully, running up a long string of wins throughout the years 1931-32, while losing very few along the way. A regular at both the big Manchester venues, his potential had certainly not gone unnoticed by the Belle Vue Syndicate, who, though using him frequently, had never had him under contract, Joe being managed, first by Tom Chapman, then by his father-in-law, Jack Hunter of Oldham, and later by Billy Metcalf of Liverpool. Though Metcalf handled his affairs, Rostron's training was done in a room above the Britannia public house in Oldham, where Hunter was the licensee.

One day Rostron was approached by Harry Fleming, who told him that in his opinion Joe had a lot of talent, but would be far more likely to succeed in the game if he were to join the Belle Vue set-up. Not only would he then have the backing of a powerful organisation behind him, but he would also have the advantage of superior training facilities plus top class sparring. Having three champions at Belle Vue was a great achievement, but with Rostron in the stable they were confident they could make if four.

Joe told Fleming he would talk it over with his dad, to whom he was very close. When father and son discussed the offer the first name to come up in the conversation was that of Norman Hurst. They had not the slightest doubt that the rumours that Hurst was behind the syndicate were quite correct. Whenever he was in town he would spend a lot of time at Belle Vue, and Rostron had once overheard him discussing the seating arrangements with Jackie Madden, telling Madden to increase the number of ringside seats for a forthcoming show. This in itself was proof to the Rostrons that Hurst's involvement went far beyond that of a sports journalist.

Something about the set-up made Rostron senior uneasy. He had never been too keen on Norman Hurst and was also dubious about the terms which had been suggested. To get in solid with the big boys was very tempting, but supposing Joe ran into a losing streak. The chances were that they might turn their backs on him. In any case, the Rostrons were a little old fashioned. Though the money was always welcome, they still valued the sporting side of boxing. Finally it was decided to leave things as they were for the time being, with Joe continuing under the management of Billy Metcalf.

The episode, however, caused the Rostrons to think long and hard about Joe's future. He had begun his working life as an apprentice in the tailoring department of the local Co-op Society, but had never completed his training, eventually making boxing his full time occupation. Although only twenty-three, he had been fighting professionally for almost eight years, and both father and son were well aware that boxing was, to say the least, a very uncertain business. Rostron senior's advice was that Joe should think seriously about his long term future, while at the same time continuing with his boxing career.

It did not take Joe long to decide what he would like to do, and in the summer of 1933 he applied to join the Nottingham police force. In the meantime he was matched with 'Battling' Charlie Parkin of Mansfield, in an eliminator for Jack Casey's Northern Area Middleweight title. Rostron was very confident of victory, having outpointed Parkin earlier that year. Before the return could take place, however, a letter arrived from Nottingham informing him that he had been accepted and was required to report for training a week or so later. Joe was therefore forced to withdraw from the eliminator, explaining to the promoter that having only put in his application a month or so before he had not expected to be called up so quickly.

So ended, somewhat prematurely, the career of Joe Rostron. Joe took part in 112 recorded contests, of which he won 93 and drew six. There were some outstanding names on his record, quite apart from McAvoy. In those eight years he had taken on the top Welters and Middleweights in the country, though his best weight was around ten stone ten. Joe fought Eddie Strawer five times, beating him on points on each occasion, though Eddie was a good stone heavier. He also stopped Billy Chew, drew with, then beat Jim Pearson twice, K.O.'d the formidable Albert Johnson, brother of Len, twice, and also defeated Jack Haynes, Sonny Doke, Glen Moody, Joe Lowther, Scottish Champions George Gordon and Willie Hamilton, Archie Sexton, Fred Shaw, Australian Leo Wax and the gifted Harry Mason.

Rostron considered Mason to be the cleverest fighter he ever met. After drawing with, then later outpointing the Leeds man, Joe was full of admiration for his talents.

'He could evade a blow with just the slightest movement of his head,' said Rostron. 'Then, having stood his ground, he would be in perfect position to catch you with a counter punch. And what that man didn't know about in-fighting and tying a man up inside just wasn't worth knowing.'

One of the few men to beat Rostron was Jack Casey, who stopped him in seven rounds at West Hartlepool in 1931. Recalling the fight, Joe insisted that Casey was easily the hardest man he had ever faced, including McAvoy.

'Tough? You could hit him flush on the chin with everything you had, and still he'd keep on coming. He just walked through everything. If you'd clouted him with a shovel I doubt if it would have had any effect. D'you know, I don't think he could feel anything!'

# Chapter 15

## The Perfect Punch

It's more than likely that McAvoy would have fully concurred with Joe Rostron's assessment of 'Cast Iron' Casey – right up until the afternoon of Sunday, November 12th, 1933, that is. For on that day Mac squared up to one Jack Forster, a handsome young fighter from East Anglia, at Royton.

Forster, who claimed to be Champion of the Eastern Counties at both Welter and Middleweight, certainly came with a formidable reputation, having got the better of such excellent scrappers as Jack Haynes, Billy Bird, Bert Danahar and Jim Maloney, though he was not regarded as too much of a threat by the McAvoy camp, who were at that point more concerned with getting a crack at Marcel Thil. Possibly they underestimated the unheralded East Anglian, who was, in fact, highly rated by many experts.

As always, Mac was in superb condition for the fight and received the usual rapturous reception from his loyal Royton fans. Forster turned out to be a neat boxer with a solid punch, but Mac soon discovered that he could outspeed his opponent and found him surprisingly easy to hit. The problem was, that the punches were having little or no effect, for Forster could soak up punishment like a sponge, which proved very disconcerting to the heavy-hitting Rochdale fighter, as round followed round with the imperturbable Forster quite happily absorbing everything that came his way.

Not only did he stand up to anything McAvoy could throw at him, but he was also very adept at breaking up Mac's fierce bursts with a powerful left jab, which, combined with some nifty footwork, invariably got him out of some very tight corners. Several times though, he was forced to take full-blooded rights to the jaw and some really crunching body shots, but never once did Forster even look like going down.

At the end of twelve rounds the Middleweight Champion was a clear winner, but finished up very frustrated and with two hands that felt as though he'd been punching a brick wall. Though McAvoy got the verdict it was the rugged Forster who received the applause of the sporting Royton crowd for the wonderful gameness he had shown in standing up to one of the hardest hitters ever to hold the title.

The N.S.B. management were also delighted with Forster's performance and immediately announced that they would be booking him again at the earliest opportunity. As for McAvoy, he always maintained that Jack Forster was without any doubt the toughest man he had ever met. According to Mac, not even Casey, Harvey or Thil could have stood up to the bombs he exploded on Forster's iron jaw.

Though Marcel Thil was now recognised as World Champion by the International Boxing Union of Europe, and also by the British Board of Control, the position was somewhat different in America, where Vince Dundee was considered to be the World title holder by both ruling bodies, the National Boxing Association and the New York State Athletic Commission. With little progress being made in negotiations with the Thil camp, McAvoy's mentors turned their attention to the possibility of a title fight against Dundee in New York. In the meantime Mac was matched with Eddie Peirce of South Africa, a fighter with wins over Archie Sexton, Len Johnson, Jack Hyams and French-Canadian Del Fontaine.

In an interview in early January, 1934, McAvoy told reporters, 'I appreciate that this Peirce is a dangerous opponent, but he's not going to rob me of my crack at the world title. I expect to win decisively, then go over to America to fight Dundee.'

Mac, who did a large part of his training for this contest at Harry Fleming's Collyhurst gym, employed a couple of new sparring partners in Bernard Penston, described as Welterweight Champion of the Irish Free State, and Harry Briers, a six footer, who had boxed in London rings and played Rugby League for St. Helens Recs. In addition, Jack Lord, the Bolton welter, was again on hand to concentrate on speeding Mac up. With no title at stake the match was made at 11 st. 8lbs.

Peirce, taller than Mac, and broad shouldered, was reputed to be a tough scrapper who wasted no time in setting about his opponents. He was said to be pushing for a shot at the Empire title and was very eager to get a crack at McAvoy.

The South African's advance publicity, however, was to prove anything but accurate, and it was clear almost from the start that Mac was far too good for him. The trouble was that Peirce knew it too, and consequently showed very little appetite for the job in hand. Because of McAvoy's reputation as a puncher there were very few men willing to stand their ground and slug it out with him. This, of course, was quite understandable, but Peirce made not the slightest attempt to even jab and move. From the opening bell his height and reach advantages were used only to smother McAvoy's attacks, the South African being all too eager to go into a clinch at the merest hint of danger.

For the first three rounds he was guilty of the most flagrant grabbing and holding, McAvoy having to repeatedly push him off, while referee Arthur Myers warned Peirce severely time after time.

After one such warning in the third round Mac at last managed to connect cleanly, and then really poured on the leather. Peirce now showed that he was quite capable of taking punishment and stood up well under the bombardment, even landing the odd blow in retaliation. Having weathered the storm, however, he then returned to his original negative tactics, much to the annoyance of the crowd.

In round seven McAvoy held off and encouraged Peirce to come to him. This ploy had the desired effect, with the result that the South African actually won the round. But the cautious Peirce refused to press home his advantage and McAvoy had no option but to take the initiative once again. After his reluctant opponent had been warned for a low blow, Mac doubled him up with a vicious body punch, following this up with another blistering attack as Peirce retreated and the crowd yelled for Mac to finish it.

Gamely, Peirce held out under the attack, then grabbed again and hung on. There were no more high spots, Peirce using his experience and the old safety-first tactics to see him through to the final bell, with McAvoy getting the verdict at the end of twelve very frustrating rounds and Peirce leaving the hall to the accompaniment of booing from the disappointed Belle Vue crowd.

Although annoyed with himself for not having put the negative Springbok away, Mac wasted no time in worrying about it. One month later he was back in the ring at London's Albert Hall, facing Al Burke, Welterweight Champion of Australia, though actually British born.

Burke, real name Albert E. Pearce, had compiled a good record since returning to this country, but being well aware of McAvoy's power, Al had no intention of mixing it with the dangerous Rochdale man. Having a big advantage in height and reach, Burke made up his mind to keep things at long range. A good boxer, he was also exceptionally quick, and darted in and out like lightning before Mac could lay a glove on him. When in close the will o' the wisp Aussie was very clever at tying his man up, and McAvoy managed to achieve very little in the early part of the fight, while Burke's speedy left picked up the points.

For a spell in the third Burke stood his ground, scoring with some jolting right-handers. He also did well in the following round, making McAvoy miss with several hefty swings, while scoring repeatedly with neat left jabs.

Having clearly won those two rounds Burke came out for round five full of confidence, meeting McAvoy head on. It proved to be his undoing, for Mac nailed him almost immediately with a right to the jaw. But with Burke obviously stunned, McAvoy, slow for once to follow up, was quickly grabbed by the dazed Aussie, who held on to him for dear life. On being prised apart by the referee the fighters stepped back. Then Mac connected with one of his specials – a right uppercut from way down, which landed perfectly, lifting Burke off the floor and depositing him flat on his back.

McAvoy walked to a neutral corner, confident that his night's work was over, and was astonished to see Burke in the act of staggering to his feet as the count reached nine. Mac moved in, picking his punches, but Burke was covering up well, despite his distressed condition, and McAvoy, finding no opening, unleashed another powerful uppercut which tore straight through the stricken Australian's defences, landing flush on the point of his chin. Down he went as if poleaxed. Yet amazingly, he managed to drag himself up to a kneeling position before pitching forward onto his face to be counted out.

Instead of sticking to his boxing Burke had made the fatal mistake of attempting to beat McAvoy at his own game and had paid dearly for his folly. Yet his performance had been a truly remarkable one. He had shown great courage under fire and fully deserved the warm applause he was given on leaving the Albert Hall ring.

That right hand uppercut was proving to be sheer dynamite whenever it connected, for Mac had worked hard at perfecting it and delighted in using this deadly weapon whenever he saw the opportunity.

Less than three weeks later, at Belle Vue, the fans were treated to another perfect knockout when McAvoy disposed of Eddie McGuire, another South African, who, in the short time he was in the ring, put up a far better show than his countryman. Unlike Eddie Peirce, McGuire was all action, and went looking for McAvoy from the start. It was an invitation that Mac readily accepted, and there was never a dull moment as the two swapped punches in the centre of the ring, McGuire taking McAvoy's best shots without flinching and opening up a cut over the champion's left eye. This only made Mac fight more fiercely, and in round two he again produced the lethal uppercut. The rugged South African went down and stayed there.

In the dressing room afterwards McGuire told his conqueror, 'I have no complaints. You beat me fair and square. I think you'll win the World title.'

The McAvoy camp was certainly interested in a World title fight, but others were chasing them, including Ted Broadribb, who was trying to get Harry Fleming to agree to a catchweights contest with Del Fontaine, of Canada. The Belle Vue people though, had other plans, such as challenging Len Harvey for the Light-heavyweight championship. Indeed, if McAvoy could beat Harvey at the heavier poundage he would automatically become the Heavyweight champion, for Harvey had recently given weight to the formidable Jack Petersen and won that title as well.

Jack Casey, meanwhile, had also put himself in the running by beating Tommy Farr, at that time Welsh Light-heavyweight title holder, Farr being scheduled to meet Eddie Phillips for the right to challenge Harvey.

At this point the Belle Vue boys made a very smart move, matching their man with Ernie Simmons, a Birmingham-based Dubliner. Not only had Simmons beaten Farr, he also held two wins over Jack Casey. Therefore, if McAvoy could get the better of him, his claim for a crack at Harvey's titles would be considerably strengthened.

The Simmons fight was not going to be an easy ride though. For one thing Mac would be giving a lot of weight away, and to make things even more difficult his training was badly hampered by a lack of sufficient sparring partners to keep him happy. Knowing he would be taking on a much heavier man, McAvoy was really unloading his big bombs on anyone they put in front of him, with the result that there were very few fighters willing to come back for more. In desperation Harry Fleming appealed for volunteers, the inducement being £1 for anyone who could last three rounds.

It was a time of great poverty in Britain, especially in the North. There was no work to be had and very little money about. Grim-faced men, young and old, would spend their days hanging around on street corners with empty pockets and very little food in their bellies. There were so few opportunities to earn even a few coppers that some were prepared to tackle just about anything.

The five brave men who turned up at the Collyhurst gym one Thursday afternoon in April, 1934, must have been pretty desperate. All the same, the ruthless McAvoy showed them no mercy, setting about them as if they were hardened pros. Yet one fiercely determined man actually managed to stay a couple of rounds. Two others stood up to Mac for two minutes each, while the remaining two were finished within twenty seconds. It was just like leading lambs to the slaughter and should never have been allowed to happen. They were hard times all right.

On his first venture into the higher division, Mac was not only conceding height and reach, but also a stone in weight. Despite this he soon discovered that Simmons did not pose much of a threat. On the other hand the big Irishman showed a remarkable capacity to soak up punishment, and although losing round after round, simply refused to succumb to McAvoy's heavy punching. Simmons was certainly not lacking in defensive skill, but found Mac's speed difficult to cope with. Though outclassed, he gave a plucky display, but at the end of twelve rounds Mac had gained an emphatic points victory.

With suitable opponents of his own size increasingly hard to find, McAvoy was again obliged to concede weight in his next contest, against Teddy Phillips, of Canada. Phillips, who was being handled by Jimmy Wilde, had already made his presence felt in this country by accounting for George Porter, Bill Webster, Billy Adair, Jim Brooks, and Donald Jones, all inside the distance. Porter, who had stood up to McAvoy for fifteen rounds, had been knocked cold in one round by the tough Canadian.

It was an open air show, staged at Belle Vue, Jackie Brown topping the bill as he once again defended his title against Valentin Angelmann of France. In a contest which had the fans on their feet to the very end, Brown just held onto his crown, the decision, a draw, being well received.

As for McAvoy, it turned out to be a night he would never forget. In a sensational bout, with the crowd roaring for almost the whole of the eight rounds it lasted, Mac found himself in more trouble than he'd ever experienced in his entire career. Though he did not know it as he climbed through the ropes, it would prove to be a real night of horrors.

The first round was fairly even, McAvoy catching Phillips with some thudding body shots and the Canadian countering sharply. At the start of the fateful second it was seen that Mac was bleeding slightly from the nose, though in no difficulty. As the round got under way he waded into Phillips, landing several more hard blows to the body. Then, following a fierce close quarter exchange, those nearest to the ring were shocked to see McAvoy emerge from a clinch with his right eye completely closed. Mac knew at once that something had gone badly wrong.

With the eye shut as tight as a clam he was forced to tilt his head to one side to keep Phillips in his line of vision, as the Canadian, seeing his chance, tore in to finish the job. Mac fought back like a tiger to keep him at bay. He could not have known just how badly hurt he really was, but the spectators certainly did, for the injury, which was worsening rapidly, was clearly visible from many rows back. The area around the right eye was swollen to an abnormal size, and the whole of the right side of Mac's face puffed up like a balloon.

The bell to end the round didn't come a moment too soon, and as McAvoy flopped down on his stool with blood pouring from his nose, Jack Bates and Harry Fleming set to work feverishly in a desperate attempt to reduce the swelling.

What had actually happened was that, as Phillips tore in, either his head or his shoulder had smashed into McAvoy's nose, damaging the breathing passages and allowing air to escape into the face and neck, to produce the enormous swelling.

When Mac left his corner at the start of round three he was a grotesque sight indeed. Though his seconds had made great efforts to relieve the swollen area, the eye remained tightly shut, and to make matters worse it was now noticed that a swelling had begun to appear below the other eye.

Just the same Mac met Phillips in the centre of the ring and proceeded to slug it out with him, taking some hefty shots in order to get in close, where he could at least see his opponent and punish him about the body. Still, many people in the crowd were heard to cry out, 'Stop it ref, stop it!'

Between rounds Fleming and Bates subjected their man to some painful treatment as they tried vainly to get the swelling down and prise the eye open. As the left eye was also beginning to close, there were times when Mac was fighting with only half vision in his one good optic.

Still he battled on, getting in some hard digs whenever he could back his man into the ropes, and subjecting Phillips to such a vicious battering that it appeared possible that he might yet pull the fight out of the fire, despite the terrible condition he was in. Showing wonderful courage, McAvoy fought with animal-like ferocity and had the crowd on its feet and roaring him on as he laced into the Canadian. Several times Phillips appeared about to go down under the onslaught, but always managed to weather the storm, clinching whenever he could and at other times lashing back at his half-blind opponent.

Back in his corner Mac could hear Ted Broadribb earnestly advising Harry Fleming to 'Throw in the towel. He could finish up blind.'

But McAvoy would not allow it, insisting that he could still win in spite of the shocking state he was in, and out he went again to swap punches with his tormentor, who must have marvelled at Mac's pluck. At the end of each round the champion presented an horrific picture as he groped his way back to his corner to be met by his despairing handlers, who could do no more than attempt to keep his left eye at least open a little. By the end of the seventh, Harry Fleming had just about reached the end of his tether and pleaded with McAvoy to retire.

'No,' replied Mac, stubbornly. 'I can beat him. I'll get him this round.'

At this point the referee came over and took a good look at him, then walked away again. But Fleming had seen enough and insisted on throwing in the towel. Again McAvoy forbade it, and the bell rang while they were still arguing. Before Fleming could say another word Mac was on his feet and moving to the centre of the ring. Though he could see his man right there in front of him he was little more than a blurred vision. In these circumstances it was almost impossible for McAvoy to find the range and the first couple of punches he threw were well off target. He knew that this could not go on and that the referee was bound to stop it at any moment. To have any chance of landing he had to get in close, and made every effort to push Phillips back in the hope of trapping him on the ropes. No one in the hall realised it, but the end was very near. When it came it was with dramatic suddenness.

As McAvoy forced the Canadian to give ground he was stung by a fierce burst of counter punching. Then, as Phillips came off the ropes, McAvoy landed a powerful right to the jaw, followed by a left hook. Before the dazed Phillips could react he was knocked through the ropes by a terrific uppercut. He was flat out and lay motionless, his body draped over the bottom rope, half in the ring and half on the apron. Peering around to get his bearings, McAvoy stumbled to a neutral corner and the crowd went wild as Phillips was counted out.

It had been a truly remarkable victory, snatched from the fire when the odds had looked like a thousand to one against. McAvoy had never doubted for a moment that he could win, but it had still taken tremendous courage just to keep going. On reaching the dressing room he collapsed and was rushed immediately to the Manchester Royal Infirmary, being later transferred to the Manchester Jewish Hospital.

In an interview with reporters, the ringside doctor said, 'In all my experience I have never seen a man continue to fight, never mind knock out his opponent, while in such an appalling state. Emphysema, which is the medical term for the condition, occurs when a bone is damaged or broken in the nose, injuring the breathing passages and so allowing air through the nose and into the region of the face and even the neck. The victim would be in great pain, and I can tell you that McAvoy had it severely.'

Mac remained in the hospital for the best part of a week, but was assured that there would be no permanent damage. It had been a freak accident and the condition would soon clear up, but for several days he looked like something out of a horror movie and was very relieved when the swelling began to go down and he could recognise himself in the mirror. The amazing thing was that he would be back in the ring only a few weeks later.

McAvoy was now tenant of the Brunswick Hotel, a small pub in Baillie Street, in the centre of Rochdale, and living on the premises with his family, which had grown somewhat. In addition to young Joe, who was now five, there were two other children, John, who was almost four, and Leonora, aged two.

Delighted with his new venture and determined to play the role of mine host to the full, he could be seen in the bar most evenings, very smartly turned out and thoroughly enjoying himself as he welcomed his growing clientele and directed operations.

With a man of McAvoy's reputation on the premises one would hardly have expected any sort of trouble to occur, but people are liable to do just about anything in drink, and if hearsay evidence is to be believed, then such a man was Gus Finnerty. Gus was the local hard case, who has been described variously as: 'a big, idle man – very argumentative', 'a heavy drinker. Always looking for trouble', 'a man who would pick on anybody who passed him in the street when he'd had a drink', and even 'a bad 'un – similar to McAvoy'!

Gus lived in Whitehall Street on The Mount, and could be a real problem whenever he was drunk and on the rampage. At such times apparently, there was one man, a certain P.C. Swift, who could usually talk to him and calm him down. It seems a pity therefore, that Swift was not on hand the night that big Gus shouldered his way up to the bar of the Brunswick, asking where McAvoy was and threatening what he was going to do to him when he found him.

As it happened, Mac was upstairs, and on hearing the commotion, came down in his carpet slippers to find out what was going on. Unlike the gallant P.C., Mac wasted no time in trying to reason with Finnerty, he just laid him out, and that was the end of the problem.

On another occasion, Charlie Henderson was walking home through the town centre late one night with a couple of his mates, when they met an acquaintance by the name of John Fleming, who was clearly the worse for drink. Fleming, though quite a nice, pleasant fellow when sober, was one of those who tended to become aggressive once he'd had a few. When one of the Charlie's friends asked him if he fancied taking McAvoy on, Fleming replied that he not only fancied the job but would go immediately to the Brunswick and challenge him. The lads laughed as he staggered off in the direction of Baillie Street, but didn't take it too seriously, knowing that the pub would be closed by that time. However, on reaching the Brunswick and finding the door locked, the intrepid Fleming banged loudly on it, calling for McAvoy to come out and face him. After a few minutes the light came on and the door opened. Bang! Fleming saw stars and fell flat on his back on the pavement. Some time later he came to, stumbled to his feet and rubbed his jaw, then, shaking his head, staggered off home to bed.

While at the Brunswick McAvoy became the proud owner of a couple of horses, which he stabled in the pub yard. He had always loved animals, especially horses, and planned to race them. In the meantime he made sure they were exercised regularly and well looked after, paying a young lad a few shillings a week to groom them and clean out the stables each day after school.

The boy's name was Arthur Ashworth, who got the job through his father, Billy, a journeyman electrician and a close friend of McAvoy's. Arthur would later gain notoriety as a local villain, and also become a frequent guest of Her Majesty at Dartmoor and various other well known establishments. At this point in his life though, being only eleven or so, Arthur's criminal activities had progressed no further than rifling his dad's pockets in search of the Capstan Full Strength cigarettes to which Billy and his son were so partial.

Arthur hero-worshipped Mac, and is one of the few people who had nothing but good to say about him. McAvoy kept several guns and was in the habit of making frequent trips into the local countryside to shoot rabbits, along with such friends as Billy Ashworth, young Arthur often going along in the car to pass the guns to the gallant hunters as they stalked their unsuspecting prey.

One day the three of them crossed the border into Yorkshire to engage in a spot of poaching, and on the way back were stopped by a police constable on a bicycle who had heard the shooting. On seeing the guns in the back of the car he took down the names of the occupants and particulars of the vehicle. At first McAvoy and Billy Ashworth swore that they had not even stopped in the area, but when the constable questioned Arthur and Billy tried to prompt his son to back up his story, McAvoy intervened and admitted the offence, saying that he had no intention of letting the boy lie on his behalf. This side of the boxer's character left a profound impression on Arthur, and resulted in McAvoy rising even higher in the youngster's estimation.

Phil Milligan. A Royton product with the heart of a lion. He fought four world champions.

2.1

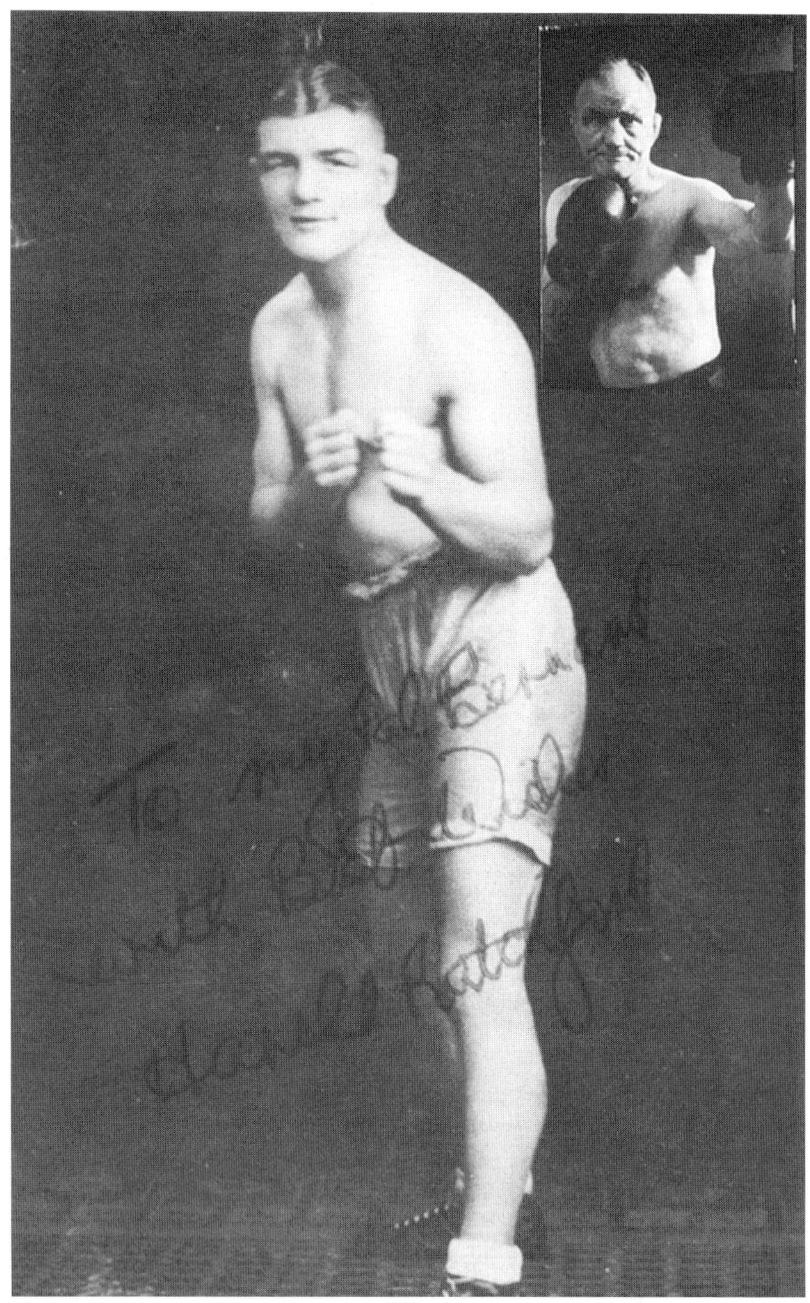

Harold Ratchford in his prime. *(inset)* Harold in his sixties – and still in great shape.

Joe Rostron, 'The Heywood Hurricane'.

A group of Royton boxers in the Isle of Man. *Left to right:* Charlie Dickenson, 'Seaman' Harry Wolfe, Jean Locatelli, Joe Tolley, Harold Ratchford and Young Mickey.

*Left to right:* Harold Ratchford, Joe Tolley and Dom Volante.

Billy Chew. The first man to beat McAvoy.

'Cast Iron' Casey – impervious to punishment.

Norman Hurst. The man behind the Belle Vue Syndicate.

The redoubtable Harry 'Kid' Furness in his fighting days – about 1930.

Harry Fleming – manager of three great champions.

Crafty Rene Devos, who taught McAvoy some tricks of the trade.

Len Harvey displays a powerful physique.

2.7

*Above left:* McAvoy the skilled horseman. *Above right:* Mac in riding gear. *Below:* Astride one of his favourite mounts in the mid-1930s.

A great champion – McAvoy proudly wears the Lonsdale Belt – 1933.

The formidable Frenchman, Marcel Thil.

# Paris 1935

McAvoy squares up to the crouching Marcel Thil.

McAvoy goes down from a low blow.

McAvoy, leaving for Paris, is seen off by his mother, Nellie, and wife Eliza.

*Above left:* 'Seaman' Jim Cox, who went the distance with McAvoy on three occasions. *Right:* John Henry Lewis, an outstanding World Champion. *Below:* Joe Lowther, who lost his North of England middleweight title to McAvoy.

# Success in America

*Above left:* The menacing figure of boxing czar Frankie Carbo, who controlled many champions including Babe Risko. *Right:* Al McCoy down in round three in Madison Square Garden. *Below:* Jimmy Smith out cold in two.

*Above:* Handsome, muscular Eddie 'Babe' Risko. *Below:* Risko blasted out in one round.

A regular Rogues' Gallery: A quartet of racketeers who infiltrated boxing in America.

Frankie Carbo – pictured at the time of his indictment in the early 1960s.

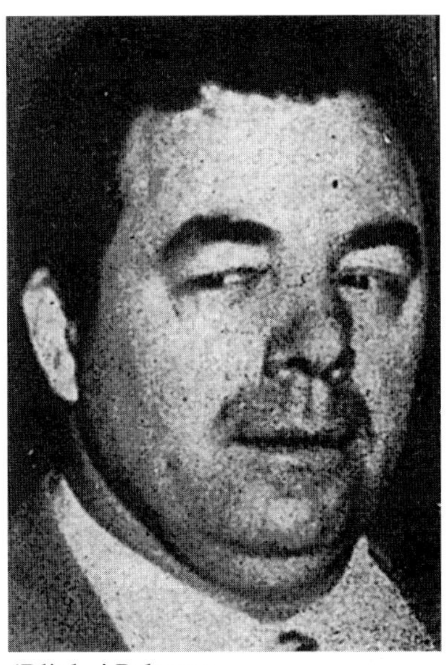

'Blinky' Palermo.

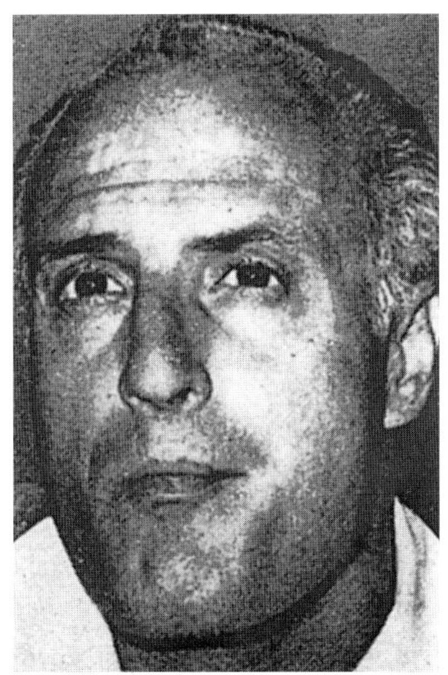

Louis Tom Dragna.

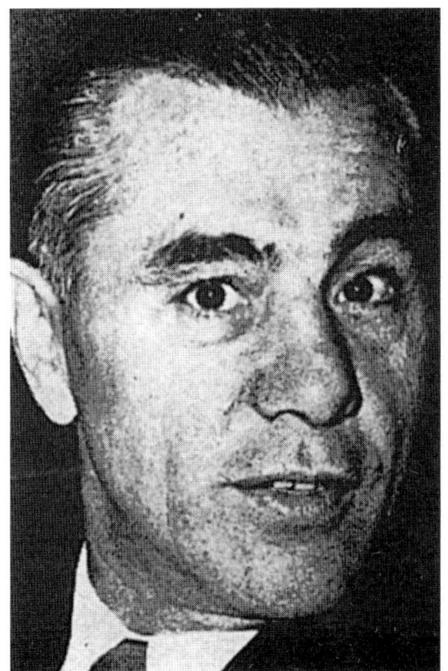

Joseph Sica.

McAvoy *(on scales)* shakes hands with Jack Petersen, to whom he conceded height and weight.

Petersen in fighting pose.

McAvoy is greeted by his family at the railway station in Manchester on his triumphant return from America.

# Chapter 16

## Parisian Misadventure

Having made a quite remarkable recovery from the horrific events experienced in the fight with Teddy Phillips, Mac decided to transport his horses to Blackpool, where he lived under canvas for a couple of weeks with one of his sparmates, in a camp at Squires Gate, much of the time being spent exercising the horses on the sands. One of them, Brunswick Boy, had previously been successful at Kirkham at Whitsuntide that year, and later won the Blackpool Turf Club Handicap.

Mac was very proud, but unfortunately was not on hand to witness the triumph, having had to return to Manchester to go into training for his next fight. Interviewed by reporters, the faithful Eliza told them that neither she nor Joe, as she called him, had backed the horse. Her husband, she said, was interested in racing only as a sport and because he loved horses, which was quite true.

Back in Manchester, Mac was already training hard for his forthcoming contest with 'Battling' Charlie Parkin of Mansfield, twelve rounds at 11st. 8lbs. Following the titanic struggle with Phillips, culminating in Mac's dramatic triumph against all odds, the Belle Vue fans could hardly wait to welcome him back, and a mighty roar greeted the highly popular 'Rochdale Thunderbolt' as he made his way to the ring.

Charlie Parkin was a clever, experienced middleweight, and though his record was somewhat patchy, it contained some good results, in particular a win over Jack Hyams in eleven rounds, a man who had always given McAvoy problems. Mac had fully recovered and looked very fit. Parkin also appeared to be in splendid shape and had plenty of support in the hall.

The Mansfield man squared up confidently as they came out for the first round and opened with several probing left leads. Mac stood off and let him come forward. As Parkin continued to advance Mac suddenly stepped in and shook him with a jarring right to the jaw, followed by another, and down went Charlie.

As he rose at nine McAvoy threw the uppercut and missed, the blow just whistling past Parkin's chin as he swayed out of its path.

Then, feinting the left, Mac banged in a terrific right under the heart and Parkin dropped flat on his face, attempted to rise as the count reached eight, then collapsed again.

Despite their disappointment at the brevity of the contest, the Belle Vue fans showed their appreciation of Mac's dynamic punching in no uncertain manner, the cheering lasting for several minutes. It was quite clear that there were no ill-effects following the ordeal of the Phillips fight. McAvoy was still on course for higher honours and the Belle Vue Syndicate made renewed efforts to persuade Harvey to put up his Light-heavyweight title.

Harry Levene, who had been appointed McAvoy's representative in London, informed the press that £500 had been deposited with the Board of Control for a match against the champion. When told of this, Charlie Rose, Harvey's manager, said, 'And we have covered it. So the match is on.' Adding, however, 'But of course, Len still has to defend against Eddie Phillips, unless the Board decides otherwise.'

It was clear that the Harvey camp was in no hurry to get involved with McAvoy again. After all, there were more promising avenues to explore, such as a World title bout against John Henry Lewis.

Extraordinary difficulties were being experienced by Belle Vue matchmaker Jack Madden in finding suitable opponents for the Rochdale K.O. King. Even Mac's willingness to give weight away was not helping matters much, for the opposition still had to have some sort of credibility or the fans would soon stop coming. There had even been talk of a meeting with the much bigger Jack Petersen,* and when asked about this Mac just shrugged and replied, 'Why not? I don't see why I can't do what Len Harvey did.'

But Madden was determined to fulfil a promise he had made to the public to bring one of the world's leading middleweights to Belle Vue. Men taken into consideration had included Marcel Thil, Vince Dundee, Teddy Yarosz, Eric Seelig, the clever German-Jewish champion, Mickey Walker, former World Champion and Cuban titleholder, Kid Tunero.

When negotiations with the Americans proved slow and unpromising, and Marcel Thil signed to defend his European Middleweight title against Carmello Candel, the only remaining candidates were Tunero and Seelig, who were scheduled to meet in Paris. A Belle Vue representative was present at the ringside with a contract in his pocket, but both fighters suffered so much facial damage

* Petersen had regained the Heavyweight title only six months after losing it, forcing Harvey to retire at the end of the twelfth round.

that it was obvious they would be out of commission for some weeks to come. With a date already pencilled in, Madden was at his wits end, and decided to try for Jack Etienne, the Belgian light-heavy who had given McAvoy such a tough contest two years before, when losing on points over fifteen rounds, a decision which had not been popular with some sections of the crowd. Etienne, having taken Mac's best punches without caving in, was considered a stern test. As well as holding a victory over Len Johnson, gained when the coloured Manchester fighter was in his prime, Etienne had also accounted for Jimmy Tarante, a rated American, and had fought a draw with Marcel Thil. Since losing to McAvoy he had won ten off the reel, and was said to be confident of his getting his revenge.

The match was made at catchweights over twelve rounds, with Mac giving away considerable poundage as well as height and reach. With his stubbly chin and muscular sun-tanned body, the Belgian looked an exceptionally tough proposition as he limbered up in his corner, and few in the crowd could have expected the fireworks they were about to witness in an explosive first round which was to take everyone by surprise, especially Etienne.

Without wasting time on any preliminaries, Mac went straight out and landed a heavy right on the big Belgian's chin which really shook him. It was obvious to the spectators that Etienne was already in trouble and there were groans from some parts of the hall, and even shouted appeals to McAvoy to take it easy, as they wanted to see a contest.

But Mac had no intention of pulling his punches and a terrific right to the body floored Etienne for a count of eight. Struggling to his feet, he was immediately nailed by a similar punch under the heart, and went down again to be counted out. The Belgian was then carried to his corner in great pain and attended to by a doctor before being allowed to leave the ring.

Mac's punching power had again proved absolutely devastating, and many in the crowd found it hard to credit that a man of such size and physique as the Belgian could be demolished in so decisive a manner.

It was now quite clear that an opponent who could stand up to McAvoy really would have to be found for his next outing at Belle Vue. One round knockouts were very exciting, but the fans were eager to see their hero extended, and Madden knew that anything less than a top overseas challenger would be totally unacceptable.

Teddy Yarosz, meanwhile, had beaten fellow countryman Vince Dundee to take the American version of the World Middleweight title.

An offer was made to Yarosz to meet McAvoy in Manchester, with the title at stake. Soon afterwards, however, a cable was received by Harry Fleming offering Mac a bout with Yarosz in Madison Square Garden, no mention being made of the title. It was decided, therefore, to wait and see if the Americans responded to the Belle Vue offer.

Though Yarosz was regarded as World Champion only in America, if McAvoy could beat him the stage would be set for a unification contest with Marcel Thil, which was sure to command big money.

With the Americans continuing to stall, however, Jack Madden announced in mid-November 1934 that he had signed 'Kid' Tunero to meet McAvoy in early December at Belle Vue. This contest was originally arranged for the Albert Hall, but was called off at the last minute when the Cuban went down with a heavy cold, following which Jack Madden got into the act, outbidding the Londoners and securing the contest for Manchester.

Tunero came with a good record, having won 48 of 52 contests, including a win and a loss against Marcel Thil, and had never been knocked out.

McAvoy's sparring partners were Fred Shaw, Ernie Simmons and Billy Vyner, a heavyweight from Wales.

Tunero arrived in Manchester from Paris several days before the fight and was installed at Hulme Boxing Club to finish his preparation. After K.O.'ing several sparring partners The 'Kid' was beginning to find the club a lonely place and an appeal for assistance was made to Harry Fleming, who very sportingly lent Vyner to the opposition, promising that the big Welshman would give Tunero a real test.

Nearly 7,000 fans were crammed into the King's Hall on the night, the higher priced seats having been sold out many days before.

When Tunero entered the ring and slipped out of his dressing gown the sight of his wonderful physique brought gasps of admiration from the spectators. A few minutes later, however, he was in dire trouble and wilting badly under a rain of vicious blows, but managed to grab Mac and hold on tightly until the referee could force them apart. After that the Kid got on his bike. He was very quick and made sure that there was always plenty of distance between himself and his heavy-hitting opponent for the next three or four rounds, occasionally darting in to deliver his own speedy combinations, then out again before Mac could catch up with him. McAvoy took the first four rounds, with the fifth fairly even. In the sixth, Mac, using a tactic which had proved successful in several of his previous fights, slowed down, allowing the Cuban to lead and come forward. As the seventh round opened Tunero appeared to have gained in confidence. He was beginning to come more into the fight and was undoubtedly being lulled into a false sense of security as he started to land a few apparently hurtful punches. Even when stung by a couple of sharp hooks to the ribs he appeared unruffled. Then, as the Kid moved into the attack himself, Mac saw his chance, and stepping in smartly, planted a beautiful uppercut on Tunero's chin. The punch carried terrific power and the Kid immediately fell forward onto his opponent, who pushed him off, the stricken Cuban then falling flat on his back, arms outstretched and quite unconscious.

Delirious with excitement, the record crowd rose as one man and cheered McAvoy to the echo. They were quite certain that it was all over, but somehow, halfway through the count, Tunero struggled to his hands and knees, keeled over again, then, with a supreme effort, just managed to scramble to his feet at nine.

As he stood there on wobbly legs it was quite obvious that nothing could save the Cuban, and at that point his chief second, Ted Broadribb, decided to throw in the towel. This action, however, was not noticed by the referee, as the towel got caught in the ropes. McAvoy moved in again and fired a left hook to the Cuban's jaw. Down went Tunero, but after a short count he was up yet again. Seeing this, Broadribb, who must have believed in miracles, snatched back the towel. But McAvoy was now determined to finish the job and drove his man into the ropes, where Tunero remained in a crouching attitude, a helpless target for the battery of powerful blows that now rained down on him. Finally, a terrific right swing toppled him over the lower rope just as the referee decided he'd seen enough. At that moment also Ted Broadribb again tossed in the towel.

It was quite a while before the badly shaken Cuban fully regained his senses. Meanwhile, Mac made no effort to conceal his delight as the fans yelled themselves hoarse. Of one thing they were certain. If their hero was not given a shot at the World title after the kind of scintillating performances he was turning in, there was absolutely no justice. According to Norman Hurst's column, however, McAvoy would without doubt be matched with Marcel Thil early in the new year.

On arriving back in Rochdale that night Mac received the personal congratulations of Gracie Fields, who was home for a busy week of personal appearances and charity work.

Only a few days after the great win against Tunero, word was received that Thil had signed a contract with promoter Jeff Dickson to meet McAvoy in Paris early in January 1935. But Mac's delight soon turned to disappointment when he learned that the Frenchman's World Middleweight title would not be at stake. Instead he would be fighting for the European Light-heavyweight title, which Thil had recently won on a foul against Martinez Alfara.

It was obvious that every possible obstacle was being put in Mac's way, yet there was no point in turning the fight down. The best thing he could do to force his way into the World title reckoning was to go out there and lick Thil. But after agreeing to the fight the Belle Vue camp were hit by a real bombshell, when it was announced that 'Kid' Tunero had been selected by the International Boxing Union as Thil's next challenger for the World Middleweight title. It appeared once again to be a deliberate attempt to sidetrack the claims of the British Champion, possibly on the grounds that he was about to compete for a title in a higher weight division. The I.B.U.'s plans, however, were quickly spiked by Jeff Dickson, who restored some sanity to the situation by stating that he was not prepared to stage the Thil-Tunero contest in Paris, as it would have no public appeal whatsoever. As it would have little appeal anywhere else in Europe for that matter, the chances of it ever taking place were just about nil.

'Much will depend on the outcome of the match between Thil and McAvoy,' Dickson told the press. 'A good showing by the British champion and the I.B.U. will probably have to think again.'

In the meantime McAvoy was called on to defend his British Middleweight title, having gone well over the normally accepted period of six months, although it has to be said that serious challengers were pretty thin on the ground. Not that there was any shortage of good middleweights around, far from it. It was simply that McAvoy was in a class of his own in this country.

All the same the Board were obliged to come up with a challenger, rather than let the division stagnate, and the man to emerge was none other than the London Aussie, Al Burke, who had lasted five rounds with McAvoy earlier in the year. Burke had earned his chance by knocking out George Gordon, of Dunblane, in four rounds, and was expected to challenge for Mac's title in the New Year.

Not surprisingly, there was only mild interest in such a contest, Belle Vue's bid of £410 being topped by that of Leicester promoter

J. Panter, who offered £550, of which McAvoy was to receive £350. The Board of Control, however, decided that this was far too low for a British title contest and extended the bidding period to the end of February 1935, leaving McAvoy free to concentrate on his very important clash with Marcel Thil.

Though the battle for Thil's title was at the Light-heavyweight poundage of 12st. 7lbs, neither fighter would be anywhere near that weight, McAvoy, in fact, being required to come in at not less than 11st. 8lbs, in order to protect the Frenchman's World Middleweight title. The contest would be fought under the rules of the European-based International Boxing Union, with a referee and two judges, one of these being W. Barrington-Dalby, the well-known amateur referee and broadcaster.

It was generally believed that McAvoy had more than an even chance of beating Thil. After all, a number of others had done it, including Fred Shaw and Jack Etienne. Thil, however, had matured late in his career and was known to be a far more formidable proposition than he had been four or five years earlier, although the question of age might well have some bearing on the final outcome. At thirty-five, Thil would be giving Mac eight years, which appeared, on the face of it, to be quite a handicap. Yet the Frenchman had been improving with every fight since winning the title from 'Gorilla' Jones, having accounted for Len Harvey, 'Kid' Tunero, Ignacio Ara (Madrid) and Gustave Roth of Brussels.

Thil would have a crowd of over twenty thousand behind him, though McAvoy would not be entirely without support. A party of 100 had already booked with one tour operator in Rochdale, while smaller groups were being put together, including one of about 60, and it appeared that the total from Mac's home town would probably exceed 250. In addition, over 200 fans would be making the trip from London.

Training was in full swing at the Collyhurst gym, with McAvoy getting through five miles of roadwork each morning and sparring in the afternoons with Fred Shaw, speedway rider turned boxer, Ian Ritchings, and Frank Hough of Battersea, known as 'The Fighting Hussar'.

All was going well, then a series of unfortunate events occurred which certainly did not help McAvoy's preparation. First, his daughter, Leonora, then three years old, was rushed into hospital with suspected diphtheria. This was about three weeks before he was due to leave for

France, and Mac was naturally frantic with worry. Though he managed to somehow carry on with his training he could not possibly have been in the ideal frame of mind for what was to be one of the most important contests of his career.

Fortunately the case turned out to be less serious than was at first feared and the child was sent home after a couple of weeks, well on the road to recovery. Mac was by then in his last few days of training and planning to wind down with a few light sessions on arriving in Paris.

Before leaving he was photographed with his wife and his mother on the steps of the Brunswick Hotel. As Eliza was not going with him arrangements had been made for her to be informed of the result by telephone. To the crowd gathered in Baillie Street, McAvoy's last message was, 'This is a very important fight for me, and I shall do my very best. I feel sure I can win.'

With that, Mac climbed into the car as the crowd cheered, and set off for London Road Station, Manchester, travelling to London that evening and staying overnight. The following morning, along with Harry Fleming and trainer Jack Bates, he flew to Paris. It was his first trip abroad and he had no idea what to expect.

Mac had trained well, despite all the worry over Leonora, but things did not run very smoothly on arrival in the French capital. There was no privacy to do any serious training, with the result that very little was achieved in this respect, and though this did not appear too serious a problem, in view of the fact that all the hard work had already been done in England, when well-laid plans are disrupted it can be very unsettling for the fighter.

The food also proved to be something of a worry. It was so different to the kind of diet McAvoy was used to, and he was not at all keen on what was put in front of him. It seems a great pity that the McAvoy camp were unprepared for such an eventuality, so that other arrangements might have been made. But Harry Fleming was used to Mac's grumbling and probably put it down to nothing more than pre-fight tension.

To make matters worse a spot appeared on Mac's left forearm, which gradually developed into an angry looking boil. It had to be treated with hot fomentations, but by the day of the fight had still not burst and was very painful. There was nothing for it but to call in a doctor and have it lanced. This operation took place just a few hours before the fight, so it can truthfully be claimed that McAvoy could not have been feeling anything like his best at what was the most crucial time of all. He may, in fact, have taken to the ring in a somewhat weakened condition. At the weigh-in he was silent and appeared very edgy. Both men were well below the light-heavyweight limit, with McAvoy scaling 11st. 0¼lb against the champion's 11st. 7½lbs.

On Mac's appearance a resounding cheer went up from his loyal supporters, and he looked down to see a group of wildly enthusiastic fans wearing red, white and blue rosettes. He waved to them, then turned away to concentrate his mind on the job in hand. When Thil appeared there was an almighty roar which seemed to go on and on, punctuated by hoots and whistles. It was an unfamiliar noise to McAvoy and totally different from the sound of a British crowd.

Mac glanced across at the stocky, bald-headed Frenchman as he entered the ring. His hairy body was gleaming, due to the fact that he was smothered in oil, something which was to cause a certain amount of controversy in the press later on.

The atmosphere in the Palais des Sports was electric, and Mac, though claiming that he wasn't really nervous, did admit later that his keenness to do well probably resulted in a state of over-anxiety, which wasn't calculated to put him in the right frame of mind for the very difficult job he was faced with.

Both men began cautiously, with McAvoy flicking out a few probing left leads as he sized his man up and tried to decide on the best way to set about opening up the champion's defence. It was not going to be easy, for Thil fought out of a very low crouch, chin well down and with almost none of his body exposed.

In the first two rounds the Frenchman did very little. His attitude seemed to be, 'Right, I've got the title. It's up to you to see if you can take it from me.'

McAvoy was now beginning to loosen up, and made up his mind to try for an early knockout. A few more sharp left jabs, a feint, and he got a glimpse of Thil's chin. Over came the right cross, but Thil saw it coming and ducked. The blow, with all of McAvoy's considerable power behind it, landed solidly on the Frenchman's rock-hard cranium. Thil didn't even blink, but Mac winced. He knew at once that some damage had been done. The hand which had given him so much trouble earlier in his career, and which had stood up under the force of all those devastating knockouts, had gone again. Mac was in trouble and knew it. Thil, however, was quite unaware that his opponent was now carrying a serious injury and Mac was determined not to make it apparent.

Despite the problem the challenger was well on top. In the third a beautifully delivered left hook sent Thil staggering back against the ropes, but as Mac followed up the crafty Frenchman managed to duck and weave his way out of trouble. In the following round McAvoy continued to be the aggressor, opening up a cut over Thil's left eye. Then, forgetting all about the injury to his right hand, Mac let the champion have it flush on the chin. At once he was in severe pain again, but Thil showed no reaction whatsoever and kept on plodding forward.

Having sampled McAvoy's best shots, Thil knew he could afford to take chances, and from the fifth onwards he proceeded to get in close and hammer away to the body. Mac now discovered just how powerful the squat Frenchman was. Though admittedly not at his best, the British champion was finding Thil a very rough handful indeed. Like Mac himself, he was as strong as an ox. Though unspectacular, and by no means a one punch K.O. artist, Thil carried a hefty dig in either hand and was as tough as teak.

McAvoy's only hope now was to try to keep the fight at long range. The Rochdale man was much more than just a slugger. He was fast and could box, but while he occasionally adopted these tactics and scored well with the left hand, he was too often drawn into rugged close quarter exchanges where Thil was clearly the master. The Frenchman's body attack was absolutely devastating that night, and the tremendous din set up by the partisan crowd easily drowned the shouts of the tiny band of loyal British fans, as Thil punished the challenger unmercifully.

For once McAvoy was being beaten at his own game as Thil sank them into the body, and the champion was not particular whether they landed above the belt or below it. Neither, it seemed, was the Swiss referee, Monsieur Devernaz, who had warned him about low punching early in the fight, for though Thil persisted with these foul tactics, which got much worse as the fight progressed and the action became more fierce, he was never spoken to again.

Between rounds Thil's body was liberally rubbed down with oil, which made him as slippery as an eel in the clinches and caused some consternation in McAvoy's corner, although it did not appear to infringe the rules.

There was no let-up as they belted away at each other for round after round, with the fans shouting themselves hoarse. First one would appear to be getting on top, then the other, but gradually it became clear that McAvoy was being slowly but surely worn down by the sheer brute strength of the balding Frenchman, whose stamina was amazing, considering his age.

From time to time McAvoy would set himself and land a solid blow flush on the champion's chin, but Thil just kept coming on. He seemed to be made of granite and always hit back with his own strength-sapping body punches.

In the closing rounds they just stood and punched it out toe to toe, McAvoy forgetting about his damaged hand as he tried desperately to pull the fight out of the fire. In any case it was now so numb that he could hardly feel it.

In the fourteenth Mac gambled everything on the punch which had put so many of his opponents out for the count, letting go with a tremendous uppercut as Thil again pressed forward. But the Frenchman neatly evaded the punch and dug a hefty right into McAvoy's body which appeared to land very low indeed. Down he went as his corner yelled foul. But there was no warning from the referee, and Mac was up at four to be met by another fusillade of vicious body punches as Thil moved in for the kill. Mac fought back pluckily but was soon on the canvas again. Fleming, intent on claiming the fight on a foul, yelled for McAvoy to stay down, but pride would not allow it, and up he struggled to face another murderous assault. But as the blows thudded into his aching ribs the bell rang to end the round, undoubtedly saving Mac from being floored again.

How McAvoy survived the last round was something of a miracle, but survive it he did, fighting back gamely and even catching the champion with some good shots of his own. But Thil was well on top and going as strongly as he had at the start of the contest, which was indeed a tribute to his remarkable condition.

There was no doubt as to the winner. Though McAvoy had put up an exceptionally gallant performance he had been well beaten, and readily acknowledged that Thil deserved the verdict.

A very disappointed McAvoy left Paris the following day with his manager and trainer, flying from Le Bourget to Croydon. Arriving in Manchester by train in the early evening, the defeated British champion was met by his wife and children plus an excited throng of boxing fans. After talking to the press, the family were driven by car to Rochdale, where they were met in Manchester Road by the band of St. Patrick's, which, striking up a lively tune, proceeded to march in front of the car as it slowly made its way towards the town centre, hundreds of people joining in the procession along the route. Outside the Brunswick Hotel Mac was hoisted shoulder high amid rousing cheers and deposited on the steps of the pub, then bombarded with questions.

Hugging his wife, he turned and put his arm around his mother, and asked her, 'How about some grub Mam? I only had one decent meal all the time I was in France, and that was after the fight.'

Mac showed his swollen hands to a reporter. Both were in a bad way, especially the right one.

'In this country,' said Mac, 'boxers are allowed to strap up their hands with adhesive tape for strengthening purposes. But on the Continent only ordinary soft tape can be used, and this is practically useless. He felt that he had scored well with his left at long range, but admitted that Thil was exceedingly strong with his body punching and had had the better of the in-fighting. Mac also mentioned that he'd been hit low on at least half a dozen occasions, and felt that if given a return he could reverse the decision. While mentioning the low blows McAvoy was at pains to point out that he was not making any excuses. In fact he had nothing but praise for Thil's performance, but not everyone was so magnanimous. Mr W. Barrington-Dalby had actually scored the fight in McAvoy's favour, and been heavily criticised for it on the Continent. Now, in a letter published in the press, he explained at great length just why he had been at such variance with his fellow judges, a Frenchman, and the Swiss referee. The gist of Barrington-Dalby's argument was that in his opinion a significant number of Thil's punches had not been delivered with the knuckle part of the glove, that he had lain on his man to an unnecessary extent, held Mac's left arm under his right while hitting with the other hand, and punched McAvoy a number of times below the belt. A few short extracts from letters published in answer to Barrington-Dalby's, would seem to clearly indicate that he was very much in the minority in his judgment that Thil had not won on merit:

'The wild statements in the British press regarding Thil's tactics, are, to say the least, very bad form.'

'All who saw the fight will agree that M. Devernaz has few equals and no superiors in this country.'

'The very fact that Thil has never been disqualified in his long career is proof of his clean tactics.'

'Though the Rochdale fighter was dead game, he was well and truly beaten by a worthy champion, who must surely be the most destructive body puncher since the days of Frank Klaus and Billy Papke.'

'McAvoy's inability to keep the French veteran at long range was a vital factor in his defeat, while the physical condition of Thil was a thing to be marvelled at.'

'McAvoy gave a very plucky display and may do better next time, but it might be wiser to let Anno Domini take further toll of Monsieur Thil before crossing gloves with him again.'

Despite the obvious merit in Barrington-Dalby's arguments it would appear that McAvoy had been well beaten on the night. Nevertheless he had put up a magnificent performance in a fight which had thrilled the massive crowd of over 21,000.

Jeff Dickson was naturally delighted, and stated that it was without doubt the greatest contest he had staged in eleven years as a promoter.

# Chapter 17

## Lumiansky

Dave Lumiansky first came to this country with 'Panama' Al Brown. He was the typical American fight manager, in style, if not in appearance. Bespectacled, and very conservative in dress, he was, nonetheless, a slick, smooth talking, extremely plausible character. An old acquaintance of Norman Hurst, Lumiansky began to be seen around Belle Vue quite a bit, and when Jackie Brown's contract came to an end in 1935 he was introduced to Lumiansky by Hurst, as also was McAvoy, whose own contract was due to run out later that year.

It was quite obvious that Hurst had big plans, in which Lumiansky, who claimed to have influential connections on the American fight scene, would play a big part. Both Brown and McAvoy were very impressed by the silver tongued American, and Jackie soon agreed to let Lumiansky handle his affairs. It was also agreed in principal that McAvoy would follow suit once his contract with Harry Fleming had run out. Fleming would continue to supervise his training, and while Lumiansky and also Harry Levene, acting as McAvoy's London agent, would be in for a cut, the man pulling the strings would still be Norman Hurst.

By far the worst aspect of the Paris trip had been the fact that he was again in trouble with his hands, especially the right, though the left was also sore and swollen. Something would certainly have to be done, or his career might well be in jeopardy. First though, it was decided that the best plan would be for Mac to take things easy for a few weeks while the swellings reduced. Apparently, Harry Fleming considered himself to be something of an expert on this type of injury. He certainly had the experience, but if the problem turned out to be beyond him, then obviously, an orthopaedic specialist's advice would have to be sought.

In the meantime, Mac was due in court at Liverpool Assizes, where he faced a charge of slander brought by one Henry Solomon Lipson, of Wavertree, Liverpool.

The previous August, on the racecourse at Squires Gate, Blackpool, Lipson, a bookmaker, had got into a dispute with McAvoy regarding a bet, the boxer accusing the bookie of being 'a Welsher' in the presence of a number of other people. Considering Mac's violent temper it would appear that Lipson was very fortunate that only words were exchanged.

At any rate, the bookie was now claiming damages, and Mac, on the advice of his counsel, reluctantly agreed to withdraw his remarks and apologise to the plaintiff, though he was still obliged to pay agreed damages and costs.

A couple of months later he was in hot water again. With the hands feeling a lot better he was back in training for a forthcoming contest against Spaniard Garcia Lluch, at Belle Vue. He was spending much of his leisure time hunting on the moors and one day drove up into Yorkshire with a friend named Bill Barnes and a couple of greyhounds. Mac stopped near Skipton and let the dogs out. Then he and Barnes followed as the animals bounded off over the fields. Whether they knew it or not they were on private land and had been spotted by a gamekeeper who soon confronted them. The police had already been sent for and a constable quickly arrived on the scene.

Shortly afterwards, before Skipton Magistrates, they were accused of game trespass on land at Coniston Cold. McAvoy explained that he had only stopped to exercise the dogs and also himself, as he was in training for a fight. When asked how he had been dressed at the time he had no option but to admit he was wearing a lounge suit, which must have struck the magistrates as rather inappropriate attire for a training run. This, coupled with the fact that he had also carried a gun, resulted in the defendants being found guilty and fined 20 shillings each, with costs.

A few days later McAvoy went into the ring against Lluch saying that he felt a bit under the weather. He was sluggish in his movements and well below his best. Though far superior to the Spaniard, he was unable to put him away and had to be content with a points win over twelve rounds.

The title defence against Al Burke was next on the agenda, Belle Vue having finally won the right to stage the contest a month after the Lluch fight. However, because of damage to a wrist, sustained in training, it became necessary to seek a postponement, the new date agreed being June 24th.

Though Burke was not considered too much of a threat, it was claimed that he had improved out of all recognition since their last meeting. He was now Southern Area Middleweight Champion and had been training in excellent company at The Ring Gymnasium in London.

McAvoy returned once more to the pure country air of Hollingworth Lake and soon recovered from the injury to his wrist. When questioned about his hands he said he was certain that they were now quite sound and that he was punching harder than for a long time. Mac did admit at a later date though, that this was not the case. His left hand, the least troublesome, was probably back to normal, but obviously there was still a question mark against the right, for he failed to produce his usual brand of dynamic punching against Burke and was again taken the full route.

Before the weigh-in, yet another problem arose when the doctor noticed that McAvoy's left eye was bloodshot and watery. This had apparently been caused by an accident in training, when a thumb had been poked in the eye. Mac assured the doctor that it was not bothering him and no action was taken. Burke, of course, was unaware that McAvoy was not a hundred per cent fit and seemed intent on adopting safety first tactics from the start. After throwing a left lead he would duck to his right and grab hold of Mac, hanging on grimly until the referee intervened. Mac was relying almost entirely on his left jab, occasionally following up with a hook, while Burke, when he wasn't holding, showed a good defence and was very quick on his feet. It was quite obvious to the spectators that if he had been more adventurous he might easily have given Mac plenty of trouble.

The first bit of excitement came in the fourth round, when, after a burst of fierce hitting by McAvoy, Burke appeared to wobble. But as Mac moved in to finish him off Burke suddenly straightened up and belted the champion hard on the chin, following up with more stinging blows to the head as Mac was forced to give ground. Recovering quickly from the shock, McAvoy hit back, and the two battled away in the centre of the ring as the spectators roared their encouragement, the sound of the bell being all but drowned by the pandemonium in the hall.

When McAvoy came out for the start of the sixth a swelling was plainly visible by the side of his right eye, which seemed to be in danger of closing as it had in the Phillips fight. But between rounds Fleming worked hard on it, with the result that the injury got no worse and caused Mac very little inconvenience for the remainder of the contest, although he was troubled by the bloodshot left eye, which continued to run, causing blurred vision.

Mac was always the aggressor and used the left hand to concentrate on his opponent's body, though Burke managed to nullify many of his punches by judicious use of the arms and elbows.

Apart from some fierce toe to toe hitting in the twelfth round there was very little to get excited about, and Mac ran out a comfortable winner, while Burke seemed quite happy to have lasted the distance.

McAvoy now owned a Lonsdale belt outright, having put three notches on it by beating Harvey, then defending it twice. His main aim though, was still a World title, and an offer was made to bring Thil to England, but the French showed little interest.

In America the position had changed very little, in spite of the fact that Teddy Yarosz had got himself K.O. 'd for the first time in his career by the then unknown Eddie 'Babe' Risko. The title had not been at stake, however, so Yarosz was still champion and therefore a target for McAvoy.

Waiting around for something to develop, Mac set about spending some of his hard-earned money, buying several horses and taking over the Royal Hunt Stables at Syke, Rochdale. In the spring of that year he moved into Strathmore, a compact, detached house at Milnrow, not far from Hollingworth Lake, while still retaining the tenancy of the Brunswick Hotel. He did not remain very long at Strathmore, however, later moving to Park Hill, Regent Street, not far from where he had been brought up.

Apart from his boxing exploits, Mac was again in the news twice that year, both as villain and hero.

At Bolton-by-Bowland he was fined five pounds twelve shillings, including costs, with the alternative of two months imprisonment, for shooting rabbits on private land.

Accompanied by two companions, he was stopped by a gamekeeper and a farm bailiff, who, after taking down the car number, demanded to know their names.

'You've got the number of my car,' Mac told him. 'I'm Jock McAvoy, the boxer.'

His companions gave their names as Mickey McGuire and Jack Johnson, both of which turned out to be fictitious, and when the gamekeeper refused to accept a bribe of ten shillings, offered by 'McGuire', McAvoy challenged the two men to fight him for the rabbits, and said, 'I'll fight the pair of you on my knees.'

The other incident, which concerned a runaway horse, showed the boxer up in a much better light. As McAvoy was driving along Manchester Road, Rochdale, he was overtaken by a driverless horse attached to a milkfloat, which had obviously bolted and was very frightened.

Rochdale's man of action didn't think twice. He simply put his foot on the accelerator, overtook the runaway, stopping about fifty yards ahead of it, and leapt out of the car. Still the horse thundered on, travelling at tremendous speed as it approached him. Mac didn't hesitate for a second. He just hurled himself at its head and grabbed the bridle, and though being dragged for some distance he eventually managed to bring the terrified animal to a halt and calm it down.

It was a busy time of the day, with plenty of traffic on the road, and there is no doubt that McAvoy's prompt and courageous action probably averted a serious accident.

At the next meeting of the town's Watch Committee, McAvoy was commended for his bravery and awarded a gratuity of two guineas, which, at Mac's suggestion, was forwarded to the local Buckley Hall Orphanage.

After his contest with Al Burke, Mac paid three visits to a London specialist for treatment to his right hand, and by the autumn it felt good again. A date was therefore arranged for Belle Vue in October, when he would meet Marcel Lauriot, Light-heavyweight Champion of France. In the meantime his contract with Harry Fleming had expired and plans were afoot for him to visit America with Lumiansky.

Lauriot was a good class fighter. He had not long before beaten the coloured American, Jimmy Tarante, and also gone the distance with Len Harvey, losing on points.

McAvoy experienced no hand problems in training and was in splendid form during a session held for the benefit of the press at Hollingworth Lake. His work on the heavy bag indicated that he was again punching his full weight with both hands, while he was extremely sharp when sparring with Jack Lord and Fred Shaw, the latter going down from a perfectly delivered left hook and being unable to continue.

Mac had Lauriot on the canvas as early as the second round, a left to be body followed by a right uppercut setting him up for the left hook which put him down for a count of eight. On rising he was met by a hail of punches, mostly to the body, and did very well to survive until the end of the round.

The Frenchman, however, recovered very well during the minute's interval and came out for round two as fresh as a daisy, forcing the action and catching McAvoy with a hard left hook to the ribs. This stung Mac into instant retaliation and he again punished Lauriot severely about the body. He also revealed some neat defensive skills, cleverly evading Lauriot's blows before coming back with quick bursts of counter punching.

The middle rounds were spoiled by too much clinching, but in the tenth Lauriot was down again from a right to the jaw. After taking an eight count he was put under heavy pressure, with Mac hammering away to the body, but managed to last out the round.

It had become obvious that either the Frenchman was exceptionally durable or McAvoy's right hand was still suspect, for he now abandoned all efforts to knock his man out and concentrated on piling up the points by means of speedy left hand work, running out a comfortable winner.

Afterwards McAvoy confirmed that his right hand had let him down again. As plans for the American trip were well advanced it was decided to allow a period of rest followed by further treatment. They were not due to depart for over a month, and Lumiansky was confident that all would be well. When McAvoy expressed his doubts Lumiansky assured him that it was not his intention to put him into the ring immediately on arrival in any case. He would have plenty of time to settle in over there and get acclimatised before going into training at one of New York's gyms.

It was during the summer of 1935 that McAvoy had first become interested in Joan Lye. Both were horse lovers, and it appears more than likely that their paths first crossed soon after Mac took over the riding stables at Syke, which is quite close to Healey, where Joan lived.

Joan Lye came from an extremely wealthy family, and at twenty-three was one of the most eligible young ladies in Rochdale. Both her father and uncle, after humble beginnings, became directors and major shareholders in the giant textile business of John Bright & Brothers. Joan's father, James, who was some years younger than his brother, married twice and had a large family, while her uncle Frederick became one of the richest men in the district and probably the greatest public benefactor in the town's history.

In 1872, when he was twelve years old, Frederick Lye began work in the grocery department of the Pioneers' Co-operative Society, later entering the offices at John Bright's, a firm he was to serve for over fifty years. An ardent admirer of Bright, one of his most vivid recollections as a young man was of being called in to witness the great statesman's will in 1878.

Frederick rose from the position of junior clerk to become vice-chairman of the company. After retiring from business he devoted a substantial part of his wealth to the benefit of the town, buying up huge tracts of lush green farmland, in total some one hundred and fifty acres, and dedicating it, in perpetuity, to the people of Rochdale, and in particular the youth of the town, for most of it is now parkland and playing fields.

Joan, like her illustrious uncle, was an outdoor type, quite pretty and possessed of the sort of self confidence and poise that comes naturally to a girl of her background. To a young man from the other side of the tracks she represented 'real class', and Mac must have been somewhat flattered at the interest she showed in him. He was by now quite famous, and in addition was tall, husky and ruggedly handsome. There can be little doubt that they hit it off from the start, in the first instance through their common interest in horses, but the fact that their backgrounds were so dissimilar quite clearly fuelled their obvious fascination for each other.

Before long Joan was visiting the stables regularly, and the two of them were often seen out riding together. So began an association which would have far reaching consequences, and a disruptive effect on their lives as well as those around them.

If Eliza suspected anything in the early stages of their association she probably said nothing about it. With a man of McAvoy's temperament she would have had to tread very carefully. In any case it was nothing new for her husband to be involved with other women, he was well known for it. But that was something Eliza had learned to live with, having now accepted that he would never change. Normally she did not worry too much, for most of Mac's clandestine affairs were usually short lived. Eliza was not to know that this relationship with Joan Lye would turn out to be something quite different.

# Chapter 18

## 'Another Hurricane Hits Our Shores'

Early in November 1935 McAvoy and his new business manager arrived in America. Mac was quite taken aback by the sheer size and bustling activity of New York City. It seemed just like all those movies he had watched in the front stalls of the Pavilion Cinema back home in Rochdale, with Damon Runyan-style characters talking out of the sides of their mouths and calling you 'Buddy'.

He was still somewhat unsure about the right hand. For although it felt sound enough it had not been given a real test since his last contest several weeks before. Lumiansky, however, bright and breezy as always, told him to 'quit worrying'. Mac was assured that if he experienced any problems while in the States they would soon be taken care of, as the Americans possessed far more know-how when it came to dealing with such injuries than did their counterparts in Britain. What Lumiansky really meant was, 'Don't worry kid. If anything goes wrong we'll get by somehow.'

Mac trained at the Pioneer Gym, and though the place was vast, he was amazed at the number of people they packed into it. There were several rings, and the gym was in full swing from morning till night. Apart from the fighters, their managers and trainers, a motley assortment of newspapermen, gangster-types and hangers-on were always in evidence, and the air was dense with tobacco smoke mingled with the acrid smell of sweat and liniment.

There was no shortage of sparring partners here, but far from being lambs to the slaughter, they were all out to give the Limey a run for his money and show him how tough they were. This suited McAvoy down to the ground. For whatever Mac's other shortcomings he was afraid of nobody and took everything they could throw at him, paying them back with interest.

The hardbitten newspaper boys around the ringside were pleasantly surprised at the way the Englishman shaped up, but would reserve their judgement until they'd seen him in a real fight, or 'when the chips were down', which was to be at the end of the month, when he would square off against leading light-heavyweight contender, Al McCoy. It was not perhaps the wisest match Lumiansky could have made, for McAvoy had gone to America with the clear understanding that a Middleweight title fight was their aim, Lumiansky having glibly assured him that with his connections it would be 'a cinch'.

True, Mac had fought for the European Light-heavyweight title, but he was nowhere near 12st. 7lbs. Getting down to the middleweight limit presented no real problems. As far as Lumiansky was concerned it was clear that one division was as good as another if there was any possibility of a title fight, and he was well aware that a win over McCoy would almost certainly open the door to a crack at John Henry Lewis, who had become champion only a few weeks before by beating Bob Olin.

McCoy, a French-Canadian, was twenty-two, taller than Mac, and at least half a stone heavier. Prior to their meeting he had disposed of a long string of contenders, including Joe Knight, Lou Brouillard, Al Gainer, Billy Jones, Joe Kaminsky, Sammy Slaughter, Lee Salvas and Charley Eagle, and apart from former champion Maxie Rosenbloom, was considered the most formidable challenger to John Henry Lewis.

A few days after arriving in New York, McAvoy got the thrill of his life when he was taken to Jack Dempsey's restaurant on Broadway and introduced to the great man himself. Dempsey had always been Mac's hero and the fighter he had tried most to model himself on. Meeting the old 'Manassa Mauler' in the flesh was one of the most exciting things to happen on the trip, in a day he would never forget. He also made the acquaintance of the legendary James J. Johnston, who ran the boxing at Madison Square Garden. Johnston, a Liverpudlian, was one of the most colourful figures on the American fight scene.

On November 20th, just nine days before the McCoy fight, Eliza Bamford received a telegram from New York which read simply:

'Arranging for you to come over. Be ready – Joe'.

Later that week a further message came through from Dave Lumiansky, which read: 'Everything arranged. Come at once'.

Eliza was soon on her way to London by train on the first stage of her long journey, the children being left in the care of their grandparents.

It was suggested at the time that McAvoy was homesick and wanted his wife beside him, and Eliza backed this up by stating that she had received over a dozen letters from him since his departure for America. There appears, however, to be something odd about this. It's possible, of course, that Mac may well have been homesick, but bearing in mind the short time he'd been away, for Eliza to have received over a dozen letters, even allowing for a little exaggeration, he would have had to be averaging practically one a day. Mac does not strike one as the letter-writing type at all. He might have managed the odd line or two, but it's very doubtful that he could have been quite as prolific with the pen as Eliza wished people to believe. She was certainly very much in love with her husband and quite willing to drop everything at short notice and travel three thousand miles to be at his side. But did Mac really send for her, or was Dave Lumiansky behind it? It has been suggested that Mac was becoming a bit too interested in one or two of the girls Lumiansky liked to surround himself with, and as the manager considered this bad news for a fighter in training, he arranged for Eliza to go out there in order to keep him in line. This could well have been the case, for, as one old mate of Mac's has stated quite bluntly, 'What? Joe send for the wife? No chance!'

Whatever the truth, Eliza duly arrived in New York, and by all accounts Mac was genuinely pleased to see her. But one can't help feeling sorry for Eliza, for it is a fact that he was at that time receiving letters from Joan Lye and also talking to her long distance on the telephone practically every day.

The match with McCoy was made at 171lbs, or 12st. 3lbs, and Al, whose handlers had obviously not paid quite enough attention to detail, was found to be overweight on the morning of the fight. As a consequence McCoy was obliged to sweat if off and was just on the weight when he came to the scales at two o'clock that afternoon. McAvoy was well inside and had no problems, apart from that nagging doubt about his hand. Though Mac had constantly expressed his concern to Lumiansky, Dave just kept on putting him off, but finally told him that the suspect hand would be treated just prior to him going into the ring, and he could rest assured that it would give him no pain during the contest.

While Mac was getting stripped for action, Lumiansky entered the dressing room accompanied by another man whom he introduced as a doctor. The 'doctor' carried a bag, and produced from it a hypodermic syringe, the size of which caused Mac to become somewhat apprehensive. After filling this up he told McAvoy to lay his hand down on the rubbing table, then proceeded to administer the injection between each knuckle, but had barely begun when Mac passed out and was grabbed by his handlers before he hit the floor.

After coming to, he felt sick and dizzy, and in no shape to go into the ring. But after being walked up and down the dressing room for a while his head began to clear and he felt a lot better. A couple of rounds of shadow boxing and he was ready. Lumiansky, who had panicked a bit, was very relieved and asked McAvoy how the hand felt. Mac said he couldn't feel a thing. His fist felt just like a lump of stone. 'Good,' said Lumiansky. 'Let's get out there and hit him with it.'

Mac did just that, and McCoy, who had been installed a slight favourite, was not only surprised at the power of McAvoy's punching, but also at the great variety of jabs, hooks and crosses with which McAvoy peppered him in the opening round. Without waiting to see what McCoy had to offer Mac took the initiative from the start, storming in, never allowing the Canadian to settle and landing with great speed and accuracy.

McAvoy's performance clearly thrilled the cynical Garden fight fans, who, instead of the correct upright stance they were used to seeing from British fighters, were treated to the unlikely spectacle of a 'Limey' who fought in true American style.

Nat Fleischer, editor of *The Ring* magazine and the doyen of American boxing writers, said that McAvoy had 'the crouch of Jim Jeffries, the speed of Jim Driscoll, the sharp-shooting of Jack Johnson and the weaving style of Jack Dempsey.'

What a performance Mac gave that night. For the first three rounds he hit McCoy with every punch in the book, before putting him down with a terrific right hander flush on the chin. He was up at four, and though Mac cut loose with both hands the Canadian managed to hang on until the bell came to his rescue.

In the fourth McCoy was down from a slip, and on rising used his height and reach advantage to keep Mac at bay, coming more into the fight as the round neared its end. In the middle rounds McAvoy dug some hefty hooks into the Canadian's ribs. His right hand felt great. He found that he could bang as hard as he liked with it and not feel a thing. It was like hitting somebody with a club, and McCoy must have been pretty tough to stand up to the battering he was taking. By the seventh, however, the novocaine was beginning to wear off and

Mac could feel the odd twinge when he landed. McCoy was getting stronger, and with McAvoy being forced to rely almost entirely on his left hand, the Canadian took the last two rounds comfortably.

But Mac was well ahead at the finish, and was loudly applauded as his hand was raised by referee Arthur Donovan. He had treated the Yanks to a great display of box-fighting and clearly convinced them that here was a Limey who was no mug and could really fight.

Back at the hotel, Eliza, listening to the fight on the radio, was absolutely thrilled, and immediately got into a taxi which sped her to The Garden. On arriving she was so excited that she dashed inside, forgetting to pay the driver, who had to follow her to get his fare.

Lumiansky was delighted. Next day they received the first of a shoal of offers for fights all over the United States, including one of two thousand, five hundred dollars for a return with McCoy. But although the money was tempting there was no point in going over the same ground twice.

The New York boxing scribes went overboard as far as McAvoy was concerned, the sports pages being packed with comment and quotes from leading figures in the fight game.

The *New York Daily News* described Mac as, 'A little middle-weight from London with the amazing habit of gnawing at his own gloves between punches, who showed the fans over at Madison Square Garden last night just how British fighters do battle.'

'Another Hurricane Hits Our Shores' was the *New York World Telegraph*'s headline, going on to say:

'Ever since Lord Cornwallis blew a costly duke at Yorktown the inhabitants of this region have been prone to regard the fauna of England as highly innocuous once the gage of battle is thrown down. But the law of averages catches up with us all. It certainly caught up with Al McCoy last night when he took a terrific drubbing from a bloomin' limey, who jolly well punched his ruddy head off. The Limey's name is Jock McAvoy, and he's very, very good.'

'At last Johnny Bull ships us a bloke who can and does fight,' said the *New York Evening Journal*. 'Jock McAvoy is the best English fighter to drop in since the day smiling Jem Driscoll came to electrify us.'

Jack Dempsey had this to say: 'Jock McAvoy is the greatest British fighter I've seen in twenty years. We want more like him in America.'

Joe Jacobs, manager of German heavyweight, Max Schmeling, said that: 'McAvoy is the best that England has ever sent us.' While Nat Fleischer stated that McAvoy would be his choice to take both the Middle and Light-heavyweight titles.'

Al McCoy, though readily admitting that Mac was a fine fighter, claimed that having to take off weight had seriously affected his chances.

Interviewed by English pressmen, Mac told them, 'Tell Lancashire, and Rochdale in particular, that I'm glad I did the trick for the old country. I like it here, because they let you go in and fight. The people are fine and have done their best to help me. I was on the heavy side and would've been faster if I'd been a bit lighter. I'll be better for my next fight, and the sooner I can get a crack at the middleweight title that Babe Risko claims, or tackle John Henry Lewis, the sooner I'll be bringing a world title home.'

Despite making the above statement, Mac insisted later that he was never interested in tangling with light-heavyweights, and that his sole aim had been to fight Risko. Of course, it should have been, but flushed with success and reading in the newspapers that after beating McCoy he was now entitled to a shot at John Henry Lewis's crown, Mac was quite happy to go along with Lumiansky, who was ready to make a deal with either one of them or both.

Not satisfied with that, the McAvoy camp also put it about that they were claiming the British Light-heavyweight title, officially held by Eddie Phillips, simply because Phillips was fighting heavyweights and was well over 12st. 7lbs. They even went so far as to issue a challenge to Jack Petersen to defend the British Heavyweight title he had won back from Len Harvey, against Mac.

Of course, Lumiansky was behind all this, but there is no evidence to show that Mac was against it. Phillips, who had won his title by outpointing Tommy Farr after Harvey relinquished it, was quite outraged and immediately let it be known that he had no intention of giving up his hard won laurels.

'I can make 12st. 7lbs quite easily,' he told the press. 'If McAvoy wants the title he'll have to fight for it as I did, not just claim it. And I'm quite willing to defend against him at any time, for any amount.'

Defending McAvoy's action, Harry Fleming told the press: 'McAvoy has fought for every honour he's gained, and would not want a title without winning it in the ring. He was under the impression that Phillips had entered the heavyweight division, and as he's already beaten most of the light-heavies in Britain, he obviously thought he had the right to register his claim.'

Throughout all this Lumiansky was talking to Risko's connections, and after some tough negotiating Mac was delighted to be told that the fight had been arranged for December 20th, just three weeks after his win over McCoy. The British champion was soon brought down to earth, however, when he learned that the title would not be at stake.

Though this may seem unfair, exactly the same thing had happened to Risko when he was paired with the previous title holder, Teddy Yarosz, their first encounter being an over-the-weight match which Risko won on a knockout. He later took the title by beating Yarosz on points.

If McAvoy managed to win, of course, he would certainly be entitled to a return with the title at stake, but having seen how poorly Len Harvey had performed in America, knowing that Len was on a par with McAvoy, and also taking into account the fact that Mac had been defeated by Marcel Thil, Risko's handlers were confident that the Englishman would not present too many problems for their boy.

Eddie Risko, a handsome twenty-three year old Polish-American ex-coalminer from Syracuse, had been almost unknown before his sensational knockout win over Teddy Yarosz the previous January.

After joining the U.S. Navy, Risko, real name Henry Pylkowsky, had won the Middleweight Championship of the Atlantic Fleet in 1931 and 1933, and had boxed in seaports all over the world before turning pro.

McAvoy was fortunate in getting the opportunity to see Risko in action, when Eddie outpointed tough Canadian Frank Battaglia in Philadelphia just a couple of weeks before he was due to face Mac. This sneak preview proved invaluable when the British champion got down to mapping out his plan of action.

After the briefest of rests Mac again went into full training. Getting his first American fight under his belt had made him feel more relaxed and confident, but after building up for the McCoy fight he now needed to shed a few pounds and went on a special diet, cutting out all fried foods and eating a lot of fish and lean meat. He would start the day with a glass of orange juice before taking to the streets for his morning run. At 10-30 he would sit down to a breakfast of bran, four or five boiled eggs and piles of buttered toast and coffee. There was no lunch, but after leaving the gym at 4-30 he would eat dinner at six. This usually consisted of tomato juice, thick soup, and either fish, chops, or a big grilled steak and a large helping of bread and butter.

In the evening he would usually visit a cinema or theatre with Eliza, and on returning to the hotel would have a sandwich and a cup of coffee before retiring.

The above diet does not strike one as being particularly conducive to losing weight, especially the large helpings of bread and butter. But this was obviously a delicacy Mac found difficult to resist, for as a child in Rochdale it would certainly have been an essential part of his diet – along with fish and chips, of course.

However, all was going well, with Mac aiming to weigh-in at around 11st. 11lbs. The big problem was still that right hand. In punching so hard with it in its 'frozen' state against McCoy, he had aggravated the injury, and was now forced to use it very sparingly in training, without, of course, making this too obvious.

The weather in New York deteriorated rapidly as December 20th drew near, with the temperature plummeting and heavy snow covering the streets. Coming from the North of England, McAvoy was quite used to the cold, but that December New York was experiencing one of its bitterest winters and seemed more like the Arctic Circle.

A few days before the fight Mac got a slight chill and developed a touch of bronchitis. It was not severe, but hampered his training to some extent, Lumiansky letting it be known later that Mac had actually spent two days in bed.

On fight night the atrocious weather was responsible for keeping the gate down, but this didn't worry Mac. He was just in there to do the job as quickly as possible. He had no option really, for after the experience of his last fight he was fully aware that the effects of the novocaine injections he had just received in the dressing room would have worn off long before the contest had gone the scheduled twelve rounds.

Mac stood in his corner, gnawing away at the thumbs of his gloves as the bell clanged to send the fighters on their way. Immediately he was across the ring, and before Risko had a chance to get set a tremendous right landed flush on his chin and down he went. More shocked than hurt, the middleweight champion scrambled to his feet almost before the referee had begun his count. Mac moved in on him like a tornado and subjected Risko to a real pasting as the crowd went wild.

In desperation the champion grabbed hold of McAvoy and tried to hold on, but Mac broke free and put his man down again with a perfectly delivered left and right to the jaw. This time Risko was up at seven, but in a very bad way and took a fearful hammering as Mac went all out to finish him. Risko, dead game, refused to go down, as Mac, snorting and snarling, chased him around the ring. But there was just nowhere to hide and it had now become a massacre, for the champion was practically out on his feet, taking punch after punch without reply, a sitting target for McAvoy's pulverizing blows. Another right to the jaw and he was down again, but pluckily dragged himself upright, battered and bleeding, at five. Knocked down yet again, he once more regained his feet after another five count. Mac now delivered a vicious combination of lefts and rights to the head, and as Risko slumped to the canvas he was sure it was all over. But astonishingly, the courageous champion somehow staggered to his feet as the count reached eight. He was in a pathetic state and one more booming right was enough to put him down for keeps. Yet amazingly, considering the punishment he had taken, Risko was still conscious and just sat there in the centre of the ring, totally incapable of climbing to his feet again, as the referee counted him out.

The Garden fans were almost hysterical. They could hardly believe what they had just witnessed. Even McAvoy's highly impressive performance against McCoy had been nothing compared to this. The World's Middleweight Champion hadn't just been beaten – he'd been annihilated, and had not managed to get in one worthwhile punch of his own. He had been put down no less than six times in a fight that had lasted only 2 minutes-48 seconds, including the count.

It was a triumph, not only for McAvoy, but for British boxing. From this day on Jock McAvoy's name would be mentioned in the same breath as those of Ted 'Kid' Lewis, Owen Moran, Jim Driscoll, Jack 'Kid' Berg and Bob Fitzsimmons, all-time greats who had taken America by storm. Now the tough guy from Rochdale had done the same. He had disposed of the World Champion in one round, and in the most convincing manner possible. It was a great pity that the title had not been at stake.

Later, in a nightclub, McAvoy, Lumiansky and company ran into Risko's party. They didn't seem too friendly when Lumiansky went over to speak to them, and after what appeared to be a heated discussion Lumiansky came back and told McAvoy that they wanted a return.

Naturally he had insisted on a title fight, but said he had not received any definite assurance on this point. The Risko camp simply wanted a return so that Eddie could have the opportunity to get his revenge. They did not see any point in discussing the middleweight title, insisting that there was clearly no chance of McAvoy making 11st. 6lbs. Lumiansky, of course, refuted this, explaining that Mac's bronchial trouble had interfered with his final preparations and resulted in his coming in rather heavier than had been the intention.

In giving his own version at a later date McAvoy wrote: 'But for being a pound or two over the weight I might have been the proudest man in the world.' Meaning, of course, that after knocking out the champion he would have claimed the title. The truth, however, is that Mac was actually 8½lbs over the weight, having tipped the scales at 12st. 0½lbs.

McAvoy also stated later that 'the weight was fixed at well over the middleweight limit in order to protect Risko's title.' But Risko scaled only 11st. 7½lbs. So, in ensuring that the title was protected, it would appear that Gabe Genovese, Risko's manager, had also made something of a blunder, for with Mac coming in at such a poundage Genovese had put his man in the position of having to give away half a stone to the murderous hitting Englishman.

The people behind Genovese, having satisfied themselves that the title was not at risk, had obviously left the details to the manager, and he was the one responsible for placing Risko at such a grave disadvantage.

At least they could console themselves in the knowledge that Risko still held the title, but their attitude appeared to be that they had in some way been double-crossed. And though they obviously felt that with both men at around the same weight there was every chance that Risko could reverse the decision, they were still not prepared to risk losing their grip on the title, preferring instead to insist that McAvoy would never be able to get down to the middleweight limit anyway.

It could be argued, however, that if they were so sure that McAvoy would find it almost impossible to make middleweight, then they could quite confidently have given him a title shot in the knowledge that he was bound to weaken himself in getting down to 11st. 6lbs.

The story has been put about over the years that McAvoy was threatened by gangsters while in a nightclub in New York. This story, which is quite untrue, has its origins in that post fight meeting with

Risko's party, and though Lumiansky's brief conversation with the opposition was anything but amicable, there is no evidence of any threatening behaviour. However, like most stories, this one contains at least a grain of truth, in that the people around Risko most certainly were members of the underworld; racketeers, then in the process of moving in on the fight business in a far more organised way than had ever been the case previously. Their menacing presence on the boxing scene, which would seriously affect McAvoy's chances of winning the title, will be dealt with in a later chapter.

The unpleasant scene in the nightclub apart, Mac and Eliza had a wonderful time in New York once hostilities were over, including an evening spent with the wide-mouthed comedian, Joe E. Brown, then at the height of his fame. On Christmas Eve they were entertained by bandleader Ray Noble and crooner Al Bowlly in the Rainbow Room at Radio City, Noble presenting them with a cake for the children, complete with miniature boxing gloves and toy boxers. They also met Rudy Vallee, who invited Mac to go on his radio show, but as they were due to sail for home early on Boxing Day, this proved impossible.

Both Mac and Eliza were agreed that the Americans, who love a winner, had treated them like royalty and they had loved every minute of it. Still, there's no place like home, and the Bamfords were just dying to get back to the smoke and grime of Rochdale and their three young children.

McAvoy was leaving New York at a time when his services were in great demand, but leaving on the understanding that he would return early in the New Year. He was just going home for a holiday, and before sailing for England he was assured by Lumiansky that Risko would be put under a great deal of pressure to give Mac his well merited shot at the Middleweight crown.

However, when the ratings were published in that month's *Ring* magazine McAvoy's name was not even mentioned in the list of Middleweight contenders. Instead, he was rated second in the light-heavies, below former champion Maxie Rosenbloom and immediately above Al McCoy and Bob Olin. It was obvious that the Americans were far from convinced that McAvoy was a genuine 160 pounder.

This was absurd, for he was still British Champion at that weight. True, he had fought more than his share of Light-heavyweights, but this had come about purely and simply because there were practically no middleweights of note left in Britain to fight. About the only leading contender Mac had not faced as champion was Jack Casey, who had been eliminated by Archie Sexton.

Lumiansky had probably made a big mistake in putting Mac in with Al McCoy. For despite the great prestige gained from his victory over the rugged Canadian, the Americans now clearly considered the most logical step was for McAvoy to take over McCoy's rating as number two challenger to John Henry Lewis.

When Lumiansky insisted that McAvoy could make 11st. 6lbs, and that he was willing to post five hundred dollars with the New York State Athletic Commission as a weight forfeit, Jimmy Johnston told him to forget it.

'Suppose he can make 160 pounds, so what? Who's going to pay to see McAvoy knock out Risko again? John Henry Lewis is the fight we want. We're all in this to make money. Right?'

Lumiansky didn't argue. He just told Johnston to go ahead and make the match. Johnston at once contacted Lewis's managers in Phoenix, Arizona, by telephone. They did not appear too eager to put their man in with the new sensation from across the Atlantic, but the Garden matchmaker was talking big money and could be very persuasive. Eventually, Lewis's people agreed to travel to New York for further discussions and the match was as good as made.

The Bamfords arrived at Plymouth aboard the *Ile de France* on New Year's Day 1936 and immediately sent off two telegrams to Rochdale, one to a friend, Bert Hulme, of Syke Road, asking him to bring McAvoy's car to London Road station, Manchester, for 9pm that night, and the other to Park Hill, where his mother was staying while looking after the children, asking her to 'keep them up' until they arrived later in the evening.

What Mac did not realise was that the town was at fever pitch in anticipation of his homecoming. This was hardly surprising after his short but explosive campaign in America, but few could have expected the tremendous reception the conquering hero was about to receive.

McAvoy's mother was so excited when she received the telegram, she decided that just keeping the children up was not good enough, and when the fighters slate-coloured saloon arrived at London Road station that evening the children, their grandmother and McAvoy's sister Rose were all aboard. Joe Bamford senior, though as proud as anyone, was now more or less housebound, and waited patiently for their return.

With the keen co-operation of railway officials the car was driven as close as possible to the platform. The train from Euston was due at 9.15, but somehow word had got around of the imminent arrival of the British Middleweight Champion, and crowds started to form long before this. The train, however, was running very late and between nine and nine-thirty the number of people in the station increased alarmingly.

The three children, young Joe, Jackie and Leonora, were hoisted onto a railway truck and aroused great interest among the spectators. There were already a number of press photographers on hand, and the arrival of several more swelled their ranks to a dozen or more. Their presence caused more people to join the mob, which had now become so dense that it was almost impossible to move.

When the London train finally pulled in at 9.50 there was a stampede, the crowd surging down the platform, with people peering into every window until the carriage containing McAvoy was located. After the door had been forced open Mac managed to squeeze out with great difficulty and hug the children. He then attempted to force his way through the excited hordes, carrying all three of them, but this proved impossible and he was forced to let go of Leonora. Then, with a child in each arm and the crowd packed tightly around him, Mac slowly pushed his way through. A little further down the platform he was waylaid by the photographers, but stopped only briefly before battling his way forward again. People tried to shake his hand and some even tried to get him to sign autographs. Bert Hulme then steered him in the direction of the car. At this point there was no sign of Eliza. She was somewhere further back, trying hard to break through. Eventually, she managed to reach the barrier, and after the family had posed for more photographs they were all bundled into the car amid thunderous cheering, Mac, after practically fighting his way in, flopping down wearily beside the driver.

The fog, which had persisted for most of the day, now lifted as the car carrying Rochdale's hero made its way up from Manchester, a distance of some twelve miles. On the Esplanade, close to one of the finest town halls in the country, waited the St. Patrick's Boys' Brigade Band, while in nearby Manchester Road people were stopping every car that came by for fear of missing the one carrying the Bamford family. Seeing this, the police soon moved in and cleared the road.

When McAvoy's car at last came into view it was spotted immediately and surrounded, with people peering in and tapping on the windows. Mac waved to them as the band struck up, and amid scenes of wild enthusiasm, led the way as the besieged vehicle slowly moved along the length of the Esplanade, turned into Yorkshire Street and proceeded to climb the hill to Wellington Street, then into Regent Street and Park Hill.

The crowd around the Bamford house was enormous, the family being hard pressed to get through the big iron gates and on to their front door. In fact, had it not been for the presence of half a dozen or so policemen there might have been a very long delay before the house was reached. Crowds of people, including large numbers of children who had been allowed to stay up for the great event, pushed against the gates and climbed up onto the walls.

After breaking through and getting safely inside the house the family was still not left alone. There was loud cheering and shouting outside, and no sign at all that the merrymakers were anywhere near ready to call off the siege of Park Hill and go home to bed. It was quite obvious that they had no intention of dispersing. Unless Mac re-appeared and spoke to them they were likely to remain camped outside his door all night. After being let out of the house by the police he stood on a wall and made a short speech, in which he expressed his sincere appreciation for the wonderful welcome he had been met with. This seemed to please and satisfy the crowd, and soon after Mac had said goodnight and gone back inside they began to drift away.

By this time it was almost midnight and Mac was dead tired and ready for bed, where he swore he intended to remain until he felt like getting up.

# Chapter 19

## Frankie Carbo and the Mob

A newspaper in early January 1936 claimed that a big London syndicate had been in touch with John Henry Lewis with a view to bringing the light-heavyweight champion to England to defend against McAvoy, but Jimmy Johnston soon put a stop to that by announcing that Lewis was under contract to Madison Square Garden. Shortly after this Mac was informed that Johnston had made the match and that he would be fighting Lewis in February or March. He would have to return to the United States no later than the end of January and would be engaging in a couple of warm-up bouts in the run-up to the title fight.

Mac was quite a celebrity now and made many public appearances locally, including what was intended to be a surprise visit to Buckley Hall Orphanage. Word of the champion's coming, however, was soon out, and as his car pulled into the school drive he was met by yet another boys' band and the strains of 'Hail the Conquering Hero Comes'. He was then welcomed by the Father Superior, made a shy speech to the boys and left a little later with their cheers ringing in his ears.

McAvoy was back in New York by the beginning of February, and on meeting Lumiansky learned that his American manager had been kept busy sifting through the many offers which had come in while Mac was away in England. They wanted him to fight Frank Battaglia, Paul Pirrone, Bill Bridges or Al McCoy again, but when all was settled Mac was informed that he would be meeting none of these. Instead, Lumiansky had arranged a trio of warm-up contests leading up to the Lewis clash, with Jack Kiernan of Long Branch, New Jersey, Jimmy Smith of Philadelphia and Anson Green of Pittsburg, all within an eight day period covering February 17th to the 24th.

Such a schedule would frighten the life out of most present day fighters, but Lumiansky obviously felt that, apart from the extra earnings it would bring in, actual combat was much better than sparring and would really sharpen McAvoy for the title fight.

It was an extremely unwise move to say the least, particularly in view of the dodgy state of McAvoy's hands, although, to be fair, a lot of people have been wise after the event. For although the problem had been in evidence for a very long time, there were obviously periods when the hands were fine and giving him no trouble at all, otherwise Mac could never have managed to get through his training in New York, and he would certainly never have agreed to take three fights in eight days had he harboured any doubts at all regarding those hands, especially with the title fight coming up soon afterwards.

As it turned out, only two of these warm-up fights took place, Jack Kiernan pulling out at the last minute through injury. Neither Jimmy Smith nor Anson Green was rated in the world's top ten, although Smith had some well known names on his record.

The Smith fight went on at New York's famous St. Nicholas Arena and drew a capacity crowd of close on 5,000. Smith was used to mixing it and attacked fiercely from the opening bell. McAvoy, of course responded immediately and the first round was fought at a blistering pace with Smith giving as good as he got. When the second round opened, Mac, instead of slugging it out, decided to pick his punches and soon succeeded in nailing his opponent with a hard left hook to the jaw. Though hurt, Smith fought back strongly, trapping McAvoy on the ropes and catching him with several heavy punches to the head.

This caused Mac to abandon his boxing and tear in with both fists flying. After punishing the American about the body Mac connected with another left hook and down went Smith for a count of nine. On rising he was badly dazed and took quite a hammering before Mac finally laid him out for the full count.

Though the right hand had again been doctored it had not been too heavily used, the left having done most of the damage.

With McAvoy again looking like a world beater Lumiansky could see riches ahead for both of them and was now talking big money with Jimmy Johnston, who was so excited about Mac's performances that he was even looking beyond the John Henry Lewis fight and talking in terms of matching McAvoy with either World Heavyweight Champion James J. Braddock, his up and coming challenger, Joe Louis, or the Italian giant, Primo Carnera.

To suggest such contests was, of course, quite ridiculous. McAvoy may have had a puncher's chance, whoever was in the other corner, but it's quite clear that money was the prime motive, while the possibility of Mac taking a bad beating does not appear to have been considered.

In the dressing room just prior to the Anson Green fight the novocaine injections were again administered, but as some considerable time elapsed before McAvoy was called into the ring he could feel the effects beginning to wear off during the early rounds and knew he would have to be very careful.

With Mac relying almost entirely on the left hand, and Green, an awkward, spoiling type of fighter, holding and wrestling most of the time, the result was an untidy, disappointing affair, which did not please the fans. At the end of ten tedious rounds Mac was declared the winner, but had not been at all impressive, though he had tried hard to make a fight of it.

To make things worse the right hand felt very sore again, and a further contest, arranged to take place shortly afterwards, against Eddie 'Kid' Wakelin, in Newark, had to be cancelled. There were just two weeks to go before Mac was due to climb into the ring for the big one. As far as the right hand was concerned he could do little but rest it as much as possible, while continuing with his general training and conditioning. It was not the ideal preparation for such an important fight, but at least he'd managed to get two quick contests under his belt, and if he could now get through the rest of his training schedule with as few people as possible realising that the right hand was nowhere near back to normal, he would simply have to rely again on the novocaine injections.

The one man who seemed to take all the problems in his stride was Dave Lumiansky, who went around as though he hadn't a care in the world. Though he didn't look much like a playboy, Lumiansky was the sort who liked to be seen in all the best places with a couple of beautiful girls on his arm, spending money, tipping lavishly and mixing with those whom he considered to be 'the right people'. He bought flowers and chocolates for hotel receptionists, slipped the odd ten dollar bill to any ex-pug he happened to run into on Broadway or hanging around the gym, and made sure that when he attended fights at St. Nick's Arena or The Garden there were always ringside seats for the bevy of beauties he liked to surround himself with.

Lumiansky was also installed in the next room to Mac at the Mayflower Hotel, which was another big expense, especially as he was seldom off the telephone. Sooner or later there would have to be an accounting, when questions would be asked regarding whose end of the purses Lumiansky's excesses were coming out of. But while they were on top of the world it never even occurred to McAvoy to keep an eye on Dave or query anything he did. Of course, his whole attention had to be focused on preparing for his fights, but later he would bitterly regret that he did not start asking questions a lot sooner than he did. There's no doubt though that Lumiansky was a slick operator who could buy and sell the likes of McAvoy, and in any case Mac was one of Lumiansky's greatest admirers and firmly convinced that he'd met the man who would make his fortune.

The truth, however, is that Lumiansky was nowhere near as well connected in American fistic circles as he liked people to believe. To be fair, he had done quite well with Panama 'Al' Brown in Europe, and his smooth tongue plus the influence of Norman Hurst had given him the opportunity to handle Jackie Brown and eventually a potential gold mine in McAvoy.

After Mac had taken New York by storm Lumiansky was in solid with Garden boss Jimmy Johnston, but other, more sinister influences were beginning to strengthen their grip on the fight business in America at that time. These racketeers and mobsters, the representatives of organised crime, were now infiltrating boxing at all levels and would eventually end up in almost total control.

To these people and the managers and promoters they manipulated, Lumiansky was no more than a small timer who happened to be acting as McAvoy's business manager. The last thing the underworld element wanted was for the title to leave the country. If such a thing happened they would be likely to lose control of that title and the earning power it represented. They had not managed to acquire an interest in John Henry Lewis, and though Jimmy Johnston was doing business with managers who had criminal connections, he himself was not directly under mob control.

In the era of prohibition, gangsters such as Owney Madden, 'Lucky' Luciano, Al Capone, 'Legs' Diamond, Vincent 'Mad Dog' Coll and Johnny Torrio had got themselves involved in boxing by buying a piece of any prominent fighter they took a fancy to. By the early to mid-thirties, as even more ruthless criminals appeared on the scene and crime became more of an organised business, the nature of their involvement in boxing also began to change. No longer did the mobsters buy in, they simply moved in and took over a fighter, using the licensed manager as a front man. This state of affairs continued to develop over the next twenty-odd years, with the men behind it becoming more and more powerful, until a stage was reached where they owned almost every big name fighter, manager and promoter in America, if only by virtue of the fact that if you didn't do business with them you were left out in the cold.

Behind all the graft and corruption lurked the menacing figure of the notorious John Paul 'Frankie' Carbo, a hoodlum with known Mafia connections and an extensive criminal record. From around 1935 onwards, Carbo, a member of the Gaetano-Lucchese crime family and a triggerman for Murder Incorporated, manoeuvred himself into a position so powerful that practically no big fight could be made and no major promotion put together unless he was in on it.

Carbo first began to get a solid foothold in boxing through promoter Mike Jacobs, who formed the Twentieth Century Sporting Club in opposition to the Garden when Jimmy Johnston was in charge there. Carbo was very friendly with Jacobs and even used his office as a headquarters, nearly always being on hand to act in an 'advisory capacity', especially when Jacobs was having problems. Mike was a very difficult man, with whom many were reluctant to do business. This is where Carbo came in. He could arrange just about anything, and though Jacobs benefited, the liaison also served to increase Carbo's influence within the game. With Joe Louis as his big drawing card Mike Jacobs was America's number one promoter for many years, while Carbo remained discreetly in the background, in close association with Mike, at the same time building up his own undercover connections in boxing. Muscling in on any manager with an outstanding fighter and declaring the mob 'in' on all that fighter's future earnings presented few problems for Carbo and his henchmen. They were well versed in graft and extortion of every kind. Of course, they were quite happy to do things the easy way, and would always make their approaches by explaining that all doors would be opened once a prospect cut them in. But as the victims really had very little choice, Carbo's failure rate was practically nil.

After Mike Jacobs' health deteriorated in the late forties it became obvious, taking Mike's age into account, that his days as a boxing czar were numbered. It was at this point that Chicago millionaire Jim Norris, head of the International Boxing Club, really came to the fore. From his headquarters in Madison Square Garden, Norris, with Frankie Carbo at his elbow, virtually ran boxing coast to coast and even arranged tie-ups with several prominent European promoters, including England's Jack Solomons.

That Frankie was on intimate terms with Norris was perfectly obvious to everyone in the game. Whenever the I.B.C. boss attended any public function or fight promotion, either in New York or out of town, the suave, enigmatic Carbo was usually in attendance. There was nothing official in their relationship, but every boxing manager knew that to break into the big time you had to do business with the I.B.C., and that the only way in was through Carbo, who was believed to have an interest in almost every prominent fighter then active. It was clear therefore, that to a great extent Carbo was running boxing and could make or break a fighter overnight. If you didn't play ball with Frankie you didn't play at all.

But every empire crumbles sooner or later, and this one began to come apart in the fifties, when Frankie Carbo was named by a prominent boxing magazine as the 'Mr Big' of the fight game, in spite of the fact that he held no license of any kind, and, had he applied for one, would certainly have been refused by any state in America.

During District Attorney Frank A. Hogan's investigation of under-cover managers, a number of those on the closest terms with Carbo were called to testify, when it emerged that no records of their finances were kept, nor did they have bank accounts, as they were in the habit of doing business strictly on a cash basis. In any case, these people were in violation of the rules of the New York State Athletic Commission, which made it a punishable offence for anyone holding a license to associate or consort with known criminals. A number of licenses were revoked or suspended, though every single one of the managers questioned denied knowing what business Carbo was in.

Soon the F.B.I. was involved, which later resulted in Truman Gibson, President of Jim Norris's National Boxing Enterprises Inc., being indicted by the California Federal Grand Jury as the man alleged to have used his influence to persuade Don Nesseth, manager of Don Jordan, to hand over an interest in his fighter to a quartet of racketeers: Frank 'Blinky' Palermo, Joe Sica, Louis Tom Dragna and Frankie Carbo.

The government's case was based on evidence of attempted extortion and threats of physical violence unless the manager turned over half of his interest in the Welterweight champion to the mob.

At a later hearing former World Lightweight Champion, Ike Williams, gave evidence which astounded those present, when he testified that he was working as a warehouseman at a salary of 92 dollars a fortnight. Though having engaged in a total of 154 contests and earned big money, he had somehow managed to finish up broke.

After quitting his manager, Con McCarthy, and attempting to manage himself, he had been unofficially boycotted by the Managers' Guild and was unable to get any work. At this point Williams had been approached by Philadelphia racketeer, 'Blinky' Palermo, a close associate of Carbo, who said he could straighten things out with the Guild if the fighter agreed to let him handle his affairs. Williams, having no alternative, went along with this and soon began to get fights again, but received very little in the way of remuneration. Under oath Ike testified that his last three contests had earned him a total of 77,000 dollars, of which he had not seen a single cent.

The testimony of Mafia turncoat Joe Valachi, at a senate hearing in the early sixties, caused more than a ripple in boxing circles when it was revealed that Sam Giancana, boss of the Chicago mob, held a twelve per cent interest in Sonny Liston, prior to Liston winning the World Heavyweight title. Others holding a financial interest were 'Blinky' Palermo and Frankie Carbo. At the time Liston's manager was Joseph 'Bep' Barone.

Top Cosa Nostra bosses behind Carbo and Palermo were said to be Carlo Gambino, Tommy Lucchese, Joe Magliocco and Vito Genovese, the man who gave Valachi the 'kiss of death' when both were incarcerated in the penitentiary in Atlanta, Georgia.

Carbo and Palermo were eventually jailed and Jim Norris forced to dispose of all his financial interests in boxing.

Now, going back to the thirties, Carbo, a man known to have underworld connections even then, first became involved in boxing when he took over a fifty per cent interest in Eddie Hogan, a promising young heavyweight. Hogan never quite made the grade, but from that time on Carbo's influence in the game began to grow. In 1935, soon after 'Babe' Risko won the middleweight crown from Teddy Yarosz, Carbo moved in and was soon acting as 'adviser' to Gabe Genovese, Risko's manager, and was therefore very much in the picture at the time of Eddie's humiliating defeat at the hands of the 'Rochdale Thunderbolt'. The following year, after Risko lost the title to Freddie Steele, it was rumoured that the mob also had a piece of the new champion, and sure enough the menacing figure of Frankie Carbo soon began to appear on the scene, though always remaining discreetly at a distance.

While Steele held the N.B.A. version of the title, both Fred Apostoli and Edward Tenet, of France, won other versions, but when Steele was beaten by Al Hostak it very quickly became evident that Carbo was still in control. Later the title passed to Solly Krieger, then back to Hostak, which made little difference to the mob. In other words, having got a stranglehold on the middleweight title, along with titles at various other weights of course, Carbo would continue to capitalize on it and also pull the strings, no matter whose hands it passed into.

So, for McAvoy to have stood any chance at all of getting a crack at the crown his manager would have had to be prepared to deal with Frankie Carbo. It's more than likely, in fact, that Carbo was with Risko's party in the New York nightclub, but very doubtful that he ever seriously considered talking business with Lumiansky. After all, deal or no deal, it would hardly have been convenient, as far as the mob was concerned, if McAvoy had won the title and returned to England with it. What sort of control would they have had then?

The fact that Mac was denied his right to fight for the middleweight crown had nothing to do with any doubts about his being able to make the weight. It was purely and simply that once Carbo and company had discovered just how dangerous an opponent the big-hitting Englishman was, they had not the slightest intention of risking the title. By beating Risko so decisively McAvoy effectively put an end to his hopes of a title shot.

John Henry Lewis, a handsome, likeable young negro from Phoenix, Arizona, had won the title the previous October, beating Bob Olin on points in St. Louis. Although only twenty-one years old, Lewis had been a pro. since 1931, and had taken part in over 50 contests, losing no more than half-a-dozen, his most recent defeat having been against Abe Feldman the previous July. He had beaten Maxie Rosenbloom three times, all in overweight matches, when Rosenbloom was champion, and held a decision over heavyweight champion James J. Braddock. Six feet in height, he was beautifully built, with wide, powerful shoulders.

In the gym McAvoy appeared to be back to his best form and greatly impressed the crowds of people who turned up to watch him go through his paces. Questioned about the suspect hand, Lumiansky assured reporters that although slightly knocked up on the hard head of Anson Green, it was now, in fact, back to normal. This, of course, was far from the truth, and Lumiansky, having told McAvoy to nurse it during training, had already made arrangements for the man with the big needle to be on hand on fight night.

Apart from that, McAvoy was feeling fit and confident. He had increased his daily run on the streets of New York from five to seven miles and was looking in excellent shape. After visiting the gym, former Heavyweight Champion, Jack Sharkey, told the press boys that in his opinion McAvoy would win. At this point, with less than a week to go before the fight, Mac was made an 11-to-10 favourite.

The Petersen contest was now definitely fixed for April 23rd, which meant that McAvoy was committed to fighting for two major titles within the space of six weeks, which was asking a lot of a man with the sort of hand injury he was carrying.

Back home in Rochdale the whole town waited with bated breath for the result to come in from America. Could McAvoy become the first Englishman to win the World's Light-heavyweight title since Bob Fitzsimmons defeated George Gardner in 1903? Of one thing they could be quite certain. Mac would give it everything he'd got. But in reality the odds were heavily stacked against him, for he would be giving away weight, height and reach to a very talented champion, who was also seven years younger. On top of that the hand had not been given anywhere near enough time to mend, and once again it would be a case of McAvoy going all out to put his man away before the effects of the novocaine wore off. Against a man of Lewis's calibre this was going to take some doing, as Mac was very shortly to discover.

Just before the fight the betting odds swung dramatically, making Lewis a 3-to-1 favourite. When the two men climbed into the ring the champion looked quite a bit bigger than his challenger, but this didn't seem to bother McAvoy in the least. The thing that did bother him, however, was the length of time he was kept waiting after receiving the novocaine injections, both in the dressing room and on entering the ring. It was claimed later that Lewis's handlers got wind of what was going on, and learning of McAvoy's reliance on the novocaine treatment, deliberately kept him waiting in order to give the drug time to wear off. Up there in the ring, McAvoy, after shadow boxing, stretching and gnawing at his gloves for some time, began to get irritated at being kept waiting and looked ready to return to his dressing room, when Lewis finally appeared.

Attacking from the first bell McAvoy worked his way in and let go with several lethal-looking left hooks, only to find that Lewis rode the punches quite easily. A master boxer, the champion was quite content to bide his time and score with the odd counter punch while he sized his challenger up. With his bobbing, weaving style, McAvoy, of the two, might easily have been taken for the American.

Coming in low in round two he now decided to make the body his target, and was more successful, until pulled up short by a neatly placed uppercut, but as Lewis tried to follow this up he ran into a hail of leather as Mac fought back fiercely, catching the champion with some hard shots to the body. In that early skirmish, though, he felt the full weight of Lewis's punches a couple of times and knew he had a tough fight in front of him.

In the fourth McAvoy began to get the better of things until a cut suddenly appeared over Lewis's left eye. Instead of causing the champion to become cautious this had the effect if spurring him on, and before the round was over he landed a heavy right cross to the chin that clearly shook the British fighter. McAvoy was in trouble, but as always, he was not found to be lacking when things were going against him and rallied strongly, standing toe to toe and slugging it out until the bell ended the round.

From then until the halfway mark McAvoy forced himself into the lead on sheer aggression, but had little opportunity to land solidly with the right, due to Lewis's clever defensive work. The hand though, was beginning to feel painful, which meant that his big plan had failed, for it was clear that the effects of the novocaine were wearing off. Far from knocking Lewis out, he had not even managed to shake him, despite having put a great deal of effort into those first seven rounds.

Mac was now in real trouble, and knew it. By the eighth the right hand was practically useless, but whatever happened he had no intention of packing it in. He knew he would have to rely almost totally on his left and backed off, trying to draw Lewis into range, then bang over the left hook. But this was a forlorn hope, for Lewis was at his best at long range. Realising there was very little sting in the challenger's much vaunted right hand, he began to force the fight more and more, driving Mac onto his back foot and punishing him severely.

After a bad ninth round, during which he was staggered several times, McAvoy came back strongly in the tenth, gritting his teeth and banging in several vicious left hooks to head and body. But after getting the best of it for most of the round he was badly shaken by a terrific left hook and was glad to hear the bell.

Despite his courageous stand, for which he was warmly applauded by the crowd, McAvoy was falling well behind and looking very tired. Still he strove for an opening and several times caught the champion with hurtful left hooks, but with no right hand to back it up was unable to press home any advantage gained. Once he did actually stagger Lewis with a hard right to the chin, but immediately regretted having thrown it, for the pain in his hand was excruciating. After that, the best he could do was to try to make Lewis miss, while scoring with the odd left jab or hook.

In spite of the overwhelming odds Mac still managed to give a very good account of himself in the closing rounds, but as the bell ended the contest he was beginning to take a real hammering.

Though he had put up a marvellous show in the circumstances there is no doubt that in the end Mac was well beaten and Lewis deservedly received the verdict, though the Garden crowd was quick to show its appreciation of the Englishman's fine performance.

There was no glumness in the dressing room afterwards. For although everyone was naturally disappointed, it was openly acknowledged that McAvoy had shown tremendous bravery in giving the champion such a hard fight when the odds were so much against him, and there was plenty of speculation as to what might have been the result had Mac possessed two good hands. Naturally there was talk of a return, which Gus Greenlees, Lewis's manager, intimated that he was agreeable to, the month of June being mentioned. But again, this was totally unrealistic. To fight Petersen in April then follow it up by taking on Lewis again just a few weeks later was really out of the question, especially as the extent of McAvoy's hand damage had not yet been determined. To Mac it felt worse than ever before and just removing the glove after the fight was a very painful operation in itself. The Athletic Commission doctor frowned and shook his head when he saw the state of it, for it was very badly swollen and discoloured. Later, however, an X-ray examination revealed that there were no broken bones, but the hand was still very badly bruised and in a highly inflamed condition.

Jack Dempsey, who had been so enthusiastic about McAvoy's talents previously, now revised his assessment somewhat, stating in an interview:

'It was a great fight, and McAvoy looked terrific for seven or eight rounds. Up to then he was in the lead, then all of a sudden he seemed to weaken and tire. In this racket you just can't afford to get tired. McAvoy is a good man, but he's just a middleweight and he can't hurt these big men. He belted Lewis at least a dozen times with his Sunday punch, but it had no effect at all. He didn't look as good against Lewis as he did against his other American opponents, but then Lewis has got class, that's why he's a champion. The truth is though, that he's just too big for McAvoy.'

Dempsey added that in the circumstances it would now be futile to talk about matching Mac with still bigger men like Braddock or Joe Louis.

These were wise words and if McAvoy read them we can be reasonably sure that he realised it, considering the way his hand was feeling.

At that time it was still extremely painful, and Mac had already made up his mind that he would seek a postponement in the case of the Petersen fight, would not submit to any more injections, and in no circumstances climb into the ring again until the injury was completely healed.

# Chapter 20

## David and Goliath

A few days after the John Henry Lewis fight McAvoy boarded the *Berengaria* for England. Besieged by reporters, he showed them his hands. They were still badly swollen, especially the right, which was very painful. All those profound resolutions made immediately after the fight, however, appear to have been forgotten, for he now informed the press that he was fairly confident that his hands would be in good shape for the Petersen fight. On arrival at Southampton he was again surrounded by newsmen and told them that he intended having a week's rest at home before going into training again. He said he was not in the least discouraged at his defeat by Lewis and was looking forward to meeting him in a return within three months.

Mac soon discovered that because of his outstanding performances in America the public was showing tremendous interest in the Petersen fight, the promoters having already taken over £10,000 in advance bookings. With the contest over a month away the cheaper seats were already sold out, the Earl's Court box office having returned nearly £3,000 to disappointed fight fans.

Of course, in normal circumstances this would have been very exciting news, but even if the hand was feeling better, McAvoy should certainly not have been thinking of risking it again, and ought to have contacted the promoters immediately to inform them he had decided to seek a postponement until such time as his right hand was completely healed. But instead, he was again carried away by the thought of what he would be losing in ring earnings and also by all the ballyhoo attached to the coming clash with Petersen.

Just over a week later he was back in training, and told reporters that he had subjected his right hand to a severe testing and was satisfied that it was in good order again. On being told that Len Harvey had challenged the winner to meet him, with the heavyweight title at stake, plus £1,000 aside, Mac said, 'I expect to beat Petersen and will be quite happy to defend against Harvey. In fact, I've already received an offer from Earl's Court Stadium, subject to my winning of course.'

It was understood that the said offer involved more than one fight and would net McAvoy at least £12,000 should he become heavyweight champion. For the Petersen fight he would be getting £4,400. Petersen himself was no stranger to big purses and was stated in one newspaper to have a bank balance in excess of £30,000, a vast sum in 1936.

Tall, well-built and good-looking, the champion, born in Cardiff, was twenty-four years old and a physical fitness fanatic, who at one time had thought of becoming a doctor. Going to sea at fifteen, he had travelled the world for over two years and also taken up boxing, fighting as an amateur for several years before winning an A.B.A. title at light-heavyweight in 1931. Within six months of turning professional he had run up a string of thirteen knockout victories, and in May 1932 became British Light-heavyweight Champion when he beat Harry Crossley on points, later relinquishing the title to campaign as a heavyweight.

In July 1932 Petersen knocked out Reggie Meen to win the heavyweight title, and successfully defended it twice, against Jack Pettifer and Jack Doyle, before losing to Len Harvey on points in November of the following year. Six months later Petersen was again champion when he forced Harvey to retire after twelve rounds at the White City Stadium, London. In December 1934 the big Welshman defended against Australian George Cook, outpointing him over 15 rounds, and held off a further challenge from Len Harvey in January 1936 at the Empire Pool, Wembley. Petersen was certainly an experienced and formidable opponent and a very popular champion, who was said to receive hundreds of fan letters every week.

There was great interest in the fight up North, with rail and coach trips being organised in Rochdale, Manchester and surrounding towns, and as the fight was scheduled to be broadcast, there would be many thousands more listening in all over the country.

It would be something of a David and Goliath clash, as McAvoy was several inches shorter than his opponent and at least a stone lighter, for even after bulking up, the challenger would be unlikely to exceed 12st. 4lbs. Although he had fought quite a few light-heavies, this would be Mac's first encounter with a full-blown heavyweight, and he was starting with the champion.

Dave Lumiansky had come over from New York to act as McAvoy's chief second. There would be no question this time of any injections. If the hand failed to take the strain Mac would again be in serious trouble, but he obviously felt that the money offered plus the chance to win two further titles, for Petersen's British Empire Crown would also be at stake, was well worth the risk.

Over 10,000 people packed the Empress Hall that night, and as McAvoy made his entrance it was obvious that quite a number of them were from Rochdale, for there were shouts of 'Up the 'Dale' and 'Come on the Hornets'.

As the two men met in the centre of the ring to listen to the referee's instructions, the difference in size was quite startling, Petersen towering over the challenger and looking down on him like a school master about to punish a wayward child.

When the contest began Mac's crouching style made the disparity in height seem even more pronounced. Petersen, though attacking from the opening bell, had clearly made up his mind to keep McAvoy on the end of his left hand while probing for an opening, then bang over the right, which was a very powerful punch. The champion, however, found Mac's bobbing, weaving style hard to fathom and had little success to begin with.

After missing with a right, Petersen took a hard left hook flush on the jaw. To Mac's dismay the punch did not seem to trouble the champion very much, and when the same thing happened in round two the challenger realised that sooner or later he was going to have to risk the right hand.

Petersen, having sampled a couple of McAvoy's best shots, now began to attack his man in earnest, but was failing to land cleanly as Mac ducked and dodged. At close quarters McAvoy was connecting with some good shots, while the champion's only success came from landing several rabbit punches, for which he was warned.

But Petersen was forcing the pace and pushing his man back, while Mac could do little, apart from occasionally leaping in and lashing out with hooks to the head. Though he had produced nothing to trouble the champion in the first half of the fight, apart from the occasional well placed counter punch, McAvoy had surprised everyone with his defensive ability, speed, elusiveness and brilliant footwork, making Petersen miss by as much as a couple of feet at times.

In the eighth Petersen had some success, catching McAvoy with a heavy blow to the body and forcing him to hang on, and in the next round Mac was on the canvas from a slip, but was up immediately. Petersen continued to do the chasing, but it was becoming obvious that the champion had neither the speed nor the know-how to pin down his elusive opponent unless he tired and slowed down. By the tenth this had begun to happen, but still McAvoy managed to keep out of harm's way. In desperation Mac threw the right a few times, though in half-hearted fashion. But each time it landed the blow proved more painful to the challenger than it did to his opponent, and little was seen of it for the remainder of the contest.

The fight had now deteriorated into a boring spectacle, with frequent clinches, and after McAvoy had again slipped to one knee without taking a punch the referee appealed to him to show a little more enterprise. But with only one hand and tiring rapidly, this was easier said than done. Just the same Mac tried his best to respond, and although having little real success, he at least attempted to raise the pace over the last three rounds.

As they came out for the final session McAvoy knew he was behind and resolved to make one last ditch effort, no matter what the consequences. Letting go with both fists he hammered Petersen about the body. But in doing so he had left himself wide open and the next moment the champion's big right hand punch thudded home, catching McAvoy squarely on the chin and putting him down on his knees, where he remained until the count reached eight.

As Mac got to his feet Petersen moved in swiftly for the kill, and with the fans roaring in anticipation of a knockout, McAvoy was forced to duck and dive desperately as the champion bombarded him with heavy clubbing blows to the head. Mac had never been knocked out in his entire career, but at that moment he was in grave danger of losing that proud record. Yet somehow, in spite of the lead in his boots, his tired limbs and the throbbing pain in his right hand, the courageous challenger managed to stay on his feet to the end.

There was no doubt as to the winner, and on Petersen's hand being raised, the man from Rochdale, completely sold out and looking utterly dejected, went over and sportingly congratulated his conqueror, who could not have been very satisfied with his own performance. Nor were the spectators, for apart from the odd burst of action there had been little to cheer about in an eagerly awaited fight which had turned out to be a most disappointing affair. McAvoy, looking stale and jaded, had turned in a very negative performance, while Petersen, with all the advantages, had not been much better. It was clearly a night to forget.

There would be no triumphant return to Rochdale this time. No bands playing or big crowds to greet him. All Mac wanted to do was slip home quietly without any fuss. Judging by the Petersen contest,

Jack Dempsey's words would appear to have been very wise ones. There is no doubt at all that McAvoy could knock out men much bigger and heavier than himself, but, of course, this is seldom likely to happen when the opposition is of good class. Yet it is interesting to conjecture on what might have been the outcome of the Lewis and Petersen fights if Mac had faced them with two sound hands.

It was obvious now that a long rest was called for. Of course, he should never have gone ahead with either of those contests, but at least there was the consolation of knowing that, apart from the £4,400 for the Petersen fight there was a tidy sum due in respect of the American tour, for which he had reportedly earned a total of £10,000. Although no one knows for sure just how many people were in for a cut, McAvoy could certainly expect to come away with a sizeable chunk of it. It was some months, however, before he received a final accounting. When he did he was not at all pleased. In fact, it would be true to say that he was absolutely staggered.

Lumiansky, after seconding Mac in the Petersen fight, was no longer around, having either returned to America or gone on to Paris, while Norman Hurst, the man behind the American trip, spent a lot of his time in London and was not the easiest man to pin down.

Don Waters, a building contractor from Edinburgh, then living in Manchester, had first met McAvoy at Belle Vue, the two striking up a close friendship and later going into business together. From the outset they found they had a lot in common. Both loved the nightlife, and although Mac was no drinker he liked to frequent Manchester's best restaurants and clubs. Don had a devilish sense of humour, which suited McAvoy down to the ground, for he was always happiest with people around him who could make him laugh.

Anxious to get hold of his money from the American trip after having been put off with all kinds of excuses, he finally managed to get Norman Hurst on the telephone and told him that he felt he had been kept waiting long enough. Hurst was at the Grand Hotel, where he usually stayed when in Manchester, and Mac was told that he could come over and pick up the cheque. Don Waters drove him there and waited outside in the car while Mac went up to Hurst's suite.

The story of what happened in Norman Hurst's hotel suite was related to the author by Waters, who, being on the spot, got it straight from McAvoy within minutes of it having taken place.

'When Joe came out he was blazing mad,' said Don. 'D'you know how much he got for those five fights in America? Less than a thousand pounds! In fact the figure was actually nearer £750. That's all he finished up with. He blew his bloody top, he did! The expenses they charged him up with were nobody's business. It was a long list. A roll of paper, just like a bloody toilet roll. He couldn't believe it. Joe told me he put that Norman Hurst up against the wall and was going to knock him through the bleedin' wardrobe. He had one hand on his throat and the other ready to punch him. He said he didn't know what stopped him.

'Oh,' I said, 'I'm glad you didn't hit him Joe. You'd have been in real trouble if you had.'

'Still, you couldn't have blamed him really. Hurst and that bastard Lumiansky had robbed him blind.

'Joe said to me, if you'd seen the bill for that bleedin' Lumiansky. I nearly bleedin' died! Flowers for the girls, so many seats for the girls, this for the girls, that for the girls.'

'He was taking these girls to the fights, to theatres and into hotels and restaurants. Aye, and it was all going down on Joe's bill.

'That Joe, of course, he wasn't such a good scholar. He was no mug, but well, I mean to say… he couldn't reckon things up as quick as what that bleedin' Lumiansky could. And that Norman Hurst… he was all right. He was well educated, he was. But I'll tell you… when Joe had him by the throat, it's a wonder he didn't knock his bleedin' head off.'

Although it was quite obvious that McAvoy had been the victim of a carve-up, its very important to put things into perspective. First of all we do not know exactly what was on the list of expenses that Norman Hurst presented to McAvoy. We only know about Lumiansky's excesses, which should certainly not have come out of McAvoy's cut, even though Mac was sometimes in attendance when Lumiansky and his entourage went out on the town.

On the other hand, no mention is made of the fact that Eliza made the trip, which would have had to be paid for out of somebody's share, presumably McAvoy's. Secondly, while in New York Mac spent a lot of time on the Trans-Atlantic telephone, talking to Joan Lye. So naturally, these calls went on Mac's bill. There would also be other personal expenses. Yet even taking all the above into account, it's quite clear that he had received a raw deal. It's also obvious that Norman Hurst was still unofficially involved in his management, otherwise it's very unlikely that he would have been the one responsible for the final accounting and the handing over of the cheque. Nor would he have wished to face McAvoy's anger had there been someone else to deal with it.

Mac had gone through hell for that money, spending many weeks away from home, submitting to a gruelling training schedule and five tough contests, plus the constant agony and anxiety suffered on account of his hands. Yet he was in for yet another disappointment. For when the cheque for the Petersen fight came through, the biggest single purse of his career, he found that his share was only £1,800.

# Chapter 21

## Upheaval

Jack Hyams was still pressing for a shot at the middleweight title, but after his recent bad experience Mac had no intention of taking to the ring again until he felt completed rested. He knew his hands needed it, and so did he, for he was now convinced that his lacklustre showing against Petersen could be put down to staleness as much as anything else; the result of too many tough fights over too short a period. He therefore wrote to the Board, informing them of the position with regard to his damaged hands, and was given a few months respite. Meanwhile, Hyams was told that he would have to compete in an elimination series to find McAvoy's next challenger.

While taking things easy, Mac was now spending as much time as possible at the Syke riding stables, where Joan Lye was usually in attendance. They were often seen out riding together, and though people gossiped, there could be no denying the fact that they made a handsome couple.

Eliza, at home with children, was well aware of what was going on, but could do very little about it. She knew that Mac's infatuation with Joan wasn't the only problem. He was a celebrity now and hated being tied down. If she nagged him and questioned him about his movements he was likely to explode. Then the children would witness another row. So Eliza kept quiet and hoped that everything would come out right in the end. As far as Mac was concerned, Eliza had turned out to be something of a disappointment. In her teens she had been nice looking and quite smart, but since having the children she no longer paid too much attention to her appearance. Though a good cook, she could hardly be described as houseproud, and was very poor at handling money, for no matter how much he gave her she always seemed to fritter it away. She had no idea how to work out her budget for food or paying the bills. He also found fault with the way she kept the house and was constantly complaining that it was never tidy. In a way his attitude was quite understandable, for he had spent lavishly on nice furniture, only for Eliza to let the children and the dogs climb all over it and wreck it. There were times when he blew his top over this, and also the fact that she ran up bills which he knew nothing about and only discovered when creditors began to press. If Eliza argued or made excuses he would be liable to land out.

Jack Pilkington has said that all McAvoy's family loved Eliza, but could not deny that Mac's anger over her lack of pride in the house was justified, yet they could never condone his ill-treatment of her. Because Eliza loved him so much and was so tolerant she always forgave him for his aggressive outbursts. Mac himself was soft-hearted underneath and usually remorseful when he realised he'd gone too far.

In Joan Lye he had found someone who was exactly the opposite of Eliza. She was strong-willed, positive and certainly not the type to be brow-beaten. In addition to which she was also intelligent, rich, young and pretty.

Of one thing Don Waters was quite certain. Mac was not in the least interested in the Lye family fortune. He was just not that type, and in any case was making good money himself. And though he might not have received all that was due to him he was still champion and therefore in a position to earn a lot more before he finally hung up his gloves.

As if all the gossiping over the champion's illicit love affair were not enough, he was still managing to attract bad publicity.

Within a couple of months of the Petersen fight Mac was back in the news, the headline reading:

*'McAVOY'S BOUT WITH A TRAMCAR'*

While driving his car in Oxford Street, Manchester, McAvoy had apparently passed in front of an oncoming tram without giving a signal. There was a collision and McAvoy's car was pushed into another vehicle. He was fined ten shillings for driving without due care and attention. Just a simple traffic offence in fact, but because McAvoy was a celebrity it warranted headlines, and though he was convinced that he was being victimised because of who he was, it is a fact that for some reason or other he managed to get into far more scrapes than the average celebrity. He just seemed to attract trouble wherever he went. And if he wasn't the cause of most of it, it can truthfully be said that when trouble presented itself, instead of using his head and either walking away or attempting to smooth things out, his aggressive attitude invariably made matters worse.

Even among people he knew, he could be extremely volatile. Don Waters told me, 'Aye, you always had to be careful. He'd give you a bloody crack as soon as look at you.'

'What, even if you were a friend?' I asked, rather naively.

'Oh, aye,' said Don, laughing. 'He didn't bloody care who you were, that Joe. Aye, he was a bugger. He was all right though. What a sense of humour he had! But if something upset him you had to keep out of his bloody way.'

When McAvoy made his return to the ring on August 3rd, 1936, there was a further court case pending, due to be heard a few days after the fight. It was a Bank Holiday Monday afternoon show at Blackpool football ground, and a big holiday crowd turned up to see if the British Middleweight Champion could regain some of his lost prestige. His opponent was Bob Simpkins of Bridlington, a decent middleweight who had beaten quite a few good men, including the Welsh champion, Dai Jones. Simpkins, hoping to break into the title picture, had challenged McAvoy, and Harry Fleming had arranged the match, which was made at 11st. 10lbs. Using the Belle Vue gym, Mac had trained under Fleming and was in great shape. After a lay-off of over three months his hands felt as good as new. In charge of the contest, which was to end in highly controversial circumstances, was Joe Tolley, McAvoy's old manager.

As usual Mac tore after his man from the start, but Simpkins proved pretty adept at keeping the fight at long range and Mac soon realised that he would have to work to create the openings. Several times in the first few rounds he managed to weave his way in and belt Simpkins around the ribs, but repeatedly ran into stiff right crosses to the head which carried plenty of sting.

McAvoy's timing and judgement of distance were noticeably faulty, clearly the result of inactivity. Just the same he looked very capable and confident, and few doubted that he would emerge the winner. As Mac settled down he began to punish Simpkins with heavy blows to the body, but the Bridlington fighter was tough and determined. He always came back with those sharp rights to the face, occasionally banging in some telling digs to Mac's ribs.

Gradually though, McAvoy was getting on top, and though still missing with most of his punches, he did manage to shake his opponent several times with big swings to the side of the head. In round six, after mixing it with Mac, Simpkins left an opening and was caught by a couple of hefty uppercuts, one after the other, but managed to hold out to the bell.

In the next round Simpkins decided it was safer to go back to his long range boxing, but could not keep McAvoy away. He was soon in serious trouble from Mac's blistering body attack and took a fearful hammering before being battered to the canvas. Slowly he dragged himself to his knees and had not quite regained the upright position when the referee reached the count of ten.

As Tolley waved the contest over a section of the crowd started to boo, and Simpkins, who was very deaf, explained to the referee that he had not heard the count distinctly. At this point McAvoy walked over and requested that the contest be allowed to continue. Having warmed to his work, he seemed keen to carry on, and said, 'That's very bad luck. It's a mistake. Let's fight on.'

But Joe Tolley would have none of it and explained that as he had already given his decision, it could not be altered, which was perhaps just as well, for Simpkins was beginning to take a real hammering, while Mac was quite happy to keep on dishing it out, but this would hardly have been in Simpkins' best interests.

Though McAvoy's timing had been way off, the most satisfactory feature of his display was the fact that his hands had stood up to it very well, for he had punched Simpkins hard and often in the closing rounds, with no apparent ill effects.

The champion's next contest was to be at Belle Vue, six weeks hence, against Albert Barjolin, an experienced light-heavyweight who had held the French title for a time after taking it from Marcel Lauriot. But first there was another court appearance, this time at Stockport, where McAvoy was charged with failing to report an accident.

William Dixon, of Highgate Crescent, Gorton, told the court that he was looking at some garden implements outside a shop in Cheadle, with his foot on the pavement and one leg over his bicycle, when he felt a bump from behind. On turning round he found that the bump had been caused by a car which had pulled up behind him. Dixon immediately got off his bike and examined it to find out if any damage had been done.

He then alleged that the motorist, McAvoy, had got out of his car and asked him what he was looking for. Dixon had asked for the motorist's name, and stated that the defendant then pushed him across the footpath with one hand and struck him on the jaw with the other, saying, 'That's my name.'

In evidence, McAvoy replied to the charge thus: 'Does he say I punched him? Well, that beats me. The man's a liar. I felt something scrape against the car, got out and found that there was nothing wrong with the cyclist. But he took a notebook out and wanted to be awkward. I asked him what damage had been done, but there was nothing wrong, so he couldn't reply.'

As there were no witnesses, Mac got away with paying costs of eleven shillings, but if the plaintiff was to be believed this was a very unsavoury incident and a further addition to McAvoy's growing list of court appearances.

When McAvoy got back into training for the Barjolin fight, which was also destined to end controversially, he found it almost impossible to find, not just suitable sparring partners, but any sparring partners at all. His hands felt fine and with around twelve stone behind the punches he was hitting with pulverizing force. Eventually his last victim, Bob Simpkins, was persuaded to join the stable, along with Pop Newman, a fighter from Leicester. The usual appeals were put out for any extra helpers who fancied their chances with the gloves on, with the offer of a pound a round to entice any brave young fellow who cared to try his luck. This time, however, there were no takers, hard times or not, and Mac was obliged to rely on Simpkins and Newman.

On the Wednesday before the fight, however, at a public workout, a lone volunteer turned up. His name was Harold Knowles of Longsight, not far from Belle Vue. Knowles courageously stepped forward and offered to take McAvoy on, saying that he'd done quite a bit of boxing in the army and was confident he could give the champion a few brisk rounds. Mac set about him as if he were defending the title, battering the unfortunate local man all over the ring before finishing him off in well under a minute.

Against his regular spar mates he was just as ferocious, but they, of course, being pros, were much better able to take care of themselves than the luckless volunteer. Simpkins, in fact, showed a surprising ability to absorb punishment, and managed to last three rounds. Newman though, was soon in trouble and finished the first round in such a sorry state that he was forced to call it quits.

All those present agreed that Mac was in superlative form and that his punching power was quite awesome. He completed the session, which lasted 45 minutes, with shadow boxing and skipping, and judging by the way he pounded the heavy bag both hands appeared quite sound, although some present were still dubious, in view of the way they'd let him down so often in the past.

Albert Barjolin turned out to be a tall, well-proportioned fighter with a muscular, tanned body, who came into the ring displaying a championship belt which he had won outright on the continent.

Once the contest got under way, however, it soon became clear that the Frenchman was unlikely to pose much of a threat, for he showed little inclination to make a fight of it and was soon backing off, McAvoy having things all his own way as he followed the retreating Frenchman and belted him about the body with both hands.

Midway through round two McAvoy banged over a heavy right to the jaw and followed up with another as Barjolin fell back against the ropes. Immediately the Frenchman signalled to the referee that he'd had enough, at the same time tugging frantically at his mouth.

As the visitor had suffered no apparent injury the spectators were at once incensed, and called on the referee to force him to continue. McAvoy was in full agreement with them, and as Barjolin came off the ropes and stood upright Mac moved into the attack once more. The Frenchman, however, refused to carry on and walked to his corner. It was then announced that he had retired injured.

Barjolin, who left the ring to the accompaniment of booing from all parts of the crowded hall, was under the impression that his jaw had been fractured, but it was later discovered that one of McAvoy's power laden blows had broken two of his teeth and driven them into the upper jaw.

Mac himself was very disappointed. He had just begun to enjoy himself and felt frustrated at the sudden ending. The hand had again stood up well and he now looked forward eagerly to his next engagement, which was just over a month away and would again be at Belle Vue, this time against Charlie Bundy, a light-heavyweight from Wales who had defeated Ernie Simmonds and drawn with both Eddie Phillips and Eddie McGuire.

In the meantime an offer was received from Madison Square Garden for McAvoy to take on Harry Balsamo, an Italian middleweight who had just beaten the highly-rated German, Eric Seelig, inside a round.

While this was being considered he was again in court for a motoring offence, this time at Preston, where he pleaded guilty to driving in a manner dangerous to the public, refusing to give his name and address, driving without a license and carrying a gun without a license.

Observed by a police constable, McAvoy had driven around a bend in Garstang Road on his off side, and over the line marking the centre of the road. A car travelling in the opposite direction had been forced to pull out of his way to allow him to get past, but McAvoy had then turned in towards his own side of the road, causing the line of following traffic to brake sharply and come to a halt.

At this point, the policeman, P.C. Bone, had intervened. According to the constable, McAvoy, on being stopped, had taken up a threatening attitude, and when asked for his name has said, 'You know my name.'

The officer said he knew him as Jock McAvoy, but would like his correct name. The defendant had then said, 'You make me sick,' and got back into his car, still refusing to give a name and address. The constable noticed that there were two women in the car with him, also a gun, which McAvoy said did not belong to him. He then drove off without even giving the officer a chance to take particulars of the car's road fund license.

It was explained to the court that the defendant had forgotten to renew his driver's license, which had expired three months before, and that the gun was a common shotgun for which no license was required, provided it was used on the defendant's own property. A list of previous motoring convictions was then read out, before the defendant was fined a total of £8-10s. He was also ordered to pay costs of £1-11s witnesses expenses plus six guineas advocates costs, and was informed that his license would be suspended for six months.

It had been rather an expensive day, and Mac was not in a very good mood as he resumed his training for the Bundy fight, to the extreme discomfort, no doubt, of his unfortunate sparring partners.

A couple of days before the fight, word was received that Bundy had taken ill and would not be able to appear. In his place, Bill Wainwright, a heavyweight from Swadlincote was drafted in. Wainwright was a giant compared to McAvoy, standing 6ft 1½in. and weighing 13½ stone.

The fight, scheduled for twelve rounds, opened quietly, with both men tentatively feeling each other out. After more than half the round had gone by with hardly a blow struck, the crowd became very restless and made sure that the fighters knew all about it.

Immediately Mac woke up and slammed a hard right into the pit of Wainwnght's stomach which sent the big man sprawling and rolling over in agony. He just managed to beat the count, but was down again almost at once from another wicked body punch, this time being saved by the bell.

McAvoy went straight into the attack as round two opened, but Wainwright came out determined to get his own back and shook Mac twice with hefty uppercuts. But McAvoy soon connected with another powerful right to put the towering Swadlincote fighter down again, and repeated the feat soon afterwards. Still Wainwright was not finished, and when he caught Mac with a heavy blow on the ear, which made the champion wince, the crowd must have felt that the fight might well develop into a more closely contested affair than the early action had indicated. But that punch only served to sting McAvoy into fierce action, and after hammering his man about the body he floored him with a thudding right to the jaw.

Again the bell came to Wainwright's rescue, but at the opening of round three McAvoy connected with the right again and this time the game Swadlincote man went down for the full count.

Mac's speed and power had been too much for the gallant substitute, who had taken some very severe punishment in the short time the fight had lasted. Wainwright had felt so confident, he had made a wager that McAvoy would not knock him out, and this had been sanctioned by the Northern branch of the Board of Control, but after the fight it was announced that McAvoy would waive his claim and that Wainwright would receive his full purse. He certainly deserved it.

McAvoy's private life was becoming more and more complicated, his association with Joan Lye having become so public that it was naturally causing Eliza some distress, especially after discussing it with him and realising that he was deadly serious about the affair. Eliza's parents also talked to Mac, pleading with him to consider the children. It made little difference. Even so, he became very angry when Eliza threatened to leave and take the children with her.

Throughout all this upheaval Mac still had to try and concentrate on his career. He was more than ever anxious to fight for a world title, but Risko's connections continued to stall. There was always the chance, though, that John Henry Lewis might give him another shot. The Belle Vue people were keen to stage the fight, but were beaten to it by Len Harvey. Len had just been appointed matchmaker at Wembley in succession to Sydney Hulls, and promptly made an offer of £4,000 to Lewis to come over and defend the title against him, in what must surely have been a unique contest, with the challenger acting as his own matchmaker.

As it turned out the fighter was less successful than the matchmaker, for Len was outpointed, though putting up an excellent show against a fine champion. Before Lewis could leave the country, his manager, Gus Greenlees, was approached by Belle Vue with an offer of £3,500 to defend against McAvoy in Manchester. Greenlees admitted that the offer was a good one and promised to consider it, along with several others they had received, including one from Paris. In the meantime Lewis was keen to return home, so nothing came of it.

There was still pressure to accept a match with Jack Hyams for McAvoy's Middleweight title, and an offer was received from Jim Wicks, later to manage Henry Cooper, on behalf of Sydney Porter of Wandsworth Stadium, London. Wicks, then acting as matchmaker, offered to put up a purse of £1,500 of which McAvoy would get £1,000. But Mac was not quite ready to put his title on the line against such a crafty customer as Hyams and did not bite.

There was also talk of another clash with Len Harvey, involving a sidestake of £500, but when nothing developed in that direction, Mac, keen to keep busy, took a fight with Rienus de Boer, light-heavyweight champion of Holland, in Sheffield.

It turned out to be a poor affair, with the Dutchman, after sampling Mac's right hand punching, getting on his bike and managing to keep out of the way for the full ten rounds. Although winning by a wide margin, Mac did not show his usual fire, and a section of the crowd, disappointed that he had not managed to put de Boer away, booed him as he left the ring.

# Chapter 22

## Tribulation and Triumph

January 1937 turned out to be quite an eventful month for the British Middleweight Champion. First he was forced to pull out of a contest with Cuban light-heavyweight, Cheo Morejon, at Leicester, having damaged his right hand again in training. His place was taken by Jack Hyams, who won easily on points.

Mac would not fight again until March, but in the meantime his problems outside the ring were mounting. After enduring over eighteen months of acute torment and humiliation, Eliza finally walked out with the children and filed for divorce. On January 15th of that year she was granted a decree nisi for the dissolution of her marriage to Joseph Bamford, known as Jock McAvoy, professional boxer. The petition was unopposed.

Mrs Bamford's case was that her married life had not been happy for a long time, her husband ill-treating her and going about with other women. She had gone to join him in America, in November 1935, and had known before this that he was associating with a woman named Joan Lye. While in America she discovered that he was receiving letters from her and had continued the association on his return, despite attempts to persuade him to break it off.

Evidence from a London hotel was also given, and Mrs Bamford, in being granted the decree, was awarded custody of the three children, plus costs against her husband. Mr Justice Langton gave her leave to write down her address in order to prevent its public disclosure, her counsel stating that Mrs Bamford feared her husband's violence if he discovered where she was living.

Joan Lye's father, James Lye, who had been very worried about the whole affair, now made renewed efforts to talk some sense into his daughter, for he realised that once McAvoy's divorce became absolute there was nothing to prevent a marriage which he and his wife were very much against. The Lyes had naturally entertained hopes that Joan would make what they considered to be a good marriage. The thought of her throwing herself away on a man like Joe Bamford must have given them nightmares. But Joan was besotted, and nothing her father could say or do would persuade her to end the relationship. In any case, she was pregnant, and though her parents would undoubtedly have stood by her and helped bring up the baby, had she chosen to go back home, she had no intention of doing so. Instead, the couple set up house together at 27 Sundial Road, Offerton, in Stockport, and on April 20th 1937, a son was born. They christened him Michael.

Less than two weeks after the divorce hearing the middleweight champion was summoned at Preston Police Court on charges of having assaulted ticket collectors Richard Bennett and Arthur Aymes.

The alleged incident had occurred just after Christmas when McAvoy had been at Preston Railway Station in connection with several horses he owned, which were being put on the train. He had another man with him, and following some minor altercation over a platform ticket was alleged to have struck the two plaintiffs, knocking off Bennett's hat and glasses and punching Aymes to the ground.

The allegations were denied, Mr A. H. Franks, of Manchester, representing McAvoy, pointing out that when his client hit people (presumably meaning in the ring) they finished up in a far more serious condition than the plaintiffs apparently had.

He also mentioned that his client, when asked his name, had said, 'You know me. Jock McAvoy or Joe Bamford.'

'There is no such person as Jock McAvoy,' went on Mr Franks, 'and the complainants know my client's proper name, yet they issued a summons in the name of Jock McAvoy. I am going to say that they did this deliberately, for the purpose of creating prejudice. I therefore move that the charges be dismissed.'

Though probably exaggerating, the complainants claimed that McAvoy had become very violent at the platform barrier, 'striking out left and right'. In view of the fact that Mac was found guilty he was very leniently dealt with, being fined ten shillings on each of two summonses. The worrying thing was, however, that he was becoming increasingly violent in public, and it was quite obvious that such conduct could not be tolerated. Up to this point nothing really serious had occurred, and there is little doubt that because McAvoy was a public figure many of the incidents in which he got himself involved were being blown up out of all proportion. But then again, why did he have to get involved so often? The main problem, of course, was that quick temper, which he had never learned to control. Mac also tended to be arrogant and full of himself, and it is perhaps significant that in a number of cases it had come out in court that when asked to give his name and address he was inclined to think that the person asking the question ought to know who he was, and was quite annoyed if he didn't.

It was around this time that McAvoy received some good news. Eddie Phillips had agreed to meet him at Wembley, with the light-heavyweight title at stake. As the date set was April 6th there was ample time to re-arrange the contest with Cheo Morejon. With the fight set for the beginning of March, Mac had several weeks in which to prepare. The hand was feeling better again, but with a title fight looming he was careful not to overtax it, working mainly with the left when it came to heavy punching on the bag.

Morejon turned out to be a powerfully built negro, almost coal black, and though an elusive, fast moving target, had a rare capacity for taking punishment.

In this fight McAvoy attempted to box his man, using the straight left far more often than usual, and though he was always in command, the Cuban himself proved very effective at long range, whereas McAvoy was totally dominant when it came to close quarter exchanges.

Every so often Mac would go all out to finish things with a fierce onslaught, but Morejon certainly won the hearts of the spectators by taking everything that came his way, remaining cool under fire, then retaliating with bursts of fast punching.

The liveliest action came in round four when McAvoy twice belted Morejon on the jaw with hard punches. Back came the Cuban, meeting Mac blow for blow and more than holding his own. But as the round neared its end Morejon was knocked onto the ropes by a sharp left hook, faltered for a moment, then, while McAvoy watched in amazement, the Cuban skipped all the way around the ring three times, as if he had suddenly taken leave of his senses, the crowd roaring with laughter at his antics.

It had not been a great contest, though quite interesting for the spectators, who had been completely won over by Morejon's spirited display and good humour. In the final round both fighters punched away non-stop, and as McAvoy's arm was raised as the winner the Cuban skipped back to his corner with a grin, apparently as fresh as a daisy and looking as if he could have gone another ten rounds.

It was reported around this time that negotiations were about to take place for a contest between McAvoy and Marcel Thil for the Frenchman's World Middleweight title, which Thil had successfully defended on February 15th against the tough French-Canadian, Lou Brouillard, the challenger being disqualified in the sixth round for an alleged low blow.

McAvoy's hand had stood up well to the twelve rounds with Morejon and he was feeling very confident as he prepared for the title fight with Eddie Phillips. But with the contest only a week or so away, Mac suddenly went down with bronchitis, a complaint which had troubled him off and on for many years. This time though it was a little more serious and Mac felt quite ill. When the doctor diagnosed bronchial influenza there was nothing for it but to seek a postponement, and the contest was put back three weeks, to April 27th. At the same time the middleweight title fight against Jack Hyams was approved by the Board of Control, Hyams having qualified for his shot by outpointing Dai Jones of Ammanford at Earl's Court that February.

In addition to the two title fights he had coming up, McAvoy was also committed to a non-title bout against the same Dai Jones, arranged to take place at Bristol on May 3rd.

Fortunately, McAvoy quickly recovered from his illness and within a very short time was back to his best form. In a public workout just one week before he was due to meet Phillips, Mac showed that he was as sharp as ever. He was not holding back with the right and was punching with great power, which was not good news as far as Eddie Phillips was concerned.

There was an air of great confidence in the Belle Vue camp. They were even looking beyond the Phillips fight to a possible encounter with Tommy Farr for the British and Empire Heavyweight titles which Tommy had won earlier that year from Ben Foord, the South African having taken them from Jack Petersen in August 1936.

Eddie Phillips was a worthy champion who had worked hard for his success. A likeable fellow, the former coach driver from Bow had begun his career in spectacular fashion, winning twenty-three contests, fifteen inside the distance. Eddie also acted as Len Harvey's sparring partner in those early days, eventually clashing with Len no fewer than four times. But although forcing a draw on the first occasion, he had never managed to get the better of the redoubtable Cornishman, though all three bouts were keenly contested affairs. Finally, after Harvey relinquished the title, Eddie became champion by outpointing Tommy Farr at Mountain Ash, in February 1935.

In contrast to McAvoy, a middleweight bulked up to light-heavy, Phillips was a natural twelve-stone-seven pounder, who campaigned a lot of the time among the heavyweights. Eddie was a solid no-frills performer with a fair dig, and could not be taken lightly, as McAvoy was soon to discover.

At the weigh-in Mac scaled 12st. 1lb 8ozs, while the champion came in at just 4ozs under the 12st 7lb limit. When the two stood together the Cockney appeared much the bigger man, which was hardly surprising, for in addition to the considerable disparity in weight, Phillips stood over six feet and possessed a powerful physique.

Before the packed Wembley Arena the challenger carried the fight to his bigger opponent from the start, tearing in with both fists and quickly nailing Phillips with a right to the body and a left hook to the head. Immediately the champion fell into a clinch, and on pulling out of it Mac tore straight in again, but left himself wide open and was tagged by a powerful left hook that dropped him to his knees. More surprised than stunned, Mac was up before the referee could take up the count and did well to evade the bombardment that now came his way as Phillips went all out for a quick victory.

Before the round ended McAvoy was fighting back and managing to score to the body. In round two Phillips tried hard to land another big punch. In doing so he left his own chin unprotected and was caught by a left hook followed by a vicious right cross which put him down heavily. He looked badly hurt but was up at eight and ready to fight back. Phillips now poked out his left to hold McAvoy off, but was hurt again and forced to clinch as Mac hammered away to the body. Eddie went back to his corner bleeding from the mouth but far from finished and came out for the third full of fight.

But he was finding the smaller man very difficult to contain and was soon in difficulties again, going down from another right for a count of two. Having allowed the Rochdale man to take control Phillips was now finding it almost impossible to turn the tide, though he caught McAvoy with the occasional well-placed right cross.

Mac looked by far the sharper of the two, and apart from the challenger's aggressiveness, Phillips was finding McAvoy very elusive as he came in, bobbing and weaving. He was being outboxed as well as out-gunned by his speedy opponent, who was proving very adept at making him miss, then banging over quick, powerful counter punches.

By the fifth McAvoy had found his rhythm and was boxing beautifully, piling up the points with sharp, accurate left hooks and jabs and at times planting a jarring right cross on the champion's chin. After being in trouble again, Phillips showed his courage by coming back strongly and catching Mac with a hard right as the round ended. In the middle rounds the champion tried his best to get back into the fight and managed to land a heavy right to the jaw, but was forced to take a couple in return.

After taking quite a battering in the ninth, Phillips recovered so well that in the next two rounds he began to take the play away from McAvoy and get well on top, giving the challenger quite a drubbing in round eleven and more of the same in the twelfth.

The thirteenth, however, saw a dramatic change in fortunes. Mac came out determined to take control and battered his opponent non-stop about the body until Phillips began to visibly weaken. Though badly hurt and fighting for breath the gallant champion somehow managed to hold out to the bell, but it was clear that the end was in sight.

As the fourteenth round opened Mac began to unload those lethal bombs, but though in bad trouble, Phillips still fought back courageously, trying hard to land the one big punch that might stop McAvoy in his tracks. But he now had the scent of victory in his nostrils and a flurry of blows in the centre of the ring ended with Mac landing a power-packed right which opened up a big gash in the champion's cheek bone. A left hook to the body followed by a couple of heavy rights to the chin and Eddie was sent sprawling into the ropes and from there to the canvas. Gamely the stricken champion struggled to regain his feet, but his limbs just refused to respond as the referee counted him out. Eddie's handlers then rushed to his assistance, but it was some time before he was in a fit enough condition to leave the ring. Afterwards he was attended by a doctor in his dressing room, but soon recovered.

It was another triumphant night for McAvoy as well as for Rochdale, and there was great excitement and jubilation as the Lonsdale belt was fastened around the new champion's waist.

McAvoy had now bettered Len Harvey's record, by holding both the Middleweight and Light-heavyweight titles simultaneously.

After the fight Mac wasted no time in heading back up North, arriving in Rochdale very early the following morning and knocking up his relatives, the Pilkingtons, who were delighted to see him and thrilled at his great victory. From there he went to his parents' house before going on to see the children.

# Chapter 23

## Disaster

Had the title fight taken place as scheduled, on April 6th, McAvoy would have had a full month to get over the effects of it before stepping into the ring again. As it was he had just under one week before the contest with Dai Jones at Bristol's Colston Hall. Though it must have come as something of an anti-climax, he made no attempt to seek a postponement and went down to Bristol with the intention of seeing Jones off as quickly as possible. It did not, however, work out that way, the Welshman putting up a stubborn resistance and forcing Mac to go the full ten rounds.

There was never any question as to who would emerge the winner. In the opening rounds McAvoy made good use of the left, while easily avoiding Jones's crude swings. By the fifth he had begun to punish his opponent and succeeded in connecting with one of his 'specials', a beautifully timed uppercut, which shook the Welshman, forcing him to hang on. In the next two rounds Jones took a rare battering and was down for a count of two, but gamely attempted to get back into the fight.

In round eight, Jones, a farmer by trade, caused something of a shock, sending McAvoy to his knees with a haymaker which landed with a thud on the side of the champion's head. Mac was up without a count and again took charge, hammering the Welshman with both hands and forcing him to clinch.

The last two rounds were all McAvoy, with Jones taking a bad beating and doing well to last the distance. The plucky Welshman was almost out on his feet in the final round, but still made every effort to fight back and received an appreciative ovation at the end for his courageous display.

McAvoy, who was probably a little stale, decided after the fight that he would take a short holiday before going into training for the Hyams fight, which was scheduled for July 26th.

Following the withdrawal of Jack Doyle from a big London charity show, due to take place on June 28th, John Harding, the promoter, needed a big name to replace the Irishman and contacted Britain's new double champion. McAvoy was glad to oblige, and was matched with light-heavyweight Frank Hough, the ex-Hussar who had once helped out Mac as a sparring partner. The match was made at 12st. 8lbs, and Hough, who was at that time working with the German heavyweight, Walter Neusel, was expected to be very strong at the weight.

McAvoy had now given up the Brunswick Hotel and also his stables at Syke, but he was soon itching to get back in the saddle and joined a local riding school. On a Friday evening in June, while riding his horse over the school's fields, Mac met with a serious accident. In taking a jump the horse stumbled and while in mid-air the saddle girth broke. McAvoy went sailing over his mount's head to land with sickening force some yards further on.

Other riders at once rushed to help him, while a trainer rounded up the horse. Some of those present had seen Mac land on his head and feared the worst. As riding instructor David Jones approached he could see that the boxer was in a bad way. He was bleeding from the head and mouth, and Jones's first thought was that his skull might be fractured or his neck broken. A doctor was immediately called, and after examining him, arranged for McAvoy to be taken to Stockport Infirmary.

In an interview later, David Jones said that McAvoy bought his horse in Yorkshire. It was a thoroughbred steeplechaser and a splendid animal. Mac was in the habit of bringing it regularly to the stables to ride it, and was a very fine horseman of considerable experience.

As it turned out, nothing was broken, though the neck muscles were so badly damaged that there was now a big question mark against Mac's future career in the ring. A consultant told him that had it not been for his powerful physique and the extraordinary strength of his neck muscles he would certainly have suffered a broken neck.

They then fitted him up with a plaster collar, and on the Sunday, only two days after the accident, he was on his way home, having got thoroughly bored with sitting up in bed. He had been very fortunate, and though the long term effects would not be known for some time, one thing was certain, there could be no thought of boxing for quite a while. The charity show clash with Hough was cancelled and the Hyams fight postponed.

In the meantime there were a couple more of the inevitable summonses to be dealt with; one at Manchester City Police Court for an alleged assault on a man named Hugh Orr in Oxford Road, Manchester, and another driving offence, this time for speeding, in Central Drive, Blackpool. When McAvoy's license was endorsed it was pointed out that there were three endorsements on it already, connected with speeding and dangerous driving.

The Oxford Road case turned out to be more serious. Mr D. J. McBeth, acting for Hugh Orr, a van driver from Salford, said that in his opinion, as the defendant was a professional boxer who made his living by fighting, he could be considered a very formidable and even dangerous aggressor to the ordinary man in the street, and it was his submission that such a person, endowed with physical capabilities far above the ordinary, should perhaps, more than other people, keep his temper under the strictest control.

Apparently there had been a minor argument following a traffic incident in Oxford Road, which ended with Bamford telling the van driver 'not to be so cheeky'.

Orr then drove off, and on stopping at a garage, found that McAvoy had followed him. The boxer had threatened to report him and 'wipe him across the nose'. Orr, who claimed later that he did not know that McAvoy was a boxer, replied, 'Do you fancy your chances then?'

When Orr came out of the garage he told McAvoy that the name and address of his firm were on the van, and said, 'So go and do your reporting.'

McAvoy was then alleged to have jumped out of his car, in which Harry Fleming was a passenger, and struck the van driver a violent blow in the pit of the stomach. 'Orr was absolutely incapacitated,' went on Mr McBeth, 'and lay writhing in pain. So severe were the effects of the blow that he had to go to a doctor that night and was taken very ill over the weekend.'

Cross-examined by Mr Kenneth Burke, defending, Orr said that although he got a bit excited he did not use any bad language and denied that he had stood with his hand on McAvoy's car and refused to go away.

Herbert Finney, an ex-policeman. and commissionaire at the garage, said that Orr had made no attempt to defend himself before the blow was struck. Bamford drove off afterwards, saying, 'You got what you asked for.'

A woman witness described the blow as 'having great force behind it.'

Mr Burke said that in his opinion it did not necessarily follow that because the defendant was a boxer it was a serious matter. A man with his skill and knowledge of the boxing profession, if he had really intended to damage the complainant, could have inflicted far more serious injuries to him.

McAvoy, who arrived at the court wearing the Plaster of Paris collar, stated that he had followed Orr to the garage to report him. After he got back into his car Orr had put his hand on the door and refused to go away. He had then got out again and pushed Orr away with the flat of his hand.

'It may have been a rough push,' said McAvoy, 'but it was certainly not a punch.' He denied that the van driver had fallen to the ground.

Harry Fleming said that he had not heard McAvoy threaten Orr. He had taken Orr's question 'Do you fancy your chances?' as a challenge to fight.

In reply to Mr McBeth, McAvoy denied being annoyed because Orr had not recognised him.

'I don't go about thinking "I'm Jock McAvoy", if that's what you mean. I don't want people to be scared of me just because I'm a professional fighter.' In the circumstances McAvoy was extremely fortunate, after being found guilty of assault, to get away with a fine of £5 and costs.

Not long after this Mac, sick and tired of the inconvenience and discomfort caused by the collar, got out of bed one night, took a sharp knife from the kitchen and started to hack his way through the plaster. As the collar had been in place for several weeks, holding the neck rigid, he could feel nothing, and imagined that the injury had mended. It therefore came as a great shock, when he at last managed to remove the collar, to feel his head flop limply over to one side and a searing pain shoot through his neck. A doctor was quickly summoned and a fresh dressing applied. After that it was just a question of being patient for a while longer, during which time periodic trips were made to London for treatment by a leading manipulative surgeon, who did such a fine job on the injury that Mac was able to have the plaster removed for good just a few weeks later. After visiting the specialist in September, Mac was given a clean bill of health and told that he could get back into training. He had made a remarkable recovery from a very serious injury which could have wrecked his career.

Soon afterwards a meeting took place between McAvoy, Harry Fleming and George Wilson of Belle Vue, Wilson pointing out the heavy financial loss which had been sustained due to the postponement of the Jack Hyams fight. He now suggested a new date, October 25th, which would give McAvoy just over a month to prepare.

'That'll do me,' replied Mac.

Fleming, who was again looking after his training, protested that, in view of the fact that Mac had been out of the ring since the 3rd of May, this was too soon, but McAvoy, impatient as always, brushed his arguments aside.

'No! The promoters have been messed about enough, and I don't want to keep Hyams waiting any longer. Besides, the doctor says I'm fit to train, so let's get on with it.'

The date was therefore fixed for October 25th at the King's Hall, Belle Vue, and McAvoy, delighted to be going into action again, got stuck into his training with a will.

Without waiting to see how McAvoy fared against Hyams, Mr A. J. Elvin, the Wembley promoter, had forwarded contracts to John Henry Lewis in America, and was hopefully awaiting their return.

Belle Vue's King's Hall was not big enough to hold all who wanted to see McAvoy defend his title against Jack Hyams, the Jewish fighter from London's East End. Though beaten by Mac twice before, Hyams could never be underestimated. He was a crafty, experienced pro., who was always capable of springing a surprise, and there was much speculation as to whether McAvoy would be able to catch up with him.

The most important question, of course, concerned Mac's serious injury and long lay-off. Would he still be the same explosive fighter as before? Would he be capable of standing up to the strain of a gruelling championship contest over fifteen rounds? He had shaped well in training, reducing his weight gradually from over twelve stone and coming in just one ounce inside the middleweight limit.

Both boxers received an enthusiastic reception as they climbed into the ring. Mac had not defended the middleweight title for over two years, and Hyams, who had been a contender for some considerable time, was determined to take the Lonsdale belt back to London with him.

The challenger started well, spearing McAvoy with a rapier-like left as Mac came in with his usual forcing tactics, then moving smoothly around the ring as the champion followed him doggedly, keen to get in close enough to set up one of those blistering body attacks. Several times Hyams made Mac miss with big right swings. An accomplished spoiler, the Cockney was very clever at tying up an opponent and difficult to catch with a clean shot.

In the early rounds McAvoy did all the chasing, with Hyams backing away and being quite content to score with the occasional left jab. But each time Mac eased off, the challenger would step in with a sharp right cross, hurting Mac and stinging him into action. Hyams would then immediately go into reverse again, using the ropes as he cleverly ducked and weaved his way out of danger. Until the fifth round it was a real cat and mouse affair, with McAvoy trying hard to corner his elusive opponent, and Hyams, boxing coolly, keeping out of trouble and picking up points with that educated left hand.

It was Hyams though, who brought the contest to life in the fifth when he suddenly stopped back-peddling and caught McAvoy with a cracking left hook, followed by a perfect right cross to the chin which halted the champion in his tracks. Mac was now driven onto the ropes, but though shaken, he fought back like a demon, causing Hyams to back off again. Having failed to press home his advantage, the Londoner returned to the old hit and run tactics.

As the fight progressed, Hyams produced similar bursts of aggression from time to time, which were very effective, and had he been prepared to open up and attack more often he might well have gained the initiative. As it was, he invariably adopted a more cautious approach, using the ring, poking out his left and falling into a clinch whenever danger threatened. He was well aware of McAvoy's great strength and had no intention of slugging it out with him.

Mac plodded after him relentlessly, but was having great difficulty in cornering the crafty Cockney. On the rare occasions that he did, Mac would set up a strong body attack, but Hyams showed shrewd defensive qualities, taking many blows intended for the ribs on his elbows and arms.

Then, in round six, disaster struck the Londoner. Crashing a heavy blow through Hyams' guard to the pit of the stomach, Mac quickly switched his attack, banging in a sharp left and right to the head, the last punch causing a large gash to appear under the challenger's left eye and blood to spurt out. It was the turning point, for a large bump now appeared, and with the eye closing rapidly Hyams was in desperate trouble. Unless he could pull something special out of the bag it was obvious that he would be unlikely to last the distance.

McAvoy now attacked ferociously, while Hyams, though badly handicapped, tried everything he knew to turn the tide. But with the injury worsening it was clear that he was fighting a losing battle. Retaliating gamely, he caught Mac several times with solid right crosses, which appeared to have no effect at all on the tough Rochdale man. By the tenth the swelling on the courageous challenger's cheek had almost closed his left eye and it was obvious that he could not hold out much longer.

Hyams looked a sorry sight as he came up for the eleventh round. But McAvoy showed him no mercy, throwing punches non-stop and battering his half-blind opponent around the ring. It was the champion's best round of the fight and he hit Hyams with some tremendous punches, including a couple of vicious uppercuts which almost tore the Londoner's head off his shoulders. Hyams was in such a bad way at the bell that he could barely make it to his corner, and it came as no surprise when his seconds called the referee over and retired their man.

Having already won a championship belt outright, McAvoy was presented with a completely new replacement, on which he had now put the first notch, the same, of course, applying to the light-heavy-weight belt he had taken from Eddie Phillips.

It was a magnificent achievement, and all the more remarkable in view of the serious neck injury he had sustained not many months before. It appeared that the enforced rest had given Mac's hands a chance to heal, for he was certainly punching with all the old venom, and feeling no ill-effects.

Alban Mulrooney, from Macclesfield, in Cheshire, was the next to feel the weight of McAvoy's mighty fists, when he stepped into the ring with him at Hanley a month after the Hyams fight.

As a former sparring partner, Mulrooney knew plenty about Mac and must have felt that this would stand him in good stead. But after sampling a couple of those rib-benders, the Cheshire man spent most of the first round going from one clinch to another. In the second he decided to try and box at long range, showing a nice straight left. But just when he appeared to be settling down Mulrooney was rocked by a right to the body that knocked most of the fight out of him.

Somehow he managed to hang on till the end of the round, but was felled by a right to the chin almost as soon as round three had got under way. Mulrooney jumped up without taking a count, but was knocked down three times more before the referee decided to call if off.

There was one more fight before the end of 1937, the Belle Vue management bringing over Vasile Serbanesco from Rumania. Serbanesco, who claimed both his country's light-heavy and heavy-weight titles, was a big man, and McAvoy would be conceding considerable weight. Just the same, before either the I.B.U. or the B.B.B. of C. would sanction the match the Rumanian's record was carefully scrutinised.

Mac was very impressive in training, and his sparring partners were again given a rough time. Serbanesco also used the Belle Vue training facilities to complete his preparations, and though the protagonists naturally trained at different times of the day, a little spying went on just the same, the reports indicating that the big Rumanian was a more than useful fighter with a strong right hand punch.

This bit of intelligence turned out to be absolutely correct. Apart from giving away plenty of height and weight, Mac found himself well out-reached and could not find the range at all in round one. In the second Serbanesco drove the British champion back onto the ropes with a long spearing left and following right crosses, and Mac had to fight hard to avoid being overwhelmed. It was quite clear that, unlike many of McAvoy's opponents, Serbanesco had not come just to stay the distance, and Mac soon felt the weight of that dangerous right hand before he managed to drive his man back with stiff body punches.

After this he decided to work at close range, and this tactic paid off almost immediately, for he soon began to punish the Rumanian about the body, while at the same time making him miss with those viciously aimed rights to the head. Boxing very cleverly, McAvoy easily took the third, and though Serbanesco was still very aggressive, his long, straight punches and big swings were just not connecting. Finishing the round with a flourish, Mac belted his man heavily to the ribs before the bell rang, and returned to his corner knowing he was well on top.

The Rumanian, however, was still very strong, and the crowd could be justified in feeling that the contest was far from over and might well go the distance. The next round, however, was to prove the last. McAvoy opened by scoring with two crisp left hooks to the jaw. Then Serbanesco, retreating, landed with a powerful right to the face, driven downwards. They then went into a clinch, from which the Rumanian emerged with blood pouring from a deep cut over the left eye.

Whether the injury had been caused by a punch was not clear, but for a moment, Serbanesco, realising the seriousness of it, seemed undecided about carrying on. Then, having made up his mind to have a final fling, he set about McAvoy in determined fashion. Mac met him head-on and the crowd were treated to a rare scrap as the two battered away at each other right up to the bell. On close inspection the gash was found to be a very bad one, extending across the eyebrow and down the side of his nose. The Rumanian was therefore forced to retire after four exciting rounds, in a fight, which, had it not ended prematurely, could well have turned out to be one of McAvoy's sternest tests.

As 1937 neared its close Jim Lye was given the not unexpected bad news that his daughter was planning to marry McAvoy, Eliza now having obtained her decree absolute. Having failed to talk some sense into Joan, Lye now decided to discuss the matter with McAvoy himself and invited the fighter to Mount Healey, his luxurious home in the hills above Rochdale. Mac was at once struck by the opulence of the place, but if he was overawed he did not show it, though he was, of course, on his best behaviour.

Jim Lye, a jolly, red-faced man with thick white hair, was an easy sort of man to get on with in normal circumstances, though it's doubtful if he was feeling all that jolly on this particular occasion. His wife, Dorothy, tall, slim and elegant, was the daughter of Dr Hayle, a Rochdale physician who had died young. She could not, therefore, be said to have enjoyed a particularly affluent childhood. Nevertheless, she was very much aware of her position as the wife of a wealthy company director, and though quite a nice lady, tended to be somewhat starchy, causing McAvoy to feel rather uncomfortable in her presence.

Taking him away from the women and into an adjoining room, Jim Lye first of all attempted to outline to McAvoy all the hopes and plans he had always had for his daughter's future, whereupon Mac reminded him that Joan had a mind of her own, a fact he could hardly deny. When the question of money finally came up McAvoy pointed out that although he might have come from a deprived background, he had climbed to the top of his profession and was a very successful man in his own right, both materially and in terms of achievement. Again, Lye could not refute this, and Mac went on to make it very clear that he was not interested in Lye's money. He quite understood why his prospective father-in-law felt the way he did, but the plain fact was that the two of them were very much in love, and that all they cared about was being together. When reminded that he was the father of three other children, apart from Michael, Mac explained that although they meant everything to him, he was divorced from their mother and therefore free to marry. We can safely assume that Jim and Dorothy Lye did not give the couple their blessing, or even acknowledge that they accepted the situation, but there was obviously nothing more they could do about it.

On December 20th, 1937, Joseph Bamford, aged 30, married Joan Alice Lye, 25, at Stockport Register Office. It must have been a sad and humiliating day for Eliza, for she still loved Joe and would stand by him through thick and thin for the rest of her life.

Nineteen-thirty-seven had been a very successful year, not only for McAvoy, but also for that other famous Rochdalian, Gracie Fields. In May she was given the Freedom of the Borough, and in

November, along with comedian, Norman Evans, also from Rochdale, Gracie starred in the Royal Command Performance at the London Palladium.

The show, which was broadcast on the wireless, drew a vast audience, with Gracie having the distinction of being the only artist on the bill to give an encore, and of course getting the audience to join her in the chorus of *'Sally'*. Norman Evans, later to become famous for his 'Over the Garden Wall' sketch, treated the Royals to an amusing piece entitled 'Joe Ramsbottom at the Dentists', which brought the house down.

When the honours list came out on January 1st, 1938, Rochdale was delighted to learn that Gracie Fields had been awarded the C.B.E. Soon afterwards the *Rochdale Observer*, obviously very proud of Gracie and her achievements, announced the opening of what they termed 'a portrait fund', an appeal to the public of Rochdale for contributions with a view to commissioning one of the country's leading painters to produce a portrait of Rochdale's most famous woman, the donations to be made in shillings.

The *Observer* itself started the ball rolling by pledging 500 shillings, while high on the first published list of subscribers was the name of the philanthropic Frederick Lye with a contribution of 100 shillings. Within three weeks 4,000 shillings had been raised. By mid-February, when Gracie received her award at Buckingham Palace, over 11,000 shillings had been received from an enthusiastic and generous public, in spite of the fact that the area was in an acute state of depression, with unemployment rife.

The *Observer* then announced that James Gunn, one of Britain's finest living painters, had been commissioned to carry out the work. The portrait was completed by late October and the presentation made at the Regal Cinema on November 5th before an audience of 3,000, with many more, who had been unable to get in, cheering outside.

Gracie, then living in her villa in Capri, came up from London where she was working, and received a rapturous reception as her car passed along the Esplanade after the ceremony.

# Chapter 24

## A Rift in the Marriage

The beginning of 1938, and still nothing had been settled regarding McAvoy's projected World title shot against John Henry Lewis. First it was reported that the champion was suffering from a serious nose injury, then came word that it was not so serious after all and that the date would soon be announced. Next, a hitch over terms, for after Lewis's purse had been agreed there was further haggling over boat fares and the number of people he intended to bring over with him.

While all this was going on, Charles Lucas, the Australian promoter, cabled an offer of £2,500 for McAvoy to meet Ambrose Palmer in Australia. McAvoy, becoming very impatient, let it be known that unless Lewis made his mind up soon he was likely to accept the Australian offer and also take other fights while over there.

But apart from being informed that Jack Hyams wanted another shot at the British middleweight title, preferably in London, about the only thing to materialise was a match with up and coming Leicester fighter, Bill Hardy, Light-heavyweight champion of the Midlands and a very promising young prospect who was expected to give McAvoy a stiff test. Hardy, managed by George Biddles, had beaten Frank Hough, Jack Strongbow and Scottish Light-heavyweight, Tommy Henderson. In fact, Henderson was engaged by McAvoy as a sparring partner and assured Mac that Hardy was no pushover. Just the same Bill appeared very cautious at the start, working behind the left hand and attempting to keep well out of range. When McAvoy caught him with a sharp right to the chin it seemed that his caution was fully justified and he was glad to fall into a clinch. Several times McAvoy trapped the Leicester man on the ropes and went to work on the body, but Hardy knew how to handle himself when it came to in-fighting and was able to smother and hold on, frustrating Mac and nullifying his efforts to get in a telling punch.

For the first five rounds Hardy put up a sound performance, but the fight was beginning to deteriorate, and after Bill had been caught with a stinging left hook followed by a powerful right to the jaw, he grabbed Mac and seemed more intent than ever on making it an untidy, mauling affair. Both fighters were spoken to by the referee, with the result that Mac came out for the sixth in more determined mood and tore into Hardy with a vengeance, hammering him about the body and shaking him with another vicious left hook. A full-blooded right to the ribs had the Leicester man gasping, then quick as a flash, McAvoy landed a heavy right to the jaw and Hardy went down. There was no chance at all of him beating the count, and it was some minutes after being carried to his corner that he had recovered sufficiently to leave the ring.

McAvoy's next contest, against Frank Hough, was arranged to take place at the National Sporting Club. Hough had been very disappointed when robbed of the chance to meet Mac previously, due to the riding accident. He had been doing well and was confident of springing a surprise. At this juncture, however, Len Harvey, who had previously been more interested in challenging Tommy Farr for the British and Empire Heavyweight titles, decided to get in on the act.

Farr had become British and Empire Heavyweight champion by beating Ben Foord, who had taken the titles from Jack Petersen. But with Farr lined up to meet Joe Louis for the world crown, Harvey, realising that he was in for a long wait, now decided to challenge for the British Light-heavyweight title once again and suggested a side-stake of £2,000, to which McAvoy immediately agreed.

The Board, having decided to recognise Hough as a legitimate challenger, now accepted Harvey instead. Both Harringay and Wembley were keen to stage the battle and each came in with a substantial offer, Harringay promoter Sydney Hulls eventually getting the match with an extremely attractive bid. The fighters would share fifty per cent of the gate up to £7,000, with anything above that amount being split between the two of them. For several weeks they could not agree terms. Then, in accordance with the Board's rules, they were summoned to attend an emergency meeting of the stewards at Board headquarters. McAvoy was not present, and was represented by Harry Levene, his London manager. Levene soon arrived at an agreement with Harvey, who was again managing his own affairs.

The fight was set for March 23rd, and with several weeks to go it was decided to slip in a warm-up contest for McAvoy at Belle Vue, on February 28th, against Walter Van Buren, Light-heavyweight Champion of Switzerland. But a few days before the fight, word was received that the Swiss had been forced to withdraw due to a hand injury. At such short notice it was far from easy to find a suitable replacement, but eventually the matchmaker came up with Jack Strongbow, of West Hartlepool, a full blown heavyweight.

The great weight disparity presented Mac with very few problems, however, for Strongbow was soon in difficulties, going down for counts of eight in both the second and the third. The big man, though taking a fearful hiding, showed rare pluck, fighting back spiritedly and occasionally landing himself, with clubbing blows to the head. In the fifth he was put down late in the round, again for an eight count, but the bell rang before McAvoy could follow up.

Immediately the sixth got under way Mac dropped the West Hartlepool man with a left hook. Strongbow, badly hurt, struggled gallantly to his feet, only to be caught cleanly on the point of the jaw by another perfect left hook which put him down for the count.

While McAvoy began his preparations for the defence of the light-heavyweight title at the Belle Vue gym, Len Harvey went off to Jack Straw's Castle, a hotel on Hampstead Heath, which had long been a popular training camp.

McAvoy was in tip top form in training, punching with devastating effect and raring to go. Meanwhile, in the Harvey camp all was not well. About a week before the contest was to take place Len knocked his left hand up while sparring, and was forced to request a postponement. This was granted, the new date being April 7th, but the news, coming at a time when McAvoy was just reaching his peak of fitness, did not put the champion in a very good mood. Having to slow down his training might just result in the sharp edge being lost. Still, there was very little he could do about it, except take it out on those around him. All fighters get a little edgy just before a fight, but none more so than McAvoy. At such times he was best left alone. It certainly did not pay to argue with him, but Harry Fleming, who was still supervising Mac's training, had been with him long enough to know how to handle him.

McAvoy finished off his training at Knutsford, in Cheshire, on Monday, April 4th, three days before the fight, and travelled down to London the following day. Both Fleming and Mac himself were well satisfied with his condition and fully confident of beating off Harvey's challenge. At the weigh-in McAvoy was nearly half a stone under the light-heavyweight limit at 12st 1¼lbs, while Harvey, who had had to take off a few pounds, came in at 12st 6lbs.

Harringay was packed to capacity, and as the fighters climbed into the ring the film cameras set up to record the contest began to roll*.

Both men looked to be in excellent shape, and when the bell sent them out for the opening round Harvey adopted his familiar upright

* In addition to being filmed by the newsreel cameras this was the first contest ever shown on television (closed circuit) in Britain.

British stance, while McAvoy, crouching low in typically American style, worked his way in close and cut loose early on with a stinging left hook to the body followed by another to the head. The second punch did not land cleanly and Harvey immediately tried to clinch, but Mac crashed in several heavy blows to the mid-section before Len managed to grab him and hold on.

This was to be the pattern over the first few rounds, Harvey waiting for Mac to come tearing in, then attempting to block or ride the punches before countering sharply. Harvey's immaculate left hand was very much in evidence in the first round, a straight punch of real power. But quite early on it suddenly went again and from then on was of little use as an effective weapon.

McAvoy soon became aware that he was fighting a man who was now labouring under the sort of handicap with which he himself was only too familiar, yet he also knew that Harvey possessed a right hand punch like the kick of a mule, and that, like Mac, he was always at his most dangerous when his back was to the wall.

But Len's troubles were only just beginning, for in round three he sustained a bad cut over the right eye. Seeing blood, McAvoy attacked the injury and managed to land a couple of hard shots close to the wound before Harvey could grab him again. Mac was now well on top and Harvey looked a sorry sight as he returned to his stool at the end of the round, with one side of his face a mask of blood.

Harvey's corner did a good job on the eye during the minute's rest and managed to stop the bleeding, but Len seemed more intent on protecting the injury during the next couple of rounds than in scoring points. From time to time the eye bled profusely, but the cornermen were always able to staunch the flow between rounds.

It was now, with everything going against him, that Harvey showed what a truly great fighter he was, bringing into play his considerable defensive skills, blocking or evading the punches, making McAvoy miss by inches, tying his man up in the clinches or turning him against the ropes as he rushed in, then sliding smoothly out of range. Surprisingly, in view of his double handicap, Harvey was not employing the holding and spoiling tactics to anywhere near the same extent as he had in their previous contests, but relying on pure defensive boxing, backed up by deadly accurate counter punching from that right hand, which invariably carried the full weight of those powerful shoulders behind it.

For the next two rounds McAvoy did all the attacking, yet for all his aggression he managed to achieve very little, and in round five was brought up short when the retreating champion suddenly decided to stand his ground. Getting a glimpse of McAvoy's jaw as he tore into the attack yet again, Harvey connected with the sort of bomb that would have poleaxed most fighters, and for a moment Mac saw stars as the punch exploded on his granite chin. Harvey tried to follow through with another and McAvoy was forced to break ground and cover up. A couple of quick jabs and Harvey again brought over the right, catching Mac on the side of the head then hammering him about the body. Mac was not at all comfortable when forced onto the defensive, but somehow he managed to hold out to the end of the round.

But Harvey was now brimming with confidence and seemed able to penetrate McAvoy's defence almost at will, probing for an opening with the damaged left hand, then banging over the right to head and body with uncanny accuracy. Mac appeared to have lost all his rhythm and as round six drew to a close he was again caught with a powerful right which landed flush on the jaw with such force that the champion sagged at the knees and almost went down. Only sheer guts and determination kept him upright. But he was in such a bad way that another right must surely have ended it. To Mac's great relief, however, the bell sounded as he swayed back helplessly against the ropes, and it was all he could do to make his way unsteadily back to his corner.

Despite his success, and the desire to get it over with as quickly as possible, Harvey was taking no chances. He was quite content to keep his boxing together and wait for another opening. This suited McAvoy, who needed time to settle down and shake off the effects of that gruelling sixth round. Over the next three Harvey was well on top and edging in front in the scoring.

In the tenth, however, things took a turn in the other direction, when McAvoy scored with a hard left hook to the jaw then followed up with a powerful right which caused Harvey's knees to buckle. Reeling back against the ropes, the challenger was wide open and had Mac followed up immediately he might well have finished his man off. But once again he was outwitted by the crafty Cornishman, who amazed Mac by grinning at him. McAvoy might well have concluded that the grin proved that Len was badly hurt. Instead the thought flashed through his mind that Harvey was foxing. For a moment or so he hesitated, then it was too late, the chance was lost. Those few vital seconds were all a cute old campaigner like Harvey needed to weather the storm. When McAvoy at last moved in he was grabbed and held.

Mac struggled desperately to free himself from Harvey's vice-like grip, but Len just clung on until his head had cleared, then neatly turned the champion into the ropes and slid away out of danger.

Harvey had proved once again that when it came to skill, ringcraft and sheer cunning, he was the master. McAvoy realised only too clearly that with two thirds of the contest gone he would really have to increase the pressure to be sure of emerging the winner. Len, on the other hand, having survived a very close call, and still feeling the effects of it, went back on the defensive. He knew Mac would come after him and he was right. As the champion came in with both fists flying Harvey was almost overwhelmed at times. Still he remained cool, managing to evade most of Mac's big bombs while attempting to whip in the right counter.

But either some of the steam had now gone out of Harvey's punches or McAvoy was getting stronger as the fight wore on, for the champion was unrelenting and several times he really shook his man with tremendous blows to the body which Len did well to withstand.

As they came up for the final round there could have been very little in it and both men went all out to clinch victory in a barnstorming finish which had the fans on their feet cheering themselves hoarse.

Of the two, McAvoy appeared the fresher, with Harvey, face covered in blood and looking all in, fighting on instinct alone. If it was all on the last round, then Mac had probably shaded it. But to the Rochdale man's surprise and disappointment, referee Percy Moss had no hesitation in raising Harvey's hand as the winner and new champion.

The fact that he was able to do this without even consulting his scorecard seemed to indicate that McAvoy's all-out aggression throughout most of the contest had not impressed Mr Moss as much as Harvey's gallant rearguard action and superb defensive qualities. And though the verdict was not greeted with any display of dissent, it's true to say that opinion was sharply divided as to whether or not it was the correct one.

McAvoy was naturally upset at losing one of his titles, and very sad to have to hand over the second Lonsdale belt. While having the greatest respect for Len Harvey and his wonderful ring artistry, Mac still felt he had done more than enough to win. But like all fighters in those days he had been brought up to accept defeat sportingly and did not hesitate to congratulate the battered but triumphant Cornishman as the belt was fastened around his waist.

With time to reflect, McAvoy's disappointment was soon tempered by the knowledge that he stood a very good chance of winning the title back, for he was well aware that no other light-heavyweight in the country had much hope of beating Harvey. Also, there was every possibility of Len turning his attention once more in the direction of the more lucrative heavyweight crown. So, with no serious challenger on the horizon for his middleweight title, Mac continued to campaign in the light-heavyweight ranks, and a month later travelled across the Irish sea to take on Marcel Lauriot, the French champion, whom he had beaten two and a half years previously at Belle Vue.

This contest, at Dublin's Theatre Royal, was arranged to take place around midnight, following that evening's performance. On the bill were pianist Charlie Kunz and comedians Sid Field and Norman Evans, the latter, of course, being well-known to McAvoy through his Rochdale connections.

Around the time of his previous meeting with Lauriot, Mac had been experiencing severe problems with his right hand and had been forced to nurse the injury, boxing cleverly and being forced to settle for a points win. This time he was obviously out to show that with two good hands he could dispose of the Frenchman in short order, and this is precisely the way it turned out.

In round one Lauriot seemed at a complete loss to fathom McAvoy's bobbing, weaving style, and had great difficulty in laying a glove on him, while Mac constantly found the target with accurate left jabs. Twice in quick succession he banged over the following right to Lauriot's chin, and though the Frenchman was obviously hurt he managed to complete the round without having visited the canvas.

McAvoy must have decided that as the hour was late it was time to bring the proceedings to a close, for after round two had opened with a brief close quarter skirmish, he measured Lauriot with the left, then laid him out with a tremendous right cross flush on the chin. The Frenchman lay there spreadeagled, with absolutely no hope of beating the count. He was spark out and had to be picked up and helped back to his corner.

Between the Harvey and Lauriot fights Mac was booked for another court appearance, this time at Bolton, where he was prosecuted for speeding and driving without insurance. After entering a plea of guilty, Mr Adam F. Greenhalgh, the fighter's legal representative, asked the court not to suspend his client's license, as he lived in Stockport, trained in Manchester and regularly visited Rochdale. Unimpressed, the magistrates imposed a £5 fine and suspended McAvoy's license for five years. This was quite a blow. For apart from the extreme inconvenience, Mac was a man who loved cars and enjoyed getting out and about. On his asking when the ban would come into force, he was informed that it was instant, and that he would not even be permitted to drive his car home from the court.

The fact that he was now settled with Joan Lye at Sundial Road, Offerton, Stockport, had not resulted in Mac turning over a new leaf. He could never resist temptation of the female kind, and plenty came his way. He was always on the lookout for it in any case, and a little thing like a driving ban was hardly likely to cool his ardour. Besides, he always had several mates around him who were similarly inclined, so he was never stuck for a driver whenever he fancied a night out.

But Joan Lye was not the sort of girl to let a man walk all over her, even if his name was McAvoy, and soon there were arguments, sometimes over little things, but more often than not brought on by Mac's philandering and exacerbated by his totally off-handed determination to do just as he pleased and come and go as it suited him. Even his close friend, Don Waters, no angel himself, could see that Mac was going too far. It was clear to him that Joan was not the kind you could take for granted and he advised Mac to steady up and begin to show her a little more consideration. But McAvoy was never one to listen to advice and just brushed it aside, saying, 'Oh, she's all right. You know how they are. They think a fellow should sit at home every night and listen to the wireless. Well, that's not for me. Never has been. I'd go bloody mad.'

Apart from the fact that she was inclined to ask too many questions, Mac seemed quite happy with Joan. Her mother, however, was beginning to get on his nerves, for Dorothy Lye seemed to come visiting almost every other day. She would arrive from Rochdale in a chauffeur-driven car, and being naturally interested in the baby and also her daughter's happiness and well-being, would enquire as to how the couple were settling down in their new home and so on. There was no problem until Mrs Lye began to make suggestions and give advice. Mac, of course, took this to be 'interfering' and from then on he began to nurture an intense dislike for her, which was probably quite unfair to the woman. It was simply the classic mother-in-law situation, but Mac would never compromise over anything, and so a further wedge was driven between the couple. It came to the point where, whenever the mother-in-law arrived, Mac went out.

A lot of his time was still spent in Rochdale, for he liked to see his parents and the rest of his relatives as often as possible. It had not taken him long to discover where Eliza was living, and he called to see her and the children very regularly. Whenever he'd had a row with Joan he would sit down and tell his troubles to Eliza, who was by no means a vindictive person and always lent a sympathetic ear.

He was now riding again and as keen as ever. During the summer of 1938, when there was very little doing on the boxing front, he spent a lot of time in the saddle, and considering the seriousness of his accident the previous year, it's surprising that he was not at least a little cautious. But in fact he seemed just as reckless as ever. One day his mount reared up suddenly and fell on its side, pinning Mac's left leg underneath it. The result — another trip to the Infirmary, where it was discovered that the leg was broken below the knee. This, of course, meant another long lay-off, and the cancellation of a contest in Sheffield against Emile Lebrize.

With McAvoy confined to the house for long periods there was more friction, and within a couple of weeks he was off again, being picked up by one of his mates and hobbling out of the house with the aid of a walking stick, his leg encased in plaster. It seemed that nothing short of complete immobilisation could keep him in, irrespective of whether he was happy at home or not.

Joan was by now very disillusioned. It was clear that the unlikely relationship between two people, who, though born in the same town, yet coming from such starkly contrasting backgrounds, was finally turning sour. Joan tried very hard to save the marriage, but had come to realise that this man, whom she still loved, and who could be so tender one moment and so callous and thoughtless the next, was by no stretch of the imagination her idea of a real husband and father. She now accepted that, despite his constant reassurances, he was the kind of man who expected to enjoy all the advantages of a happy married life while at the same time retaining his freedom, just as if he were still single, gallivanting around while the dutiful little wife ran the home and looked after the family.

Joan had become very unhappy, and after considering her position very carefully, decided to talk things over with her parents. After that she made her decision. She would leave her husband and take the baby back to Rochdale. Mac was very angry and more than ever certain that his in-laws were at the root of the trouble, which was, of course, quite untrue. As usual, as far as marital problems were concerned, Mac himself was the one most at fault. At first he tried to talk her out of it, and when that didn't work he flew into a rage. It made no difference. Joan, a very positive sort of person, had not come to her decision easily, but now that she had she would stick to it come what may.

After Joan left, Mac found himself alone in the house at Sundial Road, and though he liked his freedom he had no intention whatsoever of living the life of a bachelor. He therefore made immediate plans to sell the house, packed his things and went back to Eliza. At a later date, when Joan obtained her divorce, Eliza was named as co-respondent!

At Stockport Domestic Court, on August 6th, 1938, Joseph Patrick Bamford, alias Jock McAvoy, agreed to pay a maintenance order of eleven shillings a week to his wife, Joan Alice Bamford, of Mount Healey, Rochdale.

McAvoy, arriving at the court with his lower leg in plaster and leaning on a stick, heard the chairman of the bench tell the assembly that the husband had admitted persistent cruelty, and as agreement had been reached between the parties, the magistrates would make an order on those terms, provided that the money was paid weekly, through the court. Mac was also ordered to pay costs of £10.

Not long after this McAvoy got rid of the plaster cast and was soon back in light training. The break had been quite a serious one and had necessitated nearly three months in plaster. In view of this Mac made another amazing recovery. By late September the leg had built up sufficiently to enable him to do roadwork and generally intensify his training. Several contests were planned over November and December, and when Mac took the ring for the first one, against Jack Strongbow at the Tower Ballroom, Birmingham, on November 2nd, he was just itching to go.

Although he had previously K.O.'d the West Hartlepool man in six rounds he would be giving away two stones, Strongbow weighing 14st. 1lb against McAvoy's 12st. There was also the question of blowing away the cobwebs, for he had been out of the ring for six months. But from the opening bell McAvoy looked fast and sharp as he peppered Strongbow with accurate left jabs, following up with heavy shots to the mid-section. In attempting to guard the body, Strongbow exposed his chin, and Mac sent over a hard left hook which put the big man down for an eight count.

Round two followed a similar pattern, but in the third Strongbow decided to open up and slung several big rights at McAvoy's head. In doing so he again left himself wide open. Mac, seeing his chance, thudded in a right to the body followed by a left uppercut and Strongbow was down again for another count of eight. In the fourth he took two counts of seven and looked very unsteady on rising the second time. Mac immediately stepped in and dropped him with a crunching body shot. Somehow Strongbow dragged himself up at six, and a right to the jaw floored him again for what would surely have been the last time had the bell not come to his rescue.

In the fifth the gallant Strongbow was knocked down once more, but again struggled gamely to his feet. As he was now bleeding badly and in no condition to continue, the referee very wisely stopped the contest.

Almost three weeks later at the King's Hall, Derby, McAvoy comfortably outpointed Irishman Joe Quigley, who adopted safety first tactics throughout the fight. There was far too much holding, with McAvoy being unable to open up in the face of blatant spoiling tactics, and the crowd were not slow to show their displeasure.

Only a week after this McAvoy was back at Belle Vue, with ex-Hussar Frank Hough in the opposite corner. Hough was known as a tough customer with a heavy punch, and Mac knew that he could not afford to take chances against the Londoner, who was acknowledged to be one of the best light-heavyweights in the country.

As usual McAvoy took the initiative, but found Hough quick to counter. In the third Hough surprised Mac by catching him with a neat uppercut which jerked his head back, and followed this with a hard right to the jaw. McAvoy immediately rallied and there followed a thrilling toe-to-toe slog which had the crowd roaring. There were several similar bursts of action in the next two rounds. Then in round six, with the contest very close in the scoring, McAvoy suddenly pulled one of his specials out of the bag. As usual a powerful blow to the body paved the way for the finisher, a perfectly delivered right cross to the chin, which put Hough flat on his back. Though he tried hard to rise, the game Hussar's legs simply would not respond and he was counted out. Back in the dressing room, Hough, still somewhat dazed, was full of admiration for his conqueror, his first words to reporters being, 'Can't he punch!'

McAvoy finished off the year by travelling to Leicester on December 6th and stopping Jack Robinson of Nottingham in two rounds. Robinson, way out of his class, was down three times in the first round and taking his third count in round two when the referee stepped in to halt the proceedings.

These easy victories, while being gained against bigger men, had hardly extended McAvoy, but had served to sharpen him up after the long lay-off, and before the end of the year he was informed that 'Ginger' Sadd, of Norwich, had been nominated to challenge for his British middleweight title in the New Year. McAvoy was pleased. Apart from the opportunity of a good pay day, the fight would provide the chance to get a further notch on the second Lonsdale belt.

Following his gallant losing battle with Joe Louis, Tommy Farr was in great demand in America. Realising that he could make a lot more money over there than he could in Britain, the British Heavyweight Champion decided to stay on. He informed the Board that he would be unavailable to defend the title for some considerable time, and was therefore prepared to relinquish it.

As Eddie Phillips had already eliminated Ben Foord, the Bow man was matched with Len Harvey at Harringay Arena, in December 1938, with the title at stake. Harvey won on a foul in the fourth round and so became Heavyweight Champion for the second time. Farr's Empire title was not included in the package, and would be fought for at a later date.

# Chapter 25

## World Title Chance

Early in 1939, with the threat of war in the air and McAvoy all set to take on the pride of Norwich, bad luck again stepped in to deliver a knockout blow, when the unfortunate British champion was struck down by diphtheria, a disease that was quite prevalent in Britain at that time. He was then living at 2, Navigation Road, Altrincham, with Eliza and the children, and was taken into the local isolation hospital. Being strong and fit, Mac was, of course, far less vulnerable than most victims of the disease. Nevertheless he was very poorly to begin with, and was kept in for over a month, the title defence being cancelled indefinitely.

On being discharged Mac felt nothing like his old self and knew that it would be foolish to risk his title too soon against a man of Sadd's calibre. The fight was eventually rearranged for May 22nd at Belle Vue, giving him over three months to recover fully from his illness and get himself back into shape. But the enforced lay-off only made Mac more determined, and as usual he made a rapid and quite remarkable recovery, being back in the gym within a couple of weeks of leaving the hospital and taking on Frenchman Emile Lebrize before the end of February. The match was made at 12st. 9lbs, and Lebrize, a contender for the European light-heavyweight title, was expected to give the recently recovered McAvoy a good warm-up fight.

On the day of the contest Mac was again under the weather, suffering from a heavy cold. Perhaps because of this he decided that he was in no condition to travel the full distance, for halfway through round one Mac dropped the Frenchman with a left to the body and a powerful right to the jaw. Lebrize went down like a log and did not move until carried to the corner by his seconds after the count had been completed.

McAvoy soon recovered from his cold and just over a week later was again in action, this time at Liverpool Stadium against Tino Rolando, an Italian light-heavy who towered over Mac and outweighed him by more than half a stone.

In the early rounds McAvoy found it difficult to get close enough to land his heavy shots to the body, but when he did the Italian appeared to absorb them well and by the middle rounds was coming more into the fight with some forceful bursts of his own.

As usual against the bigger men, McAvoy found that he was much quicker than his opponent and was able to evade most of Rolando's ponderous counters. By the seventh Mac's great strength was beginning to show as he punished the Italian about the body, and several times Rolando appealed to the referee, indicating that some of McAvoy's blows were landing low. But this was not the case and his protests went unheeded.

However, by the ninth the Italian was still there and looking likely to last the full ten rounds. The end, though, was not far off and came with dramatic suddenness, when McAvoy unleashed a tremendous left hook to the pit of the stomach. Rolando dropped to his knees, gasping for breath, but somehow managed to rise at eight. Mac stepped in quickly, landing a powerful blow to the chin which sent the Italian down again, and Rolando was in the act of staggering to his feet at the count of ten when the referee intervened.

Mac was now back to his best form and ready for his contest with 'Ginger' Sadd, for which he was to receive a purse of £600. Meanwhile, a series of events were taking place which would give him the chance of challenging again for the World light-heavyweight title, albeit a British version.

In October 1938, after successfully defending against Al Gainer, John Henry Lewis gave up his light-heavyweight crown to take on Joe Louis for the heavyweight title. A month later 'Tiger' Jack Fox also beat Gainer to gain official recognition as Lewis's successor (in New York State only). Fox held the title for a little over two months before being knocked out in nine rounds by Melio Bettina.

On January 25th, John Henry Lewis's heavyweight title aspirations were shattered in one round by the lethal punching 'Brown Bomber', and following rumours that John Henry had serious eye trouble, it was considered highly unlikely that he would ever fight again. Yet a little over three months later he was on his way to England to take on Len Harvey once more, in what was claimed to be a contest for Lewis's World Light-heavyweight crown. As he had never lost it in the ring, and as no universally recognised champion had emerged, this was felt to be acceptable in Britain, if not in America, where Bettina was preparing to defend against Billy Conn, in a contest which would in fact produce, in

Conn, a worthy champion. Unfortunately for Lewis, and subsequently Len Harvey, John Henry failed to pass a medical ordered by the British Boxing Board of Control and had no option but to return to America and enforced retirement.

In place of the Lewis contest Harvey contracted to defend his British and Empire light-heavyweight titles against McAvoy on June 15th, and immediately wrote to the Board suggesting that the contest should also be recognised as being for the World title, which was now considered vacant in this country. To McAvoy's delight the Board agreed. He was now in the unique position of being set to defend his British Middleweight title and challenge for the World light-heavyweight crown, plus Harvey's domestic titles, all within a period of three weeks or so.

McAvoy, however, was too experienced a campaigner by now to fall into the trap of counting his chickens. He was well aware that to place less importance on the encounter with 'Ginger' Sadd than the big fight beyond it might well prove disastrous. In his preparation for the defence of the middleweight title, therefore, he was as thorough and as single-minded as always.

If there was any cause for anxiety at all it lay in the fact that he would be obliged to get down to 11st. 6lbs, a weight he had been nowhere near since his last defence over eighteen months before, then build himself up again to a solid twelve stone plus for the clash with Harvey, all within the space of a few weeks. Whether any of this would have an adverse effect on his strength or his stamina remained to be seen.

Training under Jack Bates at Belle Vue, McAvoy felt supremely confident. He might at times have been in dubious hands as far as his management was concerned, but he had been very well looked after training-wise, throughout the thirties. The weight came off gradually, and though he felt just as strong, he was noticeably quicker as May 22nd drew near.

Over in Norwich, Arthur 'Ginger' Sadd's preparations were going just as smoothly, and there was great excitement locally at the prospect of a British title going to East Anglia. Sadd, an extremely skilful boxer, had built up quite a reputation.

Starting in 1932, he had faced the best in Britain, including such redoubtable warriors as George Rose, Len Wickwar, Harry Corbett, Dave McCleave, Ben Valentine and Jack Hyams, winning the Eastern Area welterweight title by beating 'Seaman' Jim Lawlor in 1935. Two years later Ginger won the area middleweight crown, which he was to hold until 1949. Before getting his title chance against McAvoy he had taken part in well over a hundred contests, a clear indication of the great depth of talent around in those days.

On Thursday, May 18th, the challenger's workout was watched by a large crowd, which included the Mayor of Norwich, the Deputy Mayor, the Chief Constable and several of the city's aldermen. On the Saturday Sadd rested up and was given a civic send-off by his fellow townspeople before setting off by road to Manchester on the Sunday, the day prior to the fight. Excitement in the East Anglian capital was at fever pitch, with several hundred fans travelling to lend their hero vocal support. Those left behind would no doubt be glued to their wireless sets, for the fight was to be broadcast on the B.B.C. by Richard North, with inter-round summaries by W. Barrington-Dalby.

Six thousand fans packed into the King's Hall that Monday night, and it can truthfully be said that not a single one of them could have been disappointed at the quality of the contest or the performances of the principals, for the fight turned out to be a real classic.

From the outset, McAvoy was the aggressor, tearing in with the obvious intention of scoring an early victory. But Sadd proved to be so quick and clever that for the first few rounds hardly a solid punch was landed on the Norwich man. While successfully evading McAvoy's constant flow of potentially lethal blows, Sadd was extremely accurate with his counters, and his brilliant left hand was seldom out of McAvoy's face.

So effective was Sadd's work that it was not until the ninth round that McAvoy at last nailed him with a really damaging punch. But though Ginger was momentarily stunned, he managed to remain cool under pressure and box his way out of trouble. In doing so he showed the crowd that he possessed courage as well as great skill.

From that point on, McAvoy, always carrying the fight to his man, gradually began to gain the upper hand, and though Sadd continued to give a brilliant display of defensive boxing, he was now getting caught more, though absorbing the punches well.

In the last couple of rounds Ginger picked up his workrate as the fight built up to a thrilling climax, but at the final bell referee Moss Deyong had no hesitation in raising McAvoy's hand as the winner, though it had been a very close contest.

The combatants were warmly applauded by the capacity crowd, especially the challenger, who had put up a wonderful performance and treated the spectators to an outstanding exhibition of classical boxing.

McAvoy, of course, had played his part in making it a fight to remember, but the general opinion seemed to be that 'Ginger' Sadd had proved to be by far the most talented fighter to challenge for McAvoy's middleweight title. Had he possessed the punching power to match his superb ringcraft and undoubted courage a new champion might well have been crowned that night.

Yet without taking anything away from Sadd, it's quite possible that getting down to the weight on this occasion had robbed McAvoy of some of his power, for in the closing rounds he had landed blow after blow without any noticeable effect on the challenger.

'Ginger' Sadd went on to campaign for another twelve years, meeting top men like Ernie Roderick, Dick Turpin, Freddie Mills and Don Cockell, before retiring in 1951 without ever getting another shot at the title.

When in his seventies and in poor health, Ginger was still a great fighter, with vivid memories of the old days and his contest with McAvoy. In a letter dictated to his friend and constant companion, Raymond Cole, he told the author: 'I remember what a great fight it was. For some time in the contest I thought I'd got him, but at the finish I had no complaints about the result, though it was very close and I would dearly have loved a re-match, but it was not to be; what with the war, and other fine, deserving contenders waiting for a crack at the title – and believe me there were many outstanding fighters about in those days.

'The Belle Vue crowd were a very knowledgeable lot and gave me a warm and sporting reception. Jock's attitude to me and mine to him were what you would expect from one true professional to another – a mixture of friendship and a mutual love of the game.

'What a fighter he was. He never dished out anything he couldn't take himself. I saw stars several times that night. Jock was a very hard man indeed, who never liked to take a backward step. He was always coming at you from one bell to the next, and he could break your heart if you let him.'

With the driving ban still in force, McAvoy was getting sick and tired of having to rely on other people to chauffeur him around. He had now begun to dabble in second-hand car dealing and the fact that he was not allowed to drive was proving a severe handicap.

In early June, 1939, Mac made an application for the return of his license, although the suspension still had over ten months to run, pleading that it was vital that he should be allowed back on the road as he had his business to run, and also that he was due to take on Len Harvey in a title fight and was finding it difficult to get to and from training. Since the ban, he had been paying a driver £3 a week, and it had so far cost him over £150.

Mr P. Butlin, McAvoy's legal representative, said that although his client had twelve convictions of various kinds he had never had an accident, which was not strictly true.

Mr E. Fielding, the Borough Prosecutor, told the court that the police had made inquiries since the suspension and had no complaint to make, thus leaving the door open for the Bolton magistrates to remove the ban. However, the chairman, Alderman J. P. Taylor, said that after having given the application very careful consideration, the bench had decided that it would be premature to remove it at that time. A disappointed McAvoy was therefore obliged to soldier on and concentrate on his forthcoming fight with Harvey, who had beaten Larry Gains only four months previously to add the vacant Empire Heavyweight crown to his British Light-heavyweight and Heavyweight titles.

As usual Len set up his training camp at Jack Straw's Castle on Hampstead Heath, while McAvoy, obviously believing that a similar set-up would benefit him also, made arrangements to train at The Green Man, Blackheath, but could not settle and moved on to Shoeburyness. However, as things turned out, the South-East did not suit him either, and it was soon decided that the party should return North and again use the facilities at Belle Vue, where Mac felt much more at home.

After this rather unsatisfactory start to his build-up for Harvey, Mac got down to some serious training and worked himself into superb condition.

Around this time McAvoy's sparring partners included Paddy Lyons, an up and coming young middleweight from Dewsbury, in Yorkshire, and two Canadians, Ken Robinson and Cal Rooney, both of whom were also members of the Manchester Ice Hockey team.

As usual, McAvoy's handlers experienced the greatest difficulty in finding enough sparring to satisfy the insatiable Rochdale Thunderbolt, and those brave enough to go in with him had to withstand some pretty rough treatment. Fortunately, the two Canadians were tough lads who knew how to take care of themselves, while Paddy Lyons considered it a wonderful experience to get into the ring with a fighter of McAvoy's class, even though, as Paddy later remarked, 'I was asking for trouble.'

Paddy was certainly asking for trouble the day he managed to put McAvoy down while sparring. He was delighted with himself, but when Mac got to his feet with a snarl he knew just what to expect and was forced to cover up as the champion tore into him like a wounded buffalo and hammered Paddy non-stop until the round ended.

As Mac reached his peak in training he would get meaner and more savage, and Lyons, later to become Northern Area Middleweight Champion, recalled an incident around that time which clearly illustrates this.

'I remember one time when they were short of sparring partners – well they were always short of sparring partners for Mac. Cal Rooney had injured his forearm and was going about with it in plaster up to the elbow. As it was near enough healed, Cal, a big strong fellow, volunteered to go in with Mac, just to help out, and so somebody got a big pair of scissors and cut the plaster off.

'Well, things got a bit rough, and after McAvoy had belted the hell out of Rooney, who was doing him a favour, don't forget, a bit of ill-feeling must've crept in, and Mac grabbed him while they were in a clinch, did a cross- buttock on him and slammed him down onto the floor, then spat on him!'

Those present were naturally appalled at this outrageous and disgraceful behaviour, but Paddy, no lover of McAvoy as a person, was nevertheless a great admirer, and is firmly convinced that this vicious streak in Mac's nature was one of the factors that made him such a formidable fighter.

'When Mac fought, he really fought,' said Paddy. 'There were no half measures, even in training. He'd come at you as if he hated your guts. In fact he did, while you were in that ring with him. It was like going into the lion's cage. He'd be practically spitting blood. You could see the viciousness in his face. He was a real terror!'

With admission prices starting as low as half-a-crown, the show was expected to draw a huge crowd. In the chief supporting contest Eddie Phillips was pitted against the big colourful Irishman, Jack Doyle, who smoked a pipe and found it very difficult to apply himself to any serious training. It was to be a joint venture, with Wembley boss Sir Arthur Elvin combining with Sydney Hulls, the Harringay promoter, to stage the show at the White City Stadium, Shepherd's Bush. Helping with the organisation was the then little known Jack Solomons, later to become a major promoter in his own right.

The weigh-in, at the Stadium Club, Holborn, was well attended, and Harvey caused something of a surprise by having to pay a second visit to the scales before coming in at just under 12st. 7lbs. McAvoy had no such problems, being well inside the limit at 12st. 3lbs. As well as fighting for the British version of the World light-heavyweight crown they would also be contesting the British and Empire light-heavyweight titles.

It was to be the fourth and final meeting between these two great fighters, and though Harvey had made his debut nearly twenty years before, both were around the same age, with Len due to celebrate his thirty-second birthday the following day and Mac some four months his junior.

Waiting in the dressing room is one of the hardest things a fighter has to cope with, and McAvoy certainly had a long wait that night, for the roads leading to the stadium were so congested that both Harvey and Jack Doyle were held up in the traffic and arrived very late. A further delay was caused by the unruly behaviour of a section of the huge crowd, when several barriers were broken down and spectators on the popular side commandeered some of the better seats. At this point, the crowd, still pouring in, was estimated to be in excess of ninety thousand.

Eddie Phillips caused something of a sensation, when, having previously disposed of Jack Doyle in two rounds, he proceeded to knock out the handsome Irishman in the first. Over a hundred of the Londoner's supporters clambered into the ring to mob the winner, causing a further delay before they were cleared out.

Eventually the big fight got under way, with both boxers opening cautiously before Harvey scored with several sharp left leads to the face as McAvoy tried to get in close. After coming out of a clinch Harvey threw one of his sneak punches, a hard right cross to the jaw which shook Mac, causing him to tear in with both hands to the body, but before the round ended Harvey caught him with a powerful left hook to the jaw.

McAvoy was always the aggressor, with Harvey relying mainly on clever left hand work but tossing over the occasional dangerous right cross. In round two, Len, chased by the bustling McAvoy, went down from a slip, but quickly regained his feet as Mac came in to follow up his advantage and more than held his own in a fast exchange. In the third Mac banged in a heavy right which landed under the heart, but Harvey retaliated immediately, forcing McAvoy to give ground.

McAvoy continued to press, but by the fifth it was seen that there was some damage around his left eye. Still the Rochdale man attacked, while Harvey seemed quite content to back off and score with well placed counter punches. Whenever McAvoy put him under too much pressure the Cornishman would grab and hold until told to break by the referee, Mr C. B. Thomas. It was at these moments that McAvoy had to be on his guard against those sneak right-handers at which Harvey was so adept.

Round six ended with Len's left cheek looking badly bruised and McAvoy's continuous aggression enabled him to take the seventh by a clear margin. In this round Mac showed that he too possessed a great deal of skill by repeatedly piercing Harvey's defences with a series of speedy left jabs.

At the halfway mark McAvoy appeared to be leading by a narrow margin, but this could well have been wiped out had Harvey managed to connect with a tremendous right that missed Mac's chin by a whisker. Mac immediately lashed out in retaliation with a vicious left hook which also missed the target. Before the round ended Harvey was caught by a hard right to the body and a left to the jaw, but recovered well and cleverly boxed his way out of trouble.

The ninth turned out to be one of Harvey's best rounds, for though McAvoy carried the fight to him, the Cornishman remained cool, though damaged about the eyes, and in the latter part of the round he suddenly scored with a series of fast left hands to the head, followed by a jarring right to the body. McAvoy was put under tremendous pressure for the remainder of the round but was fighting back strongly at the bell.

Harvey now had the advantage and knew it. As round ten opened the Rochdale man's condition and toughness were really put to the test as he was forced to take several left hooks to the head followed by a heavy right to the solar plexus. In the eleventh he was caught by another hard right as they came out of a clinch, for which Harvey was roundly booed by a section of the crowd. Still McAvoy refused to surrender the initiative, trying hard to catch Harvey with one of those big right hands to the chin, but generally getting the worst of it over the next couple of rounds.

McAvoy was now showing signs of slowing down and was twice caught again with punches on the break, but came back strongly before round twelve ended, catching Harvey with a hard left hook as the Cornishman retreated.

In the thirteenth Harvey landed one of the best punches of the fight. After connecting several times with hard rights to the head, he banged over a left hook that really shook Mac. But instead of retreating he fought back with tigerish ferocity, though obviously in a dazed condition, and when the round ended the Rochdale man looked very much the worse for wear as he returned to his corner.

Round fourteen was to provide the most dramatic and thrilling moments of the entire contest. McAvoy, having made a remarkable recovery following the gruelling thirteenth, was off his stool in a flash and met Harvey with a tremendous right to the jaw which really shook the champion. Two more rights thudded home, quickly followed by a left hook flush on the chin and Harvey was in real distress.

Roared on by the crowd, McAvoy went in for the kill, trapping Harvey in a corner and hammering away with both hands in an effort to finish him off. At this moment the Cornishman was the closest he had ever been to a knockout defeat, and as another sizzling left hook exploded on his jaw he sagged at the knees and almost keeled over. Somehow though, he managed to keep his feet, back-pedalling desperately in an effort to get out of the way as Mac chased after him, throwing punches non-stop as he vainly attempted to pin the fleeing champion down and apply the finisher. Harvey had taken a tremendous amount of punishment, but was still on his feet and grabbed Mac at the first opportunity, holding on like grim death until forced to break by the referee. As Mac tore after him, snarling and snorting, Harvey got on his bike again, using every foot of the ring and calling on all his vast experience and ringcraft to survive the round.

As they came out for the final session Harvey appeared to have recovered from his ordeal, but McAvoy was clearly determined to take up where he'd left off in the previous round, throwing murderous rights at his opponent's head and again putting Harvey under fierce pressure. But Len had no intention of getting caught again and used his left hand to keep the fight at a distance as he moved smoothly around the ring. Whenever danger threatened he would go into a clinch, and try as he might McAvoy could not land another telling blow.

At the final bell the referee went to a neutral corner, and, amidst the greatest tension, slowly totted up his scorecard. Fully a minute elapsed before he finally looked up, then slowly he crossed to Harvey's corner and raised the Cornishman's hand.

It was a bitter disappointment to Mac, who was quite convinced that he had won by a clear margin, an opinion shared by many around the ringside. Of the four contests in which these two great rivals engaged, McAvoy won only one, but two of the others were desperately close.

These statistics do not necessarily prove Harvey was the better man, especially when their respective records against top American opposition are taken into account. But there can be no denying the fact that McAvoy could never quite solve the problems posed by Harvey's superb defensive skills. Len was always just that little bit too clever for him.

Harvey was now the proud holder of five major titles: a version of the World Light-heavyweight crown, plus British and Empire titles at both Heavyweight and Light-heavy. A magnificent achievement by a truly great fighter.

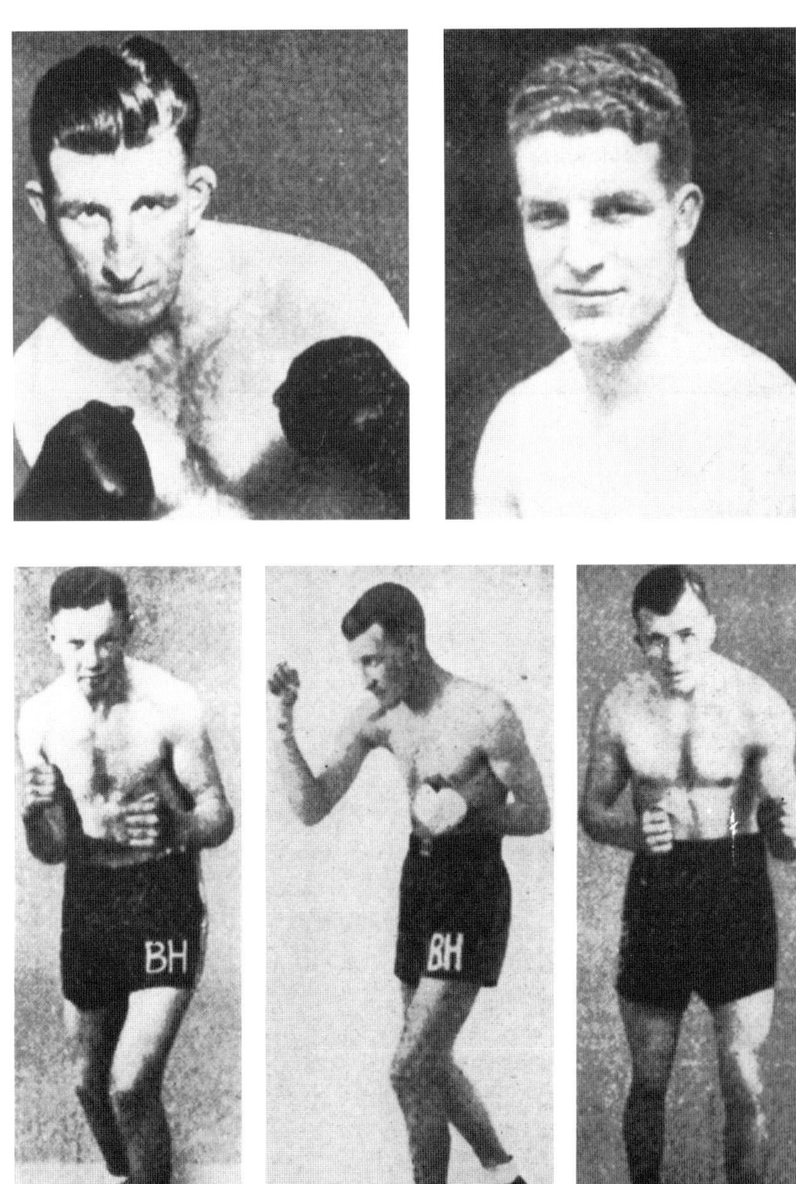


A quintet of McAvoy victims: *Above left:* Al Burke.*Above right:* Marcel Lauriot. *Below, left to right:* Bill Hardy, Bill Hood, 'Battling' Charlie Parkin.

The devastating effects of McAvoy's lethal fists.

*Right:* Mac gnaws at the thumbs of his gloves as heavyweight Jack Strongbow is counted out

*Left:* The French light-heavyweight champion Marcel Lauriot is K.O.'d in the second.

Jack Etienne, Belgian light-heavyweight champion, who was dispatched in only 66 seconds.

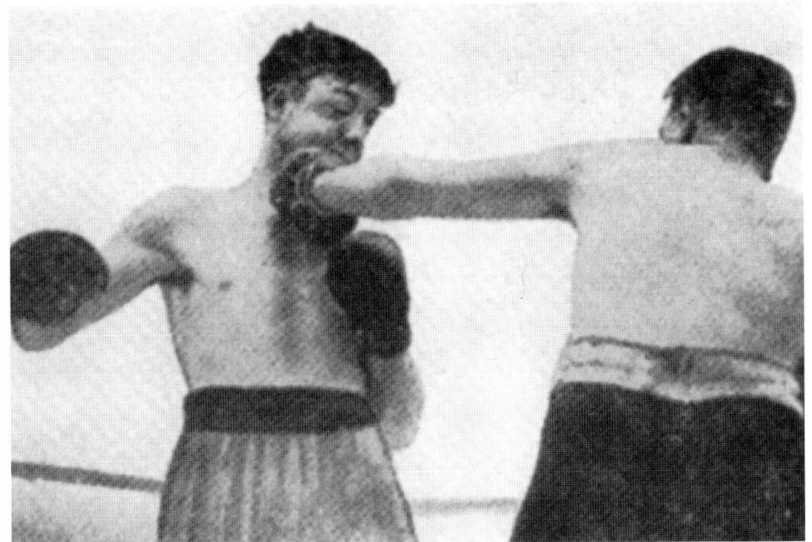

McAvoy's face grotesquely swollen as Teddy Phillips presses home his advantage.

The end for Teddy Phillips–McAvoy comes back from the dead to knock out his tormentor in the eighth round.

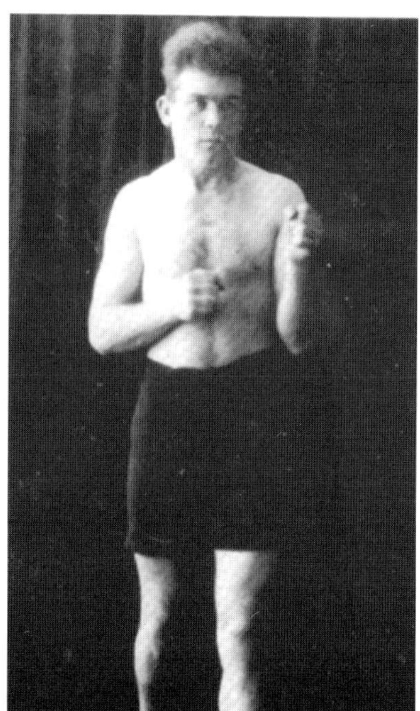

*Above left:* Archie Sexton. *Above right:* George Porter, who took McAvoy the distance. *Below:* Archie Sexton flat out in round ten.

Jack Hyams, East End Jewish battler, who faced McAvoy five times.

South African middle-weight champion, Eddie Peirce.

*Left:* Eddie Phillips of Bow.

*Right:* McAvoy K.O.s Phillips to win the light-heavyweight title.

McAvoy was at one time the holder of three Lonsdale Belts, one of which he won outright.

3.7

Ginger Sadd

Bill Wainwright

Eddie McGuire

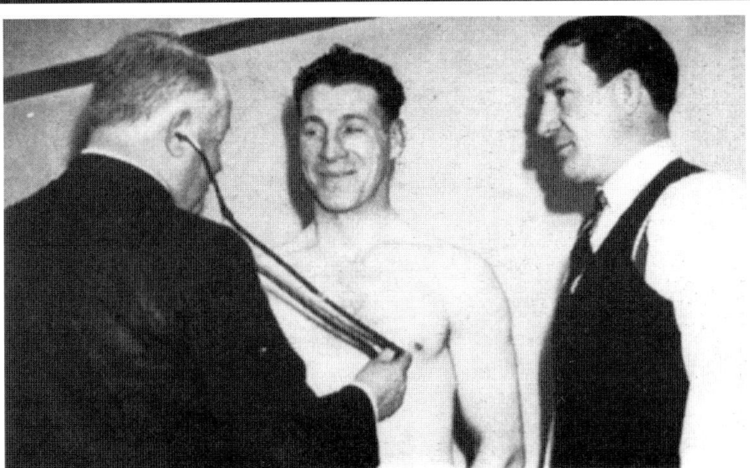

*Top:* Harvey's immaculate left hand jolts McAvoy's head back when Mac lost the light-heavyweight title in 1938. *Centre:* Unusual shot of Len Harvey, showing his powerful shoulders. *Below:* Harvey passes the doctor as McAvoy looks on.

Harvey nails McAvoy with a perfectly delivered left hook.

McAvoy in training at Belle Vue in the late thirties.

*Above left:* Joe Tolley back in uniform in World War II. *Above right:* McAvoy pictured in the gym. *Below:* Mac spars with Glen Moody at his Hollingworth Lake training camp.

Freddie Mills.

3.12

Mac wearing calipers, on Blackpool promenade in 1949.

*Souvenir from Blackpool*
*1949*

•

With the Compliments of

**JOCK McAVOY**

*Retired Undefeated*
*Middle-Weight Champion of*
*Great Britain and British Empire*

*Winner Outright*
*Lord Lonsdale Belt*

•

Sts. Lbs. Ozs.

Weight ............

The above picture shows the front and back of the postcard which McAvoy filled in and signed after weighing holidaymakers.

The great Len Harvey–
a champion at three weights

Jock McAvoy in middle age.

McAvoy proudly displays the Lonsdale Belt, surrounded by an admiring group of old-time fighters. Second from the left is Jackie Brown.

Two great champions–McAvoy with Joe Louis. The familiar face in the background, between them, is that of the late actor Peter Adamson.

Crippled by polio–McAvoy near the end of his life.

# Chapter 26

## War

During the summer of 1939, even though war had not yet been declared, there was already frantic activity throughout the country as Britain prepared to face the inevitable conflict. Food controls were introduced and ration books issued, along with gas masks. Air raid wardens were enrolled and 'black-out' practice organised. There were sandbags everywhere, and air raid shelters were being hurriedly thrown up. In Rochdale, nearly 3,000 had been erected by November, with many more well on the way to completion.

There was only one topic of conversation – war. The talk was all about Adolf Hitler and his gang and the threat of bombing. Already thousands of children were being evacuated from prime target areas like London, and it was clear that if the German bombers did attack Britain the industrial North would come in for its share of attention. The uncertainty of it all, as much as anything else, was very frightening, and the public awaited each news bulletin with the greatest trepidation.

Boxing was just about the last thing on people's minds, and on that fateful September day, when Neville Chamberlain solemnly announced to the nation that Britain was at war, planned promotions were shelved, gymnasiums closed and many young men volunteered for the forces without waiting for their call-up papers.

The first batch to be conscripted were those between eighteen and twenty-seven, but many others above that age immediately volunteered for active service, including a number of famous fighters, among them Eddie Phillips and Len Harvey. Len, in fact, joined up within a few days of war being declared and became a sergeant-instructor in the R.A.F.

There is no record of McAvoy rushing off to the recruiting office, although he was quite prepared to help out in other ways, such as giving exhibitions or appearing on charity shows for War Relief. In November of that year Mac signed to meet Jack Hyams in a non-title fight in Manchester.

Mac had continued dabbling in the second hand car business, though still struggling along without a driving license. A couple of weeks before the Hyams fight he again applied to the Bolton magistrates for the removal of his driving ban. Mr E. Fielding, the Borough Prosecutor, informed the bench that McAvoy was doing very good work going round army camps, boxing exhibitions, for which he received no payment, not even expenses. In the circumstances he could see no reason to oppose the fighter's appeal. To Mac's delight the ban was removed.

Around this time there was some talk of McAvoy fighting Australian champion, Fred Henneberry, for the Empire Middleweight title, considered vacant by the Board of Control, but nothing came of this and when Mac faced Jack Hyams in November, 1939, he had not had a serious contest for over four months, a lengthy spell in those days and not to Mac's liking at all, for no matter how well he trained, he always suffered from ring rust when out of action for more than a few weeks.

The promotion, in aid of the *Daily Dispatch* and *Evening Chronicle* War Relief Fund, was staged at Belle Vue, and a good crowd was in attendance. Unfortunately the main event fell well below expectations, with neither man showing much initiative or relish for a fight.

Hyams was probably just cautious, but McAvoy had other things on his mind. His father had been very ill for about three weeks before the fight and Mac had travelled to Rochdale frequently to see him during that time. As the old man's condition had worsened Mac became very worried, which naturally affected his training, and the champion approached the contest in the knowledge that his father was now dangerously ill in Rochdale Infirmary.

When Joe Bamford senior died on Sunday, November 19th, aged 73, the tragic news was kept from his son, the intention being to wait until after the fight before informing him.

One newspaper later claimed that someone unthinkingly let the secret slip out in the dressing room just before the fight, causing McAvoy great distress, but Mac himself later stated that this was incorrect. In fact, he was told immediately after returning to his dressing room at the end of the contest. Nevertheless, it still came as a terrible blow and one can quite easily understand the reason for his lacklustre performance. He had been very close to his father, who, though initially opposed to his son becoming a professional fighter, had been subsequently won over and took a great pride in Mac's wonderful exploits in the ring.

As far as the Hyams contest is concerned, there is very little to report, for the fighters failed to provide any excitement whatsoever, with Hyams constantly on the defensive and McAvoy plodding doggedly after him, while the spectators showed their displeasure by resorting to slow handclapping as they became thoroughly bored with the whole tedious affair. No one was sorry to see the contest reach its conclusion, with Mac being declared the winner after ten of the dreariest rounds ever witnessed at Belle Vue.

By the end of the year the nation had recovered somewhat from the shock of being plunged into war, and though fearful of the horrors still to be faced, people began to realise that life must go on and were making every effort to get back to some sort of normality. Promoters began to plan shows again, though on a limited scale, and McAvoy was hopeful of getting the chance to defend his middleweight title, for another win would make a second Lonsdale belt his own property. There was always Jack Hyams to be considered, but after the Belle Vue debacle there was little enthusiasm for a further meeting between the two. Apart from a young coloured middleweight from Leamington Spa named Dick Turpin, the obvious choice appeared to be 'Ginger' Sadd.

First, however, Sadd was required to fight an eliminator against Bert Gilroy of Scotland, who put himself firmly in the title picture by beating the Norwich man at Newcastle in March, 1940. Belle Vue then secured the McAvoy-Gilroy match, but Mac was so disappointed to be offered a purse of only £375 that he announced in a letter to the *Daily Dispatch* that he had decided to pack the game in. On the following day, however, the *Daily Express* published an interview with the fighter in which he was quoted as saying: 'I have not quit the fight game. I've a long time to go before that happens. I'm just standing out for a principle.'

But times were hard, due to the war, and because he knew he had very few options, Mac eventually accepted. Unfortunately, Gilroy was forced to pull out following an injury, and the fight never did take place.

On April 29th, 1940, McAvoy met Jim Berry of South Shields at Belle Vue. Berry, a clever southpaw, who was extremely difficult to nail with a solid punch, had beaten 'Ginger' Sadd and strongly fancied his chances against McAvoy, who by now of course was considered to be nearing the veteran stage.

Knowing that a good showing would pave the way to a shot at the title, Berry set about the job with a will, going forward confidently and landing plenty of good punches in the first couple of rounds, at the same time frustrating all of Mac's efforts to catch him with a telling blow by employing clever defensive tactics.

Again McAvoy was not at his best and was making heavy weather of the job. Berry, gaining in confidence, began to get a little more adventurous and caught Mac with a few good shots. After five rounds Berry was ahead on points and came out for the sixth determined to press home his advantage. Then came disaster for the South Shields man. With the sixth well under way he walked straight into a tremendous left hook, which, had it been a couple of inches lower, would surely have put him flat on his back. As it was, the blow caught Berry full in the mouth and immediately the blood began to flow freely, causing the referee to stop the contest.

McAvoy had not been impressive and knew it. Though obviously not quite so eager and energetic as he had been ten years before, he still trained hard. The real problem was that to remain sharp he needed more fights, and though boxing had revived to some extent, major promotions were few and far between. At the outbreak of the war McAvoy had been averaging five to six hundred pounds per contest. Now he was being asked to accept around half that amount. Even these offers were slow in materialising, and during the summer of 1940, with little prospect of a decent payday on the horizon, Mac found it very difficult indeed to motivate himself sufficiently to get into the gym and work out.

Then out of the blue came the offer of a bout with Freddie Mills, an up and coming young battler from Bournemouth, then serving in the R.A.F. McAvoy was very glad of the chance to get back into action and was pleased to accept, the contest being fixed for August 8th, at Liverpool Stadium, long known as the 'Graveyard of Champions'.

When war broke out one of the first to join up was Joe Tolley. He had retained his military connections since the First World War, and at the onset of hostilities in 1939, though still very busy as a referee and M.C., he was also an active member of the L.D.V.* Joe's first posting was to the P.O.W. camp at the Glen Mill, Oldham, where, along with a company composed mainly of veterans, he was assigned to guard some of the first German prisoners captured by the British forces. These were, in fact, U-boat men, picked up after wreaking havoc on allied shipping in the Atlantic, before being hit themselves.

Joe was probably quite happy to be back in the army. It was a

* Local Defence Volunteers.

cushy posting, very close to home, and though he was allowed a fair amount of freedom he took the job very seriously. It was not long, however, before his Commanding Officer found out about Joe's background and asked him to organise a boxing show. It had been quite a while since he'd actually put on a promotion of any kind, but once having agreed to stage the show Joe decided that he would make a first class job of it. To do this he knew that he needed a star attraction and lost no time in contacting his old protégé, Jock McAvoy. Mac agreed at once to bring a sparring partner along and box an exhibition, and Tolley was then left with the problem of putting together a supporting bill.

Meanwhile, young Albert Tolley was also in uniform and stationed less than a mile away with the 47th Squadron, Royal Tank Regiment, at Furtherhey, Lees, where he was training as a wireless operator. One morning Albert was called into the R.S.M.'s office and told that his father was on the telephone regarding a boxing show. He was allowed to speak to him and Joe asked Albert to find out if there were any boxers at the Furtherhey camp. Albert told him that he had already seen two or three lads doing some training, and Joe asked him to bring one over to the Glen Mill and box him on the McAvoy bill.

When the evening arrived Albert turned up with a lad of about eighteen named Harry Kelsall and boxed a six round exhibition with him. McAvoy was already there, chatting to his admirers while he waited for his sparring partner to put in an appearance. Albert had not seen Mac for several years, and though they knew each other very well, there had always been an element of mutual dislike in their relationship. He was hardly surprised, therefore, when the champion acknowledged him with no more than a curt nod.

After Albert had changed out of his boxing gear he discovered that there was a problem. Though it was now quite late in the evening, McAvoy's opponent had still not turned up. According to Albert: 'Mac was standing there with my Dad and getting very impatient at being kept waiting. Of course, he'd never had any patience and it didn't take much to get him annoyed. Anyway, we stood around for a bit – Mac was grumbling away and pacing up and down. He was getting more and more irritated and my Dad could see this. Anyway, eventually he turned to me and said, "Why don't you go in with him Albert?"

'Well, I looked at my Dad. For a start, I'd just done six rounds, and found it very hard going. Well, I hadn't boxed for over five years.

'But in any case, to get into the ring with McAvoy, a champion, who weighed over twelve stone at that time to my nine and a half – and don't forget, with Mac there was no such thing as an exhibition. I'd seen him in training, and I knew that whoever went in with him – it didn't matter who they were, or if they were big or small – he always knocked hell out of 'em.

'I knew he didn't like me, so that made it even worse. I thought – this is it. It's curtains for me here – and I also knew that my Dad meant it. He didn't care. He was a showman through and through. As far as he was concerned it was just a case of the show must go on, and if somebody happened to get a good hiding, even his own son, it was just too bad.

'Anyway, at the last minute this other fellow arrived – and didn't I breathe a sigh of relief. Because he'd have hammered me, there's no doubt about that. I'll tell you, I've never been more pleased to see anybody in my life than that sparring partner!'

Not long after the split with Joan Lye, McAvoy bought a house at Poynton, Cheshire, on which he neglected to pay the rates, being later summoned at Macclesfield Magistrates Court for the sum of two pounds, twelve shillings and sixpence. By that time he was living at 2, Navigation Road, Broadheath, Altrincham, in a grocer's shop, with Eliza and the children, the eldest of whom, young Joe, was now ten.

Between boxing engagements, which were few and far between, McAvoy was still doing a bit of car dealing, though in a very small way. He was really on the fringes of the trade and consequently often associated with people who could best be described as somewhat shady.

In 1939, McAvoy's close friend, Don Waters, was heavily committed financially to a housing development, which was abruptly curtailed with the outbreak of war. It was only by his astute handling of a tricky situation, which could quite easily have resulted in personal bankruptcy, that Waters managed to extricate himself from the dilemma. After paying off his bills he was left with around four hundred pounds and had lost his business.

Being above the call-up age, Waters was assigned to war work, but after injuring his spine in an accident while testing aircraft engines, he rented a piece of land at Longsight, Manchester, and began buying and selling second-hand cars. He was soon joined by McAvoy, who realised that going in with Don gave him the opportunity to set himself up in a solid, well organised business, with excellent prospects for the future.

The two of them embarked on the new venture with great enthusiasm. Though the scope of the operation was somewhat restricted, owing to the scarcity of petrol, they did fairly well in the circumstances, buying and selling cars for sums in the region of twenty and thirty pounds and managing to make a small profit.

Becoming more ambitious, they moved to a new site in Altrincham, where the owner of a large petrol station, with whom McAvoy was friendly, provided them with an adjoining forecourt, which they rented. Mac was on the site most days, buying and selling and also going off to collect vehicles, while Waters ran the office and kept the books. At the same time Mac was also operating a one man taxi business; running around late at night and picking up fares to boost his income, which was very necessary, taking into account his family commitments.

At one point he also decided to take over a butcher's shop in Hyde Road, almost opposite the Belle Vue speedway track. As meat was strictly rationed, the shop was open no more than a couple of days a week, with Mac being allowed only enough supplies to cover the customers who brought their ration books to him. Eliza ran the shop most of the time, but McAvoy often helped out.

The first time Waters called at the shop he was both amused and astonished to find McAvoy behind the counter in a butcher's apron. 'He didn't know the first bloody thing about the job,' said Don, 'but there he was, chopping up the meat with a big cleaver and calling it all steak.'

A further complication now entered McAvoy's life in the shape of Renee Garrett, a tall, slim, extremely pretty young salesgirl, and it was not long before he was picking her up each evening outside Marks and Spencer's store in the centre of Manchester, where she worked. Don Waters was often in the car with him and could see problems ahead as the affair began to blossom. It came as no surprise, therefore, when McAvoy left Altrincham to set up home with Renee just a few miles away in Heald Green. Soon afterwards the grocer's shop was sold and Eliza had little option but to return with the children to Rochdale.

# Chapter 27

## Fiery Freddie

When Freddie Mills was called up into the R.A.F. at the beginning of 1940 he was twenty years of age, but already a thoroughly experienced pro. Starting in 1936, he had compiled a very impressive record, with 56 fights behind him, of which he had won 42 and drawn six, among the latter being a gruelling twelve rounder against Nat Franks at Plymouth and another over ten rounds against former McAvoy opponent, Eddie McGuire. In all, Freddie had faced the South African three times, the other two contests resulting in a win apiece. Mills had also beaten 'Battling' Charlie Parkin three times, and after losing to Dave McCleave had twice K.O.'d the talented Londoner. In June, 1939, Freddie had been comfortably outpointed by 'Ginger' Sadd, but reversed this loss in the early months of 1940, when he also outpointed Jim Berry, Ben Valentine and the Jamaican, Stafford Barton, although in each of these contests Mills had enjoyed a considerable weight advantage.

In the late thirties Freddie had gained valuable experience by travelling the fairgrounds of the West Country with Sam McKeown's boxing booth. The booths were great breeding grounds for fighters and also provided the opportunity for them to keep in top shape between contests, for as well as taking on all-comers a boxer also benefited from the fact that there were plenty of other pros to work out with. Travelling with the booth certainly played a big part in Freddie's fistic education and helped make him the outstanding fighter he later became.

Totally devoid of science, Mills was tough, strong and possessed the heart of a lion. At this point in his career he was the sort of hungry young scrapper that McAvoy himself had been some ten years earlier.

Freddie's only problem was his size. Though he still talked of fighting for the middleweight title, he had already outgrown the division and was much more comfortable at twelve stone plus, so with the match made at 12st 9lbs, it was obvious that Mills would have a substantial weight advantage.

While Mac travelled the short distance from Manchester in comparative comfort, Mills, owing to wartime restrictions, was forced to hitch-hike from the R.A.F. camp at Netheravon in Wiltshire, all the way to Liverpool, where he managed to find himself accommodation for the night in a services hostel.

Nevertheless, on entering the ring he appeared cocky and full of beans. Freddie knew full well that this was his big chance. Up to this point he had earned very little in the ring and considered the £50 he was getting for the McAvoy fight to be quite a decent purse. A win over the famous Rochdale Thunderbolt would surely lead to bigger things and Mills was determined to fight harder then he had ever fought before. He was well aware that he was up against a hard, experienced campaigner, who had beaten some of the best in the business. But Freddie was confident that his own ruggedness and non-stop aggression would be more than enough to take the veteran out of his stride.

Mac was favoured to win, but Freddie left his corner like a tornado and attacked his illustrious opponent as though he had every intention of pulling off an early victory. Almost at once he discovered that there was a lot more to McAvoy than the tough slugger he had heard all about, for as Mills tore in with all guns blazing, he was stopped short time and again by a ramrod left jab as solid as many a right-hander he had taken in previous fights. McAvoy's greatly underrated boxing ability was very much in evidence in the early rounds as the eager Freddie, possessing apparently limitless energy, continually roared in, throwing plenty of leather but making little impression as Mac cleverly slipped his punches, tied him up inside and frequently blasted back with sharp, deadly accurate counters.

It was clear from the start that there was quite a gulf in class between the fighters, yet one thing which must have worried McAvoy was the fact that his own best punches appeared to be having little or no effect on the rampaging Freddie.

McAvoy had certainly not lost his punching power. But the truth was that at this stage of his career Freddie Mills possessed almost unbelievable toughness and durability. It was only later, after he had been unwisely thrown in with top class heavyweights and taken some fearful hammerings, that his punch resistance began to wane. At the time he faced McAvoy, Mills was capable of soaking up tremendous punishment while still marching forward to deliver his own crude, clubbing blows.

After failing to stop Freddie's tank-like rushes with a series of right handers flush on the chin, Mac set about slowing his man down by subjecting him to the renowned McAvoy body attack, but even those pile-driving left hooks and jolting rights under the heart failed to do the trick.

At the halfway mark Mac was certainly ahead in the scoring, but in round six he knocked his right hand up and knew that from then on he would have to call on all his skill just to keep out of trouble. It was now that his experience came in handy, for he attempted to put his young opponent off by talking to him in the clinches, calling him 'son' and pretending to encourage him with such remarks as 'Well done,' and 'Come on now, keep punching.'

At first Freddie was rather taken aback, but eventually realised that Mac was trying to 'old head' him. He was not falling for that and belted away all the harder, clearly getting the better of the closing rounds by virtue of his greater work-rate and non-stop aggression.

There was some question as to whether Mills had done enough in the second half of the contest to wipe out McAvoy's early lead, but the referee was in no doubt and promptly raised the Bournemouth man's hand at the finish.

Mac was disappointed. He had been hoping to challenge Harvey yet again, and knew that his loss to Mills might well result in Freddie getting a shot at the Light-heavyweight title ahead of him. He had certainly found Mills a handful, but put his inability to stop his younger opponent down to ring rust more than anything else. He simply wasn't fighting often enough and resolved to press for more contests, even if it meant accepting smaller purses, which it almost certainly would.

When the chance came to meet 'Battling' Charlie Parkin, in Nottingham, just two weeks after the Mills fight, Mac jumped at it, and though still below his best, he was able to handle the Mansfield man with ease once he got the range.

Parkin, at that time Northern Area Middleweight Champion, was on home territory, and encouraged by the noisy local fans, fought with plenty of spirit, showing a neat left hand and the occasional stinging right cross, which McAvoy was very adept at evading.

In the second round, after making Parkin miss, Mac dropped the Mansfield man for an eight count, but Charlie recovered well and managed to keep out of further trouble until the end of the fifth, which was fairly even. On coming out for round six Parkin ran into a real hurricane, being floored a total of five times as McAvoy at last found his best form, punishing his game opponent unmercifully, while Parkin, urged on by his supporters, continued to stagger to his feet, only to be knocked down again. Following his fifth visit to the canvas, the referee very wisely stepped in to halt the slaughter.

After witnessing McAvoy's explosive punching the Nottingham fans wanted more and the local promoter duly obliged, matching him with Eddie McGuire, who had matured considerably since being knocked out by Mac at Belle Vue over six years before.

The fight went on just two months later and showed beyond doubt that while McGuire had clearly improved, McAvoy had most certainly gone back. The South African appeared much the speedier man, and was in and out with rapid combinations while Mac was still thinking about it. But though he might be slower than of old he had lost none of his renowned toughness and McGuire's punches had little effect on him as he plodded purposefully forward, ever hopeful of landing the one big punch that might turn the fight his way. Once or twice the Springbok was caught with a hard shot, but always managed to box his way out of trouble, and after ten rounds McGuire was declared the winner.

McAvoy knew he had put up a poor show by his own standards and must have also realised that he was not the force he had once been. Yet he still held the British Middleweight title and was determined to cash in on it. In any case he was very anxious to put the final notch on that second Lonsdale belt. But like a good many other top sportsmen, Mac was clearly a victim of the war and was fully aware that unless a title fight could be arranged in the near future he might well have to consider retirement.

Over the next few months there was talk of title challenges from McGuire, Sadd, Gilroy and Dick Turpin, but again nothing materialised, and the following year, 1941, was well advanced before McAvoy got the chance to fight again, when he was offered a contest at the Seymour Hall, Marylebone. The opponent? Jack Hyams – who else?

They would be meeting for the fifth time, and knew each other's moves backwards. But though fighting Hyams again was not a very exciting prospect, it was a pay day, and Mac had very little option but to accept.

By the time the contest took place, on October 20th, 1941, McAvoy had been out of the ring for twelve months, but had trained very hard and looked in excellent shape, though still weighing in at around twelve stone. Jack Hyams, who was giving away around half a stone, was now Lance Bombardier Hyams of the Royal Artillery. He was determined to avenge those four defeats and knew he would never have a better opportunity.

But ring rust or not, McAvoy had a goal of his own – to finally knock out the wily East Ender, who had proved so tricky in their previous encounters. If he had bided his time he might well have got a better result. As it was, Mac's aggressiveness in the opening rounds only served to make Hyams more cautious than ever, with the result that he made every effort to keep things at long range and was quick to grab and hold whenever Mac managed to corner him.

This was the pattern over the first four rounds, then, having coped fairly well with McAvoy's early rushes, Hyams began to retaliate strongly over the next two rounds. Settling into a rhythm and boxing steadily, he scored well with accurate left leads, occasionally banging over a stinging right cross before Mac could counter.

But despite Hyam's neat work McAvoy was well ahead going into the eighth, having forced the action in almost every round. Then, after missing narrowly with a right to the chin, Hyams was badly shaken by a vicious uppercut which caused him to sag at the knees. Desperately, he tried to clinch but was heavily punished as Mac went in for the kill and finally slumped to the canvas. That Hyams managed to stagger to his feet at nine was a great tribute to his gameness, but how he contrived to last out the round was nothing short of miraculous. Too bemused even to grab and hold, Jack instinctively ducked and dived as he was driven around the ring by the savage, snarling McAvoy, and though he took another long count, the East Ender was still on his feet when the round ended.

Hyams was all-in and could barely drag himself to his corner, but recovered his breath somewhat during the minute's rest, and for the last two rounds was forced to call on all his considerable defensive skills to last the distance, for though McAvoy made prodigious attempts to end it, and had his man in real trouble several times, he was never able to land solidly enough to put Hyams down for the count.

At the end of ten rounds McAvoy was given the nod. It was to be the final encounter between the two, and there is no doubt that though Hyams had never looked like winning any of their five contests he had always proved a worthy opponent.He had faced McAvoy at practically every stage of the Rochdale man's career, yet, mainly by virtue of his superb skill and ringcraft, had defied all Mac's efforts to score a clean knockout.

McAvoy ended the year 1941 with a return engagement against

Jim Berry, who claimed to be anxious to get his revenge after what he felt had been a very unsatisfactory conclusion to their previous bout.

They met at the Royal Albert Hall in what turned out to be quite a remarkable contest. Berry came out confidently, and taking the initiative from the start, peppered McAvoy with both hands to head and body. An awkward southpaw, Berry could be very dangerous with a long right driven over the top, and caught McAvoy several times with this punch early on, causing Mac to chase him like an enraged bull in an effort to pin him against the ropes and hammer him about the body.

But the clever Geordie was never happier than when leaning back against the hemp and inviting an opponent to hit him. By ducking, twisting and dodging, Berry proved almost impossible to catch with anything like a solid blow, and treated the appreciative crowd to a marvellous exhibition of defensive boxing that had McAvoy seething with frustration.

Mac was now even more determined to catch up with this box of tricks, who was making him look very crude indeed, and in a further exchange, with Berry again delighting the customers with his wonderful antics, McAvoy suddenly connected with a punch that knocked him clean through the ropes. Amazingly, the acrobatic Geordie grabbed the middle strand with both hands and performed a somersault, landing back in the ring and onto his feet.

The roar of applause from the crowd made Mac see red and he now attacked Berry so fiercely that Jim was forced to give ground rapidly. In the fourth round McAvoy punished his man severely with heavy body shots, finally bringing him to his knees with a real pile-driver to the solar plexus. Berry somehow beat the count, but was soon down once more from a powerful hook to the body. Again he regained his feet and managed to survive the round. But it was clear that the end was in sight and Berry was soon in trouble again in the sixth, when Mac had him down for a further count of nine before dropping him for good with another pulverizing body blow.

Despite his advancing years, McAvoy had shown that he was still a formidable force, and could now look forward to the possibility of a title defence, for 'Ginger' Sadd had beaten Dave McCleave in a final eliminator for Mac's middleweight crown, the Norwich man winning on a cut eye retirement.

It was a contest, however, which appeared to arouse very little public interest, and while McAvoy waited for some promoter to set up the match he was nominated to meet Freddie Mills in an eliminator for Len Harvey's British and Empire light-heavyweight titles. Harvey's world crown would also be at stake, this being, of course, the British version only. Promoter John Muldoon, who had also staged the Berry fight, secured the contest for the Royal Albert Hall. It was to take place two months hence, in February 1942, and Mac was delighted to be given the opportunity to gain his revenge against the former milkman from Bournemouth, who was still carrying all before him.

By this time Mills had left his old manager, Bob Turner, who had guided him from his earliest days, but who, like Joe Tolley, had been persuaded to sell Freddie's contract for a comparatively small sum. The new manager was Ted Broadribb, better known in his fighting days as 'Young Snowball'. Broadribb was a very hard man to deal with and had a quick, explosive temper, but he was very shrewd and certainly knew his business. Once in Broadribb's hands, Mills made rapid progress, but even the indomitable Freddie began to have doubts when his new manager started to match him with heavyweights. At first, with the opposition not too formidable, he did well, winning and losing to Tom Reddington of Salford, knocking out big Welshman, Jim Wilde, and outpointing Jack London, later to become British Heavyweight Champion. It was at this point in Mills's career that the second meeting with McAvoy took place.

Muldoon's promotion aroused considerable interest, with the fans turning out in force to see what they believed would be a keenly fought contest between two very rugged men. As things turned out they were doomed to disappointment, the fight lasting less than a round and ending in the most unsatisfactory circumstances.

Both fighters were well inside the stipulated weight, Mills, at 12st 5lbs, being the heavier by three pounds. McAvoy opened briskly with a sharp left and right to the head, and as Freddie came charging in he was met by a right to the body which had little effect. Mills now attempted to rush his man into the ropes, but McAvoy tied him up quite easily. As they broke, Mac banged in another right to the body, but Freddie, ignoring it, tore in again, arms flailing away in characteristic style.

After a couple of brief exchanges McAvoy went down from a slip, but was up at once, and after touching gloves the fighters resumed the action, Mac leading off with a left to the face. Suddenly the Rochdale man felt a searing pain in his lower back. It was so bad that he immediately stopped boxing and gasped, 'Hold it, Freddie – my back – there's something wrong.'

Mills just stood there gaping in astonishment, while his corner yelled at him to keep punching. But Freddie, seeing that his opponent was helpless, still hesitated. The roar of the crowd faded to a murmur as McAvoy, a look of agony on his face, indicated to the referee that he was unable to continue. Before any further action could be taken, however, the bell rang to end the round. McAvoy, in great pain, was helped to his corner, but was unable to sit down on his stool. The injury, in fact, was such that the stricken fighter found it impossible to manoeuvre himself through the ropes and had to be lifted bodily over them and carried to his dressing room.

While Mills was being declared the winner Mac was given an injection by the doctor before being transported to St. Bartholomew's Hospital, where the injury was diagnosed as a strained muscle behind the left kidney. Exactly how this had been caused was never clearly ascertained, but the sudden onset of it had instantly immobilized McAvoy, who was in pain for some days afterwards and was forced to rest completely for several weeks.

Cursing his bad luck, Mac told reporters that he intended asking Mills to give him a return, but Broadribb wasn't interested. He only wanted Len Harvey, and four months later, at Tottenham Hotspur football ground, Freddie faced an aging champion who had not had a serious contest since outpointing McAvoy at the White City three years before.

Twelve years older than his eager young challenger, Harvey was battered to defeat inside two rounds, Freddie's crude, clubbing blows knocking him clean through the ropes and onto the press tables, where referee Eugene Henderson counted him out.

Freddie Mills would go on to even greater things, eventually dethroning Gus Lesnevich to win the undisputed Light-heavyweight Championship of the world in July 1948. Along the way through he was to be the victim of a number of glaring mis-matches, the worst example being his total annihilation at the hands of the giant American, Joe Baksi, in November 1946, when Freddie absorbed a fearful amount of punishment which almost certainly had a lasting effect on his health.

# Chapter 28

## Bad Company

During the years that Don Waters associated with him, McAvoy's private life was in constant turmoil, and there can be no doubt at all that most of the problems were of his own making, his womanizing, chronic impatience and mean temper landing him in all sorts of trouble.

It has been said that he would make advances to any woman he fancied, even when her husband or boyfriend was present, but Don Waters refutes this; adding, 'Mind you, if he was really keen he'd make it his business to go and sort her out when she was on her own.'

When asked if McAvoy knew Gracie Fields, Don laughed, and replied, 'Oh aye, he knew her all right. Gracie thought a lot about Joe. She had him up on the stage once at a theatre in Rochdale. She was married to Monty Banks at the time and he was there too. From what I could gather he wasn't too happy about the way Joe was making up to Gracie. Because she made a bit of a fuss of him Joe thought he could take liberties with her, but she told him where to go. Well, Joe didn't like that. He couldn't stand being knocked back. From then on he didn't have anything nice to say about her. She was no good and all this sort of thing. Aye, after that he didn't want to know her.'

Waters also recalls the time McAvoy called to pick him up at his bungalow and was feeding a pony in a nearby field when the farmer appeared and said, 'I wouldn't touch that pony if I were you.'

'Don't worry about me,' replied McAvoy, 'I can handle horses.'

'Maybe you can,' said the farmer, 'but I don't want you handling any animal of mine.'

After further words were exchanged McAvoy became very annoyed and told the farmer, 'If I get hold of you I'll knock your bloody head off.'

At that the farmer very unwisely approached in a threatening manner, whereupon he was grabbed by the shirt and knocked flat on his back, spark out.

At some later date, McAvoy, while in the company of Don Waters, again met up with the farmer, and much to Don's surprise proceeded to apologise. The rift was soon mended, but not before it had become quite obvious to Waters that the real motive behind McAvoy's uncharacteristically compromising attitude was to get an introduction to the farmer's wife, a good-looker, whom Mac had clearly taken a fancy to.

McAvoy was always very fond of cars, especially big flashy ones, and was constantly buying and selling them. One of his favourites was a blue Lincoln Continental in which he proudly roared around the Cheshire country lanes and the streets of Manchester.

Mac and Renee were extremely happy for the first couple of years they were together. Though he had returned to Eliza after his marriage to Joan Lye broke up, they had not re-married, and he was free, therefore, to go ahead and marry Renee in the spring of 1942. She was 26 and he 34. Not long afterwards a daughter, Josephine Patricia, was born. Mac idolised her, but sadly, even this important event in his life did little to change his basic attitude to marriage and the responsibilities that go with it.

The family was now happily settled at Burns Road, Cheadle, Cheshire. But after a while Mac was off gallivanting again, out most nights with his mates and forever on the lookout for 'talent'. If Renee complained she did so at the risk of incurring her husband's wrath and igniting that explosive temper, for he never liked to be questioned or asked to account for his movements, and would fly off the handle at the slightest provocation. At times like these no person within range, whether male or female, was safe, and though he would never use his fists on a woman he was not averse to landing out with a swift backhander.

Gradually the rows became more frequent, resulting in the inevitable tears, recriminations and remorse. When Don Waters called at the house one evening he found McAvoy there alone and in a very black mood. On enquiring as to what was wrong, Waters learned that Renee had left, taking the child with her. 'Well, Joe,' said Don, 'you're a bit hard on her you know. You can't go on like that with a woman.'

'I don't care,' replied Mac. 'I'm going out tonight to find her. I've got a good idea where she is. You can come with me.'

'Now you're not getting me involved,' said Don.

'Come on,' said Mac, 'you can drive me.'

Waters then went on to reveal what happened next. 'Well, we got down into Levenshulme. How he'd found out where she was I don't know, but we got into this street, then crept up a back passage. He was looking over these garden walls..., and then he spotted her through a window. "There she is," he said, "I've bloody found her. You go and get the car started."'

'Then he just vaulted over the back gate – very fit man you know – and he did no more than bash the bleedin' door in. I hurried back to the car and the next minute he comes out of the back yard with her over his shoulder kicking and screaming, the kid running along behind. Then he just bundled 'em both in the car and away we went. That's the kind of fellow he was.'

Don Waters related the episode in his usual jocular, amusing style. Though he was well aware of his old friend's many faults, he obviously had great admiration for him and several times during our interviews his reminiscences would be punctuated by such asides as: 'What a bloody character that Joe was', 'He could be a bugger', and 'Aye, but he was a great fellow you know'.

The catastrophic loss to Freddie Mills took place in February 1942. During the remainder of that year and for the whole of 1943, Mac was inactive, though through no fault of his own. There were very few boxing shows taking place, most of the fighters being in the forces anyway, many serving overseas, and sport in general was forced to take a back seat to the bloody conflict being fought out in Europe and the Far East.

The newspapers allotted very little space to boxing during this period and any hopes that McAvoy may have entertained about picking up the threads of his career appeared to be fading. He was now in his mid-thirties and must have realised that if he did not get back into action before long the chances of any future ring earnings would be virtually nil.

Then, in the early part of 1944, 'Ginger' Sadd was again nominated to challenge McAvoy for the middleweight title and contracts were signed for the contest to take place in Ginger's home city of Norwich, the champion to receive a purse in the region of £650. It was not a very large sum for a title defence, but after such a long period of idleness, with nothing at all coming in from boxing, McAvoy was only too pleased to accept it. He was also keen to get back into top condition, for the will to fight was still there, and having something to aim for again, he embarked on his training with great relish and enthusiasm.

Then came the big let-down. Either the promoter had got his sums wrong or he was finding the tickets hard to sell. Whatever the reason it soon became clear that unless McAvoy was prepared to take a hefty cut in his purse there was every possibility that the show would have to be called off. Mac was extremely angry and insisted that, as he was prepared to honour his contract, the promoter should be forced to do the same. The Board of Control, however, no doubt taking into account the fact that wartime conditions were making life very difficult for everyone, did not agree, and insisted that McAvoy compromise. Mac, feeling that he had already compromised by accepting a very modest purse in the first place, quite understandably dug in his heels and refused in the circumstances to go ahead with the fight, whereupon, he was told that the Stewards of the Board of Control had decided to fine him £200. McAvoy refused to pay and was promptly informed that the Board had declared the title vacant.

Disgusted with this shabby treatment, Mac realised that there was now very little future for him in boxing and resigned himself to planning for a life outside the game. Though he had long since disposed of the grocer's shop and was no longer in the butchery business, he was still driving his taxi, while the used car operation continued to tick over steadily, though by this time the impatient McAvoy, not having made his fortune out of it, was becoming somewhat disillusioned. He was never short of so-called friends and hangers-on, who were always very free with their advice, and after a while Mac began grumbling and complaining that the business did not seem to be making much progress.

In fact, they were doing quite well, despite the severe wartime restrictions. For McAvoy, however, the novelty had begun to wear thin, and it was not long before the partners were at odds, with Mac constantly criticising and finding fault with the way things were being run.

'Of course,' says Don, 'Joe could fall out with anybody. Aye, it didn't take much. He never trusted anybody. Always thought people were against him. That's how we came to fall out over the cars really. He somehow got the idea that I was having more out of it than he was. I told him to go through the books. It was all down there in black and white. But he wouldn't. He just wouldn't listen to sense. He'd obviously made up his mind to pack it in and that was it. You couldn't talk to Joe. You could never reason with him. I mean, we could've had a very successful business. But no, he'd had enough. Sell all the cars – sell the lot and split the money – that was Joe. So we did. But we remained friends and still went out together. In fact, I used to see him two or three times a week after that.'

Around the end of March, 1945, with the marriage going through another very sticky patch, Renee again left her husband, taking the child with her.

When he found she had gone McAvoy flew into a towering rage, which was later replaced by a smouldering, angry sullenness and a dogged determination to find her. Suspecting that she had been confiding in her brother Reg, a fireman living in Torquay, McAvoy set off to the south coast by car, taking with him a couple of cronies from Manchester.

The upshot of this ill-advised expedition was that five weeks later all three were in court at Paignton, Devon, charged with assaulting one Reginald Howard Garrett, McAvoy's brother-in-law.

Pleading not guilty, McAvoy explained to the court that he had been anxious to trace his wife's whereabouts, but that Garrett had insisted he could not help. Suddenly, said McAvoy, he felt a blow to his head, so he struck out at Garrett. As the plaintiff was about to strike him again, McAvoy's friends intervened. The evidence showed that Garrett had received a heavy blow on the ear, causing it to split.

McAvoy was sentenced to two months imprisonment and ordered to pay seven guineas costs, while his cohorts, John Thomas Garvey and Herbert Anderson, of Longsight and Moss Side respectively, were each fined £5, with 3 guineas costs.

It was stated that among McAvoy's numerous convictions were three previous ones for common assault. Notice of appeal was lodged by the defence. As this was later upheld McAvoy narrowly escaped going to gaol.

In the summer of 1945, the war in Europe finally came to an end and the whole atmosphere in the country seemed to change overnight. Everywhere there was jubilation and a great spirit of optimism for the future. People looked forward to getting back to normal living after the long hard years, but it would be some considerable time before the ration books, the petrol coupons, the air raid shelters and the queues for coke disappeared. In the meantime, everyone wanted to get out and enjoy themselves. With the blackout now a thing of the past places of entertainment boomed, the film industry entered an era of unparalleled prosperity and sport rapidly re-organised to come back with a vengeance.

London promoter, Jack Solomons, rubbed his hands and prepared to cash in with a big show at the Tottenham Hotspur football ground, matching Jack London, conqueror of Freddie Mills, with Bruce Woodcock for the British and Empire Heavyweight titles. Casting around for attractive supporting contests, Solomons offered McAvoy a bout with George Howard, a good all-round fighter from Finsbury Park.

After several years of conducting his own affairs, with, it must be said, very little success, McAvoy was now in the hands of the wily London manager, Harry Levene, who arranged for Mac to be handled by Wally May, Len Harvey's old trainer and one of the best in the business. McAvoy set about the task of getting back to full fitness in his usual determined manner. Always a hard worker in the gym, despite the constant grumbling, Mac soon began to shed weight and after a few weeks was looking sharp and confident.

Solomons' enterprise was rewarded with a highly successful show, almost forty thousand people turning up to see Woodcock knock out London in six rounds to become champion. But the old favourite was not forgotten, for when McAvoy entered the arena a might roar greeted him. He was down to 11st. 8lbs and his superb condition belied the fact that he was getting on for thirty-eight years of age and had been out of the ring for well over three years.

Waiting for the first bell like a caged tiger, Mac tugged at the thumbs of his gloves with his teeth and prepared to show the huge crowd that he was still Britain's best middleweight.

Poor old George Howard never knew what hit him. Coming out of his corner like a whirlwind, McAvoy was across the ring in a flash and immediately whipped over a wicked left hook that felled the Finsbury Park man for a count of eight. On rising, the bewildered Howard made a valiant effort to fight back but was simply overwhelmed, being knocked down twice more in round one before taking the final count in the second.

McAvoy felt good and was soon in action again, knocking out Johnny Clements of Coatbridge, Scotland, in six rounds three weeks later at Portsmouth, and following this with an eight rounds points win over Welsh Middleweight Champion Tommy Davies, in Swansea, on September 10th, 1945. The latter was an outdoor affair, with rain falling steadily throughout. Lacking motivation, Mac was not particularly impressive, and though he put Davies down in round four he was unable to keep him there, the determined young Welshman fighting back strongly to floor McAvoy in the final round. The decision in

Mac's favour did not meet with the approval of the majority of the rainsoaked local fans. Still, at thirty-eight he had given his opponent thirteen years, an exceptional feat in itself.

This was to be McAvoy's final appearance in the ring, for though he could still put 'em away, a lot of the old zip had gone, training was becoming a grind, and worst of all, as far as Mac was concerned, the purses he was being offered were hardly worth the trouble.

There was some money put by, but taking into account the effort he had put into his eighteen years of campaigning in the ring, it added up to precious little. Mac wasn't much of a businessman, though a real trier, being prepared to have a go at almost anything, and over the next couple of years, during which time the marriage was decidedly rocky, he continued to dabble in all sorts of small time business ventures, usually connected with cars.

Unfortunately, he still tended to attract the wrong type of company, and because of his name he was always surrounded by hangers-on and backslappers, among whom was one Wilfred 'Bunny' Hughes, whose friendship Mac could well have done without.

Hughes was the kind of man who harboured an intense dislike for anything that entailed hard work. A keen betting man, he was in the habit of idling away his days in pubs and betting clubs, while dreaming up get-rich-quick schemes of one sort or another. In the evenings he could usually be found at the dog-track, one of his favourite haunts. The possessor of an appalling criminal record, Hughes was a very persuasive and convincing conman, who took a great delight in exploiting the gullible, though it must be said that while exhibiting a wonderful talent for separating his victims from their goods and money, he was woefully inept when it came to covering his tracks, due mainly to bad planning in the first place.

While Hughes' activities stretched as far afield as Liverpool and London, he often made the basic error of conning people right on his own doorstep, which inevitably resulted in speedy detection followed by further incarceration. As he lived in Rochdale, it's quite probable that Mac had known him for some time. In any event, it was not long before the two of them were knocking about together. Though about five years McAvoy's junior, Bunny could buy and sell Mac, who was clearly impressed by Hughes' smooth manner and agile brain, which he much preferred to employ in concocting apparently foolproof moneymaking schemes rather than settle down to earning an honest living. It was well known that Hughes mixed in dubious company, and for this reason alone Mac would have been well advised to give the man a wide berth. It would appear, however, that the lure of easy money was too strong to resist.

In the spring of 1947 Hughes worked out a plan for obtaining a motor vehicle by using a dud cheque. The operation, carried out in Salford, was so neatly executed that Hughes not only emerged the richer by a couple of hundred pounds, but was sublimely confident that the said cheque could in no way be traced back to him. So delighted, in fact, was the irrepressible Bunny that he could hardly wait to stage a repeat performance. This time, however, he had made up his mind to gamble for higher stakes and decided that an accomplice would be required.

So it was that one May morning, Hughes, accompanied by McAvoy, visited The District Bank at Heaton Chapel, Stockport, and opened an account by depositing £47 in cash. He then obtained two cheque books. From there they went to the Davenport Garage, where McAvoy was well known. The boxer then introduced Hughes to a salesman, Harry Lane-Smith. The smiling conman told Lane-Smith that he was a doctor practicing in Rochdale, and also mentioned that his wife worked as a midwife in the same town. He said he was looking for a good car and had noticed a Rover in the forecourt which appeared to be just what he wanted.

The three men then went for a trial run in the car. On returning to the garage Hughes agreed to buy the vehicle and at his suggestion all three adjourned to a nearby cafe to discuss the deal, Hughes apologising for his unshaven appearance, explaining that he had been out most of the previous night on a serious case.

After leaving the cafe, Lane-Smith and Hughes returned to the garage, while McAvoy sat outside in his car. In the office, Hughes produced a cheque book and glibly informed the salesman that he would pay by cheque as it was more convenient. Slightly perturbed at this, Lane-Smith went out to the car, and telling McAvoy that the 'doctor' wanted to give him a cheque for £950, asked the boxer if he thought this would be all right.

'Yes,' replied McAvoy, 'it's okay.'

At this, the salesman returned to the office, took the cheque and handed over the car keys. Within a matter of two hours the vehicle had been re-sold to a Manchester garage for £610, Hughes insisting on cash, saying that he could not take a cheque for income tax reasons.

It had been as simple as Hughes had forecast, but how McAvoy, being so well known in the area, could have expected to get away with it, is beyond comprehension. His blind faith in the Rochdale conman had clearly impaired his judgement and common sense. Four days later Hughes was arrested at Salford dog-track in connection with the previous fraud, and remanded in custody. He told the police, 'You're on the wrong horse. I know nothing about it.'

By this time the dud cheque passed at Stockport had been returned by the bank. It did not take the law long to connect Hughes with that job also. Soon afterwards the police were knocking on the door of a house in Wellington Road North, Heaton Chapel, Stockport, where McAvoy and his family were now living, with a warrant for Mac's arrest. After being remanded on bail for one day he appeared in court at Stockport, along with Hughes, charged with 'Intent to Defraud', following which, both were remanded on bail for a further fourteen days.

When the two were brought up at Manchester Assizes a month later, Mrs Mary Stewart, chief clerk at the Davenport Garage, told the court that she had been very surprised when Hughes said he was a doctor, adding that she had never before set eyes on such a disreputable looking medical man.

Mr O. F. Christensen, a director of the garage, said that he had previously done business with McAvoy and that he would have trusted him enough to let him have a car on a sale or return basis anytime.

Pleading on behalf of McAvoy, Mr H. Burton submitted, 'If you want to stage a fraud do you take a disreputable looking tramp along with a two days growth on his chin and try to pass him off as a doctor? There is not one shred of evidence to show that my client ever obtained anything by false pretenses. So far as conspiracy to defraud is concerned, the facts simply do not bear this out, and I submit that there is no case to answer. The magistrates however, strongly disagreed. Hughes, described as a General Dealer, was found guilty and sentenced to eighteen months, which was hardly surprising, for when arrested he was found to be in possession of £193 in cash plus two cheques, one for £14,800, the other for £11,300, both made out to himself.

The judge, Mr Justice Staples, told him, 'You have an appalling record and a thoroughly bad Army record also. You like to do things on the twist and the crook. You have candidly shouldered most of the blame in this affair and I have no doubt this is true. You got hold of this stupid giant and found him very useful for your purpose.

To McAvoy the judge said that although he may have been led

down the garden path by Hughes, he obviously knew that there was some funny business going on regarding the cheque.

'You are a man,' said the judge, 'with a reputation known all over the world, and you have thrown it out of the window by getting mixed up in this sort of business. I know that you boxing fellows are much easier to lead astray than to knock out, for you have more in your fists than you have in your heads. You have been a fool, but I'm going to give you a run for your money by binding you over. Don't come here again.'

To which a very relieved and uncharacteristically humble McAvoy replied, 'I never will be back, sir.'

Though having only recently retired from the ring, Mac was already beginning to feel a has-been. Perhaps it was just his imagination, but the host of so-called friends and supporters now seemed much less keen to seek him out, to shake his hand and ask for an autograph. This should not have surprised him, for even McAvoy must have been well aware of how fickle the public can be, and he must also have realised that Freddie Mills, Dick Turpin and Bruce Woodcock were the names on everyone's lips. Mac was yesterday's news and he didn't like the feeling at all. He was in the same situation that all fighters find themselves in once their careers are over. But then McAvoy wasn't just any fighter. He'd been at the top since 1933. Twelve years a champion, a great champion, retiring undefeated. How could they forget so quickly?

Of course, the truth was that Mac was by no means forgotten, but being out of the limelight after such a long reign as King was a terrible blow to that massive ego, and it would obviously take a very long time for him to come to terms with the reality of his situation.

If Mac had been difficult to live with previously, he now became even more so. Yet Renee was very resilient and tried her hardest to be understanding and supportive. The embittered ex-champion drew much love and comfort from the presence of Pat, his young daughter, now two years old, while his mother was, as always, available whenever he needed to confide in her.

Nellie Bamford and her son had remained very close. Since the death of her husband Nellie had led something of a nomadic existence, moving house a number of times, always within the Rochdale area, without ever seeming able to settle. Mac visited her regularly and always made sure that she was never short of a bob or two. She still enjoyed a glass of Guinness and had no money apart from her pension.

Nellie had never been particularly thrifty and was now living in what could only be described as rather poor circumstances, in addition to which she was not in the best of health. Sitting there with her in a shabby one-up-one-down cottage reminded Mac of Turner's Yard and the first home the Bamfords had occupied on arriving in Rochdale. It saddened him to think that his mother had come full circle only to finish up living like this; old, sick and very lonely. That day he made up his mind to do something about it. Nellie would come and live with him. There was no other way.

Renee's reaction to this decision is not known, but it would have made little difference in any case, once Mac had decided, for no woman was ever going to come between him and his mother, not even his wife. He felt very strongly that she needed him now, and he was going to make sure that she was well looked after for the remainder of her life.

As it turned out, Nellie was not destined to survive for much longer. She passed away just a few days after Christmas 1945, and no doubt died a happy woman, for her beloved Joe remained by her side to the very end.

Nellie was buried in Rochdale Cemetery in the grave of her husband. Her age is given as 77, which is incorrect, as her birth certificate clearly states that she was born in 1872, making her only 73 at the time of her death.

# Chapter 29

## Struck Down

Following the unfortunate episode with the notorious Wilfred 'Bunny' Hughes, from which he was very fortunate to escape with such a light sentence, McAvoy resolved to steer clear of such company in the future. His record showed that although an extremely violent man, both in and out of the ring, he was not normally in the habit of engaging in fraudulent activities. It was quite clear that he had himself been taken in by Hughes and was more a fool than a villain. Just the same his name had again been dragged through the mud, this time in connection with what could only be described as a very serious crime.

With his fighting days behind him, a marriage which would have worked, given a fair chance, now very shaky indeed, and little or nothing on the horizon in the way of career prospects, the future appeared uncertain to say the least. Worse, however, was to come – far worse.

About a month after the trial McAvoy began to feel off colour. The first symptoms seemed innocuous enough; sore throat, headache, aches and pains in the limbs and a rise in temperature. It appeared to be a simple case of 'flu, but after being seen by a doctor Mac was taken to hospital, reported by at least one newspaper to be suffering from a nervous breakdown. The problem, however, was far more serious than that. The ache in his lower limbs now passed into a stage of weakness, followed by the first signs of paralysis. The doctor's worst fears were then confirmed. McAvoy had become a victim of the dreaded disease, poliomylitis, or infantile paralysis, at that time reaching epidemic proportions in this country.

As the name indicates, child victims far outnumber adults, and as the scare intensified warnings were given out by the medical authorities, strongly discouraging children from attending places where crowds gathered, such as cinemas and swimming baths, especially in hot weather. Where possible, all operations for the removal of adenoids or tonsils, and immunisation against diphtheria and whooping cough were ordered to be postponed, while particular care was to be taken to protect food from flies and the highest standards of cleanliness observed at all times. The epidemic was so serious that it would be no exaggeration to say that the nation was in the grip of fear.

Upon the disease first being suspected the patient is put to bed and the affected limbs completely rested. At this point splints are often introduced to give adequate rest to the affected muscles, which are very tender. The paralysis often spreads from the lower limbs upwards. If the diaphragm and respiratory muscles become affected the patient is unable to breathe properly, and unless placed in a respirator, or iron lung, without delay, death can ensue.

At first McAvoy was too ill to appreciate fully just what was happening to him. Then the shock of being told the grim news hit him a thousand times harder than he had ever been hit in the ring. Paralysis had now occurred in the legs and for several days he lay there utterly devastated. When family and friends visited they found him in the depths of despair and in no mood to talk or listen to their expressions of sympathy. He could only lie back and whisper, 'Why me... why me?'

It was some weeks before he was able to face up to the reality of his predicament, and a glimpse of the old fighting spirit now began to surface. He was angry and ready to fight back.

'I'm not letting this bloody thing beat me,' he told Don Waters, 'I'll be back on my feet before long, you'll see.'

Don's own family had, in fact, been touched by the disease, his daughter Margaret having been struck down. Fortunately, however, early diagnosis and treatment had resulted in the virus being arrested. The girl had shown great courage and was making rapid progress towards recovery. Mac was determined to achieve a similar sort of success. In a letter to his former manager, Harry Levene, he wrote:

'I'm not throwing in the towel. I intend to go on fighting. The specialist says that I'm out of danger now, as it's stopped developing. They say it could be months before they'll know how the illness will leave me, and the doctor can't say if I'll walk again. I say I will. This thing won't K.O. me.'

The entire sporting world was stunned at the terrible news. The people of Rochdale were shocked and sympathetic, yet no great effort appears to have been made, other than by those closest to Mac, to rally round him. If something official had been organised it would undoubtedly have acted as a terrific morale booster in assuring the stricken boxer that Rochdale had not forgotten its great champion in his darkest hour.

It would be correct to say that for all his wonderful achievements McAvoy had never received the sort of acclaim accorded Gracie Fields, for example. Of course, there was perhaps a feeling that Mac's exploits outside the ring had reflected rather badly on his native town, although Gracie herself was not exactly whiter than white. She had long since forsaken the cobbled streets and factory smoke for the sunny climate of Capri, and after Italy formed an alliance with Hitler early in the war she had hurriedly returned to England before embarking for America. In a way the move was forced on her. If she had stayed in Britain there is no doubt that her second husband, Monty Banks, an Italian, would have been interned. The problem was that she had managed to smuggle £10,000 out of the country at a time when the limit was no more than £10.

On the credit side, Gracie did a lot of good things. She ran an orphanage at Peacehaven in Sussex, and worked hard during the war in entertaining the troops and war workers. At the very time that McAvoy was struck down, arrangements were being made for Gracie to visit Rochdale, where the B.B.C. was planning to launch her new radio show, '*Working Party*'. Huge crowds turned out to greet her and a town hall reception was laid on in her honour.

It would have been nice to report that Gracie took the opportunity to seek out Mac and pass on some words of comfort, but there is no record that she ever did.

Some weeks later he was back home and planning his big fight-back. First he had a pair of parallel bars rigged up in one of the rooms, and would painfully inch his way along them, straining every muscle in his arms, shoulders and upper body. He would work on those bars for hour after hour until red in the face. Then, completely exhausted, with sweat pouring from him, he would hang there gasping for breath and cursing his ill-luck.

If it had been solely a question of sheer guts, effort and willpower, Mac would have conquered his disability within the first month. But unfortunately the battle he was fighting was already lost. Eventually, he was told that although the disease would progress no further, too much damage had already been done to the nerves for there to be any possibility of movement returning. The limbs were simply dead and could never be rejuvenated. The paralysis was total and accompanied by a wasting away of the muscles. There was not the remotest possibility of him ever walking again.

Mac still refused to accept this and toiled all the harder, believing that mind would somehow conquer matter. Though there was now no feeling at all in the legs, he at times imagined that there was. This would then have the effect of spurring him on to greater efforts on the bars and he would battle away with the sort of spirit and fierce determination he had always shown in the ring.

But although there was absolutely no hope of any movement returning he was at least exercising that part of the body which was unaffected by the disease. This was not at all a bad thing, for it would have been quite easy to have let go completely and simply run to fat. Though gaining in weight as the months went by, McAvoy's upper body was still very muscular, the extra bulk only serving to make him even more powerful, as would later become only too apparent, for though his boxing career was now very much in the past, his fistic activities were far from over.

Mac now needed Renee very badly and she did not let him down. Not that the sudden change in his life had made him any easier to live with. If anything, his quick temper, impatience and belligerent attitude were now even more in evidence than before, which was hardly surprising, for such an affliction was bound to hit an active man like McAvoy even harder than it would the average person. But Renee went out of her way to understand and comfort him in those first trying months following the onset of the illness, when she nursed him with the kind of love and tenderness that any loving mother would have lavished on a sick child.

In those days there was very little in the way of facilities and special medical care for the chronically sick and disabled, and the greater part of Mac's day was spent sitting in a wheelchair in the modest house at Wellington Road North, just wiling away the hours. Since his mother's death he had often thought of her. He had missed her very much and she now entered his thoughts more and more. Though Renee was kind, considerate and eager to please him, she was not a patch on his Mam. No woman was. How she would have looked after him, anticipated his every want, kept his spirits up… but no, it would have broken Nellie's heart to have seen her beloved Joe crippled and helpless like that. He was glad she'd been spared the anguish of it.

At times it was necessary for Renee to drag him across the floor on a blanket. To get him into the wheelchair required a tremendous effort, and this feat was achieved with the aid of ropes slung over a beam. With a mighty pull Mac would then hoist himself up while his wife pushed the wheelchair under him. Occasionally he would go through his scrapbook, but this usually ended with him becoming depressed again and he would suddenly slam the book shut and toss it angrily to one side.

Given all the circumstances, Mac had borne his misfortune with great fortitude and shown indomitable courage in fighting back, but as the months slipped by with no change in his condition, the boredom and the feelings of despair and hopelessness began to take a firm hold on him and he would talk of suicide.

After the first flood of family and close friends, all offering sympathy and swearing to stand by him and help in every way possible, the number of visitors gradually slowed down to a trickle. One man who never lost touch, however, was old foe Jack Hyams. Jack felt very sorry for Mac and never forgot him, writing many letters over the years. Mac later admitted that those letters meant a lot to him and certainly helped to keep up his flagging spirits as month followed month with no significant improvement in his condition.

On warm summer days he would sit at the door in his wheelchair and just gaze vacantly at the traffic going by. There was plenty of time to think and his mind no doubt wandered back to the narrow cobbled streets of Rochdale and his poor but happy childhood; to Royton and those exciting Sunday afternoons of open air scrapping for just a few bob; to the day he left Joe Tolley and moved on to bigger things; Belle Vue; winning the title from the great Len Harvey; outstanding success in America and the big purses he never saw. The triumphant return when the band played and thousands followed him home… It had all come and gone so quickly… He must not think of the past, it only depressed him. Just think of the future… if there was one… But where were all those people who had fallen over themselves to be near him not so very long before? All the backslappers and so-called friends. What had happened to them? He was becoming more and more isolated. In 1948 Mac told a reporter that he felt forgotten and forsaken in adversity.

There is no record of McAvoy ever meeting up with Joe Tolley again following the exhibition he had given at the Glen Mill prisoner -of-war camp in Oldham. Not long afterwards Tolley had been posted to the Isle of Man to guard enemy aliens, all Germans and Italians living in Britain at the outbreak of the war having been rounded up and interned for the duration.

One of the first people Tolley ran into on arriving at the camp was Deno Guselli, the Barrow Italian, who had fought many times at Royton. Joe was delighted to see him and soon fixed Deno up with a soft job sorting out the mail. It wasn't long before Tolley had some boxing organised and the camp was a much livelier place from then on. At the war's end, Tolley, now well into his sixties, lost no time in getting back into the fight business as a referee. Joe's family had split up, his mother and old Maloney, his stepfather, having died during the war. Albert, now demobbed himself, was happily married and living in nearby Chadderton. Without a home to go to, Tolley soon got himself fixed up, moving in with Margaret Danson and her family. Margaret lived in Shaw and was a sister of Harold Ratchford's wife, Nellie. She had first met Joe Tolley in the late twenties, when she had gone along to the Royton Stadium to watch Harold box, and was very much taken by the charismatic promoter, who soon began asking her out. Their association continued throughout the thirties, with no hope of marriage, for Joe had never bothered to try to obtain a divorce from Ellen, and probably never had any intention of doing so. After all, it was the best possible excuse to present to Margaret or any other lady friend who might have ideas about restricting his freedom.

Margaret was certainly besotted with Joe Tolley. Though quite a few years her senior, he was always well dressed, self confident, and quite a talker who could hold his own in any company. Margaret had waited for him throughout the war, showing little interest in other men, though she had plenty of offers. Now in her forties, she lived in the house of her father, Joe Danson, who had no objection at all to Tolley moving in. In fact, the two men were of a similar age and got on quite well together.

Though now settled and apparently quite happy in Shaw, Tolley, despite the advancing years, still could not bring himself to focus his attention entirely on one woman. One night he was spotted by a district nurse as he entered the house of a widow in High Crompton, less than a mile from Margaret Danson's house. Unfortunately for him the nurse was not at all the discreet type and promptly informed a friend – none other than Nellie Ratchford, who in turn lost no time in passing on this titbit of information to her sister.

Joe arrived home that evening to find his bags packed. Margaret was livid, and after giving Tolley a piece of her mind, suggested that as he was obviously interested in visiting the young lady in High Crompton, he might like to move in with her. Though somewhat taken aback at the sudden turn of events, Tolley, who had lost none of his old resourcefulness, did just that. Within the space of half-an-hour or so he had departed from one mistress and moved in with another, an attractive young woman at least thirty years his junior.

From his new base, Joe, in between romancing his young lady friend, was spending a lot of time on the road. He was still one of the game's top referees and simply carried on where he'd left off in 1939, travelling up and down the country several days a week and often arriving home in the early hours. For a man of his age it was a hard, demanding life, but he loved it, and being a tough old bird, just thought he could go on for ever. Joe remained a smart man, always well turned out and very proud of his chin-in-chest-out military bearing. Though things had obviously changed since the thirties and his social life diminished somewhat, he could still dig up an old flame in most of the towns he visited regularly.

But though he refused to admit it, even to himself, he was most certainly beginning to slow down. After a night's refereeing he would often arrive in Manchester so late that he would have to rely on one of the newspaper vans to get a lift up to Oldham, seven miles away. From there he then had to make his way to Shaw, a few more miles further on, usually on foot.

One night in 1946, while refereeing at Liverpool Stadium, where he was a great favourite, Joe began to feel ill during the course of a heavyweight bout he was handling. He felt slightly sick and had a tightness in his chest. Later he told Albert that he could hardly remember anything about the fight or the verdict he had given at the end. In the early hours of the following morning Joe got off the train at Rochdale station. There were no cabs about at that time, nor any other form of transport. So, attaché case in hand, he set off for home on foot. It was a long hard slog for a man in his condition, especially the last mile or so, which was a steady climb. By the time he reached High Crompton and flopped into bed he was almost dead on his feet.

Several days later Albert received a message from the lady friend to say that his father was very ill. On arriving at the house he was shocked at his Dad's appearance. Almost overnight Joe had grown old. All the hard living, irregular meals and the sixty Goldflake cigarettes he had smoked every day over a period of many years had now caught up with him. As for the lady friend; from being the mistress of a smart, if elderly, lover, who bought her nice clothes and took her out often, she now found herself playing nursemaid to a grumbling old man who simply could not stand to be cooped up in the house, despite the fact that he was far from well.

She now wanted him out, and told Albert so in no uncertain terms. Before any decision could be taken, however, Joe took a turn for the worst. He began to ramble and became so unstable mentally that the doctor ordered his removal to the psychiatric block of the Oldham and District General Hospital at Boundary Park.

Within a couple of weeks he was much better, and though his general health was still poor his mental condition soon returned to normal. The only problem was that Joe was again without a home to go to. Surprisingly, perhaps, he now turned to Albert for help. The two were very different people, with little in common. Albert, a sober, reserved, clean living young man, had always disapproved of his father's morals and way of life, and couldn't help thinking back to the time Joe had got one of his regular girlfriends, a waitress named Molly, into trouble. He could not marry her of course, but when a daughter, Mona, was born, he lavished on the child all the love and attention he had never given Albert. This was in the mid-twenties, when Albert was around twelve or thirteen and needed his father as much as any of the other lads he knocked about with needed theirs. But Joe had never paid him much heed, just used him really, and only ever talked about business when he was at home, which was not very often anyway. Now he was asking if he might move in with Albert and his wife, and though very uncertain about the wisdom of such an arrangement, Albert knew he could not let his father down. Soon afterwards the move was made.

Joe was reasonably happy at Chadderton. He did not go out much and would occasionally receive visitors; friends from the old days who wanted to talk about boxing. He would then manage to drag himself out of his lethargy and put on a show for them. For an hour or two he would be something like the Joe Tolley of old, the centre of attention, laughing, joking and monopolising the conversation.

Generally speaking though, his health was now very poor. He had a bad chest and suffered from bouts of acute depression. Worse still, his mental abilities became somewhat impaired. The top and bottom of it was, that the great Joe Tolley was burned out, both physically and mentally. Gradually, he deteriorated, and eventually became so ill that he was forced to go into the hospital. In March, 1949, Joe took the final count at Oldham and District General Hospital.

With just the faintest trace of emotion in his voice, Albert recalled; 'He was only sixty-six when he died. Not very old by today's standards. But Joe Tolley had lived every day of his life to the full. D'you know, as far as I can remember, I never knew him to stay in the house one single evening – except for the time he broke his ankle. Then he stayed in one or two nights at the most. Soon as he could hobble he was off out again.

'Some people live till they're ninety, but go nowhere and see nothing. Compared to Joe Tolley, they haven't lived at all. What a showman he was. What a character!'

# Chapter 30

## Fighting Back

It's doubtful if the news of his old mentor's passing occupied McAvoy's thoughts for very long. He was much too concerned with his own troubles. After many bitter months of sweating, straining and fighting to get the legs going he was finally forced to face up to the harsh truth. He would never walk again. Though the upper body was as powerful as ever, the legs had now shrivelled to the point where they resembled matchsticks.

Don Waters' daughter, Margaret, on the other hand, turned out to be one of the lucky ones, eventually regaining ninety-seven per cent movement. Don was naturally very happy that his own battle had been won, but sad for his friend who was at a very low ebb indeed.

Gradually, however, Mac began to show his true fighting spirit, realising that to simply sit there feeling sorry for himself was not going to help at all. Slowly, and only after a great conscious effort, he began to pull himself together. He was fitted with calipers and given a pair of walking sticks. Characteristically, he put every effort into learning to first of all balance himself, then walk with a sort of stiff-legged gait. He also arranged to have his car specially adapted, eliminating all foot controls, so that despite his disability he would be able to drive quite comfortably.

Now at least he could get out again. This made a big difference to Mac and he was soon to be seen with old friends in Manchester and Rochdale, apparently enjoying life again. He still felt very bitter that such a disaster had befallen him, but at least he was no longer housebound. Over the years he was to have a whole series of cars specially refitted, and though he had days when he didn't feel quite up to the mark, he usually managed to get out several times a week just to break the monotony.

Though he was now on his third wife he still kept in touch with the first two, calling round to visit Eliza quite regularly. When Eliza re-married, her new husband, Reg Holt, was none too keen on his wife entertaining his predecessor and Mac's visits eventually dropped off. Unfortunately, Eliza was not destined to have a happy marriage, and after a while she and Reg Holt separated. McAvoy's main purpose in visiting Joan Lye was to see his son, Michael, who was growing up big, strong and healthy.

Around this period the possibility of a new interest appeared on the horizon. Joe junior, Mac's eldest son, a well-built lad of nineteen, who up to this point had shown little inclination to get involved in the fight game, now told his dad that he had had the gloves on and was training with some other lads in an upper room of the Cloverdale Hotel in Rochdale.

McAvoy received this news with mixed feelings. On the one hand he was pleased and proud to think that at least one of his sons might well follow in his footsteps, while on the other, the thought of all the shady, unreliable and downright crooked characters to whom he himself had fallen prey, filled him with considerable apprehension. Nevertheless he resolved to help in any way possible. If only he could have got into the ring and sparred with the boy, what a difference it might have made. Still, at least he could give his son the benefit of his own vast experience. Of course, he had very little idea of young Joe's capabilities and could only hope that he had at least inherited some of his father's renowned strength and toughness.

As Joe junior had been christened Joseph Patrick Bamford, after his father, it was decided that Joe Patrick would be an appropriate name for him to fight under and one with a nice ring to it. When Joe made his debut at Salford Stadium in February 1949, his dad was at the ringside, and though Mac chatted casually with the many friends and acquaintances who came over to have a word with him, inside he was far more keyed up than he could ever remember being for any of his own fights, even the big ones.

That night, however, things worked out very well, young Joe scoring a three round knockout over Paddy Daley of Salford, an experienced scrapper. Unfortunately, this early promise was not to be fulfilled. After a couple more wins, both on points, Joe drew his next contest and then dropped a points decision to Hal Smith of St. Helens at Liverpool Stadium. After that he seemed to lose interest and it soon became clear that his heart was not really in it.

A middleweight like his father, young Joe was only moderately talented, and nowhere near dedicated enough to have any hope of succeeding, and eventually drifted out of the game. Mac was disappointed, but wise enough to realise that unless the desire and dedication are there, no amount of advice and coaching can make a boy into a champion.

McAvoy's other son, Jackie, also did a bit of sparring, but nothing ever came of it. Unlike his brother Joe, a pleasant, uncomplicated sort of lad, Jackie turned out to be something of a problem, being in trouble with the police on a number of occasions, with drink usually at the root of it. Mac was very concerned about him and tried to help as best he could. On one occasion he made a serious attempt to set Jackie up in business, taking him along to see Don Waters, who was then running a haulage company and was able to fix him up with a lorry with which to go into the demolition business. At first he seemed to do well, but after a while he lost his enthusiasm and the project eventually folded.

McAvoy himself was feeling the pinch. Apart from £25 donated by the British Boxing Board of Control, which had paid for the wheelchair, Mac had received very little help from anyone, and what capital he had managed to accumulate was almost exhausted. As state benefits in those days were hardly enough to manage on, he knew he would have to start earning a living again as soon as possible.

As a first step, a wool shop was purchased in Eccles New Road, Salford, which Renee ran, while Mac, at the suggestion of some of his friends, set about cashing in on his fame by taking a pitch on Blackpool promenade. There he sat, day after day, all summer long, in an armchair. By his side stood a weighing machine and a large board, on which were displayed a number of photographs depicting the various stages of his wonderful career. After stepping onto the scales to be weighed, members of the public would chat to the great champion, shake his hand and receive a signed postcard size photograph.

The few pence each transaction brought in did not add up to a fortune by any means, but it certainly helped keep McAvoy off the poverty line. At Blackpool he was assisted by several old friends from the world of boxing, among them 'Spud' Murphy, Johnny Tarpey, and Jackie Madden, the Belle Vue matchmaker who had shared so many of those glorious moments back in the thirties, and who was now determined to do whatever he could to help.

Many people, of course, viewed the old champion with pity, which was the last thing he wanted. It was obviously a great come-down for him and a big blow to his pride. In later years Mac was to say that he had never wanted to be a peep show and had hated every minute of those long days on Blackpool front. All the more credit to him then for having had the courage to do it, rather than remain at home feeling sorry for himself and simply relying on state charity.

While the terrible tragedy which had befallen Mac had certainly turned his life upside down, it had by no means changed his temperament. He was still quick to take offence or lose his temper, and many are the stories of him landing the old K.O. punch on anyone who had the misfortune to incur his displeasure.

There is no doubt that some of these tales are greatly exaggerated, but one in particular is too persistent not to have at least some substance. This is the one about Mac landing his sleep-producing left hook on some hapless stranger foolish enough to get too close to the car window while arguing with him. As there are several versions of this anecdote, it is not beyond the bounds of possibility that it occurred on more than one occasion.

As we all know, it's not at all difficult to get into an argument with another motorist, and the story goes that when this happened McAvoy would feign deafness so as to lure the person he was arguing with just that bit closer. When his victim came within range, the left would explode on his chin with a fearful crack and Mac would calmly slip his car into gear and drive off.

Don Waters recalls visiting The Windmill, a pub in Rochdale run by McAvoy's elder sister, Rose, and her husband. After entering the bar Mac would usually prefer to stand, in order to give himself a break from the long hours of sitting, and after propping himself up with his back to the wall he could put the sticks to one side and balance quite comfortably with the aid of the calipers on his legs.

On this particular evening, while Don was getting the drinks, he noticed two hefty fellows standing at the bar and was told that they were a couple of all-in wrestlers. After a while one of them spotted McAvoy, and turning to his companion, said:

'You know who this is, don't you?'

'No, I don't,' was the reply.

'Course you do, it's Jock McAvoy. You know, the boxer.'

'Oh, him,' said the other man, 'Oh aye, I've heard of him.'

Don immediately sensed that Mac did not like the wrestlers' manner, and when another slighting remark was passed, McAvoy, who was no more than a couple of feet away, asked:

'Why're you picking on me?'

'Ah, nobody's picking on you,' replied the wrestler, whose attitude was both off-hand and aggressive.

That was enough. McAvoy immediately let him have one on the chin and that was the end of that.

One night at Belle Vue he is said to have struck the well-known boxing writer, Gilbert Odd, probably over something he'd written about him. Mac was in calipers at this time and the scene was witnessed by a number of people, including ex-British Middleweight Champion, Johnny Sullivan, who related it to the author.

During the 1950s McAvoy was often seen at the ringside at many of the Northern Halls. He would also drive over to Rochdale quite frequently for a few hours out with Len Collinge, Billy Ashworth and one or two other old friends. He never drank much but enjoyed company and a laugh and a joke. Surprisingly, perhaps, in view of his disability, Mac had by no means lost his appetite for the opposite sex. He was still very good looking, powerfully built and dressed smartly. According to Don Waters he was still chasing females, despite his handicap. I put it to Don that this was very hard to believe.

'It's quite true,' he replied. 'Oh aye, he was a bugger for the women.'

'You don't mean to say he was just as bad as before he got the polio?, I ventured.

'Bad?' exclaimed Don, 'if anything he was a bloody sight worse. It was only his legs that were gone, nothing else. Apart from his legs he was quite normal.'

Though Don's description of a rampant McAvoy still on the chase does seem a little exaggerated, at least it's good to know that Mac was enjoying himself up to a point, and not letting his illness dampen his spirits completely. As the sixties approached, however, he did begin to slow down somewhat. He seldom went to boxing shows anymore and occasionally suffered again from periods of depression.

Then came a lucky break. Mac had had his eye on a piece of land at Hall Lane, Partington, in Cheshire. His idea was to acquire the land and move into the property, Inglewood House, which stood on it. Then, if he could get a license, he hoped to raise enough money to put caravans on the site and rent them out, feeling that the income would help set him up for the rest of his life.

In those days of post-war restrictions licenses were required for just about everything, and were very difficult to obtain. However, due largely to the influence of a certain Cheshire M.P., who happened to be a keen boxing fan and a great McAvoy admirer, the license was eventually granted and the enterprise set in motion. One or two friends, such as Billy Ashworth, helped out. Billy, an electrician, travelling over from Rochdale to light up the site for Mac.

The business was jointly owned by McAvoy and his wife. Renee was very keen on the new venture and worked exceptionally hard to make a go of it, doing all the cleaning and taking care of the upkeep of the caravans as well as handling some of the paperwork. McAvoy himself was very much involved of course, dealing with the movement of tenants, answering the telephone and generally controlling the operation. There is no doubt that the caravan site changed Mac's life for the better. It was a new interest and proved to be very therapeutic. Though he still liked to get out, he was not nearly so restless, and for a time all went smoothly.

McAvoy's older children often came over from Rochdale and got on well with Pat, who was growing up fast. It was through her that Mac was able to indulge his love of horses once again. Making sure that she received expert tuition, he bought her a horse which she soon learned to ride quite expertly. Eventually, with further training and her dad's enthusiastic coaching, Pat was good enough to enter competitions at gymkhanas. This was a good period for Mac. He delighted in watching his little girl competing and the two of them spent many a weekend travelling to shows all over the country.

There can be little doubt that Pat's presence on the scene went a long way towards holding the marriage together, but as she got older that would change. For the moment though, all was well. The business was successful and the family reasonably happy.

By the late fifties, Pat, now well into her teens, had become very successful in showjumping, and Mac entertained hopes that she might reach the top. Then, unaccountably, she seemed to lose interest and eventually gave it up. Her father felt that perhaps he himself was to blame for having driven her so hard when she was young. Even so, Mac lived in hopes that she would one day pick up the threads of what had undoubtedly been a highly promising career.

In 1960, in a newspaper interview, McAvoy was asked what he missed most in life since being struck down by polio, and replied, 'A walk along the country lanes. Mind you, when I could walk I either ran in training or went by car. Walking just seemed a waste of time. Now I'd give anything to throw away these sticks and be able to take a stroll around my home here in Cheshire. Everyone says what a nice quiet fellow I am these days. I just tell them that if you can't fight or run away, there's no point in being any other way.'

This last statement, however, was far from accurate. For though it was true that Mac could not run away, he could still fight if he had to. In 1969 he was granted an injunction in the Chancery Court in Manchester, restraining a gypsy neighbour, Uriah Burton, from trespassing on his land.

It was the culmination of a long-running feud between the two men, for Burton, known in the gypsy community as 'Big Just', had been a thorn in McAvoy's side for some considerable time. Big Just's own caravans were pitched on land adjoining McAvoy's in Hall Lane and the gypsies had tended to encroach, as well as generally make a nuisance of themselves.

If McAvoy had been on his feet rather than in a wheelchair the trespassers would hardly have been likely to take such liberties. Even so, they seriously underestimated the ex-champion. Burton was, by all accounts, a fighting man himself. Known as 'King of the Gypsies', he was apparently well versed in bare knuckle brawling and a much feared figure among his own people. But the man wasn't born who could frighten McAvoy, disabled or not. Mac was now turned sixty and only a couple of years earlier had spent some time in Withington Hospital after suffering a heart attack. Nevertheless he insisted on confronting Burton, and the story goes that Mac propped himself up against a wall, raised his fists and dared the big gypsy to take him on. Very wisely, Burton declined, and the matter was finally settled in court.

In 1962 McAvoy was invited to appear on a B.B.C. television programme, with Victor Bernard as interviewer. Asked to bring along the Lonsdale belt he had won outright, Mac was forced to reveal that he had sold it for £450 when down on his luck some years before. He also appealed in a newspaper to the person who now possessed it to give him the chance to buy it back.

McAvoy had sold the belt to a Blackpool rock manufacturer, but on the day the television programme was due to go out, Mr Colin Leslie, a Manchester antique dealer, informed the B.B.C. that he had bought it for £750 some time previously, and had kept it in his safe. He was prepared, he said, to let McAvoy have it for what he himself had paid for it.

The result of this revelation was that Mac was able to handle the trophy again, if only for a little while, it then being announced that he would negotiate with Leslie to buy it back.

For some reason or other, however, no deal was struck and the belt was again lost sight of until December 1967, when a Manchester businessman, Mr Eric Rigby, who stated that he had owned it for five years, showed great kindness in presenting the belt to the old champion soon after his sixtieth birthday.

The belt in question is one of the original trophies awarded by the National Sporting Club, the first of which was presented by Lord Lonsdale to Freddie Welsh of Pontypridd, following his great victory over twenty rounds against Johnny Summers at the National Sporting Club in Covent Garden, in November 1909. Following this, the N.S.C. awarded championship belts for all the weight divisions, thereby giving itself a monopoly, in a sense, on all British title contests. To win a Lonsdale belt outright a fighter had to put three notches on it by winning three British title contests at the same weight, though not necessarily in consecutive order. Though the N.S.C. has long since gone out of existence, and the Lonsdale belt is now awarded by the British Boxing Board of Control, the same rules still apply, the only difference being that after winning a title, a boxer must now make three successful defences before the belt becomes his own property.

# Chapter 31

## Tragedy

Though the caravan site was successful, McAvoy was by no means a happy man. He had not managed the financial side of the business too well, and Renee, who had worked very hard to make it pay, became disillusioned. Mac was once again subject to fits of deep depression and had several times threatened to take his own life. The couple rowed constantly, with Renee often getting so upset that she would go off and stay the night with her sister.

In this atmosphere the business was bound to suffer, and rather than see all her hard work disappear down the drain Renee somehow managed to raise enough money to buy out her husband's half of the enterprise.

Pat, meanwhile, had married, and was living next door in Hall Lane. She too was involved in the business. She had always worked well with her mother but found her father a very difficult man to please. Mac had never been easy to live with, but now, in his early sixties, perhaps through no fault of his own, he was far more irritable and cantankerous than he had ever been. There were times when he felt that everyone was against him, and though his son, Joe, who now had a family of his own, occasionally came over to visit him, he felt isolated; cut off from his old friends whom he seldom now had any contact with.

Early in 1969 a terrible tragedy befell the Bamford family, when McAvoy's youngest son, Jackie, was found dead at his mother's house in Kilworth Street, Rochdale. Jackie, aged thirty-eight, was estranged from his wife and children and living with Eliza, who made the shocking discovery in the early hours of the morning, after her son had returned home from a night's drinking. It was later discovered that Jackie had taken a drug overdose, but evidence given at the inquest seemed to indicate that the possibility of him having taken his own life was extremely unlikely. His wife, Maria, told the Coroner's court that her husband, from whom she was legally separated, had visited her on the day prior to his death and had enjoyed himself playing with the children, leaving in a happy frame of mind and telling her he would call again at the weekend.

Jackie's mother, Eliza, said that her son was suffering from a rash and had been taking barbiturates to help him sleep. She had left him two capsules, as prescribed by the doctor, and gone to bed. The bottle containing the rest of the capsules she had placed under her pillow when she went to sleep. Her son had called in to say goodnight and had then gone downstairs again. Next morning she found him lying dead on the hearth. At no time had he ever given any indication that he intended to harm himself. On the night in question he had been out drinking, but she had no idea how much he had consumed.

Dr. Shrigley, who carried out the post mortem, said that as well as 70 milligrams of alcohol, he had found 2 milligrams of barbiturate in the bloodstream, indicating that the deceased had taken nine or ten sleeping capsules.

The Coroner, Mr. A. Coupe, said that in his opinion it seemed extremely unlikely that the deceased had taken his own life. He was very critical of Boots, the dispensers of the capsules, whose labelling of the bottles containing lethal drugs was, in his view, highly unsatisfactory, with no dosage stated and no warning against taking the capsules in excess. The tragedy hit Eliza very hard, and from that point on her health deteriorated rapidly. She died two years later, aged sixty-one. Mac, who visited her right up until the time of her death, was also very badly affected by his son's untimely passing, and it is not surprising to learn that on a number of occasions he broke down and wept. It was a blow from which he was never to recover.

In the summer of 1971 McAvoy and his wife separated, Renee leaving the house and staying away for several weeks. Pat continued to operate the caravan site, but eventually Renee returned. As she was now the sole owner of the business she saw no reason why she should not be there to look after her own interests. But though Renee was back the marriage was not resumed, the couple living what amounted to separate lives under the same roof. And though she made every effort to avoid clashing with her husband, relations were very strained and it was not long before they were arguing again.

November 19th, 1964, turned out to be yet another day of rows and angry scenes. It would be easy to place the blame squarely on McAvoy's shoulders. He was awkward, irritable and ready to flare up at the slightest thing. But the truth is that the marriage had simply reached the point of no return. Renee had had enough. She could see no future whatsoever in the relationship, and there is no doubt that if she could have found a way out she would have taken it. She was in quite a good position financially and by all accounts had worked very hard to get there. She owned not only the business, but also the family home, Inglewood House. Even so, the future seemed bleak indeed. The marriage might be over but she was still tied to a sick, crippled husband who was making life hell for her. Renee was torn between loyalty to a man whom she had once loved and felt that she could not now abandon, and plain common sense, which told her that in remaining together they were just tearing each other apart emotionally.

That evening young Joe received a telephone call at his Rochdale home. It was Renee, who sounded very upset. She told him that his father had consumed a great deal of whisky and that they could not get him into bed. The impression Joe got was that McAvoy was the worse for drink and in a helpless state. He immediately set off for Partington.

Joe had been very worried about his father for some time. He was aware that since being forced to sell his share of the business McAvoy had felt very insecure, and this had put an even greater strain on the marriage. He had started to drink more than was good for him, which was, in itself, a sure sign that he was extremely unhappy, for Mac had never been a drinker. Joe also knew that his father had lost the will to live, and had, on a number of occasions, talked of doing away with himself.

Joe arrived at Inglewood House to find McAvoy in a very argumentative mood, but far from helpless. He immediately turned to Renee and told her that his father was not drunk. On hearing this remark McAvoy blew up and the rowing between he and Renee started all over again, the two of them going at it hammer and tongs, while Joe vainly attempted to calm things down. According to Joe, some of the remarks passed were very personal and the scene finally ended with Renee telling her husband that she was leaving and that she intended to claim the house, a statement which she later denied having made.

That night Renee returned to her sister's house in Manchester, while Joe, worried about leaving his father there alone in such a depressed state, tried to persuade Mac to return with him to Rochdale. At first he refused, and while they were talking, Pat, who had been on what she later described as 'a night out with a friend', called in to see her father, but only stayed for a few minutes before going into her own house next door.

Soon afterwards Mac agreed to accompany his son to Rochdale and gathered a few things together. As they left the house Mac said he would let Pat know where he was going and Joe waited outside while he went in. A few minutes later he heard a terrible row going on inside. He also heard what he later described as 'a strange man's voice'. It appeared that the man was a friend of Pat's and Mac had taken exception to his being there. He accused them of having an affair and said that it was 'all wrong'.

When he came outside he was upset and angry and told Joe that he was not going to leave after all, and hobbled back to his own house. Joe followed and tried hard to talk him round, but was unable to get him to change his mind and in the end had no option but to return to Rochdale alone.

Joe was extremely worried, but as these upsets were nothing new in McAvoy's turbulent life, he obviously felt that it would blow over and things would eventually settle down again as they always had, and all would be peaceful again until the next time. If this was in fact the case, he had, unfortunately, totally misread the situation, for McAvoy had reached the end of the line. The loss of the use of his legs, ill-health, the tragic death of his youngest son and a shattered marriage, had brought him to his knees. It would appear that the discovery of Pat's infidelity was the final blow, at least in his own tortured mind. For his little girl, whom he had loved so much, also to let him down, was more than he could bear. It was no longer a question of having lost the desire to live, he was now determined to put an end to his life.

In the early hours of November 20th, McAvoy's son-in-law, George Thomas Clarke, a driver, who had been married to Pat for six years, heard his name being called. He got up at once and let himself into the house next door, where he found McAvoy lying on the floor of the bedroom. Clarke lifted him up and helped him into bed, then sat down and talked to him for a while. McAvoy seemed very drowsy and at length he grasped his son-in-law's hand and said simply, 'Goodbye.'

He then dropped off to sleep so quickly that Clarke became alarmed and tried to wake him up. Unable to do so, he realised that something was wrong and called an ambulance. It was too late, Jock McAvoy was dead. The date was November 20th, 1971, his sixty-fourth birthday.

The inquest, at Altrincham, heard that the former champion had struggled along for twenty-four years after being struck down by infantile paralysis. During that time he had frequently suffered from periods of depression and had often threatened suicide. His wife, Renee, told the court that he had attempted to take his life several times and on one occasion had slashed his wrists.

'I think this would have happened at some time,' she said, 'although there was nothing about the argument that night that would have set it off.'

Denying that she had ever said she was going to claim the house, Renee added, 'I own it. There was no suggestion that I would turn him out. I signed an agreement some months ago giving him the right to stay in the house for life.'

After Dr Richard Jennings had stated that the cause of death was barbiturate poisoning, a verdict of suicide was returned.

McAvoy was dead, but true to form, his name would remain in the headlines for some months to come. First, a row blew up when it was mentioned at the inquest that permission had been given by McAvoy's family for the boxer's brain to be used for medical research. It was later stated in a newspaper that the brain would be examined at a hospital's neuro-surgery unit in Wickford, Essex, but the widow was quick to refute this, as also were Joe Bamford and his sister, Leonora Jasper.

Having put a stop to the proposed tests, Joe and Leonora, who had been named as joint executors in their father's will, were soon faced with another battle, when Renee and her daughter Pat attempted to have the will, which was described as 'home-made', set aside, by appealing at the Manchester High Court, Chancery Division, on the grounds that McAvoy was 'not of sound memory and understanding' when he made it. They also alleged that Joe and Leonora had exerted undue influence on their father to change his original will, made only one year before, and which the plaintiffs claimed should be considered valid.

In a note attached to the home-made will McAvoy stated that he and his wife rowed constantly, and that as a result he had been very unhappy. She was well placed financially, he said, and he had made no provision in his new will for her because she would eventually inherit her mother's property.

After hearing all the evidence the judge refused to set aside the home-made will, made only five weeks or so before McAvoy's death, in which he left the bulk of his £16,000 estate, including the National Sporting Club belt, to his son Joe. Leonora received a bequest of £1,000. McAvoy's children by his first marriage appear to have had the rough end of the stick for most of their lives, so perhaps justice had been done.

Jock McAvoy, alias Joe Bamford, was buried at Rochdale Cemetery on November 26th, 1971. A light drizzle was falling as the coffin was lowered into the ground, watched by a large number of mourners, including representatives from the British Boxing Board of Control and the Boxing Writers' Club, plus many relatives and friends.

It would be true to say that a great sadness was felt throughout the town that day. McAvoy made many enemies during his lifetime. Yet even those Rochdalians who had criticised his behaviour outside the ring could not help but feel very proud of his wonderful sporting achievements.

The champion was buried in a grave already occupied by his son Jackie and his first wife, Eliza, whom he had survived by only eight months. The headstone engraving describes him as:

'Joe, Jock McAvoy, 1908-1971, aged 63', which is, of course, incorrect, as he was born on November 20th, 1907, making him just 64 on the day of his death.

In 1977, Bernard Fahy, an ex-policeman, took over as licensee of the Brunswick Hotel, Baillie Street, Rochdale, the pub McAvoy had run back in the thirties. Bernard, a great McAvoy fan, appealed for help in assembling a display of memorabilia, with which to adorn the walls of one of the rooms in honour of the great Rochdale fighter. Many people rallied round, including Mr Norman Hill, a local man who had been a close friend of McAvoy and who was able to loan four sets of gloves, each of which had been used in a championship contest. In addition, many photographs and press cuttings were contributed by boxing fans in the town.

On the display being completed, in May of the following year, a grand opening was held at which boxers, ex-boxers and fans of all ages attended. The pub was crammed that night and the venture proved a great success. The highlight of the evening was the exhibiting of the N.S.C. championship belt which McAvoy had won outright and which had meant so much to him. As the belt, one of the last to be made in solid gold, was brought along to the Brunswick by Joe Bamford, junior, it was presumably still in the family at that time. However, at some later date Joe disposed of it and the belt passed through several pairs of hands before being acquired by Manchester boxing promoter, Jack Trickett.

Just how good was McAvoy? Out of a total of 147 traceable contests he won 132, 91 inside the distance, drew one and lost 14. He was never knocked out or stopped, and only failed to finish on two occasions; against Billy Chew in his very early days, and at the tail end of his career in the second Freddie Mills fight, losing both contests on retirements. In the former, McAvoy later claimed that he was just too exhausted to carry on. This is quite correct, but the fact is that he was well beaten in any case by a more experienced man. The Mills fight had hardly got under way when a slip caused the unfortunate injury to his back, so we will never know if he could have gained his revenge over Freddie. At that stage of his career, perhaps not, but very few people would have given Mills any chance at all when McAvoy was at his peak, certainly not at the middleweight limit and probably not at light-heavyweight either, despite the fact that Freddie went on to win a World title in that division, for the man he beat, Gus Lesnevich, while being a good champion, was no John Henry Lewis. After losing to Joe Rostron and Jim Pearson, two very talented Northern fighters, Mac took ample revenge by whipping both convincingly in return contests.

One man who certainly had the edge over McAvoy was Len Harvey, who won three of the four bouts the pair engaged in. Harvey was a superb boxer with a knockout punch in either hand. He knew every trick in the book and possessed a defence that was almost impregnable. Yet his showing against top American opposition was far from convincing. McAvoy, on the other hand, took America by storm. The Yanks admire raw courage and a bold adventurous fighting spirit, qualities McAvoy possessed in abundance and which he could back up with speed and punching power. He went over there and licked them at their own game and they loved him for it. Unfortunately, once he had shown his hand, those in control realised just how dangerous he was, and as a result he was denied his rightful crack at the world middleweight title.

During an illustrious career spanning eighteen years he fought them all, from welters to heavyweights, yet he was a natural middle-weight, and it is at this poundage that he should be judged. Harvey matured into a solid light-heavyweight, and it would probably be safe to say that while McAvoy ultimately proved himself superior at 11st. 6lbs, he could never quite get the better of Len at the heavier weight.

Most old timers insist that McAvoy was the greatest middleweight this country has ever produced. The late Nat Basso, veteran manager and M.C., a man who graced the game for over fifty years, remembered seeing Mac fight at Belle Vue back in the thirties, and insisted that none of the present day middleweights could have lived with him.

'Listen,' said Nat, 'you could have lined them up around the ringside. McAvoy would've taken them on one after the other and knocked out every one of them.'

The late Paddy Lyons had no hesitation in stating:

'He was the best. Let's put it this way, in my opinion Randolph Turpin wouldn't have lasted five rounds with him. That's how good he was.'

When reminded that Randy had outpointed the great Sugar Ray Robinson to win the World title, Paddy was quick to reply, 'Yes, and if Robinson had fought McAvoy, and he'd boxed as he did against Turpin, Mac would've knocked him out.'

When I began my research I was assured by a number of people in Rochdale that Len Collinge, Mac's closest boyhood friend, was no longer alive. Then I heard that this might not be so. A reliable contact informed me that he had seen Len and told him that I was in the process of writing this book and would no doubt like to talk to him. Apparently he had been less than enthusiastic, insisting that he had nothing to tell me and did not wish to be interviewed. Despite this unpromising piece of information I decided that I had to try and make contact, and eventually succeeded in tracking him down.

It was a row of old people's bungalows quite close to the Ogden Street area, where Len and young Joe Bamford had played as boys. I had a problem getting the old lady in the first house in the row to understand what I was saying. Then, realising she was deaf and dumb, I wrote on a pad the name LEN COLLINGE. Immediately she smiled and nodded, then pointed out the house to me. I knocked and waited. After a few minutes the door was opened no more than six inches and I saw the face of a very old man peering out at me. The hair was white and the face grey and gaunt. But the moment he spoke I could tell that the mind was still sharp. When I told him what I wanted he frowned and shook his head. Still holding the door firmly, he looked away from me, then snapped:

'No, I've nothing to say. He's not worth writing about.'

'But you and he were close friends.'

'That's right, we were.'

'Then why...'

'He was a bastard! I don't know why he had to turn on me. He knocked me down in the street.'

'Oh... was this before he got the polio?'

'No... no after.'

'But.., there was another side to him I'm told. He could be very kind as well as violent. Some say he was soft hearted underneath.'

Len shook his head again. 'I've seen him punch people for practically no reason at all. I don't want to talk about him. He was a bastard! We'd been friends all our lives and he knocked me down in the street.'

With that old Len started to close the door. Realising that there was very little point in pursuing the matter, I thanked him and left.

It would be something of an understatement to describe McAvoy as a controversial figure. His private life, in fact, was a disaster. Many people got hurt, usually those closest to him. When his name wasn't in the papers in connection with boxing it could usually be found in the police court columns, and though many of the offences with which he was charged were not of a serious nature, others most certainly were. Many consider him to have been a bully. Perhaps he was. But this was one bully who was no coward underneath, of that there is no question. Yet this does not excuse his behaviour, which was at times unpardonable. A trained fighter with two potentially lethal weapons, his fists, should not take advantage of his obvious superiority over others. A champion is someone to be admired and looked up to, especially by the young. He shoulders a great responsibility and should never abuse his position nor take any action which might disgrace the title he holds.

McAvoy, it would appear, made little attempt to live up to these ideals. Perhaps he felt that in clawing his way up from the bottom he had received no favours from anyone and therefore owed nothing either to boxing or to society in general. For a good proportion of his career he was badly managed, ill-used and poorly rewarded for his brilliant success in the ring.

At the beginning of January 1936, on McAvoy's triumphant return from the United States, the great Jimmy Wilde wrote:

'If New Year Honours were awarded in boxing Jock McAvoy would naturally take the highest rank. His smashing victory over America's official World Champion, Babe Risko, was the outstanding British achievement of the year. McAvoy has shown that the pure-bred British fighter is just as courageous as was the immortal Tom Sayers, whose epic bravery against the giant American, John Carmel Heenan, makes the most thrilling fight story I have ever read.'

Of course, no one expected Jock McAvoy to appear on any New Year's Honours list, as had John Bright and Gracie Fields. Yet in his own way McAvoy did just as much as either to help put Rochdale on the map. But though he has become part of the town's folklore, no statue in the town square or magnificent portrait in the local art gallery exists to remind future generations that from their town came a man who fought and triumphed over the world's best.

McAvoy was not the sort of man who could be easily overlooked. So it must be concluded that he has been deliberately ignored. To the ordinary people of the district, whether boxing fans or not, Jock McAvoy has become a legend. Yet as far as local officialdom is concerned he appears to be very much a forgotten man.

Why should this be so? It has certainly nothing at all to do with the fact that he was born in Burnley. Only a brief period of his life was spent there and he was identified with Rochdale throughout his career. The truth could only be that had he been considered a credit to the town during his lifetime, there is little doubt that his magnificent deeds in the ring would most certainly have been commemorated in some way or other.

So many people admire McAvoy for his prowess as a boxer, yet feel that outside the ring he brought shame on the town rather than honour. But surely the fact that this great fighter, after losing the use of his legs, endured over twenty-four years of mental anguish, should be enough to induce even the most vindictive among us to forgive and forget.

In any case, it is the view of many that a sportsman should be judged purely on the basis of his achievements, leaving aside all other issues. Certainly then, the time has come for the town to endow some sort of permanent, if posthumous, tribute to this great athlete – Jock McAvoy, The Rochdale Thunderbolt.

# Selected Bibliography


Bacup Times.

Blackburn Times.

Boxing News.

Burnley Express.

Colne Times.

Green Final, Oldham.

Lancashire Evening Telegraph.

Nelson Leader.

New York Daily News.

New York Evening Journal.

New York World Telegram.

Rhyl Journal.

Rochdale Observer.

Rossendale Echo.

Rossendale Free Press.

Todmorden District News.

# Jock McAvoy's Record 1927-1945

| **1927** | **Opponent** | **From** | **Result** | | **Venue** |
|---|---|---|---|---|---|
| Nov. 6 | Billy Longworth | (Royton) | W K.O. | 2 | Royton |
| Nov. 27 | Bert Hilditch | (Shaw) | W Rsf | 6 | Royton |
| **1928** | | | | | |
| Jan. 27 | Billy Chew | (Darwen) | L Ret | 8 | Haslingden |
| Mar. 19 | Teddy Cox | (Todmorden) | W K.O. | 7 | Todmorden |
| **1929** | | | | | |
| July 4 | Frank Ormerod | (Nelson) | W K.O. | 1 | Burnley |
| July 14 | Jack Ogden | (Chadderton) | W K.O. | 3 | Royton |
| Aug. 6 | Billy Chew | (Darwen) | W pts | 10 | Burnley |
| Aug. 14 | Eric 'Basher' Bargh | (Morecambe) | W Rsf | 4 | Morecambe |
| Aug. 28 | Jack Jukes | (Tyldesley) | W Rsf | 6 | Morecambe |
| Sept. 17 | Bob 'Tiger' Ennis | (Halifax) | W K.O. | 1 | Burnley |
| Sept. 25 | 'Seaman' Douglas | (Warrington) | W Ret | 6 | Morecambe |
| Sept. 29 | Billy Chew | (Darwen) | W pts | 15 | Royton |
| Sept. 30 | Jack Ogden | (Chadderton) | W pts | 10 | Fleetwood |
| Dec. 2 | Jack Harrison | (Hanley) | W Ret | 4 | Hanley |
| Dec. 5 | 'Soldier' Jones | (Rhyl) | W Rsf | 2 | Rhyl |
| Dec. 6 | Ted Abbott | (Doncaster) | W Ret | 6 | Blackburn |
| Dec. 15 | Lud Gresvig | (Norway) | W Ret | 2 | Royton |
| Dec. 20 | Billy Horner | (Leeds) | W Ret | 4 | Preston |
| Dec. 27 | Griff Williams | (Denbigh) | Drew | 10 | Rhyl |
| 1930 | | | | | |
| Jan. 12 | 'Marine' Davies | (Portsmouth) | W K.O. | 6 | Royton |
| Jan. 24 | Sid Aldridge | (Bath) | W K.O. | 4 | Preston |
| Feb. 7 | Jack Ogden | (Chadderton) | W K.O. | 2 | Haslingden |
| Feb. 9 | Andy Ross | (Barrow) | W K.O. | 5 | Royton |
| Feb. 14 | Fred Oldfield | (Doncaster) | W pts | 12 | Preston |
| Feb. 28 | Bill Lee | (Wrexham) | W K.O. | 3 | Rhyl |
| Mar. 7 | Bill 'Shocker' Bowman | (Penrith) | W K.O. | 3 | Penrith |

| 1930 | Opponent | From | Result | | Venue |
|---|---|---|---|---|---|
| Mar. 10 | Fred Blything | (Wolverhampton) | W pts | 15 | Stourbridge |
| Mar. 16 | Jack Wilkinson | (Warrington) | W K.O. | 2 | Royton |
| Mar. 21 | Fred Oldfleld | (Doncaster) | W Ret | 8 | Haslingden |
| Mar. 28 | Jim Pearson | (Bamber Bridge) | L pts | 12 | Preston |
| Apl. 13 | Ted Lewis | (Wigan) | W. K.O. | 6 | Royton |
| Apl. 14 | Dai Beynon | (Merthyr) | W K.O. | 5 | Blackburn |
| Apl. 25 | Joe Rostron | (Heywood) | L pts | 12 | Preston |
| May 25 | Eddie Strawer | (Rochdale) | W K.O. | 10 | Royton |
| June 11 | Billy Green | (Pontypridd) | W Rsf | 14 | Morecambe |
| July 26 | Eddie Strawer | (Rochdale) | W K.O. | 6 | Royton |
| July 30 | George Porter | (Nottingham) | W pts | 15 | Morecambe |
| Aug. 10 | 'Farmer' Jackson | (Doncaster) | W pts | 12 | Royton |
| Aug. 27 | 'Seaman' Jim Cox | (Wigan) | W pts | 12 | Morecambe |
| Sept. 14 | Jim Pearson | (Bamber Bridge) | W K.O. | 7 | Royton |
| Sept. 30 | Billy Delahaye | (Pontypridd) | W Rsf | 2 | Manchester |
| Oct. 3 | Patsy Flynn | (Lambeth) | W K.O. | 3 | Preston |
| Oct. 14 | Joe Rostron | (Heywood) | W pts | 15 | Manchester |
| Oct. 22 | Joe Lowther | (Leeds) | W pts | 15 | Morecambe |
| Nov. 2 | 'Seaman' Jim Cox | (Wigan) | W pts | 15 | Royton |
| Nov. 4 | Tate Evans | (Maesteg) | W Rsf | 15 | Manchester |
| Dec. 14 | Jim Johnson | (Newcastle) | W K.O. | 2 | Royton |

| 1931 | | | | | |
|---|---|---|---|---|---|
| Jan. 11 | Bill 'Shocker' Bowman | (Penrith) | W pts | 15 | Royton |
| Jan. 22 | Charlie McDonald | (Sunderland) | W pts | 15 | Liverpool |
| Feb. 16 | Dick Burt | (Plymouth) | W Ret | 8 | Manchester |
| Mar. 8 | Charlie Keeling | (Nottingham) | W K.O. | 3 | Royton |
| Mar. 30 | Paul McGuire | (Sunderland) | L dis | 4 | Manchester |
| Apl. 3 | 'Seaman' Jim Cox | (Wigan) | W pts | 12 | Bolton |
| Apl. 15 | Sonny Doke | (Battersea) | W pts | 15 | Morecambe |
| Apl. 19 | Johnny Seamarks | (Bedford) | W K.O. | 3 | Royton |
| May 11 | Fred Shaw | (Shipley) | W pts | 15 | Manchester |
| May 24 | Sonny Doke | (Battersea) | W pts | 12 | Royton |
| June 21 | Con Van Leowen | (Holland) | W Ret | 5 | Royton |
| July 11 | Jack Bottomley | (Leeds) | W K.O. | 1 | Rochdale |
| July 19 | Jack O'Brien | (Belfast) | W Ret | 3 | Dublin |
| Aug. 10 | Joe Lowther | (Leeds) | W Ret | 8 | Manchester |
| | **(Northern Area Middleweight Title)** | | | | |
| Aug. 30 | Jack Hyams | (Stepney) | W dis | 8 | Leeds |

| 1931 | Opponent | From | Result | | Venue |
|---|---|---|---|---|---|
| Sept. 7 | Jerry Daley | (Pen-y-graig) | W KO. | 2 | Manchester |
| Oct. 12 | Alfred Pegazzano | (France) | W Rsf | 3 | Manchester |
| Nov. 6 | Paul McGuire | (Sunderland) | W Ret | 2 | Blackpool |
| Nov. 16 | Billy Adair | (Bethnal Green) | W K.O. | 2 | Manchester |
| Nov. 22 | Sonny Doke | (Battersea) | W Ret | 5 | Royton |
| Dec. 20 | Ernie 'Red' Pullen | (Cardiff) | W KO. | 1 | Royton |

| 1932 | | | | | |
|---|---|---|---|---|---|
| Jan. 17 | Jack Marshall | (Accrington) | W KO. | 2 | Royton |
| Feb. 2 | Ex-Seaman Albert Harvey | (Chatham) | W pts | 15 | Manchester |
| Mar. 1 | Jack Etienne | (Belgium) | W pts | 15 | Manchester |
| Mar. 21 | Len Harvey | (Plymouth) | L pts | 15 | Manchester |
| | **(British Middleweight Title)** | | | | |
| May 9 | Edwin John | (Chelsea) | W Rsf | 6 | Manchester |
| May 29 | Bill Hood | (Plymouth) | W K.O. | 2 | Royton |
| June 19 | Sandy McKenzie | (Glasgow) | W K.O. | 1 | Royton |
| June 28 | Billy Thomas | (Deri) | W Rsf | 3 | Blackpool |
| July 4 | Carmello Candel | (France) | W pts | 10 | London |
| July 18 | Jack 'Cast Iron' Casey | (Sunderland) | L dis | 14 | Manchester |
| | **(Northern Area Middleweight Title)** | | | | |
| Aug. 1 | Tom Benjamin | (Wales) | W Ret | 5 | Blackpool |
| Aug. 31 | George Brown | (Stepney) | W pts | 12 | Morecambe |
| Sept. 11 | Billy Roberts | (Bishop Auckland) | W Ret | 3 | Royton |
| Sept. 30 | Phil Green | (Bath) | W Rsf | 2 | Rawtenstall |
| Oct. 12 | Tommy Moore | (Royston) | W K.O. | 3 | Morecambe |
| Nov. 7 | Ted Coveney | (Highbury) | W K.O. | 4 | Blackburn |
| Nov. 25 | Mihail Fubea | (Rumania) | W Rsf | 4 | Manchester |
| Dec. 7 | Hans Siefried | (Germany) | W pts | 10 | London |

| 1933 | | | | | |
|---|---|---|---|---|---|
| Jan. 30 | Glen Moody | (Pontypridd) | W Rsf | 6 | Manchester |
| Feb. 13 | Les Ward | (Woking) | W K.O. | 6 | Royton |
| Feb. 20 | Ernie 'Red' Pullen | (Cardiff) | W K.O. | 3 | Blackburn |
| Feb. 27 | Leonard Steyaert | (Belgium) | W K.O. | 8 | Manchester |
| Apl. 10 | Len Harvey | (Plymouth) | W pts | 15 | Manchester |
| | **(British Middleweight Title)** | | | | |
| May 14 | Jack Hyams | (Stepney) | W pts | 15 | London |
| June 12 | Oddone Piazza | (Italy) | W pts | 10 | London |

| 1933 | Opponent | From | Result | | Venue |
|---|---|---|---|---|---|
| Aug. 21 | George Brown | (Stepney) | W pts | 12 | Manchester |
| Oct. 9 | Archie Sexton | (Bethnal Green) | W K.O. | 10 | Manchester |
| | **(British Middleweight Title)** | | | | |
| Nov. 12 | Jack Forster | (Norwich) | W pts | 12 | Royton |
| **1934** | | | | | |
| Jan. 29 | Eddie Peirce | (South Africa) | W pts | 12 | Manchester |
| Feb. 28 | Al Burke | (Shepherd's Bush and Australia) | W K.O. | 5 | London |
| Mar. 19 | Eddie McGuire | (South Africa) | W K.O. | 2 | Manchester |
| Apl. 30 | Ernie Simmons | (Dublin) | W pts | 12 | Manchester |
| June 18 | Teddy Phillips | (Canada) | W K O. | 8 | Manchester |
| Aug. 13 | 'Battling' Charlie Parkin | (Mansfield) | W K.O. | 1 | Manchester |
| Oct. 8 | Jack Etienne | (Belgium) | W K.O. | 1 | Manchester |
| Dec. 3 | Kid Tunero | (Cuba) | W Rsf | 7 | Manchester |
| **1935** | | | | | |
| Jan. 14 | Marcel Thil | (France) | L pts | 15 | Paris |
| | **(European Light-heavyweight Title)** | | | | |
| Apl. 8 | Garcia Lluch | (Spain) | W pts | 12 | Manchester |
| June 24 | Al Burke | (Shepherd's Bush and Australia) | W pts | 15 | Manchester |
| | **(British Middleweight Title)** | | | | |
| Oct. 7 | Marcel Lauriot | (France) | W pts | 12 | Manchester |
| Nov. 29 | Al McCoy | (Canada) | W pts | 10 | New York |
| Dec. 20 | Eddie 'Babe' Risko | (U.S.A.) | W K.O. | 1 | New York |
| **1936** | | | | | |
| Feb. 17 | Jimmy Smith | (U.S.A.) | W K.O. | 2 | New York |
| Feb. 27 | Anson Green | (U.S.A.) | W pts | 10 | Philadelphia |
| Mar. 13 | John Henry Lewis | (U.S.A.) | L pts | 15 | New York |
| | **(World Light-heavyweight Title)** | | | | |
| Apl. 23 | Jack Petersen | (Cardiff) | L pts | 15 | London |
| | **(British and Empire Heavyweight Titles)** | | | | |
| Aug. 3 | Bob Simpkins | (Bridlington) | W K.O. | 7 | Blackpool |
| Sept. 14 | Albert Barjolin | (France) | W Ret | 2 | Manchester |
| Oct. 26 | Bill Wainwright | (Swadlincote) | W K.O. | 3 | Manchester |
| Dec. 1 | Rienus de Boer | (Holland) | W pts | 12 | Sheffield |

**1937**

| | | | | | |
|---|---|---|---|---|---|
| Mar. 8 | Cheo Morejon | (Cuba) | W pts | 12 | Manchester |
| Apl. 27 | Eddie Phillips | (Bow) | W K.O. | 14 | London |
| | **(British Light-heavyweight Title)** | | | | |
| May 3 | Dai Jones | (Ammanford) | W pts | 10 | Bristol |
| Oct. 25 | Jack Hyams | (Stepney) | W Ret | 11 | Manchester |
| | **(British Middleweight Title)** | | | | |
| Nov. 23 | Alban Mulrooney | (Macclesfield) | W Rsf | 3 | Hanley |
| Dec. 6 | Vasile Serbanesco | (Rumania) | W Ret | 4 | Manchester |

**1938**

| | | | | | |
|---|---|---|---|---|---|
| Jan. 24 | Bill Hardy | (Leicester) | W KO. | 6 | Leicester |
| Feb. 28 | Jack Strongbow | (West Hartlepool) | W KO. | 6 | Manchester |
| Apl. 7 | Len Harvey | (Plymouth) | L pts | 15 | London |
| | **(British Light-heavyweight Title)** | | | | |
| May 6 | Marcel Lauriot | (France) | W K.O. | 2 | Dublin |
| Nov. 2 | Jack Strongbow | (West Hartlepool) | W Rsf | 5 | Birmingham |
| Nov. 21 | Joe Quigley | (Sligo) | W pts | 10 | Derby |
| Nov. 28 | Frank Hough | (Battersea) | W K.O. | 6 | Manchester |
| Dec. 6 | Jack Robinson | (Nottingham) | W Rsf | 2 | Leicester |

**1939**

| | | | | | |
|---|---|---|---|---|---|
| Feb. 27 | Emile Lebrize | (France) | W K.O. | 1 | Manchester |
| Mar. 9 | Tino Rolando | (Italy) | W Rsf | 9 | Liverpool |
| May 22 | Arthur 'Ginger' Sadd | (Norwich) | W pts | 15 | Manchester |
| | **(British Middleweight Title)** | | | | |
| July 10 | Len Harvey | (Plymouth) | L pts | 15 | London |
| | **(World Light-heavyweight title — British version, also British and Empire Light-heavyweight Titles)** | | | | |
| Nov. 20 | Jack Hyams | (Stepney) | W pts | 10 | Manchester |

**1940**

| | | | | | |
|---|---|---|---|---|---|
| Apl. 29 | Jim Berry | (South Shields) | W Rsf | 6 | Manchester |
| Aug. 8 | Freddie Mills | (Bournemouth) | L pts | 10 | Liverpool |
| Aug. 26 | 'Battling' Charlie Parkin | (Mansfield) | W Rsf | 6 | Nottingham |
| Oct. 28 | Eddie McGuire | (South Africa) | L pts | 10 | Nottingham |

**1941**

| | | | | | |
|---|---|---|---|---|---|
| Oct. 20 | Jack Hyams | (Stepney) | W pts | 10 | London |
| Dec. 8 | Jim Berry | (South Shields) | W K.O. | 6 | London |

| **1942** | **Opponent** | **From** | **Result** | | **Venue** |
|---|---|---|---|---|---|
| Feb. 23 | Freddie Mills | (Bournemouth) | L Ret | 1 | London |

**(Final Eliminator British Light-heavyweight Title)**

**1943**
Inactive

**1944**
Inactive

**1945**

| | | | | | |
|---|---|---|---|---|---|
| July 17 | George Howard | (Finsbury Park) | W K.O. | 2 | London |
| Aug. 7 | Johnny Clements | (Coatbridge) | W K.O. | 6 | Portsmouth |
| Sept. 10 | Tommy Davies | (Cwmgorse) | W pts | 8 | Swansea |

| **Contests** | 147 |
|---|---|
| Won | 132 (91 inside distance) |
| Drawn | 1 |
| Lost | 14 |

W (Won) L (Lost) K.O. (Knockout) pts (Points)
Rsf (Ref stopped fight) Ret (Retired) Dis (Disqualified)

# Index

**NB.** An asterisk * in this index indicates that the entry is located in a footnote on the page listed.